A history of postwar Britain 1945–1974

C. J. Bartlett

Longman

Longman Group Limited London

Associated companies, branches and representatives throughout the world

Published in the United States of America by Longman Inc., New York

First published 1977

Library of Congress Cataloging in Publication Data

Bartlett, Christopher John.
    A history of postwar Britain, 1945–1974.
    Bibliography; p. 339
    Includes index.
    1. Great Britain – History – 20th century   I. Title.
DA588.B28   941.085   77-3000
ISBN 0-582-48319-0
ISBN 0-582-48320-4 pbk.

ISBN 0 582 48319 0 cased
         0 582 48320 4 paper

**Set in 10 on 11 point Times
and printed in Great Britain by
Richard Clay (Chaucer Press) Ltd, Bungay, Suffolk**

Contents

And the things that strike us as so very serious and important, they'll all be forgotten one day or won't seem to matter. The curious thing is, we can't possibly know now just what will be thought significant and important, or what will seem pathetic and absurd.

Lieutenant-Colonel Vershinin, in *Three Sisters* by Chekhov.

For Roger and Nigel

Preface

Given the treatment of the period, as a whole or in part, by other authors such as W. N. Medlicott, L. A. Monk and Mary Proudfoot, or in collected works edited by D. McKie, Vernon Bogdanor and others, I have not attempted to cover all aspects of the period in the proportions that might be considered ideal – especially if space were no object. I have tried to elaborate upon those elements in the story which I consider the most important, so that particular emphasis is given to foreign policy, the retreat from empire, the nation's economic and chief social problems, and the main causes of the ups and downs experienced by the Labour and Conservative parties. The role of scientists and engineers in postwar Britain has also seemed in need of particular analysis. By selection I hope that there have been gains in explanation without too many losses in other respects.

I am indebted to so many people for assistance of all kinds in the preparation of this book that it is impossible to make individual acknowledgements. Many indeed made their contributions long before Professor W. N. Medlicott suggested that I should attempt such a work. Colleagues in the University of Dundee, especially but not only in the department of history, have been a constant source of help and advice. I am greatly indebted to the services provided by the university library. For the typing of the manuscript I have to thank Mrs Young and Mrs Greatorex of the history department. My wife, as usual, has undertaken many chores and in particular has braved my reluctance to listen to any criticism. Equally without her encouragement I am sure this book would never have been completed.

C.J.B.
December 1976
Broughty Ferry

Abbreviations

AEU	Amalgamated Engineering Union
AUEFW	Amalgamated Union of Engineering and Foundry Workers
BBC	British Broadcasting Corporation
BMA	British Medical Association
BMH	British Motor Holdings
BOAC	British Overseas Airways Corporation
CBI	Confederation of British Industry
CENTO	Central Treaty Organization
CND	Campaign for Nuclear Disarmament
DEA	Department of Economic Affairs
ECSC	European Coal and Steel Community
EDC	European Defence Community
EEC	European Economic Community
EFTA	European Free Trade Area
FBI	Federation of British Industries
ICI	Imperial Chemical Industries
IMF	International Monetary Fund
IRA	Irish Republican Army
IRC	Industrial Reorganization Corporation
NATO	North Atlantic Treaty Organization
NBPI	National Board for Prices and Incomes
NEC	National Executive Committee (of the Labour party)
NEDC	National Economic Development Council
NEDO	National Economic Development Office
NFU	National Farmers Union
NHS	National Health Service
NIC	National Incomes Commission
NIER	National Institute Economic Review
NIESR	National Institute of Economic and Social Research
NIRC	National Industrial Relations Court
NUGMW	National Union of General and Municipal Workers
NUM	National Union of Mineworkers
OECD	Organization for Economic Cooperation and Development
OEEC	Organization for European Economic Cooperation
PEP	Political and Economic Planning
SDLP	Social Democratic and Labour Party (Northern Ireland)
SEATO	South East Asian Treaty Organization
SHAPE	Supreme Headquarters Allied Powers Europe
SNP	Scottish National Party
SSRC	Social Science Research Council
TGWU	Transport and General Workers Union
TUC	Trades Union Congress
UDI	Unilateral Declaration of Independence (Rhodesia)
WEU	Western European Union

Chapter 1

Introduction to the postwar era

The impact of war

The year 1945 has only a limited claim to represent a turning-point in British history. It is true that the war ended both in Europe and the Far East, the first nuclear weapons were tested and used, and a Labour government was elected to power in Britain for the first time with an overall majority. But in many respects the years of peace were a continuation of the years of war in different circumstances. Furthermore, if it is idle to speculate as to how British history might have developed had there been no war, it is important to see the continuity from the 1930s into the 1940s. The contemporary desire to condemn that earlier decade, both with respect to foreign and domestic policies, was so strong in the 1940s that the gap between the two periods tended to be exaggerated. Nevertheless, from about 1940 one can detect an acceleration, an intensification and consolidation of certain trends, as well as some real changes of emphasis. Without the war it is hard to imagine so great a determination to prevent a return to the heavy interwar levels of unemployment, so much interest in the creation of universal social services, or so ready an acceptance of so much government interference in the life of the nation. British recognition of the nation's changed place in world affairs was less complete; the new dependence on the United States brought about by the war – both in the working of the British and the world economy, and in the maintenance of Britain's global interests – was grudgingly acknowledged at best. Finally, there was little realization of the stimulus given by the war to the political consciousness of non-white peoples, and certainly no awareness that Britain's imperial role would be at an end in less than twenty years.

An American, George Ball, argued in 1968 that the defeat of Germany and Japan had strengthened the illusion that Britain was still a great power. Yet whatever the gap in strength that separated Britain from the United States and the Soviet Union – and despite Britain's war-damaged economy – there could be no question in the 1940s of Britain's place as number three in world affairs. No other nation was in the same league, nor seemed likely to be for many years to come. Germany, Italy and Japan were defeated, France was in need of a long period of convalescence, and China was internally divided and impoverished. Great as was the sense of physical loss occasioned by the war in Britain, there was also a special feeling of pride in Britain's role in the defeat of the Axis, and in the management of the nation's war effort. The early failures had given way to remarkable scientific, industrial and military success. It was possible to believe that the war achievements made the prewar failings less excusable and the future itself more manageable. But this new-found confidence meant the British entered the postwar years in a less radical and self-critical mood than some countries whose political, economic and social systems had been shattered by the conflict. Certainly no revolutionary reappraisal of Britain's world view seemed called for, and even at home the concern by 1945 was with reform and adjustment rather than with any fundamental challenge to the nation's ideas and institutions. Indeed, the outlines for the most important of those changes deemed necessary had already been drawn during the war itself. Although in practice the postwar years were to demonstrate that some problems had been gravely under-estimated, Britain's political leaders, though sometimes sorely pressed, did not need to question seriously their basic assumptions for many years.

There has been much debate as to the degree to which British society was transformed by the Second World War. It has been questioned whether 'a people's war' led to 'a people's peace'. But Professor Marwick has cut through semantic and doctrinaire arguments with his sensible conclusion: 'The change, then, is not in basic structures, but in ideas and in social attitudes and relationships, in how people and classes saw each other, and, most important, in how they saw themselves.'[1] By such tests, attitudes were significantly different by 1945 compared with 1939.

In the first place, the war brought about a considerable convergence in the thinking of Britain's two main political parties, even if it required the Conservative defeat of 1945 and Labour's grim experience of government from 1945 to confirm it. At the same time the circumstances of war not only brought to an end the soul-destroying unemployment of the 1930s; they also made its return seem unacceptable and unnecessary. The claims of the underprivileged to more security, comfort and dignity in their lives were greatly strengthened. Harold Macmillan commented in October 1942 that the war was providing full employment upon whose continuance people would insist: the present system of government would fall unless popular demands were met. The critical years of 1940–1, when Britain was near to defeat, both created and demanded an exceptional measure of national unity. There was the 'Dunkirk spirit', but a price had to be paid to maintain it. Many of the promises made in the First World War had not been fulfilled. More was needed this time. Amid talk of the evils of the Nazis and the fight for freedom, *The Times* commented appositely as early as 1 July 1940:

If we speak of democracy, we do not mean a democracy which maintains the right to vote but forgets the right to work and the right to live. If we speak of freedom, we do not mean a rugged individualism which excludes social organization and economic planning. If we speak of equality, we do not mean a political equality nullified by social and economic privilege. If we speak of economic reconstruction, we think less of maximum production . . . than of equitable distribution.

The News Chronicle added on 18 August 1941: 'No man is truly free who is not free from social want.' Anglican, Catholic and Non-conformist church leaders joined in a letter to *The Times* in December 1941 in a plea for more social equality. Slum children evacuated to rural areas and to that emerging 'third England', identified by J. B. Priestley in *English Journey* (1933), had opened people's eyes to the basic facts of poverty in a way that the most detailed of surveys and analyses could not.

With the passage of time since 1945, and the discovery of the weaknesses in postwar social and economic policies, verdicts on the domestic performance of the coalition governments of the 1930s have tended to soften. Britain has been credited with the world's most advanced social services in 1939: the welfare state was standing, if incomplete, and in scaffolding;[2] state influence over the economy was increasing (if full-scale nationalization was shunned) so that the state interventionists of the 1940s were able to build highways where many footpaths already existed. Collectivism was not a total novelty in the 1940s. In the prewar midlands and south of England there were many anticipations of the 1950s, with new housing estates, the spread of car ownership, the progress of chain stores all helping to blur the old lines between the lower middle classes and better-off manual workers. Economic historians have demonstrated how the 1930s, for many, were years of modestly increasing prosperity. This 'third England' that was emerging in the south and midlands might have lacked style, but it enjoyed many solid comforts.

At the same time, whole regions of the north of England, Scotland, Wales and Northern Ireland remained blighted by unemployment and inadequate social services. Under one-third of the houses built between the wars were for rent from local authorities. About one-third of the population lived in or dangerously near a state of poverty; perhaps 10 per cent of the population – the ratio was worse among children – were badly undernourished. It is significant that whereas Britain had much the same infant mortality rate as the Netherlands in 1920, by 1937 the Dutch had made significantly more progress. There were wide variations in Britain according to class and region. So deeply rooted did many social and economic problems appear, and so much part of the existing order that there were those who then queried whether they could be overcome by parliamentary means alone. In 1933 Professor Harold Laski asked: 'If Labour attains an electoral majority and thus dominates the House of Commons, will capitalism meekly abdicate before its onset?' The Labour Party, however, reaffirmed its faith in 'political democracy', and in 1937 its leader, Clement Attlee, made much of the need to win over new supporters, especially among the less hidebound of the professional classes who were discontented with the failings of the current system. That such a parliamentary strategy was feasible and desirable received much encouragement during the war, when Labour itself in 1940 joined the Churchill coalition and, through increased familiarization with the corridors of power both in government and business, gained confidence in its ability to lead without fear of serious resistance from the citadels of privilege. The war too, encouraged the use of new methods, ideas and personnel. Massive government involvement at all levels and ranges of the nation's life became customary, and in some degree more tolerable. Not least there was some practical implementation of the thinking of or associated with the greatest economist, John Maynard Keynes.

Among that mixed bag of individuals of the 1930s, who did so much to lay the foundations of the thinking of the moderate left and right of the 1940s and 1950s, John Maynard Keynes was seen as the most influential. Whatever his debts to others, whatever the failings of *The General Theory* (1936), however much he was misunderstood or his thinking oversimplified, he above all helped to erect a bridge of economic theory across which the moderate pragmatists of both left and right could communicate. Keynes argued that capitalism was not necessarily self-regulating, nor yet outmoded. As he saw it, the state should be 'the guiding influence' over consumption; 'a somewhat comprehensive socialization of investment will prove the only means of securing an approximation to full employment'. Ownership of the instruments of production was not important:

. . . *apart from the necessity of central controls to bring about an adjustment between the propensity to consume and the inducement to invest, there is no more reason to socialize economic life than there was before*. . . . *It is in determining the volume, not the direction, of actual employment that the existing system has broken down.*[3]

John Strachey was one of the left who was impressed by this reasoning. Keynes, he argued, showed democratic socialists how the state could control capitalism through financial and economic instruments. 'In so doing he helped to show the peoples of the West a way forward which did not lead across the bourne of total class war: a bourne from which the wage earners of the West recoil, now that they can see its raging waters.'[4] Advocates of more radical change, such as Professor G. D. H. Cole, lamented the success of Keynes among Labour supporters.

On the Conservative side, Harold Macmillan was among the first to be attracted to Keynesian thinking, but others soon followed, interested in the challenge to the concern with balanced budgets and hopeful that more effective measures against unemployment would now become feasible. The possibility that government could drastically influence the level of demand was especially appealing. The work of other groups and individuals before the war should not be forgotten, with Lloyd George and the Liberals pressing for an ambitious public works programme as far back as 1929. Bodies such as Political and Economic Planning (PEP) and 'The Next Five Years Group' also made their contributions. Nevertheless it is worthy of note that experiments in deficit finance in the United States and Sweden in the 1930s had not been markedly successful, and it was important that the war not only necessitated new approaches to the management of the economy in Britain but also launched the world on the great mid-century boom. Keynes himself doubted in 1940 whether it was politically possible for a democracy to test his theories save in the circumstances of war. One year later there appeared Kingsley Wood's 'stabilization' budget, the first attempt at a fairly direct application of Keynesian remedies to meet the danger of inflation generated by the war.[5] This was a move pregnant with many possibilities, the budget being drawn up to try to establish the 'output potential' of the economy, and what cuts were necessary in private consumption to meet the needs of a nation at war without serious inflation. One moved from the budget as a 'book-keeping statement' of government income and expenditure to its use as a cardinal instrument of state policy.[6] Revolutionary, too, was the fourfold increase in taxation, an increase unthinkable in peacetime, yet which would provide the basis for postwar state social and economic activity.

The war also made a great impact upon social thinking and policy. Most obviously, from the outset, fears of heavy civilian casualties as a result of enemy bombing prompted inquiry into the medical services. These gave added force to the concern already expressed by the British Medical Association (BMA) over the lack of coordination. In 1936 the Cathcart Commission had urged the adoption of a comprehensive approach to the medical services in Scotland. But the expected needs of war brought a greater sense of urgency. There were more than 1,000 voluntary and over 2,000 municipal hospitals in Britain, many of them poorly staffed, equipped and administered. Often the local authority institutions were 'still flavoured with the stigma of the poor law', some institutions having developed from former poorhouses, and used as depositories for the old and chronically sick.[7] A national hospital service was necessary for war victims, nationally directed and financed. War proved a great leveller in standards of treatment, both up and down, and as early as 1941–2 there was government recognition of the need for a postwar coordinated hospital service for all. No fundamental changes in ownership or finance were as yet envisaged, but an invaluable fund of information was being collected for use by postwar reformers.

The same spreading and levelling effects operated in other medical and social services. Given the growing shortages, it was only common sense to make special – and universal – provision for the especially vulnerable, such as expectant and nursing mothers, babies, and young children. Free or subsidized milk was introduced from 1940, and by the end of the war milk consumption had nearly doubled. Such were the improvements in medical and nutritional care that in 1944 the infant mortality rate was the lowest on record, and nowhere had the drop been more impressive than in Scotland. Other health statistics were reassuring. Full employment, reasonably steady prices for key commodities and their assured provision through food rationing were also playing their part. The overall impact of the war was to increase the dependence of many even among the better-off on state services, and once this occurred the remnants of the poor law and workhouse traditions that still underlay some of these services could not long survive. Domestic servants were not easily found, even when they could be afforded. The war also diminished the self-reliance of poorer families and neighbourhoods, calling away many of those who had formerly tended the old and sick. Only the state could cater in the aftermath of a heavy bombing attack. The strains on family life were reflected in the higher rates for juvenile delinquency, divorce and illegitimate births, and in the great increase in the employment of married women. More cases of parental neglect of children were reported. Increased action by public authorities was inescapable: recourse to them was no longer an almost automatic sign of poverty. The idea that the poor must be responsible for their condition was clearly in retreat. In 1941 the personal means test replaced the hated family means test. Yet as late as 1946 the Curtis Committee had to report that some children under the care of local authorities were still living in nineteenth-century all-purpose workhouses.

On the whole the poorer sections of the community could feel that in this war at least the 'profits' had not been wholly reserved for the wealthy. If income redistribution was not dramatic – the top 10 per cent' share fell from 38 to 30 per cent – average weekly earnings rose by 80 per cent against a cost of living increase of only 50 per cent. The coal-mining communities in particular made badly needed gains, climbing from eighty-first to fourteenth place in a wages league of 100 industries. The growing scarcity of labour was a crucial weapon; trade union membership rose during the war by one-third to 8 million, and union strength was also reflected in the growing incidence of strikes. The TUC was able to influence decisions at a national level, and the new power of labour was reflected in the appointment to Churchill's government in 1940 as Minister of Labour of Ernest Bevin, General Secretary of the Transport and General Workers Union. Churchill himself described the unions as the 'Fourth Estate'. Popular expectations were rising, but there were also deep fears lest the wartime gains should evaporate with the return of peace. As the danger of a German invasion receded, interest in reform mounted, with Labour backbenchers such as Aneurin Bevan beginning to harass not only the coalition government as a whole but also their own leaders in the cabinet for more positive action.

Certainly some prodding was necessary, for Americans as well as his own colleagues noted how grudgingly Churchill turned his attention to matters other than the war. Nor were Labour ministers necessarily responsive to pressure from the left. Attlee and Bevin declined to act on Laski's demand that the war should be used to effect a social revolution: to attempt to do so, they argued, would divide the nation in a time of peril. Nevertheless they hoped that Labour's role in the war, including its part in the extension of public services, would guarantee the party either an influential place in any postwar coalition or victory at the polls once the Axis had been defeated. Herbert Morrison and Sir Stafford Cripps, within the government, were anxious to begin the planning of postwar social changes. Bevin also turned his mind to such matters, especially in education, regional development and industrial efficiency. To many socialists he might seem a tepid reformer, but he was an intensely practical man. As a great organizer he understood and used power better than most. He was very conscious of the enormous economic problems that would face any government after the war. Attlee's views were similar. When, at the Labour Party Conference in 1943, a few voices were raised in favour of the dissolution of the coalition, he replied that the party could do more to promote its long-term aims by remaining within the government. Indeed, a continuance of the coalition into the peace was privately not ruled out by the Labour leaders, as they recalled Lloyd George's electoral triumph in 1918 and feared a possible repetition under Churchill. Perhaps, too, the immensity of postwar problems could best be met by a coalition, and on the Conservative side Churchill, Eden and Halifax were often drawn to that solution.

The wartime coalition also caused some unease among Tory backbenchers: they saw too much covert socialism. But for a group of progressive Conservative MPs, who formed the Tory Reform Committee, there was too little positive government action. They wished to project a new party image. Lord Hinchinbrooke urged the rejection of the 'Whigs' and 'money barons' in the party, and a return to the spirit of Disraeli and the quest for 'one nation'. Quintin Hogg described the 'New Conservative' in 1944 as one who did not fear modern forms of public control. For him, schemes of social security were not destructive of enterprise. 'Social democracy' and work for all must be the aim; privilege based on wealth or birth and not on skill had served its purpose. David Eccles spoke out for 'a just distribution of . . . national income'. There were several contradictory currents at work within the Conservative party. The majority of the rank and file clung to prewar attitudes and policies, but among the leaders Anthony Eden was reflecting on the possible diminution of business influence in a reconstituted party. R. A. Butler and Harold Macmillan were influential progressives, and the great electoral defeat of 1945 was to strengthen their hands. Meantime Churchill himself was reluctant to engage in much long-term planning for the future, fearing that the nation would be unable to foot the bill for ambitious reforms for many years. He readily shared the fears of the Treasury in 1944 that too much attention was being paid to a 'Brave New World' and too little to the 'Cruel Real World'.[8]

Yet some general government statements on such matters as health, social security, employment and education were necessary for public morale. Already, as a product of prewar interest, the Barlow Commission had spoken out in January 1940 against the great congested and unhealthy conurbations, pleading for a more balanced distribution of population and for an attack on regional unemployment. It also argued against the long-held belief in regional industrial specialization, a nineteenth-century tenet that only began to weaken in the 1930s. The war appeared to demonstrate the efficacy of taking work to the workers, and of industrial diversification. The Uthwatt and Scott Reports dealt specifically with urban and rural problems. The Ministry of Town and Country Planning was set up in 1943, and a Distribution of Industry Bill was carried through Parliament in the first half of 1945. The development of New Towns was envisaged. But of most interest to the public was the 1942 Beveridge Report, with its proposals for a far-reaching and universal scheme of social insurance against 'interruption and destruction of earning power, and for special expenditure arising at birth, marriage or death'. Mass Observation reported in its November 1942 *Bulletin* that many people expected the war to be followed by a return to mass unemployment and less money. Beveridge affirmed the need for a successful battle against the five 'giants' of want, disease, ignorance, squalor and idleness. *The Manchester Guardian* of 2 December 1942 described the Report as the most important social project since Lloyd George's National Insurance Bill of 1911. A hesitant government was left in no doubt of the public's desire for action. An 85 per cent poll was recorded in its favour. Labour backbenchers, and some Conservatives led by Quintin Hogg, pressed hard for action.

The final government commitment was somewhat tentative. There were similarly rather generalized promises on a national health service, urban renewal, a housing programme, and on high and stable employment. Beveridge himself published a book in 1944 entitled *Full Employment in a Free Society*, attacking government policy as too cautious. The government was not alone in its doubts. British employers asked how exports could bear the cost of Beveridge's plans, though there had been a realistic attempt to cost their recommendations. Keynes commented on Beveridge's hope that unemployment could be maintained at an average of 3 per cent: 'No harm in aiming at 3 per cent unemployment, but I shall be surprised if we succeed.' His own expectation was around 6 per cent, while Bevin, in April 1943, thought that up to 8 per cent unemployment could be regarded as normal labour turnover, and that emergency state action would be required only beyond that point. There was more general agreement that full employment, if attained, could lead to serious inflation, and there was much interest in the sort of controls that might be introduced. Beveridge himself talked of the need for compulsory arbitration or some unified wages policy involving the TUC. Mrs Joan Robinson in 1946 believed the state would increasingly control and direct labour the further unemployment fell below 2 per cent.[9] The TUC itself spoke of the need for great labour self-control in periods of full employment, but looked to the government for assurances on price controls as well as full employment. Not surprisingly traditionalists within the Treasury were worried, and the 1944 white paper on employment was an untidy compromise, with only tentative proposals as to how a postwar slump might be resisted.

These reservations by contemporaries should be borne in mind by later critics of the initiators of the broad lines of British economic policy in the 1940s when full employment later gave rise to problems of its own – especially its contribution to inflation. Those in positions of authority or influence in the mid-1940s were not unaware of the difficulties, but, as will be seen, postwar developments had a way of gaining a volition of their own. The acute postwar labour shortage, intensified by National Service, accustomed the nation to an unemployment rate of much less than 2 per cent – a figure that was neither expected nor initially sought.

Interparty suspicion and rivalry further hampered postwar planning. Vague agreements in principle could leave major differences as to detailed implementation. Party leaders were sometimes closer in their thinking than they could admit to party rank and file, each wing alert to any threat to nationalization or private enterprise. There were some interesting ambiguities in the same individual. Thus Lord Woolton found some Conservatives dangerously near to socialism in their readiness to use state power against poverty, but he himself felt that building controls, for instance, would be essential in the immediate postwar years. Indeed, despite much Conservative rhetoric against controls, there existed a widespread consensus in government as to their indispensability in the first years of peace. Sir John Anderson, as Chancellor of the Exchequer in 1945, foresaw perhaps five postwar years during which considerable control of the economy would be necessary to strike a correct balance between exports, reconstruction and consumption, and to avoid the mistakes that had helped to bring about the shortlived and damaging boom that followed the First World War. Within the Board of Trade from 1943 there was increasing interest in controls, not merely in the context of exports and inflation, but in the location and modernization of industry, and of town and country planning as a whole.

In the longer term, it is true, the Conservative party continued to hold reservations as to the extent of state intervention. It preferred to see state action as an exceptional and temporary measure, professing concern lest individual initiative and independence should be discouraged. In the context of social and health services Conservative policy at this stage was likely to be less comprehensive and ambitious than that of Labour. Conservative readiness to have some recourse to public control fell short of Labour's desire to nationalize many basic industries. Sir Alan Bullock described the future of the coal industry as 'the touchstone of British politics'. Certainly it occasioned a heated debate in the House of Commons in October 1943. Churchill strove manfully to cool passions with the reminder that the philosophy of his government could be none other than 'Everything for the war, whether controversial or not, and nothing controversial that is not *bona fide* needed for the war'. Government control of the mines would continue until a newly elected postwar Parliament could resolve the matter. In 1944 when the Reid Committee reported on the state of the mining industry, nationalization was not mentioned, and Reid himself privately opposed such a solution. The Committee did agree that some new authority and structure would be needed to carry through the vital tasks of reorganization and modernization. Bevin had hopes that the course of events would never allow the coal-owners to re-establish themselves. But he was less sure of the future of the railways. He was also told by Churchill that the highly controversial Trade Disputes Act of 1927, with its restraints on the freedoms of trade unions, must also stand. Its repeal was one of the first acts of the Attlee government. In fact, interwar economic conditions had been the chief constraint on the unions.

The great achievement in social legislation of the time was the 1944 Butler Education Act. Such controversy as it occasioned lay not between the two main parties, but with the religious denominations and with the local authorities affected by the extensive reorganization. A separate Act in 1945 made provision for Scotland. The 1944 Act was acclaimed by most Labour supporters as 'the victory for the common child' with its provision of secondary education for all. This had been a Labour party aim since 1921. The Hadow Report of 1926 seconded this view, and had also advocated the raising of the school-leaving age to fifteen. Action on the second point was frustrated by the war although progress was being made in the replacement of the all-ages elementary school with the introduction of the 'modern' school for eleven-year-olds and over. Even in 1940, however, secondary education in England and Wales absorbed only 19 per cent of all public expenditure on education compared with over 27 per cent ten years later. In 1938 only 4,000 pupils proceeded to university who had not attended a public school. Even in 1950 under 7 per cent of the seventeen-year-old age group were still at school. Professor R. H. Tawney had long argued that 'the hereditary curse' upon English education was its organization on lines of social class. Furthermore, as W. O. Lester Smith commented in 1949, the 'grey eminences' of education before 1939 'came usually from the public schools and older universities. Neither elementary nor technical education could have had the same appeal for administrators who, unlike Kay-Shuttleworth, had learnt a lot about Mantua, but little about Manchester.'[10] The war, however, both increased the popular demand for education, and underlined the many deficiencies in the existing system, not least the nation's need for more scientists, engineers and technicians.

The resultant Butler Act appeared to meet most interests very successfully in the circumstances. The proposed secondary education for all presented no challenge to the prestigious public schools. For many middle-class families there was a saving in fees with so many grammar schools now falling wholly within the state system. The Act did not establish any form of organization for secondary education; rather it promised education according to the 'age, ability and aptitude' of the individual pupil. In practice local authorities developed almost exclusively a tripartite system of grammar schools, the less academic secondary schools, and a few technical schools. Fifteen became the leaving age from 1947. This tertiary system was supported by much interwar educational theory, though there were those who already argued the impossibility of devising a satisfactory selection system at the age of eleven. But the advocates of multilateral or comprehensive schools made little impact at this time, and their defence by G. D. H. Cole in 1947, for instance, was somewhat hesitant. Few questioned the government's claim that a diversified educational system would not impair 'social unity . . . but would open the way to a more closely knit society'. The apparent broadening of the doors of entry into grammar schools for the brighter working-class child seemed achievement enough. The Attlee government, it was later asserted, left too much to the experts in Curzon Street. Only in the 1950s was there a real growth in complaints that the 1944 Act had failed to create genuine equality of opportunity, and that the chance had been missed to forge 'a public system of education genuinely capable of serving a classless democracy'. By then about one child in five was securing entry to the grammar schools; the secondary modern schools were not in general receiving the attention promised, while technical school development was negligible. A few comprehensive schools had been opened. Educational planners were also taken by surprise by the postwar rise in the birth-rate. Further unexpected burdens were thrown on the schools when rising living standards made it possible (and rising aspirations provided the motivation) for many more children to remain in full-time education after the age of fifteen. The school population of 4·5 million in 1945 had been increased by about 50 per cent within ten years.

At the end of the war Lord Woolton expressed unease over the built-in snobbery in favour of education directed to 'black coat' occupations, which strengthened the 'recording' class at the expense of the productive. Bevin, as Minister of Labour, had been dismayed by the shortage of technically qualified workers. So great was the need that there was a fourfold increase in the training of workers through day release. The technical colleges, with limited resources, served the nation well, but after the war and until the mid-1950s they were given little opportunity to expand, despite the continuing high demand for post-school courses. True, the nation's resources were strained, but there was no room for complacency when the nation was so far behind the United States and Germany in the provision of technical education. Apart from the doubling of the output of university science and technology graduates, there was the creation of specialist colleges such as that of Aeronautics at Cranwell (1946), the National Foundry College, Wolverhampton (1947), and the National College of Rubber Technology (1948).

The 1944 budget not only promised tax reliefs for industrial reconstruction, but was also more generous to industrial research. Some concern was shown in Britain at the greater success and efficiency of the United States in the practical application of research, though Britain herself had made great strides in the development of radar and other electronic aids, in automatic gunnery control, and jet propulsion for aircraft. With the defeat of Germany in 1945, Britain held a world lead in jet engines. She had also made some contribution to the development of the atomic bomb, though a long road stretched ahead before she herself could produce nuclear weapons or energy. In medicine, too, the impulse of war had been felt, with major developments occurring in the use of penicillin, sulphonamides and blood transfusion. The role of the scientist, with many other professionals, had been elevated: they had emerged from their laboratories and back rooms into the forefront of decision-making, taking up operational analysis as well as giving advice on new equipment and weaponry.

The Civil Service had similarly been reinforced with new brains during the war, though former academics may sometimes have been imaginative rather than practical. Professional economists had rarely been thus employed before the war, or had shown much inclination. But Keynes had always subscribed to Marx's dictum: 'The philosophers have hitherto interpreted the world in various ways; the thing is, however, to change it.' Of Keynes himself Lord Robbins later wrote that he could be rude, rash, arrogant and impractical, but he was 'the magician who held you entranced, even against your judgement and your will. . . . [He was] the most remarkable man I have ever met.'[11] In general both economists and statisticians advanced in status and influence in these years, with other innovations following the 1941 budget. Quantitative planning and national income analysis developed, so that *The Times* could describe the 1944 budget as 'an instrument of broad economic policy', departing from the 'old saving of candle-ends'.[12] Much of this varied expertise departed from the government services after 1945, but affairs could never again be quite the same. Government had been forced to use new methods, to take account of new needs and desires, to draw upon new personnel and skills, and to enter new realms of activity.

The war uprooted individuals and families: unfamiliar environments and experiences increased receptivity to new ideas. In their different forms both the United States and the Soviet Union presented alternative models that encouraged higher expectations. Radio, already important, was an instructive and liberating as well as a morale-boosting force. The BBC began increasingly, if still cautiously, to see itself as a forum for public discussion, and made use of the hitherto suspect intellectuals of the left. Some Conservatives viewed educational activities in the armed forces with great unease. They were unnecessarily fearful, though the following description must have fitted the odd occasion:

In the strange isolated vacuum of military service, the smoky Nissen hut with its eager lecturer and its willing listeners, who are glad of the variation in their dull routine, visions expand and notions of improvement take a buoyant wing.[13]

Nora Beloff found fellow-students, who had started the war cynical and disillusioned, ending it with more confidence in parliamentary democracy. Certainly wartime opinion polls, and the by-election successes of Sir Richard Acland's Common Wealth party were further pointers to the growing radical and restless mood. If relatively few shared Michael Foot's vision of the quest for a socialist Britain – 'For me it is the Klondyke or bust' – Attlee was right to diagnose a swing in the mainstream of opinion in favour of more planning and welfare.

Felix Frankfurter, an American jurist, commented at the height of the Second World War that Britain's future prosperity depended on the release of 'thirty million of under-educated, under-developed, under-advantaged Britons into the exercises and adventures of a better social structure'. Barbara Wootton in *End Social Inequality* (1941) con-cluded that British public life was administered by people with too little firsthand knowledge of the average person's life, an ignorance of which they were serenely unaware. Even at the level of the elites themselves, communication between the different professions was often poor, R. L. Meier for instance, in the *British Journal of Sociology* for 1951, drawing attention to the 'bane' of specialization in science and engineering, and to the complex social stratification which existed within those professions. 'The class barriers tend to prevent communi-cation. . . . Each stratum uses a different jargon, moves in its own social circle, and has a recognized groove for promotion and advancement.' The war had done something, if not enough, to break down some of these barriers between and within classes and occupations. The shake-up at the time seemed remarkable: the achievements impressive: Seebohm Rowntree felt that 'the social and economic life of the nation had been uprooted by the war as by an earthquake'. With the advantage of hindsight the disturbance appeared less impressive, or the use made of the period of upset more limited. Britain in fact remained a highly complex society with a subtle and manifold distribution of power as illustrated by Professor Finer in his study, *Anonymous Empire* (1958). What had happened, and what explains the 1945 Labour government, was both a growing confidence and assertiveness on the part of those passed by in the patchy prosperity of the 1930s, and a limited leftward movement among the amorphous middle classes. There was greater acceptance of the need for and the feasibility of a better ordering of British society. There was a new mood in the air when Lord Beaverbrook could complain that *The Times* read like an expensive version of the communist *Daily Worker*. But the new temper was not extremist, nor set for all time.

The 1945 election

As victory drew nearer in Europe in the winter of 1944–5 so it became evident that Churchill's wartime coalition could not last much longer. Churchill himself wished to postpone its dissolution if possible until after the defeat of Japan which, early in 1945, was not expected to occur until some eighteen months after the fall of Germany. His task would be eased with Labour in the government if relations with the Soviet Union should deteriorate – and in Churchill's view this seemed all too likely. Already he had received valuable support from Bevin in the British struggle against communist and other left-wing forces in Greece. Delay would also enable Churchill to make a start with his own 1943 Four Year Plan for the recovery of Britain. The military case for the continuation of the coalition was good, but the task of postwar reconstruction was now becoming the first priority. On the pace and detail of that reconstruction there were broad differences of opinion between some leading ministers. The wartime truce between the parties was rapidly breaking down, and each was increasingly anxious to shape postwar Britain according to its preconceptions as well as to gain the maximum credit with the electorate for any acts of policy or promises of action that occasion might afford. As early as 5 October 1944 the Labour party had announced its intention to fight the next general election (the last had been in 1935) as an independent party. Pressure was building up within both parties in favour of an early end to the coalition. Churchill was under strong pressure from influential colleagues such as Lord Beaverbrook for a quick election to maximize his electoral appeal as the nation's great war leader. Churchill overcame his own doubts to offer the Labour party the choice of a July poll or the continuance of the coalition until after the defeat of Japan. Attlee carefully put the pros and cons of these alternatives to Labour's National Executive Committee (NEC) on 19 May. He was forcefully instructed to demand in return either an immediate end to the coalition or an October election. Churchill's refusal of an autumn dissolution meant the end of his first ministry on 23 May – the general election was to be held on 5 July. The politicians had probably blundered into the best solution. The war with Japan, unknown to them, had only three months to run. A decisive start to postwar reconstruction was thus needed at once, and yet, as Attlee noted, in its last months the coalition was loath to act.

Few guessed in June–July 1945 that Labour was about to win one of the great electoral victories in British history, though, with hindsight, the pointers to the outcome were evident enough. Churchill, of course, appeared to bestride the political stage like a colossus; the only question seemed to be the size of his majority. The Conservative Central Office hoped for a majority of at least fifty. Yet Churchill's claims to lead the nation in peace were not so obvious as his qualities in war. Support or admiration for Churchill in any case did not necessarily induce support for the Conservative party, at whose door was laid the responsibility for most of the disappointments of the 1930s. The Conservatives had held or shared power for all but three of the last thirty years. Some swing against them was almost inevitable, especially when voters' thoughts tended to dwell more on bread-and-butter issues than on the recent victory. Disappointed Conservatives after their 1945 defeat looked around for special causes, such as the supposed (but exaggerated) superiority of Labour party organization in many constituencies and the powerful polemical writers who supported the left. Against the latter the Conservatives had little apart from Quintin Hogg's spirited *The Left was Never Right* (1945). In the election campaign itself the Labour party had rather the better of the exchanges, both in content and presentation. Of the Conservatives the best that could be said was that they showed more 'stark realism' and dwelt more on present problems than on future promises and criticism of the past.[14] Full employment and the Beveridge Report were accepted but balanced by emphasis upon the virtues of private enterprise. The party relied too heavily on the personal stature of Churchill and the socialist bogy. Churchill himself often displayed a remoteness from everyday life and feelings, and never more so than in the notorious broadcast when he tried to establish some connection between socialism and totalitarianism. Nevertheless he was almost certainly an electoral asset to his party, given the popular impression of its record in the 1930s. Labour, meanwhile, promised more than it could perform: good use was also made of the question: could the Tories be trusted to deliver the goods? The most important issues for the electorate were housing (by a long chalk), full employment, social security and a comprehensive health service. On all these issues Labour evoked the most confidence. Nationalization was not a major issue, and on the vexed question of the coal mines the Conservatives themselves did not appear averse to some state control.

Labour was also careful to make a strong bid for those among the middle classes for whom private enterprise was not a sacred cow. The party had always been a heterogeneous body, drawing inspiration from Morris, Dickens, Ruskin and Carlyle as well as Marx, and later from the Webbs, Lloyd George, Keynes and Beveridge, not to mention the general influence of nonconformity, the Bible, American contributions from Henry George and Jack London. The pragmatists within the party had always been influential, and from the late 1930s many more had moved in their direction. Bevin's successor as general secretary of the Transport and General Workers Union, Arthur Deakin, had turned from an interest in the 'socialization of industry' as late as 1940 to the vaguer position of a 'planned economy' with only selective nationalization. Deakin became one of Attlee's most powerful postwar allies. Indeed, the nationalization of iron and steel was only included in the party declaration of April 1945 against the wishes of Morrison and Arthur Greenwood. Morrison thought the steel industry too 'complicated and troublesome' for public ownership, and tried to make efficiency the yardstick of policy. At the Blackpool Party Conference in May 1945 he agreed that socialized industry would provide a firm economic base for social reform. Real progress would be impossible on rotten economic foundations. Morrison often spoke of the need for Labour to represent 'all the useful people', and Attlee himself made a neat debating point when he argued in February 1945:

It is now many years since Karl Marx gave a slogan, 'Workers of the world unite. You have nothing to lose but your chains.' It was never true of this country that the workers had nothing to lose. It has been less true with the passing of the years. If it had not, the Trades Union Movement would have been a failure.

Such, too, were the views of Bevin, whose aim was a humanized, modernized, but only partially socialized Britain. Sir Stafford Cripps, after a varied political career, and about to become one of the key figures in the new government, was now convinced that government possessed most of the powers required by Labour without recourse to general nationalization. He feared that the postwar problems facing the country would be too great for dogmatic solutions to be risked. He was moving closer to Bevin's concern to amend the failings of capitalism rather than to abolish it. Leaders of this stamp provided reassurance to voters who recoiled from doctrinaire socialism. Attlee was careful to emphasize the independence of the parliamentary party lest the more extreme ideas of the party's current chairman, Harold Laski, should frighten off support from the moderate centre. Attlee in memoir and interview said little, but in so far as brevity permitted his impatience with Laski and those of his ilk was later made very clear. George Orwell's perception of the trends in British society resembled Attlee's. He believed the most drastic changes would happen peacefully and with a show of legality, and everybody except the 'lunatic fringes' of the various political parties was well aware of this. England, he thought, was too small, too highly organized, too homogeneous – and too dependent on world trade – to want revolution or civil war. He saw the English as gentle, with an unusual respect for law and no revolutionary tradition. Although there were deep class divisions, these were nevertheless softened by the masses' indifference to political theory, and by their relatively low level of ambition. Save for the subsequent rise in crime and violence, Orwell's verdict stood the test of the next generation remarkably well.

In terms of the British electoral system Labour won a great victory in 1945, but it is important to note how far the system inflated this victory. A majority of 146 seats over all other parties was secured with rather less than half the total vote. What stood out was Labour's advance since 1935, with 3.5 million more votes (almost 12 million in all), whereas the vote of the Conservatives and their allies had fallen by 1.5 million to just under 10 million. The Liberals were still a force in terms of votes (2 million) though not in seats. The swing to Labour was impressive, yet not overwhelming. Labour had secured up to one-third of the middle-class vote, and by any calculation the Conservatives had recorded one of their worst electoral performances of the twentieth century. The torrent of Labour MPs who flooded into the new House, however, contained relatively few ardent left-wingers. There was a ritualistic (but also rather ill-remembered) singing of 'The Red Flag' when Parliament assembled, and while Harold Nicolson commented, 'I hate uneducated people having power', over half the Labour MPs came from non-manual occupations. That parliamentary conventions suffered for a while owed more to the elation and inexperience of the newcomers than to revolutionary ardour.

The start of the Attlee government

If there had been a deliberate attempt to fabricate a Prime Minister who was the direct opposite of Winston Churchill, Clement Attlee would have been a likely result. Only the inner core of toughness was similar. On 26 July, after news of Labour's triumph, Herbert Morrison tried to argue that a 1933 party decision provided that no royal request to form a government could be taken up until the parliamentary party had voted on the party leadership. The clause was not wholly clear, and Attlee, with the full support of Bevin, made haste to answer the summons from the palace while others argued.[15] In ensuing threats to his leadership, Bevin, though he sometimes grumbled, stood firmly beside him. Attlee later claimed that his relationship with Bevin was the closest of his political life. Perhaps this did not mean very much, for Attlee remained an intensely private person – almost to the point of caricature. An enigma to many of his colleagues, they often complained of lack of imagination and leadership. But he was an effective chairman of the Cabinet, he piloted his party through many storms, and was endowed with a considerable fund of common sense. In time he won the respect of the shrewd and immensely experienced American diplomat, Averell Harriman, who had dealt at length with Roosevelt, Churchill and Stalin. If luck played an unusual part in his rise to the top, once there his own doggedness and the rivalry of other claimants ensured his permanence. He appeared sufficiently left of centre to satisfy most of his party, while his respect for tradition, continuity and order assured him of much respect in other quarters. He had a special regard for King George VI. In the Commons his economical, utilitarian delivery was often singularly effective against Churchill's great rhetorical setpieces.

In the new cabinet Morrison became Lord President of the Council with the onerous task of coordinating national economic planning and development, as well as acting as chief coordinating minister for home affairs. Bevin, the new Foreign Secretary, had hoped to become Chancellor of the Exchequer, and this had been Attlee's original intention too. But Bevin and Morrison were likely to clash on the home front – Bevin's subordination to Morrison was inconceivable – and Attlee may also have wished for a stronger personality than Hugh Dalton to handle foreign affairs in view of possible differences with the Soviet Union. Bevin, had he been given the Treasury, was unlikely to have proved so well contented as Dalton with the limited successes of 1946. On the other hand, given the fact that Britain's political and economic fate was largely determined by the international context, it was probably advantageous that the government's most formidable figure should have gone to the Foreign Office. Thus the Treasury had to wait until the autumn of 1947 before circumstances and the personal force of a new Chancellor enabled it to regain its traditional place in the Whitehall hierarchy.

Attlee and Bevin had to proceed almost at once to Potsdam, where a conference of the victorious powers had been briefly adjourned while the results of the British general election were declared. The Russians appeared baffled by the unexpected outcome, but as Marshal Zhukov observed, there was no observable change in the content of British policy – only perhaps in style. As Bevin established himself, even that became less evident. He told a former American Secretary of State in September 1945 that he expected the main emphasis to be on 'power politics' in the near future, and rather shocked the American with his relative lack of interest in the United Nations.[16] In the election campaign, and at other times, there had been Labour claims that they were better fitted than the Conservatives to establish satisfactory relations with the Soviet Union. Laski, in 1945, was arguing that Labour was not committed to continuity in foreign policy, that a socialist foreign policy was possible, and that collective security was a viable alternative to alignment with the United States and a return to the policies of Eyre Crowe and Vansittart. Leonard Woolf and G. D. H. Cole were less sure of the feasibility of a socialist foreign policy, but they hoped that Britain might lead the way to a socialist Europe, and at least maintain a position of impartiality between the United States and Russia. The distinguished Italian writer, Ignazio Silone, acclaimed the triumph of Labour in 1945 with the words, 'Now Britain has the chance of leading the democratic revolution'. Richard Crossman, while recognizing Britain's current economic dependence on the United

States, hoped that Britain would 'form with the peoples of Europe a common market big enough . . . to stand up to . . . American business'. Bevin himself, when his mind turned to the more distant future, ran over various European and Commonwealth possibilities which might lessen the influence of Russia and the United States.

Variations on these ideas were not confined to the left. *The Economist* of 21 July 1945 was interested in the emergence of Britain as some sort of intermediary between East and West, while those of the right – such as Leo Amery – who feared the United States as a competitor and who still cherished ideas of the Empire and Commonwealth as the main focus of British interests, also outlined roles for Britain as a third force. During the war there had been discussions within the Economic Reconstruction Department of the Foreign Office and by interested ministers as to Britain's peacetime options. There were debates both as to the possibility of a continuance of close relations with the United States and their compatibility with the Commonwealth and Imperial Preference. There was no guarantee that American enthusiasts for a multilateral trading world would prevail after the war, while some schools of thought saw such a policy as a threat both to the Commonwealth and to the use of controls to protect Britain from postwar unemployment. In so far as any consensus developed within the government during the war, therefore, it was one which favoured the maintenance of as many options as possible. The British could not rule out the possibility that the United States might prove less internationalist than anticipated or too internationalist in a manner detrimental to British interests.[17] Thus Roosevelt himself had said that American troops would leave Europe within two years of Germany's defeat. On the other hand, while Britain might receive the aid she so badly needed for her economic recovery, she might also encounter opposition to her imperial and trading policies. In time, too, she might find her economy injured by another American depression. It was also vital that Europe should be reconstructed politically and economically as soon as possible. Britain could neither prosper nor feel safe while the future of Europe remained uncertain. General Smuts of South Africa, though welcoming American internationalism, insisted that a world equilibrium was dependent upon a strong Britain and Europe.[18]

Attlee and Bevin entertained reservations concerning the Soviet Union from the outset. Dalton, in mid-May 1945, found Attlee less optimistic over future East–West relations than he was himself. Bevin's suspicion of communists was long established, though his tough bargaining approach did not preclude the hope (at least until 1947) that some workable relationship might be established with Russia. He had a firm view of what constituted British interests; hence his opposition to a left-wing takeover in Greece. He argued in favour of a 'crowned republic', and as early as January 1945 the British TUC sent a delegation to Greece to try to bring some order out of the hopelessly factionalized unions in that strife-torn country. The young Victor Feather, a future General Secretary of the TUC, became the chief agent in that strange operation. Charges that in his foreign policy as a whole Bevin succumbed to the wiles of the professionals in the Foreign Office are absurd. Sir Alexander Cadogan's diary reveals that from his assumption of office Bevin was his own master. No more than any minister (and less than most) was he, as Aneurin Bevan claimed, 'a big bumble bee caught in a web' thinking he was 'the spider'. Indeed, in his pursuit of policies which often aroused hostility in Britain it is fitting that Lord Strang should have compared him to Lord Castlereagh. Probably no Foreign Secretary exceeded his individual influence on British foreign policy in the twentieth century: Eden himself could not entirely escape from the shadow of Churchill. At times Bevin was too arrogant, impatient and autocratic, too much the victim of his own emotions. Interestingly, however, Attlee described his egoism as that of an artist: even Michael Foot found it 'gargantuan, yet oddly inoffensive'. Largely self-taught, Bevin had an immense fund of knowledge, illumined by imagination and a sharply critical mind. If often dependent upon others for the grammatical, even the logical articulation of his ideas, he was profoundly admired by Attlee, Churchill, Acheson and many leading western European politicians. He could dip with appreciation into the fifty-year-old dispatches of Lord Salisbury as well as impress by the brute strength of his personality.

   If he distrusted the Russians and communists more than most of his party, few distrusted them not at all. Hugh Dalton at the Treasury, it is true, was at first more conscious of American hostility, and complained for some time of the Foreign Secretary's anti-communist obsessions. Aneurin Bevan, too, thought American capitalism was more likely to prove a threat to Britain than American isolationism, but he was dismayed by the manner in which Stalin's Russia occupied and controlled eastern Europe at the end of the war. Michael Foot agreed that to conciliate Russia over eastern Europe would be 'abject surrender' and a defeat for democratic socialism.[19] The philosopher, Bertrand Russell, thought Stalin's Russia as bad as Hitler's Germany. What Aneurin Bevan questioned, however, was the ability of Russia, devastated by the recent war, to menace the rest of Europe. Iverach McDonald of *The Times*, commented that as he journeyed from Calais to Russia early in 1947 so the devastation increased. The Russians as a people were 'flat with exhaustion'. If Ernest Bevin appreciated this – he certainly argued that Stalin did not want war – he still feared that events (given the instability and weakness of central and western Europe) could impose a pattern of their own. Western firmness would diminish these risks, and those of a Russian miscalculation.

   Bevin may sometimes have handled the Russians as if, as a left-wing critic wittily put it, they were a breakaway group from the Transport and General Workers Union, though Stalin and Molotov were well able to look after themselves in any rough-house. Bevin and his colleagues were also reluctant to write off eastern Europe – for emotional and material reasons. These included the customary import by western Europe of many primary products from its eastern neighbours. If little was to be expected at first from the war-ravaged territories in the east, the reconstitution of an interdependent Europe had obvious appeal. As early as 20 August 1945, following the Potsdam conference, Bevin spoke in guarded yet revealing terms to the Commons of the problem of Romania, Hungary, Bulgaria and Austria. He said: 'one thing at which we must aim resolutely, even at the beginning, is to prevent the substitution of one form of totalitarianism for another.' To these ends he continued to show interest in free elections in eastern Europe.

For the British there was the especially pressing problem of their occupation zone in north-west Germany, which had formerly drawn much of its food supply from the east, and which therefore made the treatment of Germany as an economic unity a vital British interest. Soon after the Yalta conference the Treasury, in an important paper of 7 March 1945, argued that if Russian demands on German reparations were met, and if this were coupled with the dismemberment of Germany, the whole of western Europe might be impoverished and its political stability undermined. Germany had a major part to play in the economic recovery of Europe.[20] If Soviet policy nevertheless brought about the division of Germany, Britain should be ready to consider the integration of a unified western Germany in western Europe. This explains why the British favoured a higher level of German industrial production in the immediate postwar era than did the Americans (who were still seriously divided among themselves as to future policy), though some consideration was also given to a close alignment with the French which would include strict control of the German economy to prevent the production of other than semi-finished goods. In practice, however, the British soon encountered even more obstructionism from the French than from the Russians in the treatment of Germany as an economic unit. But in the middle of 1945, the great concern was Russia. The British saw themselves paying heavily to avert starvation in their occupation zone while at the same time the Russians might be drawing reparations from Germany and in other ways adding to British difficulties. Much was made of the image of the Anglo-Americans feeding the German cow while the Russians milked her. Bevin finally secured agreement at Potsdam that payments for approved German imports should be a fixed charge on German exports, though Russian reparations from the western zones (on a reduced scale) would not be included in these calculations.[21]

Attlee wrote to General Smuts at the end of August 1945 that he hoped to avoid a real clash with Russia. He also noted that Britain had received less support from the Americans at Potsdam than he had hoped for, while the British embassy in Washington was forwarding reports of the divided opinions that existed in the United States over future American foreign policy. Further difficulties arose with the frequent failure of the then American Secretary of State, James F. Byrnes, to take the British into his confidence. His abrupt shifts in position left the British uncertain and aggrieved in the last months of 1945.[22] Not surprisingly the Foreign Office did not abandon all thoughts of spheres of influence deals with the Russians. The latter's non-interference in the Greek troubles in the winter of 1944–5 offered some encouragement here, while *The Times* strongly favoured a compromise with Russia. Yet a rigid division of Europe was contrary to Britain's material interests and her emotional commitments. Nor was there entire confidence that such deals would guarantee Soviet non-intervention in the West. In fact it was impossible to devise any policy at that time which really met British interests. Apart from the United States and Russia account had also to be taken of France. But communist strength there was disturbing, and much as Britain desired to see France restored as a major power, many years must elapse before this could take place. In these circumstances most British leaders felt happier working from the traditional island base, complemented by the Commonwealth and if possible by the United States. Anglo-French relations thus remained somewhat uncertain; British policy in Germany was dictated by harsh material needs, while the debate in informed British circles concerning Russia tended to be resolved in the spirit displayed on 25 July by Pierson Dixon (about to become Bevin's principal private secretary); in dealing with the Russians it seemed safer to act on the worse assumption.

The British public was at first ill-acquainted with this deterioration in relations with Russia, which was not confined to Europe, but which included suspicion of Russian activities at the expense of Turkey, in North Africa and northern Iran. Allied wartime differences and difficulties had received little publicity: understandably Russia's great contribution to the defeat of Germany had been emphasized, and it was not easy at first to transmit the concern felt by policy-makers and top officials. Russian action in eastern Europe caused dismay, but it could also be seen as defensive, and as a search for compensation for the massive losses sustained since 1941. The official fear that Russian influence might continue to spread in Europe, not through military action but rather as a consequence of revolutionary situations, was not easily communicated. George Orwell's *Animal Farm* was published in 1945 and served as a reminder of Stalin's Russia of the 1930s, but there was an understandable reluctance to accept that one war had been fought only to be followed by yet more great power rivalries and the possibility of conflict. *The New Statesman*, in coming grudgingly to accept the need for a British alignment with the United States and for the American loan, argued that this made it all the more imperative to avoid a breach with the Soviet Union. The Attlee government, therefore, while its foreign policy caused much satisfaction on the Conservative benches, had to proceed with a wary eye on other opinion in the country.

Chapter 2

Labour and world affairs, 1945-8

The American loan, 1945-6

Great uncertainty continued to dog Anglo-American relations. The British services would have liked to perpetuate the wartime partnership institutionalized at the highest level in the Combined Chiefs of Staff. This was not possible. If the Churchill–Roosevelt relationship had not always run smoothly, the absence of intimate personal ties was much felt until Bevin had won the confidence of the State Department. The death of Roosevelt, for instance, complicated the transition from war to peace in the Anglo-American economic relationship.

British dependence on American Lend-Lease from 1941 had provided Washington with a powerful lever with which to wring British promises of postwar cooperation in the creation of a multilateral economic order. But detailed discussions also underlined the difficulty of making real progress. American plans necessitated vast credits with which to tide over nations suffering from balance of payments deficits. Without international loans such nations would be driven to resort to import quotas, high tariffs or currency devaluation, all contributing to a return to 'beggar-my-neighbour' policies. Keynes, a restrictionist by necessity rather than persuasion in the 1930s, moved towards multilateralism during the war, but his plans to increase international liquidity through a 'clearing union' or world central bank with overdraft facilities of up to $25 billion, were too ambitious for the Americans – not least because initially they would have provided the bulk of the funds. The resultant efforts, notably at the Bretton Woods conference in 1944, to increase international monetary cooperation provided some, if rather limited, hope in the long term. But the proposed International Monetary Fund and International Bank for Reconstruction and Development could do little to meet Briain's immediate postwar problems. At the beginning of 1945 the British were hoping that, through Roosevelt's goodwill and the expected continuation of the war against Japan into 1946, it would be possible to lean on Lend-Lease while the economy began its conversion to peace. These hopes faded under a new President and in the face of an increasingly critical Congress. The sudden collapse of Japan in August meant the end of Lend-Lease long before the most pessimistic British calculations. A paper before the war cabinet on 14 August 1945 stated bluntly that without American aid in 1946-8 the nation would be 'virtually bankrupt and the economic basis for the hopes of the public non-existent'.[1]

It has been estimated that Britain had lost about 10 per cent of her prewar wealth – or no less than one-quarter if external disinvestment were also included.[2] Above all the nation was able to pay for only a fraction of the imports she needed both for current survival and for the reconstruction of her economic health. Through Lend-Lease and her ability to run up enormous debts to members of the sterling area it had been possible during the war to divert a large proportion of her former export industries to war production, so that at the end of 1944 her exports stood at only about one-third of their prewar volume. Import needs were much as in 1938, and the terms of trade had also moved against Britain; invisible earnings had fallen through the loss of one-quarter of the merchant marine, and the liquidation of over £1 billion in foreign investments. Britain's external liabilities were nearing £3.5 billion by the middle of 1945 – a sevenfold increase – yet her reserves totalled less than £500 million. It was estimated that further foreign debts of at least another £1.25 billion would be incurred over the next three years before the nation could pay its way internationally, and that, given the many changes in Britain's economic circumstances, it was expected that in order to achieve long-term solvency the volume of British exports would have to be at least 50 per cent higher than before the war. This figure was later raised to 75 per cent. Yet in June 1945 no less than 45 per cent of the nation's employable manpower was still directly or indirectly devoted to the war effort. Conversion to the needs of peace had barely begun.

In so far as the British understood their economic plight – and it is important to understand that despite rationing and austerity the mass of the British public never experienced the after-effects of war so starkly or so directly as most people in western Europe – there was a tendency to argue that their unique stand against Hitler in 1940–1 entitled them to special treatment. As *The Economist* remarked concerning the American loan on 8 December 1945: 'In moral terms we are creditors; and for that we shall pay $140 million a year for the rest of the twentieth century [a reference to the terms of the American loan as finally negotiated]. It may be unavoidable; but it is not right.' Earlier Keynes himself had been far too sanguine as to what might be won from the Americans on the grounds of Britain's contribution to the defence of democracy. With the British Cabinet, he had hopes of securing a grant-in-aid, but in Washington in the autumn of 1945 he soon found that American purse-strings were not undone with reminders that Britain had pursued a policy of unparalleled financial imprudence in the cause of humanity. More effective was his warning that without American help, Britain would be forced into the 'grimmest form of bilateralism' in international trade. In memoranda prepared for these talks he wrote of the danger at home of even stricter rationing, more complete government planning, the direction of trade 'somewhat on the Russian model', and a retreat from a world role to second-class status.[3] At the same time he believed that Britain was too weak to risk a trade war with the United States. Lord Robbins thought any British retreat from its promises on multilateralism would have been viewed by Americans as 'a plain declaration of economic warfare'.

Even so the British Cabinet several times came near to breaking off the talks with the United States when they found that nothing more than a loan was obtainable, and that of only $3.75 billion at 2 per cent interest, accompanied by other damaging conditions. In particular, Britain was required to agree to the introduction of sterling convertibility within one year of the conclusion of the loan agreements, as opposed to the five years promised under Bretton Woods. Even with these terms the American negotiators were not sure of the approval of Congress, any more than the British government could be happy about their reception in Parliament. The terms were humiliating to a proud nation. Many on the right saw the loan as yet another assault on the Empire and sterling area. Robert Boothby likened the agreement to 'Munich', and accused the government of selling 'the British Empire for a pack of cigarettes'. Beaverbrook and his press insisted that Britain and the Empire did not need the loan. Amery and many others insisted that better terms should have been obtainable. On the left there were charges that the Americans were using the loan to impede the pursuit of socialist policies in Britain. But according to Shinwell only he and Bevan opposed the agreements in the Cabinet, and though the government had recourse to the Whips to secure a reasonable vote in the Commons – as it was, the 343 in favour included some Conservatives – the general mood was one of disappointed resignation. Keynes was one of the few to offer a spirited defence. In the Lords he argued on 18 December 1945 that the only alternative was to build up a separate economic bloc: '. . . which excludes Canada and consists of countries to which we already owe more than we can pay, on the basis of their agreeing to lend us money they have not got, and buy only from us and one another goods we are unable to supply.' As late as 1947 some 46 per cent of Britain's imports originated in the Americas.

That the loan agreements were deficient, inadequate and unrealistic is clear. Professor R. N. Gardner describes the policies of both countries as doctrinaire.[4] Yet, as we have seen, the differences between them are more comprehensible than agreement; changing circumstances alone could bring about the necessary adjustments. The subsequent 1947 economic crisis, and the role of Marshall Aid in British and European recovery can leave no doubt but that the history of Britain would have been very different without this first hesitant postwar step in Anglo-American cooperation. Britain's retreat from a world role must have been hastened (a consequence not easily evaluated for Britain herself or for the world) while conditions of life in Britain would have been much harsher for many a year. Dalton, indeed, reconciled himself to the loan in the belief that without it Labour would have been able to fulfil few of its election promises. He envisaged austerity worse than at the height of the war, high unemployment – 'the near future would have been black as the pit'. Labour's chances at the next election would have been much diminished.[5] Interestingly, much American opposition to the loan agreements sprang from the belief that their effect would be to prop up both British socialism and imperialism. To some extent this was the case. American pressure against the sterling area and imperial preference proved singularly ineffective, partly because, as we shall see later, American interests required a change in policy, but also because the loan in practice facilitated the continuance of established British policies, if only for the time being. As it was, in the early months of 1946 Congress seemed loath to approve the loan, despite the assurance that it was an essential step to multilateralism. The battle was not finally won until July, by which time fears of communism and the spread of Russian influence were making a real impact on American opinion.

The slow and hesitant manner in which Britain and the United States were once mor drawing together was highlighted by the generally cool reception by American public opinion of Churchill's famous but often overrated Fulton speech of March 1946 in which he spoke in dramatic terms of the danger from communism and the need for Anglo-American cooperation. It is better understood in the light of Roosevelt's 1937 Quarantine Speech, only this time another President used Churchill to test out American opinion. Despite the ambiguous public response, Churchill was able to assure Attlee privately of growing sympathy for Britain within the American administration. This gave badly needed comfort to a government which felt gravely over-committed on the world stage, and singularly exposed to Russian pressure and hostility. If the passage of the McMahon Act, also in 1946, merely confirmed the predisposition in the American administration itself to end the wartime collaboration with the British in nuclear research, there were other signs that summer that fears of Russia were causing America's leaders to revive something of the wartime intimacy.

The Empire and Commonwealth in 1945–7

Despite the loan, Britain's economic problems were necessitating some review of her position as a world power. Some thought was being given as to what policies lay within her powers, as well as to the returns and costs to be expected from certain imperial ventures. Dalton in particular was dismayed by many of the costs, though his later rejection of the Colonial Office revealed him as something of a 'little Englander' in any case. Bevin, in contrast, dreamed of a cooperative Common-wealth, made up ultimately of self-governing states, working together to make full use of their varied resources and skills, and jointly to create a 'balanced economy'. In the shorter term he was impressed by the value of the exported primary products of certain African colonies, and he hoped to use American dependence on some Commonwealth raw material exports as a lever in foreign affairs. As for India, in June 1943 he wished to see her become a dominion as soon as possible, with an expanded industrial base which would not only relieve her domestic economic and social problems, but which would enable her to play a greater part in the maintenance of the balance of power in Asia. Already he feared that Russia might replace Japan as a source of concern in Asia, especially if China failed to establish herself as a great power after the war. Cripps, too, was deeply interested in India, and the Labour party as a whole was able to approach the question of Indian independence with rather more open-mindedness than the Conservatives.

Nevertheless, Labour did not possess a well-developed programme or philosophy either of economic development or political emancipation for the Empire as a whole. Indeed, the Fabian Colonial Bureau's ideas often provoked the resentment of Indian and African nationalists. Its idealistic and paternalistic inspiration tended to put social justice and social democracy ahead of nationalism, self-government and self-determination *per se*, at least until the mid-1950s. When other leading Labour figures came to share Bevin's fear of Russia and communism, this also created barriers between them and those who made independence the first priority. Colonial questions attracted relatively little attention even from the extreme left in the late 1940s. For the Labour party as a whole there was a tendency to lapse into the complacent belief that a satisfactory evolutionary process was taking place. As for most Conservatives, it was an article of faith that without her empire Britain could not remain a world power. Yet there were sceptics. Oliver Stanley, a Conservative ex-Secretary of State for the Colonies, had doubts as to the long-term viability of Imperial Preference and perhaps the Empire itself. He recognized that the survival of the Commonwealth was dependent on the existence of real, not artificial, mutual interests.[6]

The basic trends were not easy to distinguish at this time. Imperial unity had been impressive in both world wars, despite the protests of Indian nationalists at the start of the second. On the other hand the independence of the Dominions had long been a fact, with Australia and New Zealand beginning to follow the example of Canada in looking to the United States for security. The Great Depression had brought some strengthening of the economic links within the Commonwealth in the 1930s. Britain's trade as a whole had declined sharply, but the proportion with the Commonwealth grew, until in 1938 45 per cent of exports and 38 per cent of imports were concentrated within this region. The war brought the formal creation of the sterling area in 1940 to facilitate exchange controls (Canada was not included), and the postwar dollar shortage encouraged the continuance of these arrangements. The same circumstances led to the development and increased control of certain colonial resources, but as the debates on the American loan have already revealed, neither the Commonwealth nor the sterling area provided comprehensive answers to Britain's postwar economic problems.

Britain reoccupied all the colonial territories that had not been reconquered before the defeat of Japan in August 1945. One-quarter of the world's population and territory once again made up the Empire and Commonwealth, while the sterling area and special treaties of protection and alliance carried British influence even beyond these confines, notably in Egypt, Iraq and the Persian Gulf. But the vulnerability of Britain's imperial position, once demonstrated, could not easily be rectified. By 1945, apart from the stirrings within the colonial territories themselves, the two most formidable powers in the world, the United States and Russia, both professed themselves to be anti-colonialist. Burma was the first to secure a date for independence. The British did not at first appreciate the strength of the nationalist forces there, but speedily adjusted their policies from the autumn of 1946. Burma became independent outside the Commonwealth in January 1948. At the end of the war it was recognized that independence for India and Ceylon could not be long delayed, and during the war constitutional concessions had been granted to Jamaica, Malta and the Gold Coast.

Even before 1939 concern had been growing over the economic stagnation and poverty of many of the colonies, notably the West Indies where local disturbances had prompted a new sense of urgency. The Colonial Development and Welfare Acts of 1940 and 1945 were important innovations and there followed perhaps as much colonial development in the next ten or fifteen years as in the previous fifty. This more positive approach was reflected in the trebling of Colonial Office staff between 1940 and 1950, though the necessary experts required to serve in the colonies were not always forthcoming. There was less interest in the preparation of the colonial peoples for self-government and independence, though some initiatives were taken to try to educate new native elites in the mould of the ruling expatriates. The Colonial Office believed that it had an almost indefinite amount of time at its disposal. It moved forward with an enhanced sense of trusteeship: good government had priority over progress to self-government. Economic development was seen as good in itself, a necessary instrument against unrest, as well as in many cases a dollar-earning asset for the sterling area. In 1945 it seemed unnecessary to pay much attention to the Pan-African Conference which met in Manchester – a conference attended by figures of the utmost importance in the future history of Africa, Kwame Nkrumah, Jomo Kenyatta, Julius Nyerere and Hastings Banda.

The great imperial issue at the end of the war was India. Here it was at last appreciated that events had been accelerating. The Secretary of State for India in January 1939 had, with some reservations owing to uncertainty about the future strength of the Congress party, expected India to advance politically at the speed of a 'stage-coach rather than an express train'. Lord Halifax, a former Viceroy, believed that had it not been for the war the India Act of 1935, with its promise of ultimate self-government for a loosely federated subcontinent, might well have succeeded. Jawaharlal Nehru, however, had dismissed the measure at the time as 'pompous language, full of sound and meaning little', and it is hard to imagine the Congress settling for such a solution. In so far as the British were thinking of leaving India, they were doing so on terms which would protect their interests. Internal peace and stability were vital for economic and international reasons. India as a member of the Commonwealth was believed to be essential for imperial defence. As Leo Amery wrote to Churchill on 16 April 1943: 'To keep India within the Commonwealth during the next ten years is much the biggest thing before us.' India's strategic importance was, it was felt, confirmed by the Second World War despite her inadequate industrial infrastructure. The service chiefs reflected uneasily on the implications of India's independence, for a time hoping at the end of the war that India would become the centre of one of several Commonwealth defence groupings.

By the end of the war, however, the British had to concern themselves above all with the danger of chaos and civil war in India as their own power in the subcontinent weakened, and rivalry increased rapidly between Hindus and Muslims. What might formerly have been used as an excuse for a prolongation of British rule was now becoming an obstacle to their departure. British readiness to negotiate was not at first grasped by the Congress, and even the advent of a Labour government did little at first to facilitate constructive talks. The Viceroy and many British officials in India were viewed by the Congress as pro-Muslim and as too favourable to the princes. The Congress itself was too slow to accept that the Muslim League was a real and representative force in Indian politics. Great communication barriers thus existed between the three main parties. A British minister, Pethick-Lawrence, aptly likened politics in India to an 'Alice in Wonderland croquet party'.

Meanwhile Britain's ability to retain control of the situation was steadily diminishing. Already in October 1944 the Viceroy, Lord Wavell, had warned that the British administrative machine was running down. He saw a growing danger of communal violence, with the risk that Indians in the armed and civil services would in time become caught up in these divisions. He complained bitterly in 1945–6 of a lack of firm action by the Attlee government, arguing in particular that it should exert more pressure on the Congress. There were communal riots in Calcutta in August 1946, while the belated cobbling together of an interim Indian ministry in October, with representatives from the Muslim League and the Congress, afforded no real hope for the future. Wavell at the end of 1946 was drawing up a breakdown plan, 'Operation Ebb-Tide', providing for the progressive evacuation of expatriates from British India in the event of disaster. Dalton bleakly concluded Britain must concede independence even at the cost of a Hindu–Muslim civil war. The Attlee government was by now convinced that further delay was the more dangerous course. It decided to take the risk of announcing that the transfer of power must be effected by June 1948. It also decided to appoint a new Viceroy. This was a sensible tactical and psychological move in any case. Wavell was too suspect in the eyes of the Congress. His successor, Lord Mountbatten, was more adept in personal relations, more fluent in debate and conversation. He could be both flexible and decisive. As Allied Commander in South-East Asia he had already displayed unusual awareness of the new political forces that were at work. He had already met and made some impression on Nehru. Once in India, however, even he could make little impact on the adamantine Muslim leader, Mahomed Ali Jinnah.

The British government's new policy was not without critics in Britain, but help was at hand from the experienced and respected Lord Halifax. He grimly conceded on 26 February 1947: 'I am not prepared to condemn what His Majesty's Government are now doing unless I can honestly and confidently recommend a better solution.' Direct contact with Indian affairs soon convinced Mountbatten and his close adviser, Lord Ismay, that Britain's ability to control the situation was diminishing even more quickly than had first been imagined. Only a massive infusion of British military and administrative personnel, and a grim determination to rule India for another ten or fifteen years, could reverse this decline. At the end of April Churchill himself reluctantly acknowledged to Ismay the force of these arguments. The British, he agreed, were 'exhausted and . . . no longer interested in India'. Mountbatten and Ismay, indeed, were so dismayed by what they found that both wished to shorten the period during which power was transferred. Every delay increased the risk that Indian personnel in the civil and security services would cease to be reliable as they thought more and more in terms of their relationship with successor regimes. In the opinion of Mountbatten and the British government, the shorter the period during which power was transferred the better the safeguards against communal turmoil and bloodshed. Yet the realization that the unity of India could not be preserved opened up immensely difficult questions regarding to whom power should be transferred, and how.[7]

Mountbatten's first proposals were fiercely opposed by Nehru as too divisive. These assumed the voluntary combination of provinces into states according to their political or religious preferences. This threatened India with balkanization. V. P. Menon therefore proposed the handover of power to two states, each of which should be given dominion status within the Commonwealth, preferably under the same Governor-General in the first instance. The creation of Hindu and Muslim states would still be difficult and painful, especially in the hopelessly intermingled populations of the Punjab and Bengal, but the new plan promised greater political stability from the outset. The acceptance of both partition and dominion status by Nehru represented major concessions on his part; he had come to accept them as promising the best quick way forward. The date for independence was advanced to

15 August 1947, and preparations for the transfer of power were henceforward a desperate battle against the clock. Critics have been able to point to many mistakes in the preparations for partition, notably in the failure to take adequate precautions against the widespread violence that was to follow the announcement of the details of partition. In particular there were ample warnings of the explosive situation in the Punjab where, to divide the territory of the Sikhs, was an invitation to disaster. But those at the centre had much else to preoccupy them, not least the independent ambitions of some of the princely states. In any case, it would have been difficult to provide and control the forces needed to police such vast areas and numbers of people. Estimates of those killed in the massacres following independence vary widely; the lowest suggest something approaching 200,000 in the Punjab. Over 10 million people finally decided that they could not endure the new rulers under whom they found themselves so abruptly placed, and joined in the great migration. Even then minority problems continued, with Kashmir as a running sore between India and Pakistan, and with Pakistan itself being divided in 1971.

But in 1947 these and other disappointments lay in the unknown future. Many in Britain took special pleasure in India's decision in 1949 to remain in the Commonwealth, albeit as a republic. The negotiations were difficult, with Nehru at first opposing Indian membership. In time he came to see disadvantages for India if only Pakistan had a place in the councils of the Commonwealth. There might be other political and economic advantages for India. The negotiations also brought out Attlee's great concern for the position of the British monarch.[8] By and large the continuing relationship was welcomed in Britain, though in time it was seen that it involved both gains and losses. Indian membership of the Commonwealth encouraged other Afro-Asian peoples, as they became independent, to join. On the other hand it helped to foster illusions in Britain concerning the future potential of the Commonwealth. The question must also be asked whether the British adequately appraised the political and strategic implications of the loss of the Indian army – a crucial element in British strength in the East for over one hundred years. Did so much British concern over the Middle East and the route to India still make sense, it was later asked, and were the means for their defence still forthcoming?

The Truman Doctrine and Marshall Aid

The Chiefs of Staff's concern over the strategic implications of Indian independence has already been noted, and there is other evidence of discussion within the government of the relationship between Britain's resources and foreign commitments. Occupation forces were needed in several parts of Europe in addition to the many British military commitments in the Middle and Far East. In the summer of 1947 there were still half a million British service personnel overseas at a time of labour shortage. Even then the intention was only to reduce that figure to 300,000. By 1947 the government was under pressure from many quarters and for many reasons to cut its foreign commitments. There was always a marked reluctance among many in the Labour party in any case to support an ambitious defence policy, and especially one that now entailed both conscription and the expenditure of a higher percentage of the national product than the interwar average. Some Labour supporters opposed a British presence in the Middle East as a relic of imperialism. There were also pressing economic considerations. By 1947 the American loan was being expended more rapidly than expected. Savage winter weather early in the year temporarily paralysed much of the economy. In July–August 1947 the convertibility crisis over sterling threatened to exhaust the nation's remaining gold and dollar reserves. Dalton, backed by Cripps as President of the Board of Trade, complained repeatedly of government extravagance in these circumstances. The net cost in foreign exchange of British forces overseas in 1946 alone was put at £225 million, or more than half the balance of payments deficit for that year. It was further estimated that the nation was suffering from a manpower shortage of about half a million.

Not surprisingly British strategy with respect to several key areas of the world was far from settled in 1947. There was some debate as to how far Britain should commit herself militarily to the European continent. On the Middle East, one important example of the kind of discussion that was proceeding in the cabinet is provided by Dalton's record of a meeting at Chequers in February 1946.

Attlee is fresh-minded on Defence. It was no good, he thought, pretending any more that we could keep open the Mediterranean route in time of war. That meant we could pull troops out of Egypt and the rest of the Middle East, as well as Greece. Nor could we hope, he thought, to defend Turkey, Iraq or Persia against a steady pressure of the Russian land masses. And if India 'goes her own way' before long, as she must, there will be still less sense in thinking of lines of Imperial communications through the Suez Canal. We should be prepared to work round the Cape to Australia and New Zealand. If, however, the U.S.A. were to become seriously interested in Middle Eastern oil, the whole thing would look different.[9]

Attlee pressed these views on the Chiefs of Staff, arguing that Britain should retreat south to a line from Lagos to Kenya, and rely essentially on geographical obstacles to protect the African empire. These ideas were obviously music in the ears of the hard-pressed Chancellor of the Exchequer, and continued to attract sufficient attention for the Chiefs of Staff to intimate privately to the Prime Minister in January 1947 that they would resign unless the Middle East were held.

Attlee continued to feel that the military exaggerated the strategic value of the Middle East, but his reference even in February 1946 to possible American interest was very significant. The government could not make too much public reference to its hopes of closer relations in general with the United States in view of Labour backbench opinion and the attitude of some ministers. Nor did it wish unnecessarily to provoke the Soviet Union. Bevin gave assistants such as Christopher Mayhew and Gladwyn Jebb the impression that he did not finally despair of working with the Russians until late in 1947. At times he seemed more worried by the ultimate threat from a resurgent Germany. Within the Cabinet Dalton, Cripps and Bevan were at first more critical of the Americans than the Russians. The activities of American oil companies in the Middle East occasioned some concern – to Attlee among others, though he also saw oil as a basis for Anglo-American cooperation. In fact fear of Russia encouraged regulation of Anglo-American oil competition just as, in time, it led to cooperation in the running of the occupation zones in Germany. The two governments were closer in sympathy and understanding than was often the surface impression, the basic trend in their relations in the Middle East, for instance, being obscured by their differences over Palestine. As early as 1946 the British were able to draw some comfort from the support lent by the Americans to the skilful double game played by the Iranian Prime Minister in securing the removal of Russian troops from the north-west of his country. By July–August 1946 Anglo-American talks were beginning over Britain's need for American assistance in strengthening both Greece and Turkey against communist pressure.

The British had earlier recognized that the Russians might have a grievance over the restrictions imposed on the movement of their warships through the Turkish Straits by the Montreux Convention of 1936. Such sympathy cooled when the Russians also demanded bases in the straits and frontier revision in eastern Anatolia in 1945. American fears developed more slowly, but develop they did. Turkey was increasingly seen as another state the Russians were bent on dominating. Bevin and Truman used equally firm language in December 1945. The British reaffirmed their 1939 alliance with Turkey in 1946, and in August Turkey was assured of Anglo-American support for any firm, but reasonable response to Russian demands. American service chiefs described Turkey as the strategic key to the eastern Mediterranean and Middle East. Anglo-American staff contacts were being resumed on both Middle Eastern and European strategy at this time. The Admiralty warmly welcomed the establishment of a permanent American naval presence in the eastern Mediterranean. Encouraging, too, for the British was the American announcement in September 1946 that their occupation forces would remain in Germany for as long as might be necessary, and on 2 December it was agreed that the British and American zones should be merged to relieve their economic problems. The British were paying some £80 million a year to help feed the Germans, and though this burden would not be immediately eased, the new arrangement gave promise of future relief.

The Treasury was also warning that Britain could not continue to support Greece unaided beyond 1946.[10]

In October 1946 some Labour backbenchers protested against this new pro-American trend in British policy. But Attlee refused to listen to an appeal from twenty-one MPs for a more socialist line that was independent of both the United States and Russia. Fifty-three MPs then tabled an amendment in support of a 'third force' foreign policy. This was the first internal party crisis since the election. Morrison was able to quieten the discontent temporarily, but this idea of a western European socialist 'third force' kept recurring, notably in the Crossman–Mikardo–Foot *Keep Left* pamphlet of May 1947. The majority of the Cabinet, however, agreed with Attlee and Bevin that western Europe was too weak economically and militarily for such a policy to be feasible, at least in the foreseeable future. As Attlee put it; 'there wasn't either a material or a spiritual basis for it at that time. What remained of Europe wasn't strong enough to stand up to Russia by itself. You had to have a world force because you were up against a world force.'[11] The European economic crisis of 1947 revealed that this thinking was in no way too pessimistic. As it was, given the country's own economic problems, the government was sailing very close to the wind, for all Bevin's appreciation from bitter trade union experience of the need to keep a keen eye on what there was 'in the till'.

Those in the government who were concerned at the cost of British foreign policy did win one victory early in 1947. On 21 February, on the insistence of the Treasury, the British warned Washington that their aid to Greece and Turkey must cease on 31 March. The significance of this note has sometimes been exaggerated. The State Department had long been aware of Greece's precarious position, and the growing success of communist forces. Some assurance of American support had been given to Athens on 18 October 1946. Washington was mainly surprised by the suddenness of the British warning, but made maximum use of the note to frighten senators with the spectre of a communist gain in the Near East that would threaten American hopes of containment elsewhere in the Mediterranean and even in Europe. The British themselves were perhaps surprised by the scale of the American response, with the proclamation of the 'Truman Doctrine' on 12 March and its sweeping promises of support for 'free peoples who are resisting attempted subjugation'. More specifically, the United States assumed most of the British burden in Turkey and Greece. Not only was their survival seen in the context of the containment of Russia from Iran to Italy, but there were fears lest the British, feeling themselves unsupported by the Americans, might be driven to spheres of influence agreements with the Soviet Union.

Even more far-reaching American action was soon called for as the British and European economic problems worsened. Britain and France drew a little closer with the Treaty of Dunkirk of March 1947, which was mainly intended to provide insurance against Germany.

Bevin, too, seemed disposed to toy with ideas for closer economic cooperation with France – even perhaps the establishment of a customs union – but as the year proceeded the inadequacy of purely European solutions became all the more apparent. The Council of Foreign Ministers met in Moscow in April 1947, only to produce the most pessimistic conclusions in Bevin's mind. He informed Attlee in a lengthy letter of 16 April that the Russian object was 'to loot Germany at our expense'. On reparations for themselves, on the rehabilitation of their occupation zone, in their bid for influence in other zones, Russian policies would all be at the expense of western powers. Piecemeal Russian concessions, he argued, were a repetition of the strategy of previous conferences which brought only such settlements as the Russians desired, leaving the wider issues unresolved to the disadvantage of the West.

Therefore I stipulated that I would not be committed until I had seen the problem as a whole and could ascertain whether any decision would involve additional cost for Great Britain, whether it would provide repayment for what we had put into Germany, and whether over reparations we should be treated quite fairly.

In the light of existing Russian policy, he went on, 'I cannot see how current reparations can be paid unless they are provided from America and Great Britain', given the present plight of Germany. Bevin opposed four-power control of the Ruhr unless it was applied to Germany as a whole. 'It is quite clear what the Russians are after, namely to get into the Ruhr, to make our Zone impossible to work . . .' He feared the powers were getting 'perilously near a position in which a line-up is taking place'.[12]

The economic situation was also worsening. The severe winter of 1946–7 had possibly delayed the British export drive by nine months. Dalton anticipated that the American loan would be exhausted in the first half of 1948, a year earlier than expected. There were various causes, including the rising price of dollar goods. Cripps feared the development of worse than wartime economic conditions, with imports cut so drastically that much of the food ration would be reduced by one-third, and with timber in such short supply that house building would be limited to a mere 50,000 a year. Unemployment might also rise to 1.5 million despite the fact that at the moment the nation was desperately short of manpower. Ideally, drastic cuts in government and national spending of all kinds were called for, but the Cabinet seemed unable or unwilling to grapple with the approaching crisis. That spring the Keep Left group argued sensibly for firmer and more austere economic policies, but neither in anticipation of sterling convertibility nor during the summer economic crisis were departmental ministers prepared to slash their estimates, save under the most severe pressure.

Attlee gave no real lead at this time, and was the subject of much criticism by his colleagues. Morrison, though in overall charge of economic affairs, lacked the machinery as yet through which to act effectively. Cripps doubted Morrison's ability to plan and act effectively even had suitable machinery been in existence. Morrison was also recovering from a serious thrombosis which had incapacitated him for three months. Bevin appeared unhelpful, if not irresponsible, to some of his colleagues. He, for his part, shared Cripps's lack of faith in Morrison's economic expertise. There were suggestions that a Minister of Economic Affairs should be set up (to replace Morrison's ineffectual overlordship), but Attlee made no response. The strain of government was clearly telling on key ministers, and tempers and their sense of perspective suffered in consequence. It has also been generally asserted that Treasury officials failed to anticipate how serious a run on the reserves would be occasioned by the introduction of sterling convertibility in July. Nevertheless this widely accepted version of a divided and palsied ministry blundering into a crisis is not quite the whole truth. The government was weak, but it was not wholly inactive.

American sources reveal that from at least May 1947 the British were warning Washington of increasing financial difficulties. There may even have been some informal exploration of the possibility that convertibility might be delayed.[13] It was still difficult to quantify or give a firm date for the impending crisis: the Americans commented on the slowness with which the Treasury produced many of its estimates, and some remained imprecise to the end. But more serious was the certain opposition of Congress to any British attempt to escape from the terms of the American loan. Indeed, American officials in the early summer of 1947 were anxious to do nothing to excite Congress at a time when only a revolutionary change in American foreign policy seemed equal to the task of saving Europe from further economic decline, with the most damaging consequences for the United States itself. Both Bevin and George Marshall, the American Secretary of State, departed from the Moscow conference in April 1947 convinced that it was Soviet policy to play a waiting game until western Europe sank into poverty and chaos. The State department recognized that western Europe would soon be unable to buy more dollar goods, and might relapse into narrow nationalist autarkic policies, under totalitarian or revolutionary regimes. Communism or some other hostile political order might emerge. Even if Britain managed to resist the worst of these developments, her will and ability to oppose the Russians might be crippled, and, without Britain as an ally, many in the State Department feared that American opinion would take flight into isolationism. The peaceful multilateral trading world dreamed of by American internationalists would evaporate.

The American solution, which was to go down in history as the Marshall Aid programme, was carefully launched in deliberately low-key speeches made by Acheson and Marshall himself in May and June, but with great care being taken to alert the Foreign Office as to their significance. Bevin wasted no time in taking the initiative among western European states to secure the promise of cooperation and self-help that Marshall desired. But a visit by the American Under-Secretary for Economic Affairs to London at the end of June revealed that the British also entertained hopes of securing special financial concessions. Bevin declared: 'I think it would pay the United States and the world for the United States and the United Kingdom to establish a financial partnership.' He thought Britain had entered into obligations to end discrimination in trade and to institute convertibility three years too early. Dalton also made it clear he thought convertibility was likely to prove premature, but the conversations must have impressed all the British participants with the danger of antagonizing Congress.[14] To some extent, it would appear, the government abided by its promises concerning sterling convertibility in the knowledge that, while it was likely to have damaging if not catastrophic consequences, it was a necessary act to win American confidence, and to ensure the successful launching of Marshall Aid.

The British were indeed in a very difficult position. Since 1945 they had paid out some £750 million in gifts and loans to aid others in postwar reconstruction, but to little avail. India was dependent upon her sterling balances to avert disaster. Britain traditionally relied on her surplus with the eastern hemisphere to help meet her deficit with the Americas, but now neither she nor the east had the means to earn sufficient dollars. Indeed, some countries had difficulty in buying from Britain. Shortages of certain primary products were also holding back some sections of the British economy, including the expansion of livestock on British farms. A vicious circle thus existed which the non-communist states outside the Americas were unlikely to be able to break by their own efforts. Britain also bore the added burdens of her occupation role in Germany, of sterling convertibility, and of the sterling area itself. The terms of trade were swinging against her so that rising import prices had cut the value of the American loan by about one-quarter. The British argued that they deserved special treatment from the United States because of their imperial and world trading roles. There was also an evident fear that the creation of a European 'pool' might drag them down to the level of the others. Flashes of interest by Bevin in closer European economic cooperation came to nothing, and broadly it was British policy to accept only such cooperation with Europe as was necessary to ensure American economic aid. When the Council of Europe was proposed, Bevin declared: 'I don't like it. I don't like it. When you open that Pandora's box, you will find it full of Trojan horses.'

Bevin's talks in mid-June 1947 with the French foreign minister, Bidault, found both in early agreement that progress towards the implementation of the Marshall programme would be quicker if the Russians declined to cooperate – which they did on 3 July. Interestingly, Bevin still entertained some hopes that summer that Marshall Aid might prove a means of drawing the east European states into closer contact with the west. This would have had obvious economic and political advantages, and the Soviets may have pulled out before the possibility of Marshall Aid excited too much interest in eastern Europe. Anglo-French leadership nevertheless brought together a meeting of sixteen European states in Paris in the middle of July. A Committee of European Economic Cooperation was set up to report on Europe's needs and to prepare proposals for European economic cooperation – promise of real progress here being vital to persuade Congress that Europe was worth helping. Bevin expressed fears of communist subversion in western Europe, especially in Italy, but he was pleasantly surprised by the firmness of the French towards the Russians, despite the strength of the French communist party.

Even so, Britain's economic problems were becoming too urgent to await the outcome of these moves. Convertibility was introduced on 15 July and it was immediately evident that a larger flight from sterling was taking place than had been anticipated. There were fears in Washington of further British withdrawals from foreign commitments, commitments which the United States might have to take up at greater expense than subsidizing the British. Britain might also return to bilateral trading. But there was also some criticism of the size of the British housing programme, welfare expenditure and socialism in general, and of the disappointing level of coal production. Bevin sent an urgent warning on 25 July that the country's financial situation was becoming critical. Other warnings followed to the effect that the loan would be exhausted by the autumn.[15] Without early help, drastic dollar import cuts would be inescapable, less aid could be given to Europe, multilateral trade would be threatened, and Britain would 'no longer be able to act as the differential gear between the United States economy and much of the rest of the world'. The American ambassador in London was equally alarmed. Marshall informed Truman on 1 August that the situation was critical. Anglo-American talks were hastily arranged for the 18th. Only $700 million of the loan remained: $176 million had been lost in six days. With some hesitation the Americans agreed to the suspension of convertibility on the 21st: the last of the 1946 credits were frozen (Washington agreed later in the year to their release). Britain had to be sustained as America's main partner against the Soviet Union and for the good of world trade. Even with the ending of convertibility and the imposition of stricter controls on dollar imports by Britain and her sterling partners, British reserves fell perilously close to what was regarded as the bare safe minimum of £500 million. Nevertheless these measure sufficed to bridge the gap till Marshall Aid became a fact.

The British search for a Middle Eastern policy

All this time the British and the Americans continued to draw together over the Middle East despite their persisting differences over the future of Palestine. Given other British disappointments in this region, and the views of many in the Labour party, this partial convergence of Anglo-American thinking must surely have helped to persuade the British to cling to positions which they might otherwise have relinquished as beyond their own unaided powers to sustain.

Bevin, from the outset, was not content with the traditional instruments of protectorates, treaties and bases. If his foreign policy was not 'socialist' in the eyes of some Labour critics, he nonetheless worked with that Foreign Office school which believed less reliance should be placed on military strength, and more on voluntary partnerships between Britain and the peoples of the Middle East. 'Peasants not pashas' was the theme of one memorandum. Such a policy was hampered by Britain's economic weakness following the war. In any case the likelihood of working with the new political forces which were emerging in the Arab world was exaggerated. To many Arabs this approach was merely imperialism under a new guise. Political divisions within the states and within the region further complicated the problem, British support for one group alienating others. Attlee dismissed most of the Middle Eastern governing classes at this time as a poor lot, but agreed that the British themselves, both in government service and in business, were often slow to accept the need for change gracefully.[16]

In practice the British found their most reliable allies among the autocratic and traditional rulers, such a King Abdullah of Transjordan whose state was poor enough to find British subsidies welcome, and the sheikhdoms of the Persian Gulf. Saudi Arabia was moving into the American orbit, while nationalist aspirations and political factionalism in Iraq and still more in Egypt threatened the existing treaty relationships. Bevin toyed with the idea of developing in Kenya an alternative to the great Suez base, but in general the service chiefs found him an ally in their struggle to uphold British strategic interests in the Middle East. Although he was prepared to renegotiate Britain's defence treaties with both Egypt and Iraq on a more equal footing, and was even prepared to withdraw British forces from the Suez base in certain circumstances, he also insisted that no political vacuum should be allowed to develop in the Middle East. As early as 7 November 1945 he had asked whether the Russians were aiming, in that region, to come 'right across, shall I say, the throat of the British Commonwealth'. Field-Marshal Alanbrooke was sent on a Middle Eastern tour in the autumn of 1945 in search of allies. An initialled agreement with Egypt came to nothing in October 1946, mainly because of a collision of interest as to the future of the Sudan. Bevin told the American ambassador on 9 September 1947 that the Sudan was potentially a British base, and could be used to prevent Egypt aiding an enemy.[17]

Anglo-Egyptian relations steadily deteriorated, and the troubled domestic politics of Iraq frustrated the negotiation of a new defence treaty with Britain in January 1948. Not surprisingly the American ambassador in London reported on 11 June 1947 that the British were uncertain what bases they would hold in the region in ten years time (apart from Gibraltar, Malta and Cyprus), and in the long term they looked to good relations with the local peoples as the best defence against communism.[18]

The sterling convertibility crisis of August led to more discussion as to whether Britain could afford to stay in the Middle East, but Attlee supported Bevin in opposition to any general evacuation.[19] Concern over the cost nevertheless persisted, or at least was used by the British to try to elicit a firmer expression of American intentions in the region. There were also hopes of American backing for British plans to try to raise Middle Eastern living standards. British irrigation experts were at work in the Tigris-Euphrates area, but in general Britain lacked the resources to support major development projects. Britain further looked to Washington for aid in their frustrating negotiations with the Egyptians over the future of the Suez base, or failing the cooperation of Cairo, in the creation of an alternative base in Cyrenaica. The Chiefs of Staff insisted that the Middle East was second only if not equal to the United Kingdom as a strategic theatre in a major war, the Middle East being vital for Commonwealth communications and British oil supplies, as well as serving as an offensive air base against an aggressor. But it was necessary to win more assured American backing. A State Department memorandum of 5 November 1947 noted that:

... although the British Government has decided that the maintenance of the security of the Mediterranean and the Middle East is vital to British security, they have not made plans to implement that policy and one of the most important reasons for their indecision has been the lack of knowledge of United States policy in respect of that area.[20]

One cannot be sure how far the British were bluffing, but it is clear that earlier doubts concerning Britain's strategic future in the Middle East were gradually being resolved by the general strengthening of their relations with the United States as well as by the deterioration of relations with the Soviet Union.

The Americans for their part were fearful of a communist advance into Iran, French North Africa and Italy, Greece and Turkey. The National Security Council concluded in the winter of 1947–8:

It would be unrealistic for the United States to undertake to carry out such a policy (opposing this advance) unless the British maintain their strong strategic, political and economic position in the Middle East and Eastern Mediterranean, and unless they and ourselves follow parallel policies in that area.[21]

Anglo-American talks indeed produced from George Marshall on 4

December 1947 a promise that, provided the British did not seek exclusive spheres of influence and did not offend Middle Eastern nationalism with outdated colonial attitudes, 'parallel policies' and substantial agreement would be possible on most issues.[22] He could not, however, agree to any formal commitments. With this, perforce, the British had to be satisfied. But it was enough, given the general course of American policy. The Middle East, in any case, was daily becoming more important. In the event of war with Russia, the loss of much of western Europe seemed possible, and the Middle East would provide essential bases for air strikes against Russia. Middle Eastern oil was also becoming increasingly valuable, and with the construction of oil refineries in Britain all-important dollars were being saved. Indeed, by 1949 the Middle East was providing half the oil imports of western Europe, and the proportion was still rising. Bevin had no hesitation in defending his Middle Eastern policies as crucial to the living standards of the British working man, and to Labour critics in 1947 he insisted that he was not going to put all British interests in a pool while everybody else stuck to his own.

Given this measure of Anglo-American cooperation, the differences between the two states over Palestine may be seen in a clearer perspective. The promise to create a National Home for Jews in 1917 had led to many unforeseen consequences. By the 1930s there were many more Jews seeking entry to Palestine than had been expected. The Nazi persecution was the main, but not the only cause. The tepid response of most western peoples to the fate of the Jews strengthened the hands of those who came to insist that Jews could find no security save in a *state* of their own. In turn the Arabs could reasonably ask why the sins and omissions of the Europeans should be paid for at their expense. The sympathies of most of the Labour party, like those of Churchill, lay originally with the Jews: the widespread feeling that their horrific sufferings in Europe deserved special consideration was often accompanied by a remarkable insensitivity concerning the Arabs. Thus Eleanor Rathbone could speak of justice to the Arabs but of the entitlement of the Jews to even more on account of past suffering and their ability to do more for mankind in the future. Dalton saw no difficulty in moving Arabs to let in more Jews. Attlee, on the other hand, was impressed by the fundamental differences of Jew and Arab, and feared too the effect of an anti-Arab policy on Muslims in India. Bevin believed good relations with the Arabs were vital, but under-estimated the strength of the Zionists themselves and their supporters in the United States. He was also unfairly criticized by many of his own party for failing to act decisively in favour of partition, and thus in support of the Jews. The problem was in some respects more intractable than that of India where at least the principle of partition, though not the details, was finally accepted by both sides. The Arabs rejected partition: the Zionists demanded an independent state. No compromise was possible. Sooner or later it would be resolved by force between Jew and

Arab unless an outside power could impose an alternative solution. At first the issue turned on the rate of entry of Jews into Palestine, with the British caught in the crossfire of Jewish and Arab pressures. Hopes – very tenuous ones – that an Anglo-American committee of inquiry might find a way forward had already been wrecked when President Truman, from political necessity, had tried to satisfy Jewish opinion in the United States without neglecting America's Arab interests.[23] British, Americans, Jews and Arabs, all were at loggerheads, the nearest approach to cooperation being between the Arabs, the Foreign Office and the State Department. There were divisions, too, in the British Cabinet, and further uncertainty was introduced by military interest in 1947 in the possible creation of a base in Palestine should Suez prove untenable. Even reference to the United Nations in February did not entail any firm decision, save that the British remained adamant that they would not enforce a solution which was not accepted by both parties, and that partition should not be adopted. When therefore the United States and Soviet Union finally agreed upon partition in 1947, to the great embarrassment of the British, the latter announced that they would not assist in its implementation, and would surrender the mandate to the UN on 15 May 1948. With 80,000 British troops failing to defeat Jewish terrorism, with the cost of the occupation mounting, and with British public opinion becoming hostile to further involvement, the decision was understandable. To stay to help enforce partition would have been a fatal blow to British relations with the Arabs. According to Glubb Pasha, commander of Abdullah's forces, Bevin hoped that Transjordan would occupy eastern Palestine. Bevin also complained to Montgomery in April 1948 that British troops in Palestine were giving insufficient protection to the Arab population. The British minister in Transjordan, Sir Alec Kilbride, was highly critical of his country's foreign policy. To him it lacked purpose, clarity and a sense of responsibility. But whatever the spirit in which Britain's policy was conducted, events had in practice passed far beyond her grasp. By April 1949 the Jews had secured control of most of Palestine, while many Arabs found in Britain a convenient scapegoat for their defeat.

If, however, the British had washed their hands of one area, their interest in the Middle East as a whole had by then been confirmed by the development of the cold war and some assurance of American aid. In 1948 Francis Williams, who had been Attlee's public relations adviser, published an important analysis of Labour policy, *The Triple Challenge*. Concerning the Middle East he wrote:

So long as she remains a world power Britain cannot but be interested in varying degrees in the future of Turkey, Persia, Iraq, Syria, Lebanon, Palestine, Transjordan, the countries of the Arabian Peninsula, Egypt and the Sudan, and even Ethiopia, Eritrea and the Somalilands.[24]

This list was almost worthy of Curzon, yet should also have included

Cyrenaica. The armed forces themselves had hopes at worst of holding a line from the Taurus mountains to the Gulf of Aqaba against a Soviet attack.[25] But in June 1948 there was a penetrating insight into the future recorded in the State Department. There it was noted that the Colonial Office's insistence on the exclusion, for strategic reasons, of Cyprus (as well as Malta) from the possibility of self government, was laying up trouble for the future.[26]

Chapter 3

The domestic policies of the Labour government

The economic heritage in Britain

The Labour party, according to Professor Marwick, 'had that same ingrained democratic sensibility which had bedevilled the policies of MacDonald and Baldwin. In 1945 the Labour government had a unique psychological opportunity to be bold: but bounded as they were by the empiricist traditions of British politics they were not able to seize it.'[1] Others, employing varied arguments, have reached similar conclusions. Given growing disappointment with the course of British history since 1945 this is an understandable development. Nevertheless, as more detailed research into this period becomes possible, so the contrary argument might be strengthened, namely that, with the enormous difficulties (internal and external) under which this government was obliged to work, it is remarkable that it achieved as much as it did. Most of the party's main leaders were cautious, pragmatic people, yet they were moved by a real sense of injustice and a conviction that British society could be better ordered. Certainly they recoiled from leftist solutions on theoretical grounds as well as for hard practical reasons. The government required the willing cooperation of existing civil servants (Attlee later insisted that there was no obstructionism from right-wing bureaucrats), businessmen, and the main professions. Nor could trade unionists, with their vested interests, be forgotten. Too many upheavals would have damaged British exports, reduced confidence in sterling, or diminished the prospect of American aid. It was believed by the Labour government that a balance had to be struck between domestic reform and the nation's world role. Such changes as were instituted had mostly to be worked out in detail in office, were in some cases pushed through only with difficulty, and a generally overburdened government would have been hard put to take up other tasks. Most of the key ministers had already endured the strain of office in the wartime coalition. Cripps was driven by ill-health into retirement in 1950, and Bevin in 1951. Attlee and Morrison both experienced serious illnesses. Aneurin Bevan was in his prime, but lacked a power base, detailed programme, and all-round political skills. Finally it must be remembered that the party had neither sought nor been given a mandate in 1945 for drastic change.

Reference has already been made to the international environment which the Attlee government faced. At home there was the daunting task of making good the havoc of war and converting a war economy to the requirements of peace. There was the pressing need for the volume of exports to exceed the prewar figure by no less than 75 per cent. There were the promises in the election manifesto to be met. The government was also much influenced by the fear lest the expected postwar boom should soon collapse, as had happened after the First World War. In the past seventy years the British economy had been more troubled by recessions than by excess demand, save in time of war. As late as 15 July 1950 *The Economist* was asking whether the prophets of an economic slump would yet be proved correct: was the world enjoying only the 'Indian summer of the long postwar inflation'? In 1945 no one could predict how the economy of the United States would develop. Uncertainty shrouded the prospects of world trade in general.

The American loan at least provided the government with some temporary firm ground from which to work: indeed it may have created false confidence against which Dalton and Cripps later raised unavailing voices. Nor did Dalton himself easily wear the garb of a Cassandra, exuding too much confidence in 1946. His policy of 'cheap money' became an object of sharp criticism once persistent excess demand was apparent. The country, however, had become accustomed to low interest rates since 1932, and such rates reduced payments on government securities and sterling balances.[2] The fear persisted that the postwar demand might burn itself out within three years, whereas the time needed to reconstruct the British economy and to meet the backlog of demand created by the war was underestimated. In so far as immediate restraints were necessary – and these were considerable given the manpower and the raw material shortages – the government looked to a continuation of wartime controls, rationing and the use of taxation. Indeed, with controls and low interest rates as its instruments, the government at first proceeded with some confidence. It expected that it would be able both to encourage and control investment. Later, as concern over excess demand replaced fears of a possible slump, cheap money was driven into the shadows from 1947, though it was never wholly abandoned by the Attlee governments. There had, moreover, been other causes of inflation, and the extent of the attacks on cheap money owed much to Dalton's personal identification with it.[3]

In 1945 Labour inherited not only controls but a fairly widespread – if perennially grudging and critical – public acceptance of them. These, of course, were wasting assets, not least since the controls were designed for the much simpler purpose of winning a war rather than running an increasingly complex economy in time of peace. Similarly business and public tolerance of controls began to diminish. Even in war major differences of opinion could develop over the best use of scarce resources: in peace the demands of foreign markets and a civilian economy were still more difficult to fathom. As the *Economic Survey* for 1947 commented: 'Our national existence depends upon imports, which means that the goods we export in return must compete with the rest of the world in price, quality and design, and that our industry must adapt itself rapidly to changes in world markets.' The same document also stated that it was too early to produce a five-year plan, though one might try to devise 'a useful practical guide'. Subsequent *Surveys* showed even less interest in the future. Labour had once talked of a 'plan from the ground up', but no such document was ever devised. No planning ministry was instituted in 1945, it being left to Herbert Morrison as Lord President of the Council to coordinate economic planning and development. Morrison himself inclined to pragmatic solutions; he was convinced that the British would not tolerate drastic innovations. He was handicapped by his own lack of economic flair as well as by the inadequacy of government institutions. Rivalry with the Treasury was a further obstacle. Important institutional changes, and in personnel, were necessary in 1947 before the government could begin to exercise even that more limited control over the economy with which it was then prepared to content itself.

Although many physical controls were used by departments during the war, the manpower budget was the only method ever possessed by the War Cabinet to determine the balance of the whole war economy by a central and direct allocation of physical resources among the various sectors.[4] From 1945 negligible use was made of this instrument, though there were arrangements to try to discourage the movement of labour from important yet undermanned industries. More positive results in the pursuit of a more satisfactory distribution of labour could be expected from the use of building licences, the power of the Capital Issues Committee to pronounce on capital issues over £50,000, and the government's control of raw material supplies. Some discrimination could be exerted in favour of important export-orientated or import-saving industries, or in favour of the formerly depressed regions.

Even so difficulties could arise. Coordination over the use of scarce raw materials was far from complete. It was largely a matter of interdepartmental negotiation, with *ad hoc* judgements being the subject of many pressures. Morrison described the allocation of materials as 'the reconciliation of the irreconcilable'. Some success was achieved with the vehicle industry, the steel allocation being based on a promised level of exports. It was possible in general for broad economic objectives to be defined, and economic information and forecasts built up to guide the government in its control of imports and in its allocation of resources. Yet, significantly, the government was heavily dependent on personnel from private industry in the administration of many of its controls. Trade associations were extensively involved in their application.[5] The government was able to make use of the public service tradition that ran deep in much of the British middle class. There was also within industry widespread appreciation of the dangers of an uncontrolled return to a free market economy – the post-1918 experiences were borne in mind here too. Nor could businessmen ignore the degree to which the power balance had moved in favour of the left. Both government and industry, in fact, had many incentives to try to work together and did so with no mean success until 1947-8. The partnership, indeed, gave much protection to some of the less efficient sectors of British industry. Through the administration of price controls some businessmen were also able to achieve unusually good profits.[6] But the government itself really had little choice in the matter, since the necessary expertise was rarely forthcoming from other sources. The Civil Service was not anxious to undertake a more direct role in business. Its ethos was changing so slowly that a contributor to *The Political Quarterly* in April-June 1951 could claim, if somewhat light-heartedly, that a Victorian returning to Whitehall would have been surprised 'only by the presence of women'. Apart from its distrust of a business role, Whitehall was no longer so strong in economists and statisticians as it had been in the war. Professor A. A. Rogow has argued that the Labour government was worse served in economic intelligence than the Truman administration in America.[7] The 1946-7 fuel crisis, the 1947 convertibility crisis, and the information guiding government policy in 1950-1 all suggested serious deficiencies, even if such were far from providing the whole story. Labour's six years in office encouraged new thinking as to the manner and degree of government involvement in the economy. Although this was partly reversed by the Korean emergency, the Attlee ministry tended to concern itself increasingly with a general rather than a detailed oversight. As early as 1948 an assault on unnecessary controls was ordered in the Board of Trade and Ministry of Supply. By 1950 the government was looking to the budget and to a limited selection of controls to regulate the balance of payments as its main instruments.

Less than one-quarter of the productive capacity of industry was earmarked for nationalization. As early as June 1946 Attlee insisted at the Bournemouth party conference: 'The Government has gone as far left as is consistent with sound reason and the national interest.' The great task was to make industry more efficient and humane. The party's hostility to monopolies and cartels found expression only in the cautious legislation of 1948, and in general British industry in the 1940s continued to exist in a heavily protected world. Protection was afforded by its own internal arrangements, by government control of imports, and by its access to the markets of the Commonwealth through preferences and dollar shortages. The government was at first less active in the promotion of exports to dollar markets than might have been expected. Despite some government help there was no Dollar Exports Board until 1949. British exporters themselves had reason to fear American tariffs and other impediments to trade; it took time for fears of a great American recession to lift, but there was also a tendency to look for excuses for inaction. Bevin, despite other preoccupations, and Cripps were troubled by this slow progress. Cripps contributed to the creation of the Anglo-American Productivity Council in 1948 and the arrangement of visits by British industrialists to study American methods. The British Institute of Management's Administrative Staff College was set up at Henley, and earlier Cripps had worked for the creation of development councils in certain industries to encourage modernization. Few had materialized, and fewer achieved anything against industrialists' fears of backdoor government influence. The councils were caught in the backwash from 1948 as the high tide of cooperation between government and industry began to ebb. The Government also gave help to industry with respect to research, development and re-equipment, with about one-quarter of the cotton industry's new machinery in 1947–8 being paid for by a £10 million grant.

The recovery of British industry was greatly assisted by the conversion of much of the factory space and machinery built for arms production from 1936. Against the heavy disinvestment that occurred in industry producing civilian goods must be set the £1,000 million investment in munitions between 1936 and 1945. Never before had so much been invested in a comparable period. A proportion of this had been spent on the provision of services and communications. Among the beneficiaries had been the prewar depressed areas, including Glasgow and even the Scottish Highlands. Electrical power had been expanded by a half, tractor production doubled, and at the end of the war £100 million of machine tools were sold off to private industry – about twenty times the prewar average annual rate of purchase. Some 75 million square feet of factory space became available. The iron and steel, machine tool, vehicle, aircraft, chemical, plastic, electrical and electronic industries had all been expanded. The stimulus afforded by war needs to the development of radar, radio, even simple computers in anti-aircraft defence, provided an invaluable basis for much postwar civil development. Chemical substitutes for many raw materials had been known before the war, but the creation of the British petrochemical industry really dates from 1942. Since oil is mainly composed of carbon and hydrogen, two of the commonest chemical elements, it could be used in the production of synthetic rubber, nylon, terylene, detergents and many other useful substances. Finally, if rail and road transport, the textile and certain other industries had suffered severe disinvestment during the war, the mechanization of both coal and agriculture had been accelerated.

The war had also left a useful legacy of highly skilled technicians and technologists, and some greater appreciation of the worth of such people and of scientists. The government's new respect for the scientist was reflected in the creation of the Defence Research Policy Committee and the Advisory Council on Scientific Policy, both chaired by Sir Henry Tizard. He also chaired the Committee on Industrial Productivity, set up in 1947 to advise the government on scientific research most likely to aid industrial productivity. There were specialist committees to advise on textile research, the uses of gas turbines, and other specific problems. Radar, jet aircraft, rockets and nuclear weapons had all dramatized science, lifting it outof the pages of H. G. Wells into the real world. Science, too, had become too costly to be left solely to individuals or even private companies. There was the promise of further revolutionary developments, both civil and military, in the near future. Of particular interest was the beginning of the British nuclear programme.

Even in the course of the war itself there had been Anglo-American difficulties and differences of opinion over nuclear cooperation. Britain was firmly committed to a long-term nuclear programme with or without American help from 1941. Churchill and his intimates were convinced that Britain as a great power must have nuclear weapons. The initial British contribution to the development of an atomic bomb had been of the utmost importance: Britain's role declined sharply in the later stages of development and much was learned from the Americans, including some insights into the development of thermonuclear devices. Nevertheless there was understandable dismay when the United States broke off cooperation with the McMahon Act in August 1946, especially after Roosevelt had impressed others beside Churchill with his apparent determination that Britain should be helped not only to regain her economic strength but also to possess nuclear weapons.[8] Averell Harriman, who was American ambassador in London in 1946, also thought American conduct shabby.[9] As it was, the British, being forced to proceed on their own, broadened their research and development, and so facilitated the exciting if controversial leap into large-scale civil research in the 1950s. In 1945–6 work started on a nuclear research and experimental establishment at Harwell, the first nuclear piles and chemical separation plant at Windscale, and a gaseous diffusion plant at Capenhurst. Great secrecy surrounded the programme. Attlee took few colleagues into his confidence. Initially he and Bevin had entertained some hopes of international cooperation, including the Soviet Union, but both American and Russian conduct confirmed the predisposition among British policymakers to believe that their country, as a major power, must have her own nuclear capability. In government circles, only the mathematician P. M. S. Blackett and the scientist Sir Henry Tizard were important critics. Attlee and Bevin, while not excluding the possibility of renewed cooperation with the Americans, insisted that Britain had to be protected from a possible American return to isolation as well as be in a position to exercise some influence over the United States acting as a world power. No explicit decision to develop a bomb was taken until January 1947, and then in the general context of national defence rather than with special reference to the Soviet Union. Civil applications remained highly speculative at this stage, and without the military stimulus would not have reached a practical stage of development in the 1950s. Until at least 1952, despite the fears of Tizard, the atomic programme did not constitute a serious drain on the nation's resources.

It was, in fact, remarkable for the efficient and economic manner in which it was conducted. In the view of Professor Gowing, Britain acquired a nuclear capability for military and industrial purposes at 'a bargain-basement price'.[10] The credit for this achievement lay with government-employed personnel, men of remarkably varied talents, who had often to struggle against the lack of interest shown by, and the technical limitations of, private industry.

The uneven union of science and industry in Britain was a matter for general concern. Highly qualified scientific and engineering personnel were certainly in short supply, yet not all industries seemed aware of their need to recruit more good graduates. If demand from non-industrial sources outstripped the university output of scientists (although it was doubled to 5,000 between 1946 and 1952), systematic use was not always made of those who were available. The aircraft industry, for instance, was guilty of some maldistribution of qualified personnel. Research and design teams were strengthened at the expense of other vital, if more prosaic departments. Bright ideas proliferated, but were not always sufficiently related to the more utilitarian problems of producing a finished aircraft at the right time, at the right price, and with the appropriate capabilities to attract foreign as well as British buyers. Government interference and indecision sometimes added to the industry's problems, but the aircraft firms remained a good example of the national tendency to use scientific manpower with a definite bias in favour of advanced research. Within that bias, there was a further national emphasis on defence. As will be seen, Britain's high standing in pure science was not fully reflected in her postwar economic performance. Japan and Italy later demonstrated how much economic growth could be achieved despite a heavy dependence on imported knowledge.

Britain's industrial heritage in 1945 was thus very mixed. Some sectors possessed remarkable potential. Others, such as shipbuilding and the car manufacturers were flattered by a sellers' market. Britain had too many small car-making firms producing too many models with insufficient regard for foreign needs and tastes, and weak in after-sales services. In the first postwar years this did not matter. Cotton textiles were highly vulnerable, not only because of rising competitors using cheaper labour, but as a result of disappointing British levels of productivity (these could be as low as one-third of those prevailing in the United States). The government's ability to influence industry in general was limited, given its lack of expertise and the suspicions of both management and labour. Indeed, *The Economist* on 29 June 1946 argued that state, management and labour mutually reinforced each other in preserving inefficiency in industry. 'There is a conspiracy of labour, capital and the state to deny enterprise its reward.' Efficiency for many Labour supporters was one of the less important reasons for nationalization, political motives and concern for social justice ranking much higher. Labour sometimes sought wider support for nationalization by arguing that it would be more efficient, but the endeavour to secure control of the 'commanding heights' of the economy proved so complicated and time-consuming in itself that little positive thought was given to the question of efficiency *per se.*

The implementation of the programme of nationalization

Elements of public control and public ownership were well established in Britain by 1945. There were various local government utilities such as water, roads, sewage and cleansing. The Post Office, the British Overseas Airways Corporation, the London Passenger Transport Board, the Central Electricity Board and the Port of London Authority were all precursors to varying degrees of nationalization. Coal royalties had been nationalized in 1938 though not the mines themselves. The war added to the experience of the government in assisting with the running of key concerns. Indeed, Lord Reith as Minister of Transport, drew up a plan to nationalize the railways that was strikingly similar to that instituted in 1947.[11] Nevertheless the relative success of the wartime approaches of government to industrial matters encouraged the Labour leaders, already predisposed to caution and with much else to preoccupy them, to avoid radical experiments in the administration of the new nationalized industries, and in addition to concentrate their attention upon a few key industries. Aneurin Bevan himself declared at the 1949 Blackpool Conference, 'we shall have for a very long time the light cavalry of private competitive industry'. Many of his colleagues expected private industry to provide much of the infantry and artillery as well.

Morrison was widely accepted as Labour's expert on nationalization, even by his critics. He was able to draw on some practical experience, notably his part in the creation of the London Passenger Transport Board. Both in the relevant government departments and in the TUC some general studies of problems of nationalization had been undertaken,[12] though Shinwell could claim with some truth that detailed plans were lacking in 1945. The chosen instrument for nationalization became the public corporation, responsible to the relevant minister, who in turn was responsible to Parliament. But power in the last resort lay with the Minister and the government. Joint consultative committees with worker representation were set up, only to achieve little influence in practice. Hopes that the corporation boards would themselves include many workers were also largely disappointed. Only the Central Electricity Authority achieved significant worker representation (with Lord Citrine, an ex-union leader, as its chairman); the average was under one-fifth. There were various reasons for this. The government was anxious that the boards should be mainly staffed with people with ample managerial experience. If no special provision was made to enable working-men to gain such experience in the future, there was also a considerable reluctance on the part of a majority of trade unionists to, at best, risk their independence; at worst to give the appearance of changing sides and becoming bosses' men. There were serious conflicts of loyalty, and while unions often argued the need for more workers' influence (notably in the TUC's interim report on postwar reconstruction), they also feared that involvement in management would weaken their position as the defenders of labour. The long, hard, and divisive industrial history of Britain could not be transformed overnight by acts of nationalization.

The organization of the nationalized industries thus left much to be desired. Management remained remote – sometimes became more remote – from the workers, and was often over-centralized. Too often the 'old gang' seemed to be in power. Nor was it always possible to find first-class personnel. The National Coal Board inherited over 750 concerns and over 700,000 workers, but was able to fill few key appointments with men who had experience both of mining and of large-scale operations. It also inherited an industry with a disastrous record in labour relations. The best that can be said of the coal-owners between the wars is that they responded to unfavourable market conditions in accordance with accepted economic wisdom, and that the industry was 'seriously affected by the peculiar nature of the period'.[13] But the fact remained that its interwar record was poorer than its main competitors'. Miners believed that they had been betrayed by the government after 1918; they recalled the interwar wage cuts, and the desperate strike of 1926. There were the accumulated grievances of generations, and memories were little affected by the doubling of wages in the industry between 1939 and 1945, an advance above the national average. This was just seen as paying miners no more than their due, and in no way providing compensation for the past or security for the future. Pit production committees during the war had revealed yet again the difficulties of communication between the two sides in that industry. Despite increasing wages and mechanization, productivity had declined during the war. The unattractiveness of the work and the isolated community lives led by most miners made increased leisure preferable to higher wages once a certain level of satisfaction had been reached.

The need for drastic reorganization was recognized by the Reid Report of 1944 and by the Conservative party. The latter, in office, might have attempted something short of nationalization, but in opposition they offered only token resistance. The magnitude of the task facing the National Coal Board, which took over on 1 January 1947, was not at first fully appreciated. There had been a steady decline in coal stocks in Britain, but there were also deficiencies in the transportation of such coal as was available. Nationalization, even with adequate management and resources, could not be expected to produce significant results before the 1950s. Of some interest, nevertheless, is an American assessment of the condition of the industry at the beginning of 1947, even if it reveals much ignorance concerning Britain's housing problems and of entrenched patterns of thought and behaviour. It commented on the absence of a wage system designed to encourage productivity, on the slowness to provide housing at expanding pits, and the reluctance of miners to leave the less productive pits for new areas; it emphasized a general lack of drive, flexibility and imagination by American standards.[14] Emanuel Shinwell, as Minister of Fuel and Power, was much criticized by some of his own colleagues for the 1947 coal crisis. Effective government action called for cooperation between Shinwell, Dalton and Cripps. This did not develop. Doubtless there were faults all round. Shinwell later fared better as a service minister.

The case for the nationalization of electricity and gas was strong. Neither, as organized, could undertake ambitious and coordinated modernization and expansion programmes. There were over 500 separate electricity undertakings – seventy-five in London alone – with tariff and voltage variations from area to area. A Hydro-electric Board for the North of Scotland had been established with excellent results during the war. The British Electricity Authority came into being in 1948, with local distribution being placed in the hands of fourteen subordinate area boards. Gas supply was even more disorganized and inefficient, and legislation to set up a Gas Council and twelve Area Gas Boards was introduced in January 1948. The nationalization of the Bank of England in 1945 was largely a symbolic act – it did not, in Churchill's opinion, raise any matter of principle. To BOAC were added two more public air corporations, British European Airways and British South American Airways, the latter being merged with BOAC in 1949. Independent companies could operate charter flights, and act as agents for the corporations. Unfortunately the British aircraft industry had few suitable planes to offer. There was much complicated interplay between manufacturers, government and operators, and perhaps no small element of sheer chance, in the evolution of the Vickers Viscount into the outstandingly successful aircraft it became in the 1950s. Satisfactory air fleets were built up only after much time, trial and expense, and with a heavy reliance on American planes.

A British Transport Commission was set up in 1947 with the onerous assignment of creating a 'properly integrated system of public inland transport and port facilities'. It was provided with five executives to run, respectively, the railways, ports and inland waterways, road services, London passenger transport, and railway hotels and catering. There was much talk of the creation of a speedy, cheap, coordinated system to meet all needs, including those of the sparsely populated areas. In fact little was achieved by way of integration – Morrison would have preferred one corporation to deal with inland transport[15] – the Commission being too overburdened, and preoccupied with immediate responsibilities. It was an elusive – some would argue illusory – goal in any case. It was realizable to some extent in the case of the London Transport Executive – the heir to a well-established organization – and then only until the explosion in commuting by private car. The nationalization of road haulage was particularly difficult, given the variety of services involved. Firms were left free to carry their own goods, but could use private contractors only over short distances. In practice British Road Services emerged as a fairly satisfactory long-distance haulier, with its interconnected, regular runs, so much so that some BRS customers objected to denationalization by the Conservatives in the early 1950s. Bus and coach travel was building up to its peak of 1953-4, but success on the roads was often achieved at the expense of the railways.

The railways had served the nation well during the war, but at the cost of heavy wear and tear that had not been made good. Their tremendous wartime achievements perhaps encouraged an exaggerated belief in their future importance. The dramatic achievements of the interwar expresses helped to obscure the growing challenge of road transport. The postwar petrol shortage gave further protection to the railways. Yet the deterioration in their financial position was clear before the war. Railway pricing was often unimaginative, inflexible or hampered by government regulations. Statutory restrictions frequently put the railways at a disadvantage compared with the road operator. Railways were at their most economic in regular long-distance operation, but too much of their capacity was directed to peak hour commuter traffic, to miscellaneous short-haul goods services, and, with the return of peace, to holiday traffic which demanded extra rolling stock for only a portion of the year. The Railway Executive lacked authority under the overworked Transport Commission, the railways remained starved of capital for some years, while fares and rates were held down by government command. The railways themselves also lacked sophisticated financial management. The possibilities of diesel and electric traction were at first neglected, while new and mostly unnecessary designs of steam locomotives were authorized. It is not realistic to look for a revolutionary improvement in British inland transportation at this time, but equally it cannot be said that the policies pursued showed much promise in imagination or administrative skill.

The case for nationalizing the above industries, except perhaps for road transport, could be justified on grounds other than pure socialism. Each industry had heavy capital requirements that were unlikely to be met by private investment. The Conservatives, in consequence, devoted most of their criticism to problems of organization and accountability, and amounts of compensation for the former owners. Both parties were content with vague guidelines on coordination and the need for each industry to break even financially over a number of years.[16] The major debate over nationalization was reserved for iron and steel. This industry was not obviously inefficient or short of capital, but was clearly one of 'the commanding heights' of the economy. Therefore for both parties questions of principle and power were at stake. Dalton insisted concerning the steelmasters that their record was little better than the coal-owners. Ernest Bevin believed that the leaders of this industry had shown great social irresponsibility between the wars, failing to modernize the industry sufficiently. Aneurin Bevan had seen the steelworks in his own constituency of Ebbw Vale closed between 1929 and 1935 on grounds of economy. It was argued that public ownership of so vital an industry was an essential part of any serious attempt at state control of the economy. Sufficient steel had to be produced at the right price, and not in quantities that best suited the pockets of the steelmasters. The estimated long-term iron and steel requirements of the nation might not accord with the readiness of private enterprise to risk investment on the necessary scale. In addition, the Franks Report early in 1945, which had been accepted by Churchill's caretaker government, had stressed the need for modernization and considerable restrictions on the freedom of individual iron and steel producers to act as they chose. This did not necessarily imply nationalization, but it pointed to the need for considerable state involvement.

The Attlee government entered office little prepared to grapple with the complex task of nationalizing iron and steel with their multiple links with other firms. Attlee and Morrison were not anxious to proceed, but were prodded forward by the Cabinet. An Iron and Steel Board was set up in 1946 to provide some government supervision of the industry, and Morrison a year later explored the possibility of a compromise with its leaders, who themselves were prepared to accept a measure of government involvement. Morrison feared the disruption of the industry at a critical time, and may have noted a lack of enthusiasm for nationalization among trade unionists in the industry.[17] In the middle of 1947 he reached an agreement with the steelmasters for government supervision, but not full nationalization. The Iron and Steel Board would be strengthened and would be able to recommend the nationalization of any inefficient unit in the industry. Morrison's biographers comment:

He had produced a compromise plan which was acceptable in broad terms to most of the steel bosses and to Lincoln Evans, general secretary of the steel union, was acceptable to himself and the Prime Minister, and which he believed he could sell to the party.[18]

Only on the last point was Morrison too optimistic.

Otherwise he had produced a statesmanlike plan which, if implemented, must surely have proved preferable to the dogmatic man-handling to which the industry was subjected by both parties over the next twenty years. Unfortunately Morrison's standing in the Cabinet was not high at that time. There was also dissatisfaction with Attlee as premier, and he consequently was in no position to challenge majority party and Cabinet feeling which favoured full-scale nationalization. The entire political atmosphere in the summer of 1947 was not conducive to thoughtful discussion, with dissension and disillusionment in the party coinciding with nightmarish threats to the gold and dollar reserves. July and August were the months of the convertibility crisis. Ministers were tired, jealous, critical and uncooperative. Apart from intrigues to displace Attlee, at the end of July Dalton and Cripps were contemplating resignation over the failure to grapple with the economic crisis, while Bevan threatened resignation if steel were not nationalized. The Conservatives were gaining rapidly in popular favour (they were ahead in the opinion polls) and for some in the Labour party there were too many reminders of 1931.

An exhausting Cabinet of 7 August decided against Morrison's scheme. A promise to nationalize steel, though not necessarily in the coming session, was needed to pacify many backbenchers and to restore party morale. A Bill was finally drafted to provide for the national-isation of firms that produced more than 50,000 tons of iron or 20,000 tons of iron and steel in 1946–7. This Bill received the royal assent on 24 November 1949. At one time the delaying powers of the House of Lords appeared to threaten the government's timetable for steel, and this possibility contributed to the government's decision in 1947 to press on with legislation to lessen the powers of the other House. The Parliament Bill, introduced in 1947, received the royal assent on 16 December 1949, and effectively halved the power of the Lords to delay legislation to one year. In practice, however, the timing of the 1950 election ensured that steel nationalization could not be implemented before there was an appeal to the voters.

In many ways Labour had won a pyrrhic victory over iron and steel. Electorally it was not an asset, though Labour still narrowly won the 1950 election. Furthermore, the Iron and Steel Federation, encouraged by the government's slender majority from February, and hopeful of another election, engaged in a policy of active non-cooperation down to July 1951, and thereafter relations with the government could best be described as one of 'armed truce'.[19] Difficulties were experienced with managerial personnel at many levels. The Conservatives' return to power in 1951 undid most of Labour's work. Neither the nation nor the industry itself was assisted by the uncertainty that embraced iron and steel from 1945, although coal and other shortages help to explain why no more than 70 per cent of the 1945 development programme had been completed by 1952. This programme, in any case, had been no more than the sum of the plans of individual firms. From the vantage point of the 1950s it seemed unambitious. The Americans retained their dramatic lead in productivity, while great progress was being made in West Germany and Japan. Certainly there had existed not wholly un-reasonable fears that the postwar boom might level off in the 1950s, but the clash between government and industry, as well as technical conservatism within the industry, all played their part in the final outcome.

Agricultural and regional policies

One industry with which government had been establishing a fairly successful relationship was agriculture. Agricultural prices had fallen catastrophically from 1920 to 1933. Farming was languishing in many areas, with the acreage of arable land in decline, and the quality of much of the grassland deteriorating. Agricultural research was being put to little practical use. The recovery from 1933 owed more to the general revival in demand than to government measures, but the 1930s nevertheless represented a turning point in the relations of government with farming. State aid took various forms, such as the regulation of food imports, subsidies, help with modernization and marketing. The war greatly accelerated and intensified these developments. As early as November 1940 there were government promises that a well-balanced agricultural industry would be maintained after the war. Postwar food shortages were anticipated, with higher prices, and with Britain less able to finance food imports through invisible earnings. *The Economist* became an important convert to subsidized agriculture in March 1945. The wartime achievement had indeed been impressive, with the proportion of the nation's home produced food rising from one-third to one-half. Research, improved techniques, more machinery – especially tractors – some increase in the labour force, and a 50 per cent increase in the land under cultivation all contributed. This production drive brought some loss in soil fertility, but fertilizers, improved drainage and water supplies could be set against this. The labour force fell after the war, though farmers were now on the whole better placed to afford additional capital expenditure. Increasing costs and output complicated the task of measuring the improvement in farming income, but it is significant that it now constituted 2.4 per cent of the national income (1945) compared with 1.2 per cent in 1938–9. The cost in government aid was heavy. Thus food retail prices rose by only one-fifth during the war, whereas agricultural prices nearly doubled.

After the war agricultural expansion was sustained by continuing government aid and encouragement. The Agricultural Act of 1947 covered about three-quarters of farming produce, using guaranteed prices and deficiency payments, with subsidies to offset the competition from cheap food imports. These represented a very heavy burden on the Exchequer, but this was scarcely questioned before the 1950s, when balance of payments problems (especially dollars) became less pressing, and few problems attended British food imports. With the striking improvements in farming productivity (then rising at about 6 per cent a year) a gradual reduction in the real costs of food subsidies became possible by the 1960s without serious injury to farming confidence. The impact of research, new equipment and techniques was truly remarkable in these years. On the other hand many small uneconomic farms survived, and there were those who argued that the resources devoted to agriculture might have been profitably applied to industry to boost exports. Yet the history of British agriculture since the 1930s reads more like a success story than many sectors of British industry, with output doubling despite a 40 per cent fall in the labour force. Most impressively, its productivity, growth record and general efficiency compared favourably with the western European average. Whatever the doubts that arose in the intervening years, a strong agricultural sector was an undoubted asset in the uncertain economic conditions of the mid-1970s, and throughout the whole postwar era home-grown food helped to relieve pressure on the balance of payments.

An attempt was made by the Attlee government to provide comprehensive regulation of the use of land by means of the Town and Country Planning Act of 1947. The National Parks and Access to the Countryside Act of 1949 set aside some areas for national recreation. Until the first postwar census of 1951 there was no real appreciation of the radical upturn in the population that had developed since 1942, but the distribution of the existing population, especially the overcrowding in London and the south-east, some parts of the midlands and the north, and in Glasgow, occasioned concern. The New Towns Act of 1946 was an attempt to relieve the pressure in London and some other major cities, while the Distribution of Industry Act of 1945 was followed by a drastic cut in factory bulding in the south-east. Government efforts to promote regional development also included Board of Trade loans for industrial estates, the building of factories for rent to entrepreneurs, the improvement of local services and the purchase of land for development. Among the varied government grants and loans was the provision in a local government bill for aid to the poorer local authorities whose income from the rates did not suffice for adequate public services and amenities, all of which were important in the attraction of new industry. These various controls and incentives ensured that about half of new industrial building in 1945-7 was concentrated in old areas of high unemployment, and over a quarter in the first postwar decade. The definition of such areas was changed following the war, and by 1948 had come to embrace about one-fifth of the population of Great Britain.[20]

The continuance of full employment in the long term, however, gradually eroded interest in the development areas in the early and mid-1950s. By 1955, only about 5 per cent of the insured population in those areas directly owed their jobs to the state. Meanwhile no less than eight of the first fourteen New Towns were being built near London. Office building in the capital was allowed to burgeon and add to the city's commuter problems in the near future. The redevelopment of old city centres often brought controversial results, the loss of central living accommodation intensifying transport congestion during the day, and leaving a wilderness of concrete at night. The Second Land Utilization Survey, begun in the 1960s, found that the Town and Country Planning Act of 1947 had not resulted in such intelligent land usage as hoped: in fact, piecemeal development around cities was continuing much as in the 1930s. In a commendable desire to control and improve, planners in the first postwar generation found cities and people less malleable than they had often expected.

Labour's social policies

If any issues in particular had moved nearly half the population to vote Labour in 1945 these had been the social questions – the shortages of housing, the insecurity of the lives of so many of the population, the desire for some sort of protection from sickness and unemployment. Furthermore, as Professor T. H. Marshall observes:

The idea of the Welfare State came to be identified with the war aims of a nation fighting for its life. It is not surprising that, in England, it wore a halo which is not to be found in other countries when, in due course, they undertook the task of social reconstruction.[21]

Neither Beveridge nor Labour's legislation was without its debts to the past, just as all parties contributed to the creation of the welfare state in the twentieth century, but 'there was a flame burning within the Labour Party in those years, compounded of the struggles and sufferings of generations of working men and women, that made the achievement peculiarly its own'.[22] Two contemporary Labour figures, Bessie and Jack Braddock, began their joint autobiography with a portrayal of conditions in Liverpool in the bitter winter of 1906–07, when people queued in St George's Plateau for farthing bowls of soup, while near the mercantile extravagance of St George's Hall stood the squalid housing of the poor. Much as the practical problems and pressures of power could lessen the divide between the average Labour and Conservative minister, yet the background experience, the personal perceptions, the party heritage and folk memory could rarely be shrugged off in its entirety. Their constituencies and constituents too often bore the marks of past neglect (on the Conservative side, colleagues of Harold Macmillan noted the impact of his old constituency, Stockton-on-Tees, which had suffered badly in the depression). There were, too, the shadows of Tolpuddle, Taff Vale, the General Strike and the Depression, of Clydeside, Jarrow and Ebbw Vale. Among those so influenced was the new Minister of Health, Aneurin Bevan. A man of Celtic passion and poetry, he fought many an inner battle when faced with the ambiguities of power. For while office conferred the means to change some things, it also entailed sacrifices and compromises, and responsibility for policies with which he did not wholly agree. Less down to earth than the other outstanding contemporary product of the British working class, Ernest Bevin, he was the most dramatic, and the most controversial, politician of his age. The first years of Attlee's government formed the most creative period of his life.

The most pressing postwar social need was housing. Despite the building boom of the 1930s (the nation's stock of houses stood at some 12.5 million in 1939), only limited progress had been made against slums and overcrowding. Much property had been destroyed and still more damaged or not properly maintained during the war. After the war the demand for housing was intensified by the spurt in marriages and the rise in the birth-rate. These were respectively one-tenth and one-third above the immediate prewar average. Churchill's Minister of Housing in March 1945 had optimistically assessed the immediate need at three-quarters of a million new houses. In the longer term, three to four million houses would be required, half a million of these in a slum clearance programme. This target required building on the scale of the 1930s. In fact, greater efforts would be necessary. Bevan inherited orders for 150,000 prefabricated houses, various powers to subsidize the local authorities in slum clearance, and plans to restore the building industry's labour force, which, by the end of the war, had shrunk to about one-third its former strength. There existed, however, no comprehensive building plan. The limited suppply of building materials had to be shared among housing, factories, schools and hospitals. Some Conservative critics wanted to give private builders their heads, but this would have led to an inflationary scramble for scarce materials, and would have continued the interwar building bias in favour of the middle classes. On the other hand, the creation of a giant housing corporation under the Ministry of Works might have proved unwieldy, or, in so far as it was effective, might have been dominated by the big building firms. Bevan therefore chose to work mainly through the 1,700 local authorities, and strove to overcome their problems with generous subsidies and other government help. Most Ministry of Health housing experts favoured this approach, and the main delays in the programme arose from shortages of raw materials.

At the time of the 1951 census there were more occupied dwellings (13.3 million) than in 1931, but households had grown even faster (to 14.4 million). The excess of households over houses was thus much the same as in 1931, and this left Labour vulnerable to the Conservatives' promise in 1951 to build 300,000 homes a year. Yet the difficulties had been enormous. At the time some thought Bevan's programme too large in view of the nation's difficulties, and from the middle of 1947 he was under pressure from the Treasury and his cabinet colleagues to reduce it. Nevertheless, between 1945 and 1951 some 1.5 million additional homes were provided, and fears that economic necessity would halve the building rate by 1949 were not realized. In the circumstances Labour's achievement was rather better than it is normally painted. Bevan himself displayed a laudable, if not always attainable ambition to improve upon the existing 'twilight villages' of council houses and 'fretful fronts' of middle-class ribbon development. His successors in the same ministry did not always display so much vision when resources were less scarce.

Between 1945 and 1948 several Acts were passed to provide a network of social security schemes on the lines of the proposals in the Beveridge Report. The Industrial Injuries Bill of 1945 based benefits on more generous principles than those envisaged by Beveridge. A comprehensive National Insurance Bill was introduced in 1946 to provide both for old age and unemployment. Attlee, in a classic speech on 7 February 1946, asked:

Can we afford it? Supposing the answer is 'No', what does that mean? It really means that the sum total of the goods produced and the services rendered by the people of this country is not sufficient to provide for all our people at all times, in sickness, in health, in youth and in old age, the very modest standard of life that is represented by the sums of money set out in the Second Schedule to this Bill. I cannot believe that our national productivity is so slow, that our willingness to work is so feeble or that we can submit to the world that the masses of our people must be condemned to penury.

He also argued that the Bill would maintain purchasing power in times of recession, and would improve the distribution of purchasing power among the people.

The old idea that this could only be done through wages and profits, and not by collective provisions of this sort, is now, I think, dying. . . it is interesting to see how far, in quite a short time, we have travelled from the conception of panic cutting-down of the purchasing power of the masses, which was employed as a means of dealing with the abundance crisis of 1931.

There was strong Conservative support, with the reminder that that party, too, in office, had contributed to the scheme. It was given an unopposed second reading on 11 February. The Bill provided for contributions from employers and employees towards the payment of old-age pensions, unemployment, ill-health and injury benefits. The choice of flat-rate contributions, determined by what the poorest of those in employment could afford, found few critics at the time. But conjoined with the determination to limit the Exchequer's contribution, the result was basic pensions in 1948 below the exiguous Beveridge subsistence level. This meant the defeat of his hope that in time National Assistance would be confined to exceptional cases as the bulk of the population became entitled to full benefits. A rising population of pensioners (it increased by 75 per cent or 3 million between 1948 and 1969), inflation, and a steadily improving standard of living for the mass of the population – and therefore a changing conception of poverty as a relative rather than an absolute term – increased the difficulty of providing benefits that bore some relation to an upward-moving subsistence standard. National Assistance, indeed, was needed to supplement other benefits extensively. Overall, between 1948 and 1962, the number having recourse to National Assistance almost doubled to 2 million. Simultaneously most benefits, if usually with some delays, had risen rather faster than the cost of living index, especially after 1959.

Nevertheless, the insurance scheme, coupled with National Assistance, meant that welfare in Britain provided protection which, despite its limitations, was one of the most comprehensive in Europe. The third social survey in York provides some evidence of the impact of the new legislation as early as 1950 when only 3 per cent of the working class in that city were reported to be in a state of poverty, but that on the basis of the 1936 provision of welfare this would have increased to over one-fifth. The same survey, however, indicated that that same proportion of York's working-class population had little margin of comfort. As will be shown later, this was the more significant figure in an age of inflation and rising expectations. Meanwhile the National Assistance Act of 1948 had abolished the last vestiges of the hated Victorian Poor Law and workhouse system of relief, and had further weakened the premise that poverty was a crime or the product of personal failings.

The National Health Service completed Labour's social reforms. A government white paper of February 1944 had agreed with Beveridge's plea for a universal service that made no distinction between rich and poor. Apart from the deficiencies in the provision of hospitals already noted, there was an uneven distribution of doctors over the country, with the south of England being unduly favoured. In 1939 health insurance covered only about half the population nor did it go beyond the services of a doctor. This haphazard system had necessitated government intervention during the war, and the medical profession's own leading spokesmen in the British Medical Association had begun to talk of radical change, including payment of a large proportion of doctors' fees by the state. The profession, however, easily took fright in the face of any initiative by the state, and was haunted by the fear that even limited government intervention would develop into a Franken-stein monster of bureaucratic control. Private practice would be undermined, it was claimed, the personal relationship of doctor and patient destroyed, and the independence of the profession eroded. The long history of state involvement in public health was perhaps imperfectly understood: already the average doctor received about one-third of his income from the state. The mounting costs of medical research and development necessitated more state assistance. But it was not difficult to present Labour in general, and more particularly Bevan as the Minister of Health, in an autocratic light. Even Bevan's predecessors under Churchill had fared badly when submitting less radical schemes to the BMA, though that body recognized the need for change. As with steel, this was a battle over power. Both parties acted on the Palmerstonian principle that one fights fiercely over the smallest issues to enhance one's credibility on the larger ones.

Bevan was bent on a national hospital service to ensure a reasonable spread of facilities and staff over the country. There was much resentment over the demise of the voluntary hospitals, but their standards varied too sharply, and only the state could provide the means for an overall levelling up in quality. This was to sugar the pill of nationalization for many. Morrison opposed the transfer of all hospitals to special regional boards, but Bevan correctly argued that to await the reform of local government and build the hospital system on that foundation would cause unacceptable delay. The United Kingdom was therefore divided into twenty regional hospital groups, each of which was to have a university school of medicine. With respect to general practitioners, Bevan was determined to buy out the sale of practices, and to achieve a fairer distribution of doctors over the country. He wished to leave the patient free to change his doctor, and also free to choose to receive medical treatment as a private or national health patient, or a mixture of the two. Doctors should be free to work outside the service, partly or in entirety. He believed they should have a basic salary, plus capitation fees according to the number of their national health patients, and there should also be the possibility of private practice. In retrospect it is not easy to understand the furore that these proposals evoked. Some members of the medical profession could talk of themselves as threatened with the fate of West Indian slaves, of Bevan as a 'Medical Fuehrer' or a resurrected Cromwell. Certainly Bevan had a remarkable talent for treading on the toes of others, including ministerial colleagues.

Royal assent to the National Health Service Bill on 6 November 1946 therefore did not mean the end of the battle, with leaders of the BMA continuing to insist that the 'independence of medicine' was at stake, threatened by the potential powers of the Minister. There were divisions within the profession over the legislation, but a poll of general practitioners suggested that nearly two-thirds opposed participation on the current terms. On–off talks, in which Bevan was prepared to consult though not to negotiate, often conducted in an acrimonious atmosphere, had made no real progress by the end of 1947. The medical profession appeared to be increasingly and overwhelmingly committed against the intended system. But the profession was in an exposed position. Conservative opposition was uncertain, as the BMA itself noted. A Gallup poll found public opinion strongly in favour of the new health service.[23] Bevan spoke of standing by the 'will of Parliament', and he remained confident that the mix of basic salary, with capitation fees and private practice, the promise of better hospitals and other amenities would appeal in varying degrees to sufficient of the profession for the service to commence on 5 July 1948. Tactics and timing were also important in the negotiations, and in April Bevan set out to reassure the profession without conceding anything of substance. It was never his intention, he insisted, to turn the doctors into 'civil servants'. He re-emphasized that a whole-time salaried service was not envisaged. With gestures such as these he was able to bring about a steady collapse of the opposition, so that in practice, from July 1948, most of the profession agreed to participate in the new service within a matter of weeks. About 97 per cent of the public had registered as national health patients before the end of the year.

The service also included free dental and eye treatment. The rush for glasses in particular was greater than expected, and in February 1949 a supplementary estimate of £52 million was necessary for the National Health Service. Nearly twice that supplement was required in the following year. But costs were bound to be uncertain at first. Cries of extravagance and waste soon abounded, yet the Guillebaud Committee could report in January 1956 that the service, though costly, had in fact been absorbing 'a decreasing proportion of the country's resources since 1949–50'. Inflation accounted for most increases; inefficiency for very little. Part of the cost of the service could, in any case, be offset by the gains to the community as a whole through the general improvement in health. Its preventive as well as its curative roles should also be noted. In its first years blindness from cataracts was reduced by a quarter, thereby enabling many people (especially the elderly) to continue to lead normal lives. Unfortunately about half the hospitals taken over in 1948 were obsolete (most of these had been built before 1891), and little new building was undertaken before the 1960s. In time even former critics became more kindly disposed towards the service, not least when the increasing costs of advanced medicine were recognized. Such costs made a national approach desirable. Bevan's coordinated hospital service was much praised, and the Porritt Committee of 1962 agreed that there had been no discernible loss of independence by the medical profession. Much remained to be done, but a noble start had been made. One can only speculate whether as much (or more) would have been achieved under the initial guidance of a less abrasive minister.

Other legislation by the government included the Criminal Justice Act of 1948 which ended the use of birching and flogging as a form of criminal punishment. The government opposed the end of hanging, although 215 Labour MPs voted in favour. New protection was given to homeless children, and a comprehensive youth employment service was instituted. Aid was provided for those too poor to pay for their own legal defence. University representation in the House of Commons was abolished, as was the university and business vote (about 300,000 being affected by this loss of the second vote).

From convertibility to devaluation

It might be said that the really creative or innovatory period of the Attlee ministries came to an end in 1947. Thereafter there was some filling in of the details, but in the main they were preoccupied with running a nation and an empire in the conditions of a deepening cold war and of a hesitant British economic recovery. The government had been badly shaken by events in the middle of 1947, with crises over steel nationalization, convertibility and the premiership. It was fortunate that Attlee and Mountbatten were freeing Britain from the Indian imbroglio, that there was the promise of Marshall Aid, and that the immediate sterling crisis was being met by new economic measures, plus cooperation from sterling area members and the United States. Discontent within the party was being met with the promise of steel nationalization and a blow against the powers of the Lords.

The question of the premiership grumbled on into September, with Cripps in particular pressing for ministerial changes. He not only urged Attlee to step down in favour of Bevin, but offered a list of the leading members for a new Cabinet. Cripps would have made a splendid medieval prelate. Attlee, however, had no need of four knights. He could rely on Bevin. The Foreign Secretary had been heard to mutter against the Prime Minister himself, but for one so assured of his own abilities he was surprisingly conscious of his limitations as a party politician. He had entered Parliament too late to learn its ways. Also, as he told Cripps, he did not like the parliamentary Labour party, and 'they did not like him'.[24] As neither Bevin nor Cripps would accept Morrison, this left Attlee in a very strong position. Nor did Attlee allow himself to appear put out by Cripps's bold move. Morrison's biographers marvel at Cripps's ability to retain his reputation for integrity in the course of manoeuvres which were climaxed by his own acceptance of a new office from the man he was seeking to demote.[25] Attlee's own subsequent comment was that Cripps's egoism was that of an altruist. More than that, he possessed, as did Bevin, a growing respect for Cripps's mastery of economic affairs. The latter was therefore given the new post of Minister for Economic Affairs. The duties were comprehensive and included foreign economic policy. Fortunately the probability of disputes with the Chancellor of the Exchequer were fortuitously removed by Dalton's indiscretions to a lobby correspondent as he was about to unveil his second budget of 1947 to the Commons on 12 November. Cripps carried his existing power with him when he was appointed to the Treasury. Perhaps no other minister, even in war, came to have so much control over the economy.[26]

Cripps's abilities had sometimes run riot in the past: now opportunity and qualities were well matched. Austerity and dedication were required, and Cripps epitomized both. Hitherto he had often behaved as one with too much ambition, pride and energy to be fitted satisfactorily into any position. He had veered wildly in his political thinking, his legal successes not finding their sequels in politics. It is true that after 1947 he still failed to husband his strength intelligently. Nor was he a great master of economic theory. The devaluation of sterling in 1949 cast a shadow over his performance. His policies were greatly assisted by Marshall Aid: he had the great good fortune to retire from office before the economic problems occasioned by the Korean War and the 1950 economic boom had had time to bite. Yet if the Treasury had been consistently handled in a Crippsian spirit (and he did not believe in austerity for its own sake) the British economy during the ensuing generation could hardly have been the loser. Despite changes of course, his sincerity was unquestioned. He was the most religious-minded leading British politician since Gladstone: his main concern from the early 1940s was the moral and technical regeneration of Britain. From 1947 he admirably complemented Bevin in the struggle to contain expectations and to win the voluntary cooperation of the unions in wage restraint. It was Bevin, however, who ensured the defeat of proposals circulating in the cabinet in the winter of 1947–8 for the introduction of wage controls.[27] By and large over the next two years a remarkable measure of union cooperation was secured in the struggle against inflation.

Under Cripps the Treasury regained its old pre-eminence in financial matters. Although Dalton had begun to cut back government spending and to reduce excess demand in the economy, under Cripps there was more sense of purpose and detailed control. Donald Winch concluded:

Cripps was more at home with Keynesian terminology and methods than Dalton; his budgets were more firmly set within a framework of detailed analysis of likely future trends in the economy as presented in the annual Economic Survey. *Under Cripps a balance was established between physical and financial planning. Short-term budgetary objectives and long-term aims were brought together.*[28]

Douglas Jay later claimed that at this time planning became more realistic, and Treasury relations with other departments more constructive.[29] More attention was paid to inflation, to the interdependence of investment, domestic consumption and the balance of payments. Full use could be made of the new interdepartmental planning body attached to the Lord President's office, set up by Morrison under Sir Edwin Plowden. The government emerged much strengthened from the summer crisis. John Mackintosh noted that the cabinet by the end of 1947 suggested 'the image of a cone', with Bevin, Cripps and Morrison serving below the premier as the key coordinating ministers.[30] There was no 'inner cabinet', but much efficiency resulted from functional delegation to subordinate ministers. Morrison earned high praise as leader of the House from Conservatives such as Harold Macmillan (a very astute judge) and Lord Kilmuir. The government indeed depended too much on the health and vigour of these four men.

For the time being the cohesion of Cabinet and party was helped by the seriousness of the situation at home and abroad. Even Marshall Aid could only lengthen the period during which Britain had to bring her balance of payments into equilibrium and end the sterling area's dollar deficit. So unfavourable were the terms of trade in 1947 that even with an increase of 8 per cent in the volume of British exports compared with 1938, and a fall of a quarter in the volume of imports, this still left a trade deficit of nearly £500 million. The total overseas deficit, swollen in particular by the cost of British forces overseas, was estimated at nearly

£700 million, while the reserves fell by a little over £1,000 million. An American assessment, made at the beginning of 1948, warned that British imports could not be cut back much further without imperilling industrial production itself.[31] At least, following the convertibility crisis, members of the sterling area began to cooperate more effectively to restrict the outflow of capital, to ration dollar imports, and to encourage dollar-saving trade within the area. Particularly impressive was the rise in British imports from non-dollar areas. In 1947 no less than 46 per cent had originated in the western hemisphere; in 1948 this fell back to the prewar norm of 32 per cent as production elsewhere in the world revived. Washington proved remarkably understanding, recognizing that the economic recovery of the sterling area must now have precedence over the fight against discriminatory policies, especially in the light of the struggle to build up western strength against communism. Within the Labour party, too, the mood was sober in 1948, with Bevan at the Scarborough Party Conference warning that 'If we did not have Marshall Aid, unemployment in this country would at once be raised to one or one and a half million'. The vast majority were for the time being reconciled to anti-Russian policies, to the continuance of a British world role not so very different from that in the 1930s, to cooperation with the United States, and to policies of change within Britain which were at most reformist, piecemeal, and not the prelude to a comprehensive restructuring of the nation.

In 1948 there was an impressive increase in the volume of British exports, a result both of expanded output and of government restrictions on domestic demand. Fears of devaluation temporarily receded. Apart from taxation, domestic demand was curbed by wage restraint. In return for government assurances on profits and prices, the TUC finally agreed to conditional wage restraint in March 1948, and again a year later. A formidable ally of the government was Arthur Deakin, General Secretary of the Transport and General Workers Union. His own experience of industry had left him convinced that high wages, if unrelated to higher output, could lead to unemployment: he believed that workers must look mainly to modernized industry for prosperity in the long run, while recent European travels had impressed him with the dangers of inflation. Despite much grumbling and discontent wage rates rose on average only 5 per cent between February 1948 and the autumn of 1950, although the retail price index increased by 8 per cent. Such restraint could not continue indefinitely, but a valuable breathing space was obtained.

Relations with the employers, too, were satisfactory for a time, despite dividend restraint and in 1948 a special 'once and for all' levy on the rich. These were really of political or psychological, not material importance. Industry recognized the more tangible effect of wage restraint, and was further conciliated by the government's reliance less on direct controls and more on indirect economic management as well as consultation with employers and trade unionists. Dow pays tribute to Cripps's appreciation of the limits of public tolerance over government interference. Voluntary cooperation was his aim, and, according to Stephen Blank, writing on the FBI in 1973, he won more industrial confidence than any other postwar minister.[32]

Nevertheless, Andrew Shonfield argues that in 1948 the Labour government missed its great opportunity to introduce the sort of basic long-term planning machnery that was to be established in parts of western Europe in the next fifteen years. French planners derived inspiration from the abortive Development Councils set up by Cripps: 'the basic elements of modern planning' were present in Britain as in no other western country. Shonfield significantly adds:

The striking thing in the British case is the extraordinary tenacity of older attitudes towards the role of public power. Anything which smacked of a restless or over-energetic state, with ideas of guiding the nation on the basis of a long view of its collective economic interest, was instinctively the object of suspicion.[33]

The government continued to approach economic problems essentially on a departmental basis, with *ad hoc* coordinating committees only in a crisis, and with the Treasury striving with varying degrees of success to control departmental spending. It achieved less than it hoped in curtailing Aneurin Bevan's housing programme. The nationalized industries also went their separate ways; the chance of a national energy policy was neglected: there was no systematic examination of Britain's long-term needs. The government was repeatedly taken by surprise by short-term developments in the economy. It was also impressed by union hostility to any hints of statutory wages or manpower policy and by industry's readiness to cooperate only when and where it felt such cooperation to be in its interest. Not surprisingly Cripps, in 1950, described the budget as 'the most important control and the most powerful instrument of government'. With Cripps in particular interpreting 'democratic planning' to mean extensive consultation and cooperation with private industry, there was no one in the party to give an alternative lead. Critics were still active, but their energies were directed to questions of nationalization, foreign policy and the social services. They did not offer an alternative economic policy. Nevertheless the 1949 budget, so *The Economist* of 16 April reported, produced an 'internal eruption in the Labour Party which was only with difficulty brought under control'. Cripps warned on 6 April:

There is not much further immediate possibility of the redistribution of national income by way of taxation in this country; for the future, we must rely rather upon the creation of more distributable wealth than upon . . . redistribution. . . . Total taxation, local and national, is now more than 40 per cent of the national income, and at that level the redistribution of income entailed in the payment of Social Services already falls, to a considerable extent, upon those who are the recipients of these services.

We must, therefore, moderate the speed of our advance in the extended application of the existing Social Services to our progressive ability to pay for them by an increase in our national income. Otherwise, we shall not be able to avoid entrenching, to an intolerable extent, upon the liberty of spending by the private individual for his own purposes.

Cripps was also disturbed by the soaring cost of food subsidies, then approaching £500 million a year. His cuts envisaged a reduction to £465 million, about £100 million less than the estimated figure for 1949–50 without the changes. But even this austere budget could not protect Britain from the American recession, a widening of the dollar gap, and fresh talk of sterling devaluation, especially in the United States. Dow argues that devaluation in April 1949 (five months before it was reluctantly undertaken) would have been 'a considered move' of great value to the economy. It might also have been less drastic. The balance of trade of other sterling members with dollar countries was worsening at the same time. Cooperative efforts to cut dollar imports came too late to save the pound. Strong speculative pressure began to develop. The Cabinet discussed the problem with growing concern from the middle of June, with Cripps at first following the City argument that deflation, not devaluation was the answer. Wilson at the Board of Trade agreed. But Attlee and Morrison opposed massive cuts in food subsidies and public expenditure – there must be no repeat of '1931' – and Dalton and Gaitskell swung to their side.[34] The final Cabinet decision was eased by Cripps' absence through illness: he argued for £700 million economies on his return. Bevin opposed cuts in the armed forces, Bevan in the social services. There were resignation threats, but Attlee and Morrison secured compromise cuts of £250 million in October. Meanwhile the pound had been devalued to $2.80 in September, a cut of 30 per cent. This increased the competitiveness of sterling area goods in the United States, but its overall effects were debatable. Probably Britain devalued too late. Possibly she devalued too much, but this only became clear with the passage of time. The dollar gap was lessened mainly by America's own economic recovery. Wage restraint in Britain also played a vital part in improving the balance of trade. This was so dramatically transformed in the space of a year that Britain was able to withdraw from the Marshall Aid Programme at the end of 1950.

Chapter 4

The cold war and the decline of Labour

The evolution of the cold war from December 1947 to the emergence of Communist China

The rift which was to develop in the Labour party in 1951 over the scale of rearmament that was necessary to oppose the threat from communism was in striking contrast to the earlier closing of Labour ranks in the face of Soviet foreign policy from the winter of 1947–8. The failure of the Council of Foreign Ministers in London of 25 November to 15 December 1947 to agree on German reparations or the future governance of Germany consolidated the anti-Russian tendencies that were sweeping through British opinion. Americans observed a great change in Labour sentiments towards both the Russians and themselves. Bevin, in great good humour, informed American colleagues on 18 December 1947 that he was now assured of full trade union support in his foreign policy. His own reciprocal promise to support the TUC in the defence of free collective wage bargaining against statutory measures was a matter of deep conviction for him in any case. He added that if unions once lost their job of fixing wages they were either ruined, as in Russia, or turned to political mischief.[1] As for foreign affairs, he later described his meetings with Marshall at this time as the moment of joint decisions to halt Russian aggression.

There was, of course, still much work to be done, with Britain and the United States often not fully in step. Lewis W. Douglas, the American ambassador in London, noted in August 1948 how subordination to the United States was 'a bitter pill for a country accustomed to full control over her national destiny'.[2] The British saw themselves and their Commonwealth as of unique value to the Americans, and therefore deserving of better treatment than the other states of Europe. The expectation remained strong that in time the Commonwealth would enable them to deal with the Americans on relatively level terms. Keyed up with this hope the British were anxious to make no concessions that might jeopardize this potential. Douglas saw a tired people who felt that the world was balanced on the edge of disaster and that for once no part of the decision was in their hands. Thus they tended to be critical both of any American tendency to take risks and also of any continuing American uncertainty as to the degree of their commitment to the defence of Europe and the Middle East.

For Bevin at the beginning of 1948, Anglo-American relations had become sufficiently intimate again for him to take calculated risks in expectation of ultimate support. American official thinking differed little from his own, but Congress remained a disturbing imponderable. American policy-makers believed that without the European Recovery Programme western Europe would slip out of the American orbit, and Britain would almost certainly follow her continental neighbours.[3] American reliance on Britain was dramatically underlined in a State Department paper of 11 June 1948 which saw special value even in a Labour government, since it should serve as a focus of attraction for the non-Marxist left in Europe. Britain was the outstanding example of a likeminded nation. As for the empire, though the Americans still professed faith in ultimate self-government, they hoped the process would be evolutionary and not result in the loss of territory to an enemy. There should preferably be no hurried British retreat from the Middle East: British interest in Cyrenaica as a substitute base for Palestine and Egypt fitted in with the growing American concern for the security of North Africa. Britain's role in Malaya and Singapore was equally welcome. In so far as the State Department remained critical, it was over imperial preference and the sterling area, and the British failure to give a vigorous lead to European unity. Even on European economic cooperation British policy seemed too cautious and independent, though there was some grudging recognition of the peculiar problems posed by the Commonwealth and the sterling area. Britain's economic performance was also viewed with some dismay. Apart from Labour's suspect experiments, there was continuing criticism of the lack of real modernization and the slow rise in productivity. An otherwise sympathetic American ambassador spoke of the need for more work for less money.

It is against this background that the events leading up to the creation of the North Atlantic Treaty Organization in April 1949 must be viewed.[4] Bevin, in his 1947 talks with Marshall and in exchanges early in 1948, insisted that the time had come to begin the formation of a federation or union in western Europe, and 'if possible to bring the Americans into it'. Marshall had been encouraging so far as Congress might allow. Bevin also felt free by the end of 1947 to discuss military strategy with France. The Anglo-French Treaty of Dunkirk of 4 March 1947 had provided only a paper basis for an alliance so long as communist participation in a French government seemed possible. The fierce political and industrial turmoil in France in the last months of 1947 both demonstrated the determination and strength of anti-communist forces in France and suggested that the re-entry of communists into a French coalition government was unlikely. Bevin drew closer to France, and while not yet proposing a formal western alliance he urged the need for some closer understanding – 'a sort of spiritual federation of the West'. It was necessary to create a conviction in western Europe that further communist inroads would be stopped; he was also anxious that any German irredentist movements should develop not from eastern Germany but under western control. He envisaged Britain's links with France being extended to the Benelux states, and in time to Italy and other Mediterranean states, to the Scandinavian countries, and ultimately to Germany and Spain. The British government feared that pressure on Spain would merely strengthen the Franco regime. In time the centre might establish itself in that country, when Spain could be welcomed as a valuable economic and strategic ally of the West. Approaches to Canada early in 1948 showed that that country's response would be dependent on that of the United States. Indeed, much though Britain desired dominion support in general, American backing was always the critical element. Bevin remarked: 'The Soviet Government has based its policy on the expectation that Western Europe will sink into economic chaos and they may be relied upon to place every possible obstacle in the path of American aid and of Western European recovery.' Marshall Aid must be backed by political cohesion. Bevin went on: 'We in Britain can no longer stand outside Europe and insist that our problems and position are quite separate from those of our European neighbours.' Half-measures were useless: one must not be afraid of Russian reactions, however hostile.

There followed some intricate manoeuvring with the Americans. Bevin believed that progress in European cooperation would be much assisted by some assurance of American support: Washington wanted to be sure that the Europeans meant business – not least to impress Congress. The British were informed: 'You are in effect asking us to pour concrete before we see the blueprints.'[5] Bevin was fishing for Anglo-American defence talks in Europe on the lines of those recently held concerning the Middle East. The communist coup in Czechoslovakia in February 1948 only added further urgency to the talks, and there were fears too of Soviet pressure on Norway, as well as of the possibility of a communist threat to the Italian government before the scheduled elections of April 1948. On 6 March Bevin agreed that British military support for the de Gasperi government might be considered in certain circumstances. The Americans were certainly anxious for British assistance, especially when the occupation of Sicily and Sardinia was being considered as a possible countermeasure.[6] With the completion of the Brussels treaty on 17 March 1948 – which united Britain, France and the Benelux states for purposes of 'collaboration in economic, social and cultural matters, and for collective self-defence' – the American government was well placed to explore just how far it could carry Congress towards a commitment to the defence of Europe. Bevin had hopes of the creation of an Atlantic security system that would stretch from Greenland and Newfoundland to the Azores and Casablanca. According to the American ambassador in Brussels, Bevin also showed interest on 18 March in bringing Eire into the fold for 'common defense'. The ambassador added: 'He believes union in Ireland can be accomplished by sympathetic handling and obviously went to some lengths to flatter the Irish Chargé.' Eire later intimated that it could only consider joining NATO if it was first reunited with the North.[7] But if Eire could not be tempted, the ground had otherwise been well prepared for the creation of NATO. The deterioration of East-West relations over Germany was providing any further incentives that were needed.

By the end of 1947 the failure to make progress over the future of Germany was causing the British and Americans grave concern. The working of the bizone was still far from smooth, and its creation left many problems unresolved. There were still acute food shortages: both powers were subsidizing their occupation zones. There was a desperate need both to create a viable economy and to make some progress in the formation of a German administration. There was the continuing fear that the current situation was working in favour of the communists. True, the British, though less apprehensive than the French, had not yet forgotten all their fears of a German militarist revival. But the context was changing. As Bevin remarked to Marshall on 7 Sept. 1948, 'we are now faced by the menace of Germany allied to or occupied by the Soviet Union'.[8] Before 1948 the French had usually been the chief, or certainly the most obvious obstacle to the implementation of Anglo-American wishes in Germany. As the threat from Russia and communism became more general, so the future of Germany was discussed increasingly in those terms. Even the local British and American political and economic difficulties ran into the broader issue: whether they looked to German economic unity or zonal currency reform to ease their burdens, and whatever their approach to the future governance of Germany, their interests were bound to clash with those of the Soviet Union. Whether the Russians aspired to control all Germany, or whether they sought merely to ensure that western Germany did not menace their interests, they were obviously hostile to any moves to increase the economic and political strength of western Germany. Furthermore, the western sectors in Berlin were a constant challenge and temptation to the Soviets. The obvious Soviet tactic in the German question was to exert pressure in Berlin. Tentatively from January 1948 traffic with Berlin was increasingly obstructed until by July, save for the air corridors, the blockade of Berlin was complete.

In the western response, the British were not totally in harmony with the United States. At times Bevin was afraid that the United States might overreact; he was disposed to be conciliatory on the question of reparations both to lessen the tension and because, as he argued, the Russians were not in breach of the current reparations agreements. The existing exchange of goods with the East had economic advantages as well. But the Americans were increasingly determined that the German economy should play as large a part as possible in the recovery of Europe, and in general wished to adopt a tough line. As usual the pressure of events was soon bringing the two countries together. In April the British were not prepared to fight for Berlin in all circumstances, though they would resist an 'organized act of war' by the

Soviets. But on 24 July Bevin feared that a western abandonment of Berlin would lead to the loss of the rest of Europe.[9] On the whole the British doubted the likelihood of a deliberate act of war by Russia. Accidents, however, could not be ruled out – hence the wary eye on Washington as well as Moscow – and there was always the fear of communist-inspired strikes or riots. Throughout this time, too, there was constant worry over the fragility of western European morale – the French had no wish to relive the campaigns of 1940 and 1944 (surely the liberating Anglo-American forces would find a desert this time). Retreats into neutrality or fellow-travelling in response to further communist advances seemed likely. Hence the urgency with which Bevin pursued the creation of NATO. If there was sometimes the fear that the Americans would act too precipitately, there was the more persistent worry lest they should not join in the creation of NATO with the speed and conviction needed to sustain European morale.

Despite the Berlin blockade this was not a period when British and American statesmen on the whole feared an imminent Soviet military attack, but rather a debilitating war of nerves. Churchill favoured a showdown with the Soviets at this time, arguing that war would be inevitable once the Russians had nuclear weapons. Aneurin Bevan talked of calling the Russian bluff in the Berlin blockade by sending an armoured column along a closed autobahn.[10] The great contemporary concern was also for the internal stability of France and Italy, with the political defence moves of the time being mainly intended to improve western morale and self-confidence. Even so, British defence commitments to Europe remained hesitant without the assurance of solid American support on the continent. Great reliance was placed in the deterrent power of the American Strategic Air Command. American bombers were based in Britain, and, according to the American Secretary of Defense, both Attlee and Cripps in the autumn of 1948 saw Britain as the main base for strategic nuclear operations against Russia. Bevan's biographer found no evidence that he dissented.[11] But in 1948 it was Anglo-American air power in another role which was decisive. Contrary to expectations, it proved possible for West Berlin to be supplied from the air, even during the winter of 1948–9, and the 'air-lift' brought the blockade to an end in May 1949 despite the formation of a West German government.

Meanwhile, careful negotiations with the United States had resulted in the signature of the North Atlantic Treaty on 4 April 1949, article V of which affirmed:

The Parties agree that an armed attack against one or more of them in Europe or North America shall be considered an attack against them all and consequently they agree that, if such an armed attack occurs, each of them, in exercise of the right of individual or collective self-defence . . . will assist the party or parties so attacked by taking forthwith, individually and in concert with the other Parties, such action as it deems necessary, including the use of armed force, to restore and maintain the security of the North Atlantic area.

Good progress was also made in the economic recovery of western Europe in 1949, while the American-backed Greek government was triumphant in the civil war, aided by the break between Stalin and Tito's Yugoslavia. These morale-boosting gains were only partially offset by the first Russian nuclear test in August 1949, and by the victory of communism in China. In Britain feeling continued to run strongly against communism, with the trade union movement withdrawing from the World Federation of Trade Unions in January 1949 after long and bitter clashes with communists. The Trades Union Congress approved this step by a vote of more than six to one in September. Also in July 1949 the Labour party expelled five MPs for persistent support of the Soviet Union. Debates in the Labour party on foreign affairs now centred mainly on the respective roles of military, political, economic and social weapons in the battle against communism.

The emergence of Communist China in 1949 did not find the British and Americans in total agreement, but broadly London sympathized with Washington's desire to contain communism in the Far East.[12] Britain herself was encountering an increasing guerrilla threat in Malaya, mainly composed of local Chinese communists. Foreign Office communications to Washington on 5 January and 15 August 1949 showed alarm at the rapid progress of Mao Tse-tung's forces in China, and there were no doubts that these were wholehearted doctrinaire Marxists. A communist victory, it was believed, might have repercussions in India, Malaya, Indo-China and other areas in the Far East, and Bevin spoke of the need for worldwide Anglo-American cooperation. He believed that an anti-communist front was needed in Asia, though Anglo-American interests began to diverge a little once communist control of mainland China was assured. The United States was in no hurry to recognize the new regime, and was certainly not prepared to do so without hard bargaining and some assurance from Pekin of more respect for American interests.

Bevin, however, had to take account of left-wing opinion in Britain, and also, indeed, of some business interests who hoped that recognition might facilitate the continuance of at least some trade with China. Account, too, had to be taken of Chinese communities within the empire in the east, not to mention other local interests. India inclined to early recognition, British diplomatic tradition on the whole favoured the acceptance of accomplished facts, while there were as yet premature hopes that differences would develop between Russia and China over Manchuria and Sinkiang, and that China's enormous internal problems might moderate anti-western feeling. Furthermore the British had hopes of holding Hong Kong, and they saw no point in provoking the Chinese unnecessarily. Acheson, the American Secretary of State, was therefore unable to delay British recognition of Communist China (it was accorded on 6 January 1950) although Bevin went out of his way to assure him of continuing British interest in the creation of effective obstacles to the spread of communism, especially in Indo-China. He shared the American desire for more French concessions to anti-communist nationalists in that region.

Britain and European cooperation, 1948–52

Despite some signs to the contrary, there proved to be almost complete continuity between Labour and Conservative ministries on the question of closer relations with western Europe. It was also an issue where there was a clash of Anglo-American interests. Britain was the worst, because she was the most important, offender against American hopes for the creation of a more unified western Europe. Bevin, in the eyes of Acheson, Adenauer and Duff Cooper, at times appeared the most European-minded of leading British politicians. Acheson once found him hopeful that the Brussels treaty might lead to a 'cabinet for western Europe', from which 'common judgements' might emerge, and in which Germany might finally be included. At times he spoke with some interest of a European customs union. But his listeners perhaps failed to appreciate his readiness to air ideas while at the same time making a ruthless assessment of what he thought was politically feasible. It was soon evident that such thinking would make no headway in Whitehall. The early postwar enthusiasm of some of the Labour party for a 'Third Force' socialist Europe withered as parties of the centre and right came to dominate the politics of France, Italy and West Germany in the late 1940s. The issue even came to divide Labour from continental socialists who favoured moves towards greater European unity, despite the current revival of capitalism.

There were other obstacles too. Labour was determined to rid Britain permanently of poverty and unemployment, and feared that any sacrifice of British sovereignty might endanger that objective. Dalton, who headed the British delegation to the Paris conference at the end of 1948 to discuss closer union between the members of the Brussels treaty, was guided by this concern and by the resolve to protect British links with the Commonwealth.[13] American enthusiasm for a more united Europe also aroused suspicion. If achieved, it might deepen the divide between East and West: it might also serve as an excuse for less direct American involvement in the defence of Europe. British influence with America and in the world as a whole might suffer if she lost some of her identity in Europe – her efforts to secure special and separate treatment over Marshall Aid have already been noted. Some British gestures were, of course, necessary to relieve the American pressure upon them for a more positive role, but the American government iself was a little ambivalent, wanting both a British lead in Europe and the continuance of Britain's special relationship with itself and the Commonwealth.

Conservative enthusiasm for Europe was also suspect. The continent was an obvious forum for Churchill: a united Europe a grand theme. Early in 1947 he founded the non-party United European Movement, with Duncan Sandys as the main British organizer. But, as Harold Macmillan later noted, Churchill gave no effective institutional lead, and his speeches from 1946 betrayed ambivalence as to Britain's role in any steps to European unity. This was unfortunate, since many Europeans hung upon his words, and often read too much into them. Rhetoric was mistaken for reality. Dalton detected less enthusiasm for Europe among Conservatives when they were addressing British audiences.

In July 1948, when France proposed a customs and economic union and the creation of an all-European assembly to the Brussels treaty powers, Bevin led the opposition. Later, on 15 September, he argued in the Commons that one should start on an *ad hoc*, functional basis, although a political assembly might finally arise out of cooperation over defence and economic questions. One must not try, he said, 'to put the roof on before we have built the building'. The European integrationists, however, were trying to see the building whole, including the roof. Bevin preferred an intergovernmental approach, arguing that a parliamentary assembly might cause confusion and bitterness, especially if a national government should oppose its proposals. Finally the British agreed to the creation of a consultative assembly as well as a committee of ministers of the member states, but the former had to be clearly subordinated to the latter. There was still a fierce argument over the composition and voting procedures of the new assembly. The statute of the Council of Europe was signed in London on 5 May 1949, the five Brussels states being joined by five others. But the British had been largely successful in robbing the Council of any real powers. When some delegates, mostly French, Italian and from the Benelux group, with federalist aspirations, pressed for the extension of the Council into a legislative body, the British enjoyed majority support when they insisted on the maintenance of a cautious functional approach. Until 1951 at least, Britain had little cause to fear that progress would be made towards European unity by way of the Council of Europe. Even this did not stop the possibility of withdrawal being considered by the government.[14]

The British were also able to ensure that the Organization for European Economic Cooperation (OEEC) was set up in April 1948 very much in accord with their wishes, French supranational plans again being frustrated. As three-quarters of Britain's trade was carried on outside Europe Whitehall could feel that its concern for national sovereignty was justified. Bevin once declared that Britain 'has to be and must remain the centre of the Commonwealth itself and she must be European. It is a very difficult role to play.' This was very true. When Cripps, in the spring of 1949, showed some interest in joint Anglo-French economic planning, he was overruled by Attlee and Bevin.[15]

British economic policy always seemed 'insular or imperial rather than European', and one French socialist wittily described the NEC's June 1950 pamphlet entitled *European Unity* as a new version of 'Socialism in One Country'. Labour politicians generally remained ill-at-ease with both the continental bourgeois parties and the doctrinaire French and Italian socialists, but their suspicion of moves to European unity was a national rather than a party phenomenon. Commonwealth preference slowed trade liberalization within the OEEC, and Conservatives had no hesitation in their 1951 election manifesto in placing that preference ahead of European union. Not surprisingly by 1950 some of the continental European enthusiasts were becoming wary of British obstructionist and qualifying tactics. The time was coming when they would be ready to proceed without the offshore islanders.

In May 1950 the French foreign minister, Robert Schuman, proposed that the coal and steel industries of France and Germany, and of such countries as wished to join, should be placed under a common higher authority. His aim was both to take a step towards a federal Europe, and to make yet another Franco-German war impossible. The first aim was underlined by French insistence that countries participating in a conference to discuss the plan declare beforehand that 'their immediate objective [was] the pooling of coal and steel production and the institution of a new high authority whose decisions will bind'. If the French wished to frighten off the British, they could hardly have chosen a more effective agent – the red-rag of principle with which to provoke the pragmatic British bull. The proposals were also sprung abruptly on the British with the Americans enjoying prior consultation. Acheson later agreed that the approach to the British had been mishandled. But the French, for their part, already had every reason to suppose that the British would prove an obstacle to constructive talks. In 1949 Monnet had been exploring the prospects for closer Anglo-French cooperation, including some pooling of resources, but to no avail. British devaluation had led to some Anglo-French trading problems. If the French went out of their way to ensure that Britain did not participate in talks to establish what was to become known as the European Coal and Steel Community (ECSC), it was understandable. They had good reason to fear British spoiling tactics. The formal British refusal was made on 2 June 1950 in the arrogant expectation that the talks would make little or no progress.

Nevertheless France, West Germany, Italy and the Benelux states successfully set up the European Coal and Steel Community in April 1951; though less supranational than originally intended. British parliamentary debates on 26–27 June 1951 revealed a general consensus that this diluted supranationalism was too strong for Britain. The Six had accepted the principle of majority voting, however qualified, in the running of the ECSC, whereas both parties in Britain were insistent on a veto. The British, too, were perhaps misled by the apparent strength of their own industries: the Six combined were producing only twice as much coal and three times as much steel. British steel, it was hoped, could undersell the Europeans. There was an underestimation of French confidence, and their readiness to deal with the Germans without the British. The strength of the supranational impulse in Europe was not appreciated, and the attractiveness of Britain's own plans for tariff cuts and more limited economic cooperation was exaggerated. The French in fact feared that anything less than the Schuman plan would give them insufficient influence over the German economy. They could be sure, too, of American favour. British miscalculations were not surprising in the circumstances of 1950–1: more disturbing was their failure to show deeper understanding thereafter. But some light is thrown on the psychological and mental blocks that existed in Eden's insistence in January 1952 that Britain could not join a European federation.

This is something which we know, in our bones, we cannot do. . . . For Britain's story and her interests lie beyond the Continent of Europe. Our thoughts move across the seas to the many communities in which our people play their part, in every corner of the world. That is our life: without it we should be no more than some millions of people living on an island off the coast of Europe.

The 1950 election and Labour's uncertain future

While the first hesitant steps were being taken towards greater western European cooperation, British attention was mainly focused on the sudden intensification of the cold war, the renewal of economic difficulties in 1951, and the political uncertainty which gripped the nation as a result of two relatively inconclusive general elections in 1950 and 1951. The nation, which had firmly rejected the Conservatives in 1945, edged hesitantly to the right in 1950–1, and there was little hint in these years that a period of no less than thirteen years of Conservative rule was to follow.

It was not easy for the Labour government, in the winter of 1949–50, to settle the day for the election – whether before or after the budget. Attlee and Cripps decided on the earlier date, 23 February 1950.[16] The moment was far from ideal. Sterling had recently been devalued, and if clothes rationing had ended and there had been some relaxation in the postwar tightening of the food ration, the prospect of an early end to austerity seemed remote. Labour had lost no seats in parliamentary by-elections, but it had done badly in some local elections. The party was also suffering from internal divisions over further nationalization and over the amount of socialist content in its policies. Bevan had asserted in 1948 that socialism was about the establishment of the right priorities, and could not agree with Cripps that it was still necessary to sacrifice so much for the reconstruction of the economy, or with Bevin that no further cuts could be made in defence. He was dismayed by the timorous leadership of his colleagues: he believed that modern industrial society had broken the traditional social framework and cast individuals adrift. It was vital, therefore, to bring about 'a restatement of the relations between individual and society'. There were many in the Labour party who shared these views, but in practice the debate was often narrowed down to the question of more or less nationalization. Here Morrison could always retort that nationalization shopping lists were not vote-catchers: 'consolidation' was the answer. Bevan himself accepted that a mixed economy was what most people of the West would prefer, but the problem remained how much of each ingredient. For Bevan, public property should 'dominate'.[17]

Too much had been expected from those industries which had been nationalized, and disappointment meant that the Bill to nationalize steel and the proposal to nationalize sugar were giving much valuable ammunition and publicity to the Conservatives. Tate and Lyle built a skilful campaign around the attractive cartoon figure of 'Mr Cube' to oppose the nationalization of sugar. The image of bureaucratic interference and red tape was easily evoked. A proposal to nationalize ICI encountered local union opposition, while G. D. H. Cole now argued that equality had become a more pressing issue for the party than further nationalization. In the nation as a whole there was much less faith in planning, nationalization and controls by 1950. Thus, despite the influence of the left, Morrison was able to dilute proposals for public ownership in the party's 1949 statement, *Labour Believes in Britain*, and in the 1950 election manifesto. His aim was to appeal, as in 1945, to 'all useful men and women' – to people in professional and technical occupations as well as to the party's traditional voters. The historian of the 1950 election was indeed impressed by the degree of overlap in ideas between the two party manifestos: Labour's *Let Us Win Through Together* and the Conservatives' *This Is the Road*.[18] The left were convinced that this muting of socialism was a fundamental mistake, whereas the rest of the party trembled at the hint of every new indiscretion by Bevan and his friends. Dalton thought even the diluted nationalization proposals cost the party votes in February 1950.[19]

Labour fought to a great extent on memories of the 1930s rather than on its own record since 1945, a not unwise strategy in the light of a later constituency study of Bristol North-East by R. S. Milne and H. C. Mackenzie in *Straight Fight* (1954). This suggested that more than half the Labour voters were moved by fear of unemployment – significantly the Conservatives were now making full employment the party's 'first aim' in contrast to more cautious promises in 1945. Memories were long among the poor, whereas middle-class attention was concentrated on the more recent government controls, high taxes, rationing and austerity. Indeed, since 1938 there had been a per capita improvement in working-class consumption of consumer goods and services of some 17 per cent. Those of the middle classes had fallen by about the same proportion; the rich by over 40 per cent.[20] The gains of the poor were reflected in Rowntree's report that children from all classes in York in 1950 were heavier and taller than their 1936 counterparts. Infant mortality continued to fall. Nevertheless the constant renewal of the electorate must be borne in mind, and even the thinking of the same individual could change with the passage of time. Memories of the 1930s would weaken, just as the belief could gain ground that Britain did not always have to be subjected to so much government control and to so many restrictions on personal consumption and preference. Labour for the time being was sure of the ardent left-wing vote – it had no other outlet – and of those who wished to consolidate the gains made in the 1940s. But it had less to offer to the ambitious, and to those who had either turned against the Conservatives in 1945 or abstained.

In these circumstances the Conservative revival was less remarkable than it might seem. Voters disenchanted with Labour had no plausible alternative. Given reasonable competence and a shrewd assessment of the middle ground in British politics some recovery was inevitable. Yet, given the close-run elections of 1950 and 1951, every Conservative contribution to their improved image was of consequence. The 1945 election had been a visceral defeat, though the rejection of so many sitting Conservatives helped to open the door to new blood. R. A. Butler later remarked on the great difficulty experienced by the party in drawing level with Labour over six years, despite austerity and economic crises. The party had to 'convince a broad spectrum of the electorate, whose minds were scarred by interwar memories and myths, that we had a broad alternative to Socialism which was viable, efficient and humane, which would release and reward enterprise and initiative but without abandoning social justice or reverting to mass unemployment'. Churchill was not easily diverted from foreign affairs, and in any case he preferred to criticize Labour rather than offer hostages to the future with a detailed alternative programme, or a new Tamworth Manifesto, as Butler and Hogg demanded. Butler recalls that in the end he had to assume Churchill's approval of 'the broad statement of policy' expressed in the Industrial Charter. Personally, he wished to demonstrate Conservative acceptance of a sufficient state role to ensure full employment and the preservation of the welfare state, as well as to propound the merits of freedom and competition.[21] The Charter strove to balance the interests of employees and consumers alike. Not surprisingly Butler and some of his allies were suspect to many in the party as 'pink socialists'. The Beaverbrook press condemned the Charter, insisting that if the electorate rejected the left, 'they will turn to the Right, but never half-Right'. In this case the Beaverbrook press was not even 'half-right'.

The Conservatives were in fact far from united in their philosophy, with groups giving different degrees of emphasis to the roles of the state and the market. It would be tedious to follow these debates: much of the rhetoric in any case bore little relation to realities, even as understood

by the leadership. What really mattered was that most party feeling was
fluid and pragmatic. Quintin Hogg argued in *The Case for Conservatism* that it was more an attitude of mind than a philosophy – the
party was a constant force responding to the permanent need of a free
society for a power making for consolidation or orderly change. The
most valuable element in this creed or approach was scepticism as to the
invariable wisdom of human reason, abstract principles, and the power
of politics to put things right. If this was too often interpreted
negatively, here was still a platform on which the party could try to offer
itself as a more empirical and competent alternative to Labour. It
expressed concern for the interests of all classes, though essentially its
appeal was directed to the more affluent and ambitious elements. Given
increasing social mobility and the spread of opportunity in Britain,
these formed a growing proportion of the population.

Meanwhile efforts were being made to discourage the selection of
Conservative parliamentary candidates simply on grounds of birth and
wealth, and, though the immediate effect was small, a useful number of
able and more professional politicians won seats in 1950–1, among
them Edward Heath, Reginald Maudling, Enoch Powell and Iain
Macleod. The last-named gained early fame with a slashing attack on
Aneurin Bevan and the health service in the Commons in March 1952.
This was soon followed by his appointment as Minister of Health by
Churchill. By 1950 the party organization had been shaken up at all
levels: party research and information services were improved. The
party set out to fight the 1950 election with a more classless image –
interestingly the voters portrayed on Labour and Conservative electoral
posters were often indistinguishable, or with the Conservatives
sometimes having the more working-class appearance. The Conservative programme was a judicious mixture. It accepted full employment
and the welfare state, it included cautious promises to ease rationing
and controls, it fiercely attacked nationalization and high taxes, and
offered generalized promises of more incentives for individual effort
and enterprise.

Yet the election was a disappointment for the party. Ground was
regained among the middle classes. The Conservatives did particularly
well in the dormitory areas of large towns, especially around London.
But whereas the Labour vote fell dramatically in Middlesex, it was little
affected in the old areas of heavy unemployment. Some 450 factories had
been built in the development areas between 1945 and 1948, and
unemployment there averaged only about one-quarter of the 1937
levels. Overall Labour secured 13,266,592 votes (and 315 seats)
compared to 12,502,567 (and 298 seats) for the Conservatives. The
Liberals, with 50 per cent more candidates than in 1945, could add only
one-sixth to their overall vote: they were left with a meagre nine MPs.
The Communists fared disastrously, losing the two seats won in 1945,
though, by their increased intervention in the election, possibly
depriving Labour of up to four seats. Indeed, it is worth noting that the

Redistribution Act of 1948, and the postal vote, both worked against Labour, robbing a 3 per cent lead in votes over the Conservatives of much of its effect. Account should also be taken of other factors, such as the impact of the Liberal vote, and overall analysis of the 1950 election suggested that Labour now needed more than a 2 per cent lead in the popular vote to be sure of a parliamentary majority, and thus negate the current electoral bias in favour of their opponents.[22] Labour had clearly lost less ground with the electorate than their slender majority appeared to indicate.

With so narrow a parliamentary majority the Attlee ministry was not expected to last long, in the light of past experience. Yet neither its early demise nor defeat was inevitable. It required a combination of international ill-fortune and internal Labour feuding to bring about an election eighteen months later – an election which was still only narrowly lost.

The Labour party's internal divisions were revealed as early as May 1950 when, at a joint meeting of the National Executive and the Cabinet, Bevan, Morgan Phillips and Sam Watson battled with Morrison over the future of nationalization. In practice, the slender majority made new measures impossible. Rivalries within the party were intensified by the failing health of Bevin and Cripps: the struggle for the succession to key positions in the government and party was beginning. There was resignation talk by Bevan whenever the possibility of National Health charges on patients was mooted. Cripps warned in his budget speech in April 1950 that there could be no excuse for overspending in the NHS in the coming year, and that any expansion in one field must be met by economies in another. Bevan was obliged to accept the imposition of a cabinet committee to exercise some surveillance over NHS costs.[23]

Nevertheless, in the early summer of 1950 and indeed for some months longer, there seemed a chance that the British economy was recovering well enough for the government to gain some room for manoeuvre. An American boom and recovery in western Europe were both stimulating the exports of the sterling area, so that Britain's balance of payments problems appeared to be rapidly disappearing. Much rationing and many controls had been lifted, defence spending had been stabilized, TUC cooperation in restraint of wages was still holding, though its days were clearly numbered. During the chancellorship of Cripps a balance of payments deficit of £450 million was transformed into a surplus of £300 million. National output was increasing at about 4 per cent a year, only one-third of which was allowed to pass to domestic consumers. Personal consumption, in real terms, was a little above the 1938 level, with much fairer distribution among the population as a whole. Inflation had been slowed, and if the government had been helped by some extraneous forces, J. C. R. Dow argues that 'on the broadest questions of economic policy' it had performed with some credit. 'Only greater austerity could have greatly shortened the period of disinflation and control; and for the policy itself it is difficult to imagine a sensible alternative.'[24] Professor Hutchison commended the government for its remarkable indifference to electoral considerations, and Professor Pollard observes that the British economy was reasonably healthy compared with the rest of Europe – though given their comparative war experiences that was not saying a great deal.

The economy also appeared to be growing at a satisfactory rate in comparison with the past. Contemporary complaints of austerity and undue government interference showed only a partial grasp of realities. Indeed, Pollard thought consumption perhaps a little too high. Economists, in retrospect, have also been critical of the level of industrial investment. Too little attention had been paid to improving industrial efficiency. If one postulated that the nation's greatest need was a rapid increase in the national wealth, the government had wasted too much time over nationalization and income redistribution, and devoted too little effort to the search for positive means of increasing the national product. But Professor Pollard adds that the government was not alone in this failure. British industrialists, after two wars and the great depression, were often lacking in enterprise to a degree for which the current government could not be held responsible. External forces were swinging against the country once again, with first the trade boom and then the Korean War moving the terms of trade against Britain. The Korean War also brought a general deterioration in the international scene, and foreign affairs were to be the most immediate cause of Labour's downfall in 1951.

The Korean War

The Korean War broke out on 25 June 1950. The British Cabinet's view at the time that the communist North Koreans were the aggressors, whatever the provocation offered by the South, has received some confirmation from the memoirs of Nikita Khrushchev. The North apparently believed that the southern regime could be overthrown in a limited military operation – American intervention was not expected. The United States, however, feared that western inaction would encourage communist activities elsewhere in the world, and the British Cabinet agreed that the United States must be supported.[25] Attlee spoke of 'naked aggression' by North Korea: American and British references to the lessons of appeasement in the 1930s were not mere rhetoric. But it was also recognized in Whitehall that support for the Americans was vital to strengthen those in the United States who were wholeheartedly committed to the defence of Europe and who were opposing those Americans, such as Robert Taft, who, without retreating into isolation or wishing totally to neglect Europe, nevertheless wished to follow a less expensive and more selective foreign policy. The British readily supplied air and sea forces, but a brigade was collected with more reluctance, and then mainly to counter American critics who alleged that the British were not pulling their weight. Helped by this limited contribution the British hoped to discourage western over-commitment in Korea. As early as 6 July 1950 Attlee was listing other points of possible communist activity – Hong Kong, Persia and Greece – and the consequent need for anticipatory allied cooperation. Detailed Anglo-American discussions followed.

The Cabinet, however, faced an increasing number of problems. There was the dilemma of trying to decide how much rearmament was necessary: what the nation could afford and what it could not afford *not* to do. If there seemed the great possibility that Korea would merely prove the prelude to other and perhaps more serious communist moves, there were also fears of American adventurism, of overreaction, or of over-commitment in areas of less interest to Britain. In this explosive atmosphere it was inevitable that the highly charged question of German rearmament should come to the fore. American strategists had already been arguing that western European defence was dependent on a West German contribution, but the current crisis was needed to bring this issue into the realm of practical politics. It was a subject which was bound to cause immense controversy in Britain and the Labour party. Indeed, nothing was to divide the Labour party more sharply in the early 1950s. Bevin admitted to Acheson in September 1950 that the British Chiefs of Staff strongly favoured German rearmament, but was clearly uneasy as to the possibility of carrying it through the Cabinet and Parliament.[26]

With hindsight it has been possible to argue that Soviet military strength in eastern Europe was probably exaggerated at the time. Nevertheless there is no escape from the genuine feeling of alarm with which, for instance, Montgomery, Lord Ismay and later Eisenhower, viewed the miscellaneous conventional forces then at the disposal of NATO. Whether one took 1952 or 1954 or some more distant date as the year when Soviet nuclear strength might seem sufficient for Moscow to adopt a more positive policy in Europe, if it were so minded, the equation of conventional strength could never make sense without some infusion of German forces. British obduracy on the question of German rearmament gradually melted in September when it was recognized that American reinforcements in NATO and the appointment of an American as Supreme Allied Commander Europe (SACEUR) were contingent upon the creation of twelve West German divisions. In public, on 19 September, British, French and American ministers agreed that the creation of a national German army was undesirable, but they referred to their interest 'in principle' to German participation in an international force for the defence of Europe. Acheson praised Bevin's contribution to this outcome. Churchill had already spoken of the possibility of a European army in August, and in

October the French Prime Minister, René Pleven, produced a plan for a European Defence Community for the joint control of European military forces within NATO. Germany might contribute small contingents to a European army. The French aim was both to control German militarism by such means, and to draw Britain, if possible, into a supranational defence structure. The British, however, were determined to avoid such a fate, and at the Paris conference which opened on 15 February 1951 to discuss the proposed EDC they were represented only by an observer. The election of a Conservative government later in the year brought no change of policy. The response both of Eden and Churchill was bleakly negative.

Meanwhile the British were probably precipitate in favouring talks with the Soviet Union over the Far East as early as July 1950. More wisely in the autumn, after the rout of North Korean forces in the South, and the UN motion calling for free elections throughout Korea, the British suggested (vainly) that military operations in the North be confined well south of the Chinese and Russian borders, and a cease-fire and demilitarized zone negotiated. Whether the imposition of such restraints on General MacArthur's forces would have prevented the intervention of Communist China in November cannot be established, though the Chinese only intervened after clear warnings, and after some hesitation if a high-ranking Chinese politician who later fled to the West is to be believed.[27] Certainly in the face of MacArthur's reckless advance towards their border the Chinese had no choice. They intervened to such effect that in December 1950 it seemed possible once again that all Korea might be lost. Attlee flew hurriedly to Washington to discuss the British defence programme and the overall international situation as well as the alarm provoked by the ambiguous remarks of President Truman on the possible use of nuclear weapons. Acheson thought Attlee a 'Job's Comforter', and was dismayed by the concessions he was apparently prepared to make in the Far East, such as the admission of Communist China to the UN, as well as its recognition. Attlee, for his part, learned how American domestic politics limited the President's freedom of action. Even so, his visit perhaps did something to remind the Truman administration of the opinions of other western nations at a time when the atmosphere in the United States was dangerously emotional. Attlee could secure no immediate American help with the British rearmament programme, and indeed soon after his return British defence spending was increased yet again despite protests from Bevan and Harold Wilson. At the end of January 1951 the Foreign Office and Hugh Gaitskell (according to Dalton, Gaitskell threatened resignation on this issue) were able to insist that Britain join the United States in branding China as an aggressor at the UN.[28]

In 1951 the Korean War settled down to a costly two-year stalemate, while MacArthur was removed for insubordination. His readiness to fight a full-scale war with China dismayed the American Chiefs of Staff and European allies alike. British influence, at most, can only have been marginal, but it is interesting that Acheson singled out the British ambassador, Sir Oliver Franks, for special mention as a diplomat with whom he was able to conduct wide-ranging analyses of the international scene throughout the years 1948–52. If the British continued to find America too sympathetic towards Japan and the Chinese Nationalists on Taiwan, and too rigid in their hostility to Communist China, from Korea to Indo-China there persisted basic common interest in the containment of communism. Serious differences in detail were to become apparent only after the departure of Acheson from the State Department.

For the Attlee government the most serious consequence of the worsening of the cold war in 1950–1 was the increasing burden of defence. By the end of January 1951 the Cabinet was planning to spend £4,700 million over the next three years, or about double the expenditure envisaged at the beginning of 1950. So great an increase was partly due to American pressure, partly to British recognition that a major effort on their part was essential if they were to have any hope of influencing American policy, as well as being seen as a necessary response to the current international situation. The unpublished Dalton papers include a War Office circular of 4 February 1951 stating, 'war possible in 1951, probable in 1952'.[29] The Chinese intervention in the Korean War at the end of 1950 had caused much alarm, and even before that there had been fears that the East-West strategic balance would be gradually disturbed by the Soviet acquisition of a nuclear capability. The first Soviet nuclear test had occurred in 1949, and by 1954 it was anticipated that the Russians might be able to offset the western nuclear deterrent, thereby enhancing the value of their conventional forces in Europe. Some increase in western conventional forces was therefore necessary. At this time, too, many western strategists were far from persuaded that a major war could be determined by atomic weapons alone. This explains why so large an expansion of NATO was envisaged. Within the Cabinet Bevan continued to argue that Russian steel production was too low for her to risk war, but at the same time he favoured a western guarantee of Tito's Yugoslavia when Soviet threats in that quarter were reported.

In retrospect the contemporary charges of Bevan and Wilson that too much was being spent by Britain on armaments can be described, at least in several senses, as correct. At the time, however, it appeared more important to run risks with the economy in the search for security. The government believed that no 'unbearable strain' would be imposed on the economy if American aid were forthcoming, and if the necessary imports could be purchased in the right quantities and at the right prices. The plan to spend £4,700 million within three years was dependent to some extent on circumstances, but the fact remains that the government appears to have been too optimistic as to the nation's ability to carry new burdens without serious injury to the balance of payments, new investment and domestic consumption.[30] Adjustments

could, of course, have been made later, but before these could take place
the Labour government had fallen.

Labour's fall from power

Expectations that the second Attlee ministry would not last long did not
include the expectation that it would be followed by a long period of
Conservative rule. Labour contributed much both to their own fall and
to the subsequent Conservative ascendancy. Though one cannot
dogmatically assert that Labour's internal divisions were decisive, they
certainly played a major part in the politics of the 1950s. Personalities,
principles and events interacted to turn pre-existing tensions within the
party into serious conflict. Rearmament brought to a climax the debate
over the priorities in government expenditure, while the retirement first
of Cripps and then of Bevin meant that the Cabinet had lost two out of
its four key figures. Adequate substitutes were not to be found among
the older generation or less controversial of Labour's leaders. The
obvious claimants for advancement were Aneurin Bevan, whose
influential standing in part at least of the Labour party pre-dated the
1945 victory, and Hugh Gaitskell, aged forty-four in 1950, the
outstanding ministerial success among the younger men. This rivalry
would have been less damaging to the party had it not been for Bevan's
personality and strong identification with the left: these ensured both
his defeat and the divisive effects of the contest.

Cripps resigned as Chancellor of the Exchequer in October 1950
through ill-health. Gaitskell, then Minister of State for Economic
Affairs, and already noted for his mastery of economic policy, appeared
the obvious choice to both Attlee and Cripps. Bevan opposed
Gaitskell's appointment to the Treasury, writing in protest to Attlee and
urging a wider reconstruction of the ministry. Attlee was unmoved. He
believed that Bevan as Chancellor would not have inspired sufficient
foreign confidence. In March 1951 Bevin was no longer able to continue
as Foreign Secretary, and Attlee, without much conviction, appointed
Morrison in his stead, claiming that there was no obvious alternative
and that Morrison wanted the job. Bevan, meantime, had merely been
moved sideways from Health to Labour. The long-term hopes of Bevan
and the left on the one side and of their opponents on the other were
bound up in these appointments, and trials of strength to try to shift the
axis of government were only to be expected. Attlee had maintained the
status quo or perhaps even shifted it a little against the left.

These defeats within the Cabinet found Bevan ill-disposed to make
further concessions to help the government as its problems rapidly
mounted with the Korean War, rearmament, and the consequent
economic problems. The balance of payments surplus left by Cripps
rapidly evaporated. The cost of imports had been rising even before the
Korean War, and there was growing popular impatience with wage

restraint. The voluntary cooperation of government and the TUC was breaking down, so that in 1951 the government found itself in a dangerous inflationary situation, and with a new balance of payments crisis on its hands. Wages, prices and consumer demand were all rising at a time when the terms of trade were swinging harshly against Britain, and when additional resources were needed for rearmament. Paradoxical though it might appear, Dow describes economic policy-making under Hugh Gaitskell in 1950–1 as the most sophisticated yet attempted in Britain – 'far more reputably Keynesian' than his predecessor's. The difficulties of the Treasury must be appreciated. British imports rose by a quarter in price in 1950 and by another quarter in the first half of 1951. Export prices rose by less than half that amount. The *Economic Survey* for 1951 expected imports to cost another £1,000 million, an underestimate of only £150 million. But invisible earnings also proved less than expected, largely because of the Abadan oil crisis[31] which deprived Britain of another £150 million. A surplus of £300 million in 1950 was succeeded by a deficit of £400 million in 1951.

Many other members of the sterling area were in a similar plight, their dollar earnings being nearly halved while their dollar purchases were increasing. In consequence there occurred the most extreme swing in the sterling area's balance of payments hitherto recorded – its deficit with the rest of the world totalled some £600 million in the second half of 1951. The British government resorted to controls, higher taxes and dividend restraint, but the nation was clearly living beyond its means. Industry could not meet both export and rearmament needs simultaneously. Steel and the metal-using industries were the main bottlenecks, and here a squeeze on domestic consumers could provide only limited help. More drastic action, such as further imports cuts, as introduced by the succeeding Conservative ministry, might have been taken earlier, but the scale of the problem was not easily grasped. Nor was quick and effective coordination with the rest of the sterling area attainable, while the majority of the government continued to believe that risks had to be run on behalf of the defence programme.

This crisis brought to a head the internal divisions and rivalries within the Labour party. Ostensibly the resignations of Bevan, Harold Wilson and John Freeman on 21 April 1951 turned on the scale of rearmament, the imposition of health charges, and the balance of expenditure on the NHS as opposed to pensions and family allowances. For Bevan the health service was always a sensitive point. There had almost been a crisis between himself and Cripps over its cost a year earlier. A running battle with Hugh Gaitskell can be dated from that time. Issues and temperaments became inextricably tangled. There were other clashes of principle within the party, notably over public ownership.

Fenner Brockway in *Outside the Right* recalled the current dismay of the left at the absence of a social programme to follow that of 1945–50, and at the impossibility of paying for any that might be devised while defence spending ran so high. Richard Crossman argued in *New Fabian*

Essays (1952) that the Attlee government had lacked a theoretical basis for its reforms, so that they represented the end of a century of social reform and not, as its socialist supporters had hoped, the beginning of a new epoch. Indeed, as Ralph Miliband thought, most of the Labour party vacated office later in 1951 without deep regrets, expecting to reinvigorate the party in Opposition. Although the articulation was sometimes confused, the desire of the left to strike down capitalism, power blocs and arms races remained strong, and for them the policies and prospects of the government by 1951 presented a bleak prospect.

As for Bevan himself, his personality and motivation are so differently described by friend and foe, especially at this time, that it is hard to see in them the same person. This underlines the strength of feeling on both sides. According to George Brown, Hugh Gaitskell insisted that in his rivalry with Bevan it was all a battle for power: 'he knew it and so did I'.[32] Bevan claimed that, for him, Gaitskell represented nothing in the Labour party, or at best symbolized a swing from socialism to 'mere Liberal reformism'. The overall atmosphere in both Cabinet and party must be grasped before the real cause of the impending ministerial crisis can be understood. It was greater than the sum of its more obvious parts.

Yet there were those who felt that the split should have been avoidable: Attlee thought so himself. But the latter was working from a hospital bed in April 1951, and he favoured Gaitskell in any case. There were some attempts to smooth away the differences, but neither Gaitskell nor (more hesitantly) Bevan was disposed to compromise. Both saw concession as a sign of weakness. The struggle had begun long before the spring of 1951, and in those critical months Gaitskell's standing had risen among most of his Cabinet colleagues. Feelings concerning Bevan were usually at best ambiguous. John Strachey, for instance, sympathized to some extent with Bevan on both the health charges and foreign policy, yet he supported Gaitskell. Some were highly critical of Bevan. Shinwell later condemned him for dividing the party. Dalton came to fear him as a demagogue and even as a potentially autocratic leader. He thought him too talkative, rhetorical and provocative in the Cabinet. Gaitskell, in Dalton's eyes, had become a model minister. Attlee and Bevan were temperamentally poles apart. Michael Foot might write later of the pro-Bevan feelings of masses of socialists in the country, but many of Bevan's Cabinet colleagues saw him as an electoral liability. Bevan was the most exciting politician of the postwar era; he had immense gifts; he could be compassionate as well as ambitious, creative and flexible as well as impetuous and emotional. But he lacked the tireless, disciplined and hard-headed resourcefulness and discretion of the most successful politician. As one who once saw himself as part of a sub-group on the right wing of the 'Bevanites', Richard Crossman wrote of his tendency to smash things up.[33] Even his great admirer, Michael Foot, described his own single clash with Bevan as 'an horrific occasion'.

In July 1951 there appeared a Bevanite pamphlet, *One Way Only*, which insisted that overemphasis on the threat from Russia, and therefore on rearmament, was causing Britain to retreat from socialism, and to ignore the need for more aid to the underprivileged regions of the world. In various ways the Bevanites were actively trying to increase their influence within the party, and not without success. But there is no obvious supporting evidence for Harold Macmillan's reference to a rumour on 21 September 1951 that Bevan had 'in effect, blackmailed Attlee by threatening to withdraw his support unless the Parliament was dissolved'.[34] In fact Attlee had written to Morrison as early as 27 May 1951, raising the possibility of an autumn election. He also sounded other ministers. Attlee was most anxious that the election should precede the planned royal tour of Australia early in 1952.[35] But his hopes of May that circumstances might be more favourable to Labour in the autumn were not realized. Indeed, the situation was worse. Shinwell thought Attlee a tired man, 'resigned to defeat', though arguing he needed a new mandate to meet the pressing economic difficulties. Interestingly, most ministers do not seem to have felt the same sense of urgency for an election. Doubtless Attlee was feeling the strain of no less than eleven years of continuous office; he also had reason to fear for the unity of his party if he called upon them to support yet more austerity. With a clear mandate from the electorate and the assurance of four or five years of office during which to develop more than a strategy of survival, the situation might look different. Even a Conservative victory in the current difficult situation might prove less damaging to Labour than to try to struggle on. Certainly the Conservatives themselves took office with much trepidation. Attlee's decision was neither self-evident nor inexplicable.

The election of October 1951 was fought over much the same ground as its predecessor. David Butler thought the government made a fatal mistake when it failed either to court the centre by abandoning the nationalization of steel or to take the initiative with 'a decisive legislative programme'.[36] Neither was in fact possible, given the state of the party, although left and right could draw together for the 1951 election with a policy of public ownership only for those concerns 'that fail the nation'. Admittedly the government was increasingly giving the appearance of drifting from day to day, seemingly over-impressed by the experience of office with the limitations of power. Controls had their use in conditions of acute shortage, but otherwise they had proved clumsy, unpopular and even counterproductive. The subtler methods of overall guidance and supervision of the economy, especially through the medium of the budget, were not easily given electoral appeal, not least when government calculations appeared to be going badly astray. Some Labour ministers were also making strong defences of the mixed economy. Cripps had warned of the dangers of taxing profits too heavily, and Gaitskell followed in April 1951 with the reminder: 'In an economy three-quarters of which is run by private enterprise, it is foolish to ignore the function of profit as an incentive.' Policies of this kind based on practical experience should have accorded well with the general mood of the country, which was increasingly sceptical concerning further nationalization and undue government interference in the economy. But Labour's weakness lay in the fact that more people were coming to believe that the Conservatives could be trusted to administer the economy in much the same manner – perhaps, indeed, more competently, flexibly, and with more conviction than Labour – without in any way jeopardizing full employment or the welfare state.

Experience of austerity was also beginning to balance memories of the 1930s. Radical changes in society and in the economy no longer seemed so necessary: the possibilities of human betterment within a mixed economy seemed very real. The exhibits at the Festival of Britain of 1951 were tangible evidence of what the future held, once the priorities for export could be relaxed. There was more talk of industrial co-ownership and profit-sharing, and even a little implementation. The image of private industry had been softened a little, and Conservative talk of 'freedom' and 'enterprise' had a more confident ring. There was also a somewhat reckless Tory promise to built 300,000 houses a year. Labour, indeed, were generally on the defensive against Tory charges of the Bevanite threat, the failure of nationalization, and the cost of living. The party did strive to project itself as a better defender of the peace than the Conservatives: in fact the theme, 'You can't trust the Tories' embraced both home and foreign affairs. If there were few specific charges of war-mongering against Churchill, some observers were inclined to feel that this issue, more than any other, explained the knife-edged outcome to the election. Yet it is interesting that both Morrison and Shinwell should have been prepared to contemplate a little gunboat diplomacy of their own against Iran not long before. Once one cut through the party rhetoric the overlap between the two programmes was remarkable.

The election itself revealed that, even on the defensive, Labour's appeal in the country was still remarkably strong. The government even appeared to regain some support during the election campaign. Its record 13,948,605 votes[37] represented 48.8 per cent of the total cast: the Conservatives secured 48 per cent, and they improved on their total vote only in 1959. The Liberals contested fewer than one-third of the seats for which they had fought in 1950, and their share of the poll slumped to 2.5 per cent. This helped the Conservatives much more than Labour, though the weakness of the Liberals helped to inflate the votes of both main parties. Labour's high poll suggested much continuing suspicion of the Conservatives, though the swing to the latter was remarkably uniform over most of the country. The Conservatives also made significant gains among first voters compared with 1950. Dalton lamented that it was becoming increasingly difficult to recruit Labour supporters; the success of the welfare state was perhaps breeding apathy. The bias noted in the working of the electoral system in 1950 continued to favour the Conservatives, being worth perhaps half-a-million votes. Such were the circumstances in which the Conservatives edged to a total of 321 seats against Labour's 295. In this fashion Labour left office in 1951. They departed under a cloud, their party divided, though not without hope of victory at the next election. At the time their economic record suggested nothing so much as the unavailing efforts of Sisyphus, and only with the passage of time was it possible for their successes and failures to be viewed in better perspective. Then and since many have expressed disappointment that the government's policies had not been more radical in all aspects of foreign and domestic affairs. Few such critics have seriously considered the limited range of options open to the government, or the wide-ranging implications of their suggestions. It is true that Bevan as Minister of Health provided a personal drive that might not have been supplied by any other Labour politician in his office, and perhaps achieved more in consequence. But he was supported by a unique public demand for the NHS. Despite difficulties and disappointments, the Attlee ministries can be credited with the most solid achievements of all governments between 1945 and 1974.

Chapter 5

The return of the Conservatives: 1951–5

Conservative domestic policies, 1951–4

Conservative elation at their victory in October 1951 was tempered by the daunting economic situation. Harold Macmillan commented on 28 October: 'It is 1940 without bombing and casualties – but also without the sense of national unity.' The new ministers encountered much pessimism among their financial advisers, with the Treasury forecasting 'a continuing range of difficulties'. There were some fears that the terms of trade would remain permanently tilted against Britain, and that there would not be a sufficient expansion of world trade to facilitate yet further increases in British exports to meet the deficit. The long-term prospects were not encouraging. Any hardheaded Conservative who strongly believed in private enterprise had also to recognize that British politics since 1945, and the two hardfought elections of 1950 and 1951, had demonstrated the solidity of Labour support and the probable precariousness of that of the Conservatives, especially if they became tarred with controversy and failure. Essentially the Conservatives had gained office on the strength of Labour's weakness. There was no mandate for drastic change. Macmillan's analysis of the prospects is interesting. He foresaw, after the next election, the possibility of a Labour majority of 200 led by Bevan as premier. However, he drew comfort from the fact that Labour had fought the 1951 election, not on socialism, but on the fear of unemployment, decreasing wages and welfare, and of war. If none of these fears became a reality, we may be able to force the Opposition to fight [the next election] on Socialism. Then we can win.'[1] Unfortunately the new government faced rising prices and unemployment, and a difficult time abroad. Labour prophecies seemed all too likely to be realized.

Churchill took office aware that his party had to establish its progressive credentials in both home and foreign affairs. He had been personally affronted by the warmonger hints. Having in the past argued that Russian possession of nuclear weapons would make war inevitable, he now acted with increasing determination to disprove his own prophecy. His choice of Butler as Chancellor of the Exchequer instead of Oliver Lyttelton suggested a desire to avoid identification of his government with big business. Butler had done much since 1944 to free the party from the image which it had gained in the 1930s. As Butler said in March 1947:'We are not frightened at the use of the State. A good Tory has never been in history afraid of the use of the State.' The new Minister of Labour, Sir Walter Monckton, was an experienced lawyer-politician – he had advised Edward VIII in the abdication crises. He commented: 'Winston's riding orders to me were that the Labour Party had foretold grave industrial troubles if the Conservatives were elected, and he looked to me to do my best to preserve industrial peace.'[2] Macmillan, a forceful administrator and consummate politician, was entrusted with the vital task of meeting the promise to build 300,000 houses a year. The electoral appeal was obvious: it was a programme whose progress could readily be demonstrated and immediately felt. But its impact on industrial building was not carefully weighed. Churchill also hoped to hasten the end of rationing, reduce taxation and eliminate unnecessary controls. He wished to avoid controversial legislation, showing no great interest in denationalization save in so far as it was necessary to fulfil election promises and satisfy party opinion. All this did not amount to a very bold strategy, but the government, with so small a majority and faced by so many problems, did not appear to have a very secure future.

There was some Conservative backbench restlessness in the face of their leaders' caution. Government spending and taxation were not slashed as hoped: the commitment to full employment and the main body of the welfare state too tightly constrained the government. A Labour government might have given more attention to the social services, but if Conservative policy was not adventurous neither were the economies significant. As for economic policy Dow remarks: 'Though some shift in the emphasis of economic policy was apparent, there was probably less change in deeds than in the doctrines by which they were justified.'[3] Indeed, some analysts have concluded that Conservative Chancellors in general shone neither in economic theory nor as practical businessmen. Butler's approach to economic policy has been described as more political than that of his predecessor, and this proved both a strength and weakness. But the degree of continuity from Labour was so striking that in February 1954 *The Economist* coined the word 'Butskellism'. Significantly, too, Labour had been reducing controls in response to circumstances just as Butler, at the start of his chancellorship, felt obliged to restore them to meet the economic crisis. He did, however, in his March 1952 budget cut both income tax and food subsidies, while his economic policy overall made much more use of monetary instruments than his predecessor. The bank rate was raised in November 1951 – the first time since the war. More pressure was exerted on the banks to restrict their advances to borrowers in times of stringency.

To meet the economic crisis in the winter of 1951–2 the government cut imports, and took over the allocation of about two-thirds of the supplies of raw materials. Help was fortunately also forthcoming at the Commonwealth finance ministers' conference in January 1952, although promises to cut imports extended in Australia's case to serious reductions in imports from Britain. But with the dollar earnings of Malaya, the Gold Coast, and South Africa once more picking up, the sterling area as a whole began to enjoy a surplus. The British government's import cuts involved a considerable retreat from the recent liberalization of trade negotiated with the nation's partners in the OEEC, but an import saving of some £600 million was deemed vital for 1952. The government's measures were powerfully assisted by a dramatic swing in the terms of trade in favour of Britain – indeed, nearly half the improvement in the balance of payments was attributable to this one cause. Thus, although the volume of British exports fell by 10 per cent, the reserves were rising rapidly by the end of 1952. Britain's own export and invisible earnings gave her a comfortable surplus in 1952, while the rise in retail prices at home slowed from nearly twelve to under 7 per cent. Wage rates rose no faster than retail prices: indeed, the slackening of demand at home and abroad was sufficient to bring about a minor recession, with unemployment edging up to 2 per cent. Thus within a year of its electoral victory the new government found itself in a more favourable position than expected, much of it the product of circumstances beyond its control, but at least merited in part by the apparent firmness and conviction with which the Cabinet had set about its tasks.

From the middle of 1952 to the end of 1954 no postwar government enjoyed so favourable an economic climate. Britain was able to purchase sufficient foreign food to end rationing in 1953–4. The fall in the cost of imported raw materials, with some increase in the productivity of British industry, did much to slow the price rise, so that from the middle of 1952 to the end of 1953 there was an average increase of only 1.5 per cent, followed by a still modest increase of 3.5 per cent in 1954. The improved terms of trade also meant that most of the increase in British manufactured production could be sold at home without causing a balance of payments crisis. The minor recession of 1952 had left some excess labour and capacity that could be utilized without generating inflationary pressures. New investment did not expand until 1954. Further relief had been afforded the economy by cuts in Labour's projected defence programme. Churchill himself, as temporary Minister of Defence, had thrown himself with great gusto into the task of scrutinizing the rearmament plans. On 30 July 1952 he informed the Commons that the original programme was 'utterly beyond our economic capacity to bear'. The services' share of the production from the engineering and metal-using industries was cut from 20 to 15 per cent. Nevertheless, economists such as Professors R. S. Edwards and F. W. Paish concluded that the scale of Britain's defence effort at this time contributed to the slowness of her economic growth compared with that of West Germany. The main contemporary impression, however, was one of success, with a fairly judicious balance being struck between the economic and military needs of the nation. The coronation of Elizabeth II in the summer of 1953 thus coincided with a new mood of confidence and optimism. It did not seem wholly naive to speak of a 'new Elizabethan age'. In practice the rapid economic recovery from the 1951–2 crisis bred a dangerous complacency, discouraging any critical review of the nation's position in the world, and encouraging the belief that the economic base of the country was fundamentally sound.

It is true that when the economic situation was at its worst, in the first half of 1952, some interest in new solutions can be detected. Harold Macmillan commented on 29 February on the continuing leakage from the reserves despite the government's economies: 'It is not worth while making all these tiresome and unpopular cuts, if the leakage keeps going on through the Commonwealth, etc. We might do better to wind up the Sterling Area (except for U.K. and the Colonies) altogether.' In his memoirs he wrote:

Many of us began to ask ourselves whether Great Britain could ever become a going concern again if she continued to carry the whole burden of operating a banking as well as a trading system, and shoulder all the obligations of sterling as an international currency.[4]

Ideas were circulating in government as to the possibility of funding a large proportion of the sterling balances, leaving the rest freely convertible but at no fixed rate. Some argued that the reserves were as yet too low to bear such a burden, and certainly fears of further devaluation through a floating pound added to the pressure on sterling early in 1952. But Mr Assheton in the Commons on 12 March, 'voicing what many in the City thought' argued the case for 'an honest currency', and for the need for immediate action in case the situation worsened. 'What shall we have to do then? We shall have to let the currency run free, or devalue it, without having any reserve at all.'[5]

The possibility of convertibility and a floating pound was very much in the air in 1952. But a far-reaching set of proposals, given the code name 'Operation Robot' and discussed by the Cabinet, was finally defeated with Lord Cherwell among others helping to steel Churchill's mind against it. Convertibility could only have been purchased in this scheme with both a floating exchange rate to meet international complications and a greater readiness to use the bank rate to regulate demand at home, if necessary with drastic deflationary consequences. Cherwell argued that this 'financial jugglery' would injure relations with the Commonwealth, the European Payments Union and the United States. It would also prove politically unacceptable in Britain, endangering full employment. Convertibility would have been a risky expedient so long as there was an acute shortage of dollars, or until sterling could compete more effectively. In the circumstances of 1952 it might even have led to dollar-hungry states restricting imports from Britain in order to convert more sterling into dollars. Not surprisingly, a possible programme for a more cautious advance towards convertibility was only hammered out by government departments with the utmost difficulty in the summer of 1952. At the Commonwealth conference in December there was agreement in principle concerning the ultimate aim of convertibility, but it was hedged around with restrictions such as the curbing of inflation, the general freeing of international trade, and the availability of adequate international credit. Convertibility was gradually instituted between 1955 and 1958, without a floating pound. The Bank of England was always the strongest force in its favour, but Sir Dennis Robertson observed in 1954 that currency convertibility was:

> *not an end in itself, but a means to the promotion of a steady and abundant flow of international trade* . . . *it is sometimes necessary to be on the look-out for a certain tendency on the part of those engaged in administering a currency to be a little too much swayed by considerations of prestige – of the ability of their own idol to 'look', the other idols 'in the face'.*[6]

A. C. L. Day (*The Future of Sterling*) warned in the same year that 'a general use of sterling as an international currency can involve the British economy in costs that are not commensurate with the advantages'. Rumours of impending convertibility sometimes led to speculation against sterling in the mid-1950s. Nevertheless, it was only among those with fundamental doubts about the long-term strength of the economy that serious fears developed concerning the use of sterling as an international currency. Thus Andrew Shonfield still occupied a fairly isolated position in 1958 with his detailed warnings of the damage that was being inflicted on the balance of payments and on the domestic economy by the pound as a reserve currency and in its international roles. Tradition, prestige, a feeling of responsibility for and interest in an ordered monetary system, as well as hopes of economic gain, all help to explain why the policies in question were followed.

At home, although the economic position began to improve and despite party rhetoric, the government adopted a policy of economic liberalization with some hesitation. It needed practical success to encourage further movement. Both the budgets of 1953 and 1954 seemed highly successful, and by the end of 1954 most controls had been abandoned. Consumer demand (though not at first industrial investment) responded well to tax reliefs, while much success appeared to attend the manipulation of the bank rate and other monetary measures. Butler spoke of the introduction of incentives to work and save to replace government 'snoopers' and 'spivs'. The commitment to full employment remained an important constraint, nor was it possible to reduce significantly the massive involvement of the state in the economy, with some quarter of the working population being in its employ, and with the government being responsible for up to 40 per cent of the nation's investment and expenditure. By 1958 the government's spending as a proportion of the gross national product had been reduced to about 36 per cent, but it is important to note that defence savings provided much the largest element. In 1952 defence had absorbed nearly 11 per cent of the gross national product: this had fallen to 7.5 by 1958.

Government relations with industry were somewhat ambiguous. Experience with Labour's Productivity and Development Councils finally persuaded ministers that they were counterproductive, causing friction with unions and employers rather than bringing positive results. The difficulties of establishing satisfactory relationships, were highlighted by government dealings with the aircraft industry. Defence needs, as well as costly civil projects to try to reduce British dependence on American airliners, necessitated close cooperation, yet there were repeated disappointments. In part these arose from ministerial failures, both Labour and Conservative, to relate aircraft specifications – especially for military aircraft – to industrial possibilities, to subsequent costly modifications in design, and to government payments which varied between parsimony and extreme generosity. There was a clear need for closer and more informed communication. At the same time the government was ignoring the structural deficiencies in the industry. As aircraft became more sophisticated so there was need for more concentration of resources. The average American firm had 50,000 employees; the average British (and there were sixteen of them) only 15,000. American firms had proportionately four times as many qualified staff, and more capital equipment. Professor Beer recorded the opinion of one government planner in the early 1950s: 'We are rather disillusioned with physical programming. We prefer to get results not by commanding what must be done, but by putting out a piece of cheese and trusting that some particular mouse will go after it.'[7] But in the most advanced technological fields this was no longer enough, there being no guarantee that a mouse of the right breed or with the correct metabolism was to hand. One had either to lower one's sights or begin selective breeding.

Not all businessmen were anxious to go their own way in the early 1950s. Lord Woolton in charge of the Ministry of Materials in 1953–4, while running down government stocks of raw materials, was disappointed to find that many of the traders employed by the government were by no means anxious to return to buying materials on their own account. On the other hand, business complaints against high taxes greeted the government at every turn, though the government itself could feel that industry was often slow to take advantage of such investment incentives as were being provided from 1953. Until the late 1950s interest in regional development was fading, though north-east Lancashire was added to the scheduled development areas in 1953. Interest in industrial relations also tended to run into the sand. Some Conservatives had desired to act against restrictive practices, unofficial strikes, the closed shop, and had discussed the feasibility of non-political unions and some sort of wages policy. Joint employer–employee consultation, co-ownership and even some forms of industrial democracy had attracted attention. But the government was determined to tread with great care in the area of industrial relations. When Butler mooted the possibility of a tripartite body to try to relate wage increases to productivity, the TUC responded with a blunt negative.

The government was disposed to attribute wage inflation at this time mainly to the competitive bidding by employers for scarce labour, and it believed that inflation could best be handled through its control of the overall level of economic activity. Some use was made of courts of inquiry and arbitration tribunals, and the government made frequent appeals for responsibility in wage negotiations. Monckton, though later much criticized as an arch-conciliator or appeaser, was acting strictly in accord with the wishes of the Cabinet. In the winter of 1954–5 a court of inquiry helped to open up a whole new dimension in wage bargaining when it argued that the level of railwaymen's wages should be related to the rates for comparable jobs in private industry. This was fair, but it added to the inflationary spiral which had started elsewhere. In general, in 1953–4, wages and salaries had risen about three times as rapidly as output. The Treasury's *Economic Survey* for 1954 was full of gloomy prognostications concerning the decline in the competitiveness of British exports if internal costs were allowed to rise too quickly, but as to positive action the government believed it could only hope for a 'change in the climate of opinion' and the growth of 'voluntary moderation'. In fact, government, business and unions were tending to drift apart in an atmosphere of mutual criticism. Each was taking a narrower view of its responsibilities. The engineering employers in particular were full of complaints of government appeasement of the unions.

Conservative hesitation was also reflected in the treatment of the nationalized industries. There was much less denationalization than was expected, partially because of the hesitancy of some ministers, but also because there were fewer purchasers of sections of the steel industry, and of road transport undertakings than anticipated. Fears of renationalization under a later Labour government obviously operated to some extent, but both private users and the government itself were discovering that some parts of the nationalized long-distance road haulage service had many advantages. Regular, nationwide, interconnected operations were of value to firms such as Lyons and Cadbury. As for steel, its national importance meant that some degree of state supervision was necessary, and under the 1953 Act the government was provided with much the same sort of powers as Morrison had sought in 1947. An Iron and Steel Board was instituted under the Ministry of Supply to supervise investment in the industry, and to try to encourage coordination. Consumers were given rather better representation on this board than they had enjoyed under Labour's plans. The government also retained some reserve powers over maximum prices. But the Board's powers were basically too limited and too modestly interpreted. The industry required firm direction as to both modernization and rationalization. It is true that a major example of government intervention, the decision in 1958 to establish separate strip mills in both Wales and Scotland when the sound commercial choice would have been one larger undertaking, does not inspire confidence in outside intervention. Yet the steel firms themselves, when left to their own devices, failed on the whole to keep pace with foreign rivals, and in the early 1960s the industry had far too much outdated plant. If renationalization fears helped to inhibit investment, the steel industry seems to have added its own quota to the mistakes made by the politicians of both parties.

The early 1950s were doldrum years for the nationalized industries. They were left very much to run on the momentum imparted to them by their creators, whose thinking had been directed more to organization and control than to long-term dynamic management.[8] The Conservative government continued to employ the vague guidelines that the industries should pay their way, taking one year with another, and there were the usual exhortations on efficiency and coordination. But investment was too often conditioned by immediate needs with too little thought for expected returns in the long run. Past theoretical justification for nationalization, that it would end wasteful competition and lead to integrated services, was not reflected in the relations of the three fuel and power industries, or in those between road and rail transport. Transport nationalization had, of course, left users free to choose between them, including the right to employ their own vehicles. Selective experiment was the most that could be expected as yet in the way of transport integration, but of this there was no sign. The new government did indeed try to reduce the problems of the overburdened Transport Commission. Six Railway Authorities replaced the old Railway Executive, with full responsibility for management and operation, and the 1953 Act also required the Transport Commission to prepare plans to bring the railways up to date. The railways were just about in balance on operating account in 1955.

Further experience, however, demonstrated that decentralization was carried too far. The railway modernization plans were ambitiously prepared with too little regard for transport developments as a whole, and with insufficiently realistic or sophisticated approaches to the questions of cost. The target was a thoroughly modernized rail system which would be able to pay its way in the 1960s. Steam traction would be replaced by diesel or electric power; track, signalling, freight depots, all were to be improved. Initially it was estimated that this would require an investment of £1,200 million over a period of fifteen years. This was soon found to be too low. The chances of the railways earning a profit were lessened by continuing government restrictions on fares and rates, and by the accelerated challenge from road traffic. The car explosion dates from the early 1950s as petrol rationing came to an end, and the easing of the export drive released more cars for the home market. Incomes were also rising to enable many more people to become car owners – there was a 50 per cent increase to over 3 million between 1951 and 1955.

In the fuel and power industries coal was still king. If production continued to fall below demand, productivity was at last beginning to rise. Uncertainty as to the future, coupled with the extensive civil spin-off from nuclear developments for military purposes, encouraged the drafting of plans for a number of nuclear power stations. The first civil nuclear reactor programme had been approved in June 1952. The Atomic Energy Authority was set up in 1954 and a £300 millon ten-year programme announced. Coal production costs were expected to rise as deeper seams were dug and there were fears over the reliability and cost of foreign oil supplies. Little happened as expected. Nuclear progress was slow: the efficiency of other types of power station improved.

Neither Labour nor Conservative governments had really succeeded in mastering the broad problems of nationalization. Governments interfered too much to help themselves in the short-term management of the economy; private enterprise expected cheap service or cheap products from the nationalized concerns, and begrudged public expenditure on them; the left thought more in terms of social justice than of economic efficiency. In 1952 the Ridley Committee urged increasing competition between the nationalized industries, for example in fuel and power, but there was perhaps a greater need for a systematic investigation of pricing and investment policies to establish where low prices were creating excessive demand or inefficient usage, and whether adequate returns were being obtained from investments. There was also need for more activity to try to improve labour relations, to lessen the remoteness of management, and to try to cast off the pall of disillusionment which had settled over so much of this great experiment in British industry.

The state of the nationalized industries did not greatly concern the public. They were more conscious of the overall quickening of economic activity from 1953, with earnings rising well ahead of prices, and with goods at last refilling the shelves and windows of the nation's shops. Impressive progress, too, was being recorded in the government house-building programme, with its pledge to build 300,000 homes a year. For the period 1948–57 as a whole, house-building represented about 22 per cent of all gross fixed capital formation in the United Kingdom. In 1953–4 it rose as high as 26 per cent. In the view of many economists house-building absorbed too many scarce resources which would have been better applied to the modernization and expansion of industry, and the improvement of Britain's competitive position in the world. The government, however, could feel from 1953 that its current economic policies were on the right lines, and that there was sufficient room for manoeuvre to fulfil one of its most explicit election promises.

The scale of the housing problem left by Labour has already been noted, and account has also to be taken of the movement of population, especially to the more prosperous areas, and of rising expectations concerning comfort and amenities. In addition much property was in decay. Well over half the 13.5 million dwellings in the country in 1953 had been built before 1914. Much was privately rented, and with rent controls even the enlightened landlord was often in no position to pay for repairs when costs had tripled since 1938. The number of slum houses was still estimated at around half a million, but one-third of the housing in England and Wales fell below what was coming to be viewed as the proper standard in the 1950s (the housing situation was still worse in Scotland). Great efforts, both in repairs and new building, were essential merely to keep pace with a rapidly changing situation. Neither political party had an effective answer to the decay of so much privately rented property, Labour recoiled from the vast expense of a policy of municipalization. The Conservatives were working towards some relaxation of rent controls, but this too was to provide no answer to the problems of many private landlords. Real progress was thus confined to the provision of new housing, especially for sale to the growing number of people for whom home ownership was becoming feasi increasingly attractive. This was one of the great postwa revolutions.

Macmillan as Minister of Housing brought drive and imagir the task. He was strongly backed by Churchill and the Chancel Exchequer. His overall approach he described as one of ' Beaverbrookism', a reference to Lord Beaverbrook's app aircraft production during the war. Regional housing boards to grapple with shortages and bottlenecks. New methods and were employed, and there was some retreat from the stan down by Bevan. The party's target of 300,000 houses was twelve-month period from November 1952 to October 195? surpassed. Only in 1958–9 did house-building drop tempor; 300,000. From 1954 there was less sense of urgency, and housing in particular suffered a decline. Slum clearance and nome improvement continued. The 1961 census indeed suggested that homes and households over the country as a whole were roughly in balance. The distribution, however, was uneven, with some areas such as London suffering from acute shortages. Much of the progress was, moreover, being offset by the continuing decay of far too much property. Consequently housing once again became a political issue in the early 1960s.

Britain and the security of Europe, 1951–4

Although Churchill had returned to office in 1951 with clear, if broad, ideas on domestic policy, his deepest interest lay in the field of foreign affairs. Opinions vary as to Churchill's handling of his Foreign Secretary, Anthony Eden, at this time. Lord Kilmuir thought Eden enjoyed more independence at the Foreign Office than anyone since

Lord Rosebery in the 1890s, but George Mallaby refers to brusque interventions by the premier that were humiliating to the minister. Sir David Hunt, then a private secretary to the Prime Minister, recalls that Churchill, in his desire to meet the new Soviet leader, Malenkov, 'braved the displeasure of his Cabinet, and threats of resignation from such leading Conservatives as Lord Salisbury and Harry Crookshank, and mocked at the advice of the whole Foreign Office from Anthony Eden downwards'.[9] Churchill's age and failing health meant that he was unequal to consistent effort, but he could still intervene to great effect, as over Anglo-Soviet relations.

He also turned his attention at times to defence policy where his thought oscillated between the traditional and the revolutionary. He showed interesting foresight concerning the importance of nuclear delivery systems which could ride out a first strike by an enemy and still inflict a decisive retaliatory blow. With such forces a measure of equilibrium might be introduced into the nuclear arms race. To Parliament on 1 March 1955 he spoke of 'the value of deterrents, immune against surprise and well understood by all persons on both sides . . . who have the power to control events'. Here Churchill was contributing to a line of thought which was becoming increasingly influential in the United States, and which was worked out in depth by strategic theorists such as Albert Wohlstetter in the late 1950s. Churchill hoped that with thermonuclear weapons war would finally become an unacceptable instrument of policy, and that some progress might consequently be made towards a more peaceful world. He grasped that safety *might* prove 'the sturdy child of terror, and survival the twin brother of annihilation'. He argued that after 'a certain point has been passed, it may be said: "The worse things get, the better".'

Churchill was surprised and impressed by the progress made under Attlee towards the development of a British nuclear bomb. As Prime Minister he was able to learn more about the enormous American potential, and in 1952 he found his own Chiefs of Staff generally anxious to place more reliance on nuclear deterrence in both British and western strategy. Britain tested her first nuclear device in 1952, though some years would elapse before she possessed an effective nuclear strike force. Churchill at first found it much harder than he had expected to re-establish a close political and nuclear relationship with the Americans. His predecessors had tried to negotiate an arrangement with the Americans in 1949 whereby, although Britain would not entirely abandon her nuclear programme, she would rely on American-made atomic weapons. Such bombs would only be used in accord with 'joint strategic plans'. There had already been some slight relaxation in the 1946 American restraints on the supply of information, but hopes of further progress in 1949–50 were shattered by divided opinions in the United States, and by American fears of British security leaks, intensified by the arrest of the atomic spy, Klaus Fuchs, in January 1950. However, the British nuclear test of 1952 and the development during the rest of the decade of an effective nuclear bomber force (ultimately equipped with thermonuclear weapons) persuaded the Americans to advance towards an increasingly intimate nuclear relationship, with the revocation of the McMahon Act in 1958.

All this took time, and though Churchill was helped in his relationship with the United States by the election to the presidency in 1952 of his close wartime comrade, Dwight D. Eisenhower, the Anglo-American partnership, though unique, was not without its other problems. Britain and America were partially out of step over Iran, Egypt, Europe, NATO, Russia, South-East Asia, and trade. The British were inclined to rate themselves too highly, neither side took sufficient pains to examine each other's point of view, and it was unfortunate that Eden and Dulles, the American Secretary of State, should have found themselves so far apart in temperament and outlook. Their relations were as coldly remote as those of their predecessors had been full-bloodedly close – Bevin and Acheson smoothed away many a difference over a friendly drink. Nevertheless Britain continued to be treated by the Americans as a military ally in her own right. She was still responsible for about 40 per cent of the industrial output of the European members of NATO, even if she was in receipt of some American aid under the Mutual Security Act.

Difficulties also persisted over the degree to which Britain should involve herself in the affairs of western Europe. In their description of their intended foreign policy to the electorate in 1951 the Conservatives had placed European unity third, after Commonwealth defence and Commonwealth preference. Events soon suggested that even that rating would not be taken too seriously. Sir David Maxwell Fyfe promised the Consultative Assembly of the Council of Europe on 28 November 1951 'a thorough examination' by Britain of proposals for a European army. But Eden unequivocally told a press conference in Rome a few hours later that Britain would not contribute to such a force. Eden, in opposition, had shown little interest in the European ruminations of his leader. He had also been assured by Eisenhower on 27 November 1951 that British forces in the long run would best operate with the Americans as a strategic reserve for the West. On 1 December Eden noted that for France and Italy the purpose of the proposed European Defence Community was to pave the way for a European federation. No separate armies would be allowed except to serve as overseas garrisons.[10] Britain could not join an EDC with such objectives. Churchill repeated Eden's negative to the Commons on 6 December, and Paul Reynaud of France immediately expressed the opinion that Britain's refusal would mean the collapse of the whole scheme. He was correct, though the project took nearly three years to die. Without British participation in the EDC the French feared German dominance.

The German question and its relationship with the Soviet Union also evoked much debate in Britain. Anti-German sentiment was still strong, and there was much hostility to German rearmament. *The Daily Express* and the left-wing *Tribune* were on common ground here, and there were lighthearted references to a 'Bevanbrook axis'. Bevan himself hoped to see a united Germany with free institutions, limited armaments, and posing threats neither to East nor West. There were many variations on this theme. But Chancellor Adenauer of West Germany, on a visit to Britain in December 1951, was assured by the Foreign Office that it was government policy to oppose the neutralization of Germany: if Germany were to be reunited she must be free to join the West. Pierson Dixon, Deputy Under-Secretary in the Foreign Office, was reported around this time to be stating that the government wanted a one or two year delay in talks with Russia on Germany in order to build up western strength.[11] Russian proposals on German reunification in 1952 were certainly viewed with the utmost suspicion, being interpreted as ploys to delay or frustrate the formation of the EDC, and to ensure that any reunited Germany should not be allowed to ally with NATO. The British were anxious that Germany should not be free to return to the days of Rapallo from 1922, when it could play East against West. Russian intentions are by no means clear, but to prevent the rearmament of West Germany and its integration in the western camp Moscow may even have been prepared to abandon the communist regime in East Germany if this ensured the neutralization of Germany. According to American intelligence, East German communist leaders were warned by Moscow that they might have to play the role of Thorez or Togliatti (leaders of the French and Italian Communist parties respectively) in some future reunited Germany.[12]

A disarmed, neutralized, reunited Germany had not a few attractions in theory, and might be seen as a way forward to stabler East–West relations. But Germany as a cushion between East and West could also have turned out to be one of the air-filled variety, and thus highly unpredictable in changed or changing circumstances. For the West to have seriously explored this possibility in 1952 would have been a veritable leap in the dark, with damaging consequences for their relationship with the ruling Christian Democrat party in West Germany, and with the prospective loss of twelve badly needed German divisions. Yet if the British were at one with Adenauer and the Americans that on no account must West Germany be separated from the western alliance, Churchill and Eden, though in rather different ways, both entertained hopes of relaxing East–West tension. Churchill was not unaware of the electoral advantages that would accrue from such a relaxation. He was also fully aware of the dangers and burdens that would arise from the unchecked development of the Cold War, and the continuing nuclear race. At first he argued in Washington in January 1952 that the Russians seemed to fear the friendship of the West more than its enmity, and that therefore only western strength might reverse the position and persuade the Kremlin to seek western friendship. But the death of Stalin and the thermonuclear threat by the spring of 1953 had convinced him of the need for a new policy. His last two years in office were dominated by his desire to establish his name as a man of peace as well as of war. This hope may have tempted him to prolong his tenure of 10 Downing Street when he was no longer entirely equal to his responsibilities: it also explains the precipitancy of some of his moves.

Churchill disturbed allies, many of the Cabinet, and his own Foreign Office by proposing in the Commons on 11 May 1953 that there should be an informal meeting of heads of government of the leading powers. He warned that the West must not assume that 'nothing can be settled . . . unless or until everything is settled'. Privately he criticized the Americans for dogmatic opposition to Russia, and reflected on the possibility of a central European pact modelled on the Locarno agreement of 1925. Charles Bohlen, the American ambassador in Russia, later thought that some Russian concessions on East Germany might have been forthcoming. But circumstances favoured Adenauer and Dulles, neither of whom was anxious to talk with the Russians at that stage. Churchill himself fell ill, and the United States was agreeable to no more than a meeting at the level of foreign ministers to discuss Germany and Austria. This met unsuccessfully in Berlin in January 1954. Both Macmillan and Moran, however, found Churchill more optimistic concerning negotiations with Russia than either the Foreign Office or Eden, and throughout 1954 he repeatedly tried to break the log-jam. For Eden the main priority until October 1954 was to ensure the establishment of the EDC or some substitute, and only with western Europe thus consolidated was he prepared to begin a systematic exploration of the possibilities of East–West detente. He emerged from talks with Molotov early in 1954 convinced that the main Russian aim was the break-up of NATO, nor was there any common ground on the future of Germany.[13] Indeed, Eden, by acting less precipitately than Churchill and more flexibly than Dulles, probably struck the right diplomatic note in 1954. This was to be a year of remarkable diplomatic achievement for him, even if some of his work lacked durability.

Eden was thinking of alternatives to the controversial European Defence Community as early as December 1951. He was also determined that Britain should not be saddled with the blame should it fail.[14] He was therefore prepared to do a great deal, short of actual British participation, to try to ensure its success. With the American Secretary of State he issued a joint declaration on 19 February 1952 in which both promised to maintain forces in Europe to assist the Defence Community. This was not enough for the French, who saw it as yet further evidence of the British preference for cooperation with the United States. In April Eden tried again, with assurances of aid to the EDC so long as Britain remained a member of NATO. Eden insisted, 'we have established a formal and special relationship between the United Kingdom and the EDC. This shows clearly that, although we cannot join that community, we are linked with its future and stand at its side.'

In May 1952 a number of agreements were signed in Bonn and Paris to grant full sovereignty to the German Federal Republic, to establish the EDC, and to spell out the Anglo-American relationship with it. In fact, although French ratification of the EDC was not to be forthcoming, in the early months of 1952 the steps towards it and still more the ECSC appeared to be pushing Britain to the sidelines of European affairs. The so-called 'Eden proposals' were put forward in the spring to try to strengthen the links of the Council of Europe with the ECSC and EDC, but it was not long before the European enthusiasts had seen through this device as yet another of the British 'half-way houses'. Macmillan believed that the Foreign Office underestimated both the threat of western European developments to British interests and the capacity of Britain to seize the initiative and direct them into more satisfactory channels. Britain could not join a federation, but might be able to inspire a confederation organized more in the manner of the Commonwealth. Britain, he concluded hopefully, could participate in such a union or federation without injury to her relations with the Commonwealth and the United States. But, if he showed a little more imagination than his colleagues, it is unlikely that even proposals of this kind would have strengthened British influence in Europe.[15]

Anglo-American insistence on the desirability of an early French ratification of the EDC continued. The British were also conscious that the new American Secretary of State, John Foster Dulles, in his impatience for European unity, was anxious that it should include Britain. Dulles's famous threat in December 1953 of an 'agonizing reappraisal' of American policy should the EDC collapse could also be interpreted as a warning to themselves. But Churchill and Eden recoiled when France demanded that their forces should stay in Europe for at least another twenty years. They could only warn the French of the dangers of further delays in the ratification of the EDC. All was in vain and at the end of August 1954 the French National Assembly finally rejected the proposed community. This meant not only the end of the European army; it also left the issue of Western German sovereignty in doubt, as the Bonn agreement of 1952 established that sovereignty was conditional on the formation of the EDC. Nor could there be a West German contribution to NATO without some new agreement, and it would have been unthinkable in Britain as well as in France for German rearmament to proceed without integration in western defence in such a way as to preclude any revival of German militarism. As it was, German rearmament was already endangering the unity of the Labour party.

Eden claimed that the solution came to him, Archimedes style, in his bath one Sunday morning, but other contributors seem likely. The Dutch and the French, for instance, had both talked of the extension of the Brussels treaty to Germany and Italy in May 1952. The ensuing negotiations, however, were dominated by Eden, the circumstances fitting perfectly his gifts as a diplomat. The desire for a solution was deeply felt throughout western Europe and the Atlantic alliance. What was required was the skill and patience to fit together a complicated set of pieces. Eden was helped by the British Chiefs of Staff's readiness to enter into more precise military obligations in Europe now that Britain's commitments elsewhere in the world seemed to be lessening. Discussions on the future of the Suez base with Egypt were nearing completion, the situation in Malaya and Kenya was being stablized, and the Cypriot problem had yet to be fully appreciated. The bargaining power of the French was lessening as they had cause to fear that the United States would soon rearm West Germany unilaterally. NATO made no provision for limiting the contribution of any one member, and in other respects its structure was too loose to reassure the French. The older Brussels treaty organization of 1948, however, provided more scope, as well as emphasizing the Anglo-French relationship, and it was to this that Eden turned to provide the framework for German rearmament and reintegration into western Europe as an equal. Complex negotiations resulted in the London and Paris Agreements of October 1954 (these came into effect on 6 May 1955) by which both Germany and Italy were admitted to the Brussels treaty, renamed the Western European Union. Among its agencies was one to supervise the armaments of the member states, and in particular Germany's undertaking not to manufacture certain arms, including atomic, biological or chemical weapons. Germany's commitment to NATO of twelve divisions could not be increased without the authority of the Council of the Brussels treaty organization. Britain and America were to cooperate with France to see that West Germany honoured her promise not to revise her frontiers or to seek reunification by force. Britain gave firm promises to maintain four divisions and a tactical air force in Europe.

Eden was widely praised for his achievement. Eisenhower thought the October agreements one of the 'greatest diplomatic achievements of our time'. Churchill privately remarked that materially they altered nothing, and that their value was essentially moral. The British, in fact, were soon seeking permission to reduce their forces in Europe, but by then the peoples of the 'Six' were moving towards the formation of the Common Market so that this subsequent British equivocation was of less consequence than would have been the case earlier. Whatever may be said of British policy before or after the autumn of 1954, Eden made the correct moves at that time with assured diplomatic expertise.

Britain and the Far East, 1951-4

The Anglo-American 'special relationship' was often an ambiguous one, and never more so than in the Far East. But from the ending of the Anglo-Japanese alliance in 1922, the British had been forced to recognize that their security, and that of their empire, rested heavily on the United States. Admiral Sir David Beatty concluded in 1924 that in the absence of an American fleet in the western Pacific, 'we existed in the Far East on the sufferance of another power [Japan]'. In the more menacing year of 1932 Sir Robert Vansittart wrote: 'By ourselves we must eventually swallow any and every humiliation in the Far East. If there is some limit to American submissiveness, this is not necessarily so.' The Second World War rammed home the extent of this dependence. In 1951 the British suffered the acute embarrassment of seeing Australia and New Zealand enter the ANZUS Pact with the United States, an alliance to which Britain vainly sought admission. But the pact was no more than a full-scale admission by the Australians and New Zealanders that the United States had replaced Britain as their chief protector. As for Britain, if the Korean War had been of consequence to her only in the context of world rivalries as a whole, the emergence of Communist China with the ability to lend growing support to communists in South-East Asia was a direct threat of the first order. Anglo-American differences on policy concerning China, Formosa, Japan, Korea and Indian neutralism, and the differences between Eden and Dulles over Indo-China in 1954, must not be allowed to obscure the existence of common concerns.

Indeed, in Indo-China, so long as no French collapse seemed imminent, and so long as Acheson remained Secretary of State, Anglo-American policies remained reasonably close. Acheson informed the British ambassador in the middle of 1952 that if China intervened against the French, the Americans would not send troops but would rely on air-sea power, and a blockade of the Chinese coast.[16] It was not his aim to destroy communism in China. The British may have been undecided as to policy, but Bevin, Macmillan, and Montgomery, for instance, all anticipated to some extent the famous 'domino' theory articulated by Eisenhower in 1954.

As the French position weakened, and Dulles seemed bent on ever more extreme solutions, so Eden became increasingly active in quest of a diplomatic solution. Early in 1954 he expressed interest in some form of partition in Vietnam to stabilize the situation, to check further communist encroachments, and to protect Malaya. In Berlin in January 1954, despite the impasse with Russia over the future of Germany, there was talk of a five power conference (to include China) and Eden saw this as a possible way forward in Indo-China. The Americans first opposed the admission of China, and then continued to adopt a menacing if somewhat uncertain stance concerning the future of South-East Asia. But Eden, with a conference agreed for Geneva from the end of April, argued that while a collective defence agreement might be needed in that region, there should be no precipitate action. Diplomacy must be given its chance. The envisaged military measures were unlikely to be effective, and since one step was likely to lead to another the risk of a world war could not be discounted. Eden favoured no more than a policy of firm warning against further communist encroachment should partition be agreed at the conference. He also had high hopes that India might be able to exercise a restraining influence in Peking. As the crucial battle in Indo-China developed at Dien Bien Phu, and a beleaguered French garrison faced defeat, so harsher proposals came from Washington. Eden was unimpressed. He clung to the hope of a political compromise and of sympathetic diplomatic action by other Asian states. In strategic terms, he was now more interested in the fate of Thailand than Indo-China, though he would have welcomed the creation of a 'protective pad' made up of Laos, Cambodia and parts of Vietnam.

Dien Bien Phu fell on 7 May, eleven days after the opening of the Geneva conference. Not until 21 July was final agreement reached, with Eden playing a critical part in the cliff-hanging, tortuous negotiations. But it is important to remember the forces working in his favour as well as the obstacles in his path. There was a new French government under Mendès-France that was anxious to secure a settlement by 20 July. Both the Soviet Union and China wished to reduce international tension, and were prepared to urge restraint on the Vietminh. As for the United States, despite Dulles's withdrawal from the conference and his angry rumblings from the sidelines, the desire to resist the spread of communism did not extend to agreement in Washington as to how this should be done. Eisenhower was prepared to risk militant action only if assured both of solid Congressional support and of assistance from the British in particular among America's allies.[17] These conditions were not met. The American Chiefs of Staff were divided, with General Ridgway warning against intervention, not least because American troops would be needed, and the nation was unprepared for another Korea. All in all, those who unequivocally favoured belligerent action, both in the eastern and western camps, were in a small minority. In practice, the American government became mainly concerned to avoid identification with a compromise settlement with communists, while at the same time it looked for any opportunity to prevent their further spread. Eden was further helped by fear of a third world war and a thermonuclear holocaust.[18] Finally, India proved a useful intermediary with the Chinese.

Four states emerged from what had been French Indo-China, only North Vietnam being under communist control. The intention was for the partition of Vietnam to be only provisional. Elections were to be held in 1956 to resolve its future. The United States itself at this time was unsure as to the viability of South Vietnam, though it was determined at the very least to buy time for the rest of the region. This, too, in a more pragmatic fashion, was the British aim. Eden noted: 'I wanted to ensure an effective barrier as far to the north of . . . [Malaya] . . . as possible'.[19] Already in April 1954, faced with the possibility that all Indo-China might become communist, he had considered a guarantee of Thailand in conjunction with the United States. If, in the continuing uncertainties that followed the Geneva conference, the British would have preferred a security system that included India, the formation of the South East Asian Treaty Organization in September 1954 was a tolerable substitute. The obligations of the member states – Australia, Britain, France, Pakistan, the Philippines, Thailand, New Zealand and the United States – were less onerous than those in NATO: the treaty spoke only of 'continuous and effective self-help and mutual aid', though, depending on circumstances, the British commitment could have become dangerously open-ended. The treaty aroused only limited opposition in Britain. The government could congratulate itself on confirming the American commitment to the security of South-East Asia as a whole (it formalized a development that had been in progress at least since Roosevelt's assurances to Britain concerning Malaya shortly before the attack on Pearl Harbour) and on partially offsetting Britain's exclusion from the ANZUS pact. Given the promise that an ultimately independent Malaya would maintain close relations with Britain, including a defence relationship, and given other Commonwealth interests in the region, SEATO made good sense to British strategists in the context of the mid-1950s.

By 1954, too, the Malayan emergency was causing less concern. British authority had not been easily re-established after the war. The dramatic surrender of Singapore to Japan in 1942 had been a great blow to British prestige. The war had had devastating effects throughout South-East Asia, disrupting the economies, overthrowing the established authorities, and shattering traditional ideas and ways of life. However, the fragmented political character of the Malay peninsula – a conglomeration of principalities and colonial territories – and its racial divisions meant that no broadbased nationalist opposition to British rule could easily develop. In particular the Malays feared the very substantial minority of Chinese in their midst, and early in 1948 the British withdrew a plan for a Malay union, which would have strengthened the political position of the Chinese, and proposed instead a federation, which gave more power to the Malay sultans. British policy left many Chinese fearful as to their future in Malaya. This assisted the communists, and by June 1948 their activities had become so menacing that a state of emergency was proclaimed.

Relations between the British and the Malays were not wholly satisfactory, but they were good enough to ensure that the non-Chinese element in the Malayan Communist Party never represented more than about 10 per cent of its strength. Most Malays saw the communist guerrillas as a Chinese threat, and there was a consequent reluctance to press for early independence through fear of the political outcome once the British had left. Nor were the Malay Chinese united in their support of the communists. Many gave support only out of fear for their lives; many leaned to the communists only so long as they could see no satisfactory political future for themselves in Malaya. All these circumstances meant that the British, with the right political and military strategy, would be able to retain Malaya as the main dollar-earning member of the sterling area in the 1950s.

It took time for the British to find the answers, and in the early 1950s there was much disillusionment when, against 50,000 soldiers, and a quarter of a million police and home guards, 5,000 or so communist insurgents still appeared to be more than holding their own. The High Commissioner was murdered in 1951. The director of operations, Sir Harold Briggs, had already recognized the key importance of isolating the insurgents from sources of supply and information among the population, in this case especially the poorer Chinese in rural areas. Some half million squatters were resettled in 400 well-protected new villages and extraordinary efforts were made to insulate the population as a whole from the guerrillas and to deny the latter food. Political measures were also in train in the early 1950s. Local government was improved and there was some land reform, while the British government resisted the temptation to play off the Malays against the Chinese. Lyttelton as Colonial Secretary from 1951 insisted that racial unity and harmony were necessary preliminaries to peace, and soon afterwards the British were rewarded with the formation of the Alliance Party, representative of moderate Malay, Chinese and Indian opinion. In 1954 the British felt the political situation sufficiently improved to promise independence once the emergency was at an end. Much credit was given General Templer as High Commissioner from 1952 for the restoration of morale at a critical point, and for the new sense of vigour which was imparted to the administration and security forces. There was still much trial and error in British policy, the mixture of harshness and conciliation varied from time to time; there was much criticism, and progress was slow. The Malaya which was emerging did not accord with all political tastes, but in terms of British interests in the 1950s it was a success story. The danger was that it could breed over-confidence and encourage the pursuit of similar strategies in less suitable political terrain.

The nationalist challenge in the Middle East, 1950–5

Anglo-Egyptian negotiations on the future of the great Suez military base had been reopened in 1950. According to Egyptian sources, the Chief of the Imperial General Staff, in talks with the Egyptian premier in the middle of 1950, had warned that from ten to fifteen Russian divisions could reach Egypt within four months of the start of a war. But in the view of Cairo, such a Russian advance would be less likely if Egypt were neutral. Egypt therefore pressed for abrogation, not revision of the 1936 treaty. Bevin replied that Britain would take no steps that would leave the Middle East defenceless: she would continue to contribute to the security of her friends in the region. Britain professed herself willing to evacuate the base by 1956 but insisted on a close defence relationship. Efforts to appeal to Egyptian pride included the proposal on 13 October 1951 for a Middle East defence organization in which Egypt would be included as an equal member with Britain, the United States, France and Turkey. The Egyptians replied by repudiating the 1936 treaty,and when the British refused to recognize the repudiation, attacks on British lives and property in Egypt followed. The security of the Canal Zone was henceforward to become a major headache, locking up as many as 80,000 troops in defence of installations and equipment covering some 200 square miles and representing a British investment of about £500 million. For the British, all roads and routes in the Middle East led to Suez, and while alternative bases had been considered, both wartime experience and strategic calculations since seemed to confirm that it was indispensable.

The British were simultaneously facing a crisis in their relations with Iran – one which was seen as another test of the credibility of their claims to act as a power in the Middle East. The British-owned Anglo-Iranian Oil Company held a monopoly of Iran's proven oilfields. Iran was the largest oil producer in the Middle East, but its oil revenues remained disappointingly low. Richard Stokes, the Lord Privy Seal, argued in August 1951 that British conduct had left the Iranians with ample grounds for complaint.[20] A hesitant Iranian government was caught between British obtuseness and extremist opinion at home. In March 1951 the Prime Minister was assassinated, and the Majlis pushed through the nationalization of the oilfields and Abadan refinery against expert advice. Dr Muhammad Musaddiq became the dominating political figure in Iran for the next two years. An eccentric personality, he perhaps became the victim of his own image in the eyes of his fanatical supporters. He once remarked: 'I believe more in the moral than economic aspect of nationalization of the oil industry.'[21] But there was continuing obstinacy on the British side, especially in the eyes of the Americans, who feared communist exploitation of the crisis. The British demanded not only compensation for the nationalization of the company's assets but also damages for what they claimed was an illegal act. Musaddiq refused any compensation until Britain recognized the legality of the act of nationalization. The British clearly were afraid that any such concessions would undermine their other interests in the Middle East. The Foreign Secretary, Herbert Morrison, toyed with the idea of seizing the refinery by force in July, and waxed impatient at the caution of his colleagues that summer. Attlee wisely argued that quick decisive action was impossible – the forces were just not available – and that any act of violence would have been politically and morally disastrous, particularly for British influence in Asia. The Cabinet as a whole recoiled from force without American support.[22]

Fortunately for the British the Iranians could neither find new purchasers for their oil nor could they raise a foreign loan. The attitude of the United States was crucial. After some hesitation Washington moved closer to the British position. The Americans finally persuaded themselves that Musaddiq was not a prospective ally against communism. In August 1953 the army under General Zahedi seized power, and in the subsequent negotiations the British were persuaded to accept the validity of the nationalization decree. A consortium of eight foreign companies was to work the oilfields and refinery, the original British company taking a 40 per cent share. Iran received 50 per cent of the profits. The settlement was realistic, but the British had failed in their bid to discourage an experiment which might act as a precedent and an inspiration for others.

In Iraq, Nuri as-Sa'id, a friend of Britain, was also under pressure to follow a policy of neutrality and oil nationalization. He had warned the British government in September 1951 that it would be necessary soon to revise the 1930 treaty. Some uncertainty also surrounded Jordan following the assassination of Abdullah in 1951, though in July 1953 Britain was able to negotiate a twenty-year treaty with Libya under which some military facilities were secured. With Egypt the impasse persisted, despite American efforts to mediate. Indeed, there were British complaints that American activities were encouraging Egyptian obstinacy, especially when the American ambassador sympathized with Egyptian claims to the Sudan. Nevertheless, the seizure of power by the Egyptian army in July 1952 introduced a more constructive tone into both domestic and foreign policies. In February 1953 an Anglo-Egyptian agreement opened the way for Sudanese independence (1956) while in London second thoughts were being entertained as to the value of the Suez base.

The 1936 treaty, which Egypt had repudiated, was due to expire in 1956. The British had to act before time ran out. Faced by necessity, the defence planners began to discover strategic advantages in a smaller base on the island of Cyprus, although it lacked an adequate harbour. Installations on the scale of Suez, it was argued, might have no future in the nuclear age, while one of Britain's great needs was for a secure base from which small-scale operations might be mounted in the context of Middle Eastern politics. This would be politically impossible from Egypt, and it was this requirement which caused a British minister on 28 July 1954 to insist on nothing less than continued British sovereignty over the island of Cyprus. Sovereignty in Cyprus was required not only for the security of the base but also to ensure that it could be used in any circumstances. As far as the Soviet Union was concerned, the inclusion of Turkey in NATO lessened the need for Suez, though the British still hoped that the base could be used in a major conflict, and urged upon the Egyptians the advantages of an integrated Anglo-Egyptian air defence system.

Churchill did not follow this new military thinking with any enthusiasm, and had some sympathy for the 'Suez Group' of about forty Conservative MPs who vociferously opposed the policy of 'scuttle'. One of their leaders, Captain Waterhouse, complained that the British were losing the 'will to rule', and well into the 1960s voices could still be heard arguing that the retention of the Suez base by Britain would have averted many of the subsequent ills that befell the Middle East. In fact the British were lucky to secure the treaty of October 1954 with Egypt, which enabled them to evacuate over the next year and a half without much loss of face, and with certain assurances concerning the maintenance of the base for a further seven years. There was a clause providing for British re-entry in the event of an attack upon an Arab state or on Turkey by an outside foe (not Israel). The British unfortunately looked for a degree of pro-western alignment in Egyptian foreign policy which was not intended in Cairo, and certainly not by Colonel Nasser, soon to become premier. But disappointment brought only worse British misjudgements.

Meanwhile the British were digging themselves into a crisis in Cyprus. With its small population divided between Greeks and Turks, the British grossly underestimated both the measure of sympathy for enosis (union with Greece) that existed among Greek Cypriots and the problems that could be posed by well-organized terrorists. The Greek Cypriots showed themselves equally unmindful of the Turkish dimension. For the British the Turks were only a marginal consideration until they began to consider, from 1955, what political concessions might have to be made to the Cypriots. British efforts to crush the EOKA terrorist forces led by Colonel Grivas were unsuccessful. In Cyprus the British could not reproduce the combination of military and political tactics which was working so well in Malaya, and in their frustration they resorted in 1956 to the feeble expedient of exiling the leading Greek Cypriot politician, Archbishop Makarios, to the Seychelles.

The African awakening

The Gold Coast riots of February–March 1948 first brought home to the British the development of a new mood and consciousness among some Africans at least. This was the first African challenge to the assumption of the Colonial Office that it had almost an indefinite amount of time at its disposal to determine the future of British Africa. The Colonial Service was paternalist by tradition, instinct, and perhaps self-interest. In so far as self-government was distantly conceived, some adaptation of colonial economies and societies to the modern world was envisaged as a necessary preliminary.[23] Economic development and welfare programmes in any case were subordinated after the war to Britain's own economic interests and to her straitened circumstances. Thus even good intentions in the Colonial Service were not easily translated into effective reforms given existing attitudes, the scale of the problems and the frequent contradictions between British and colonial economic interests. Cripps wrote in 1947: 'The whole future of the sterling group and its ability to survive depends . . . upon a quick and extensive development of our African resources.' But this could lead to imbalance in the economies of the colonies, with production being geared too much to a limited range of products which could find markets in dollar areas or Britain herself. The encouragement of cash crops could even create local food shortages. Production for export often increased the white settler influence (as in East and Central Africa), disturbed the conservative peasantry, and provided grievances for the radicals and the uprooted.

Neither the economic relationship between Britain and her colonies nor the local gains and losses can, of course, be explained in simple terms. Poverty and underdevelopment were not caused simply by colonial rule. Africa was no paradise before the British arrived: nor did it become one with the departure of the colonial power. British investment and aid, and the provision of assured markets for certain colonial products must be weighed against the colonial contributions to the health of the sterling area, especially the dollar earnings of West Africa. The British provided varied expertise for much of a continent that was trying to enter the twentieth century. Nevertheless, it was steadily becoming apparent that the British, having disturbed one way of life, could not control the consequences. Even their paternalism sometimes discouraged local enterprise; their ability to meet the problems of population pressure, land hunger, growing concentrations of impoverished people around the towns was limited. Not only were popular expectations rising, but the most ambitious were determined to settle their own destinies. Such ideas spread more slowly in rural areas, and there was a tendency among the older generation of the Colonial Service to see the peasantry, and not the urban dwellers, as the true Africans. An old farmer in Barotseland assured Sir Ralph Furze, late of the Colonial Service, in 1960 that 'he wished to remain under the gracious protection of the blanket of King George V'. What mattered, however, were the views of those who could draw support where it counted, especially in the towns.

The Colonial Office had been thinking more in terms of the education of an indigenous meritocracy than of the speedy development of democratic and responsible government. No uniform pattern was imposed on the colonies, but the general approach was elitist. This was not without its advantages in the encouragement of high professional standards. It was not so well fitted to meet a rapidly changing situation, and a sudden telescoping of the time-scale of progress to self-government. Nkrumah had asserted: 'Seek ye first the political kingdom and everything else shall be added unto you.' This was an over-generous promise, but increasingly it became the prime demand in the Africa of the 1950s. For the black leaders of East and Central Africa it was an imperative, given the strength of the white communities. Without their 'political kingdom' the Africans in those territories could look forward at best to a very slow and limited advance. Tom Mboya claimed with some truth that it was not until the political unrest of the 1950s that the

Christian churches in East Africa began to see the black Africans as other than children.

The Gold Coast troubles of 1948 broke out in what had hitherto been regarded as a 'model colony'. Local grievances were exploited by the more radical nationalists. Ex-servicemen were particularly prominent, war experience having broken the mystique which formerly surrounded their white rulers. They had mixed with whites of all kinds, they had helped to defeat other whites and even to guard them as prisoners of war. The independence of India and Pakistan had been a further inspiration. But at the end of the war, to the colonial governor of the Gold Coast, the chiefs still appeared to be the dominant local force, well aware of their limitations and anxious to take advice. The creation of an all-African legislative council was seen as a great triumph but political advance of this kind (with a conservative native elite made up of chiefs, professionals and some intellectuals) was rapidly coming to an end. New leaders were gaining political support, especially in Accra. The Watson Commission reported in 1948:

The Constitution and Government of the country must be so reshaped as to give every African of ability an opportunity to help govern the country, so as not only to gain political experience but also to experience political power. We are firmly of the opinion that anything less than this will only stimulate national revolt.

But radical opinion continued to outstrip the British for a little time yet. Kwame Nkrumah and his Convention People's Party (founded in 1949) drew their main support from the urban skilled and unskilled, clerks, and primary school-teachers, and especially those whose education had not proceeded beyond the secondary stage. They opposed both the existing Gold Coast elite and the British. A state of emergency was proclaimed in January 1950, but the imprisoned Nkrumah won the 1951 election, and the Governor, Sir Charles Arden-Clarke, wisely decided to swim with the tide. Nkrumah was released to become chief minister. A relatively brief period of apprenticeship was now envisaged before the Gold Coast received its independence, and on this understanding a working relationship was established between the two sides.

Constitutional progress was also beginning to accelerate in Nigeria. A constitution introduced in 1947 had been expected to last for at least nine years without amendment. It was changed in 1951. Such events in West Africa sent a shock through the whole continent south of the Sahara. Was it, perhaps, the beginning of the end for the white man in Africa? Conditions, however, varied so much in that continent that it was not easy to judge. West Africa was far more advanced than the East. In 1948 a colonial governor described an independent *African* Kenya as unthinkable as an autonomous Red Indian republic inside the United States.[24] So perceptive a scholar as Margaret Perham, writing in *Foreign Affairs* in 1951, considered that decolonization in East Africa might occupy half a century, given the area's general backwardness and the strength of tribalism. She also saw the future too much in terms of close Euro-African relations, too little in terms of independent African development. Yet Julius Nyerere, who did so much to create the Tanganyikan nationalist movement in the 1950s, appears to have been deeply interested in the possibility of close cooperation with Britain as late as 1962. Tom Mboya wrote of the bitter struggles of Kenyan nationalists to rouse the people from their sense of inferiority to the whites. British opinion concerning the future of Kenya was somewhat confused, with many looking to the white settlers to spearhead modernization, though with local colonial officers sometimes recoiling from change and favouring the preservation of the traditional tribal society.

Unemployment, land and other grievances, as well as political ambition, explain the growth of the Mau Mau terrorist movement in Kenya from 1948. Seen at the time simply as a primitive and fanatical force – and even now not easily analysed – Mau Mau sprang from the Kikuyu tribe which had long nursed its hostility against the white settlers who farmed the good agricultural land of what had become known as the White Highlands. The white population of Kenya trebled between 1945 and 1960, and in 1952 only a little over one-third of the whites could claim more than five years residence. The White Highlands were the most progressive and valuable element in the Kenyan economy, yet they could only be a source of trouble. The white settlers wanted a permanent place – for some the dominant place – in Kenyan politics. Unlike large business undertakings with interests in many parts of the world, which could in consequence often adapt to a changing political climate, the white farmers were seeking to create a way of life in one country. When Mau Mau erupted in 1952 a Conservative Colonial Secretary warned the settlers that political progress to a multiracial society (there was a large immigrant Asian community too) would be necessary, as well as force of arms, against the terrorists. Multiracial partnership had a variety of meanings, and not only to the white settlers. It was abhorrent to most Africans who demanded majority rule. Attitudes in Britain, however, were such that even the Labour party did not unequivocally adopt the principle of one man one vote in its thinking on colonial developments until 1956. Meanwhile in Kenya the security operations were greatly assisted by the failure of Mau Mau to win support generally in the Kikuyu tribe. Other tribes were largely unsympathetic, so that while the aspiration for independence gathered strength, the political–military problem was in some ways akin to that in Malaya, and was manageable, given a British readiness to make some political concessions.

Less dramatic at the time but with more serious implications for the future was the creation of the Central African Federation in 1953. This was made up of Southern Rhodesia, a self-governing colony since 1923 and controlled by white settlers, and the protectorates of North

Rhodesia and Nyasaland. The question of some form of union had been raised before, and as recently as 1938 the Bledisloe Commission had opposed the idea in view of black African hostility. A Central African Council had, however, been set up in 1944 with sketchy powers. Northern Rhodesian white leaders approached the question of federation with care lest it should benefit the south unduly at the expense of the north, with its greater mineral wealth. A conference at Victoria Falls in 1949 was inconclusive for this reason, but interest in the federal idea was strengthened by the political gains of Africans elsewhere on the continent. White settler critics of federation diminished as the economic advantages became more promising. Through this expected economic strength, and the political cohesion provided by federation, it was hoped that white dominance would be assured for the foreseeable future. The Attlee government was also developing a hesitant and ambiguous interest in federation, partly at least because of the triumph in the 1948 South African elections of the Nationalist party led by Dr Malan. The ensuing policy of *apartheid* was anathema to British socialists, and the Central African Federation in consequence began to attract attention as a possible alternative experiment in multiracial relations. If it could harmonize both white and black interests, the federation's size and potential wealth might make it a valuable stabilizing force. There were fears, probably exaggerated, that Southern Rhodesia might otherwise gravitate for political and economic reasons to South Africa. Harry Franklin, with varied experience of the region, concluded in *Unholy Wedlock* that references by Southern Rhodesian politicians to this possibility were not serious, but were used to bluff the Attlee government into support for the federation.[25] As it was, both Cabinet and Colonial Office continued to have doubts concerning the white treatment of black Africans in such a federation. Both were aware of African hostility to the federation, and thus gave only guarded agreement in principle in 1951.

The succeeding Churchill government took rather less account of African feeling, choosing to regard it as unrepresentative or uninformed as to the advantages which the federation was expected to confer upon all races. Ministerial enthusiasm for the federation, according to Franklin, made any business pressure in its favour secondary. From the opposition benches Labour became increasingly critical of the neglect of African opinion. The white settlers, on the other hand, were dangerously over-confident, interpreting the clauses on racial partnership as according them more or less permanent seniority. Sir Roy Welensky, who became the federation's second premier in 1956, saw himself as pursuing a policy midway between that of the Afrikaners and the Colonial Office. European control would endure into the future as far as he could see. But unrest developed in Nyasaland as early as 1953 (this protectorate having been added to the federation on the wishes of Britain who could see no economic future for it on its own). Six years elapsed, however, before the British government began to awaken to the seriousness of its errors concerning the federation.

Britain as a great power in 1955

Many illusions existed in the 1950s concerning the nature and prospects of the Commonwealth, although already evidence was beginning to gather of the weakening economic ties. Discussions at the end of 1952 revealed that no further elaboration of Commonwealth preferences was possible.[26] True, the retreat from exchange controls and dollar-saving trading arrangements developed slowly, while the percentage of British investments within the Commonwealth actually increased in the mid-1950s. But British trade with most members of the Commonwealth was growing slowly or stagnating. Australia was especially anxious to pursue a more independent course. Canada, not a member of the sterling area, was one of the faster growing markets, but the United States grew faster still. British exports were also growing in western Europe (though not until the 1960s was this market to exceed the Commonwealth as a whole). Peter Thorneycroft, as President of the Board of Trade, showed particular awareness of these new developments. As early as 1954 he argued at a Conservative Party Conference that for Britain to press too hard for Commonwealth preferences could injure Commonwealth unity, and a year later, with Macmillan, he was warning the Cabinet of the beginnings of the decline of the Commonwealth as a market, although even then it was absorbing about 40 per cent of Britain's exports. Britain continued to offer Commonwealth producers a large and stable market, and was rewarded with lower food bills. But the remarkable growth of world trade at this time meant that most members of the Commonwealth, like Britain herself, were finding new openings for their products and were becoming less dependent on British manufactured imports.

These trends, by 1955, were sufficiently marked for Macmillan, who had hitherto seen the Commonwealth and European economic relationships as potentially compatible, to ask whether Britain was not in danger of falling between two stools, and whether it would not be the worse fate to be excluded from Europe. His colleagues, however, hoped to continue to strike a balance through the maintenance of Commonwealth preferences while negotiating a free trade agreement with western Europe in industrial goods. This, as we shall see, was an illusion.

Efforts to probe the future are not necessarily rewarding, but at this time the government was neither interested in nor well-equipped to engage in long-term planning. Some efforts to this end in the Foreign Office, for instance, had come to little in 1949. There was insufficient coordination between the Foreign Office, the service ministries, the Board of Trade, the Colonial Office or the Commonwealth Relations Office in the 1950s. Within the Foreign Office itself the same was true of the six departments that between them were responsible for British policy east of Suez. British policy-making remained badly fragmented, and was run mainly on traditional and departmental lines. Still more fundamental, however, was the strength of national confidence before November 1956. So great was this that it seems improbable that a better constructed government machine, even if it had produced more farsighted answers, could have implemented radically different policies. Britain was enjoying the Indian summer of her career as a world power. Not surprisingly the Conservatives were returned to office in 1955 with an increased majority.

Chapter 6

Crises and recovery, 1955-9

The Conservatives re-elected, 1955

The Conservatives had won power in uninviting circumstances in 1951. For some time thereafter electoral and other tests of public opinion favoured Labour, but gradually, as the economy strengthened and rationing ended, so the standing of the government improved. On the tests of full employment, maintenance of the welfare state, and an acceptable foreign policy, the ministry had done well, and by the winter of 1954-5 its prospects of re-election were excellent. The Secretary of the Cabinet, the future Lord Normanbrook, noted that the party had wanted an election for some time: 'The economic situation was as good as it was likely to be. In the autumn it might not be so good.'[1] This brought to a head the question of the party leadership, for Churchill was now eighty years old, his health was failing, but the old warrior was hanging on in the hope of some breakthrough in East-West relations. He could not, however, persist in the face of the party's need for a new leader before the next election, and in April 1955 Anthony Eden at last succeeded to the position to which he had so long been the heir apparent. The succession was undisputed, though this did not mean that all Conservatives had happily accepted this position since the early 1940s. James Stuart, Chief Whip to 1947, had been one of those to express doubts concerning Eden's capacity for all-round leadership.[2]

Eden was in some respects the victim of his own success in foreign affairs. It had become almost unthinkable for him to hold any other office under Churchill. Indeed, in his twenty years as a minister, he had spent all but three in the Foreign Office (only in opposition had his role been more varied). This perhaps helps to explain why, according to several accounts, the new Prime Minister involved himself more than usual in the work of departmental ministers, nervously worrying over details and failing to stand apart and above in the manner of an Attlee or a Macmillan. Prime ministerial styles and abilities differ sharply – a greater contrast than that between Churchill and Attlee, for instance, is hard to imagine, but both were effective first ministers.

In 1955, when Eden became Prime Minister, all seemed to promise well. Eden's political record was singularly good. He was not tarred with appeasement: in foreign policy since 1951 he had apparently steered a statesmanlike course in dealings both with Middle Eastern nationalists and with the communist world. He had glamour, if a hint of fragility. His background was upper-class, but not obtrusively so. He appeared a sound professional leader of a party much of whose appeal lay among those of middling means, who aspired to a car and home of their own, and the chance of a grammar school education and white collar job for their children. His was a party which stood for enterprise, change and welfare – all in moderation. Eden himself in his memoirs wrote of his dream of a property-owning democracy, a popular but vague aspiration for many Conservatives much as socialism was for many of the Labour party. He admitted to being attracted by the openness of Americans concerning money-making. To make a profit was 'not a crime but a necessity', and if money was too much admired in America, he thought it 'too despised' in Britain.[3] He was interested, also, in the possibility of 'partnership in industry', including profit-sharing and joint consultation. A comfortable compromise between the Britain and America of the 1950s seemed reasonable, and Butler had already suggested its feasibility in May 1954 when he asked, 'why should we not aim to double the standard of living in the next twenty years?'

One of the main assets of the Conservatives in 1955 was the disarray of their opponents. It is true that in contrast with 1950 and 1951 the former now had four years of growing prosperity to their credit to set against what seemed, as time passed, the years of ever greater austerity under Labour. The latter could no longer rely on memories of the 1930s (the past was no longer on their side), nor had they a great deal to offer that was new. In May 1953 Labour had even lost a seat to the Conservatives in a by-election – the first such gain by a government since 1924 – and thereafter the Tories rarely appeared at a disadvantage. Yet what was most striking about the 1955 election was not the Conservative vote – it in fact fell by 400,000 – but the collapse of that of Labour, with a drop of no less than one and a half million. The relative contentment was unmistakable. The Conservatives had done little to disillusion the electorate and something to win its confidence. On the other hand Labour's impact was almost wholly negative. Yet it is over-dramatic to write of the party fighting for its survival between 1951 and 1963, for all its divisions and confusion: one 1931 was enough. The instinct for survival reasserted itself as each election approached, though the broad triumph of the moderates in the preparation of every manifesto was balanced by the efforts of the left to increase its influence at other times. The left won battles in this fashion, but never a campaign, save, as we shall see later, in a defensive struggle allied with other party stalwarts over Clause IV to uphold the party's theoretical commitment to public ownership. Otherwise the left had little success within its own party or with the public at large in putting the case for further nationalization; the presentation lacked depth, though for Bevan it was always a critical test. He argued thus from his experience as a young miner in South Wales: the question of power was crucial, and power meant ownership. If the party pragmatists thought him doctrinaire, he took pride in the position.

No simple definition of 'leftness' or of 'Bevanism' within the Labour party is possible. Bevanite strength varied, though there was a hard core of about forty MPs. The fifty-seven who departed from the party line over defence in March 1952 included pacifists, and were indeed sufficiently heterogeneous to be known as the '57 Varieties'. Some of the most dramatic quarrels centred on foreign and defence issues, perhaps as a relief from the well-worn theme of nationalization on which there was little new to say, but also because on these issues the left could attract more support from within the party. There was also the struggle for key posts, again a battle which involved more than the left against the right or the emerging Gaitskell faction. Attlee, however, retained the leadership until the end of 1955, apparently determined to deny Morrison the crown, and content to play the part of an undemonstrative umpire. Support for Bevan continued to vary according to the issue at stake, while Bevan himself, partly as a matter of temperament and partly out of concern for ultimate party unity, had no wish to organize the Bevanites as tightly as Crossman and Mikardo urged. Perhaps he recognized its political futility.

Within the Labour movement as a whole the Bevanites were often able to draw a great deal of support from constituency workers, and from their representatives at Labour party conferences. Both the Bevanites and their opponents, however, were inclined to exaggerate the strength of the left within the constituencies. Nor was big union support for the right so solid as was often supposed.[4] The Trades Union Congress of 1951 only narrowly supported the government on health charges; a powerful minority of unions favoured extensive nationalization, and in September 1954 the TUC supported the Labour front bench on German rearmament by only four million votes to three and a half. This is not to ignore the determination of key union leaders such as Arthur Deakin, Tom Williamson and Will Lawther to smash Bevanism. They were especially outraged when Morrison was voted off the NEC in September 1952, when the Bevanites also secured six of the seven constituency seats on the NEC. Most of the leading unionists of the early 1950s were cautious men, with long experience of the ups and downs of working life, impressed on the whole by the material progress which had been achieved since the early 1930s, and suspicious of the journalists, writers and 'freelance intellectuals' who surrounded Bevan. Will Lawther, the miners' leader, denounced them as a 'group of people with anarchistic tendencies and highly inflated egos'. Deakin and Williamson both attacked the Bevanites as a threat to the unity and stability of the movement – divisiveness was a mortal sin. Bevan's own passion and impatience also disturbed many.

Bevanism was not frustrated by the big unions alone. It was a shifting minority within the parliamentary Labour party, able only occasionally to attract enough support to embarrass the leadership. It also stimulated a counter movement, to be distinguished from the traditional, pragmatic right. This was basically made up of intellectuals who rejected the theories of the left, and who can best be described as 'revisionists' or 'Gaitskellites'. These feared that Labour was becoming enervated by the prosaic practicalities of Morrison and the traditionalists, or was in danger of political suicide if it became identified with the Bevanites. The intellectual origins of the movement can be traced back to the work of Evan Durbin, Hugh Dalton and Hugh Gaitskell in the 1930s. Such ideas had lost momentum in the early years of the Attlee ministry. Only when the party seemed to lose its sense of direction and will to fight, save for the activists of the left, was it revived. The Socialist Union was set up after the 1951 defeat, and the already established *Socialist Commentary* became the organ of the revisionists in opposition to the Bevanite *Tribune*. The latter complained that socialism was being muddied with 'liberal traditionalism'. Certainly the Socialist Union was anti-Marxist. It sought a new humanitarian, ethical basis for socialism in the modern world. Public ownership was deemed less important to socialism than the struggle against a class-ridden society, poverty and squalor. As far as industry was concerned, ownership was less important than the methods and ethos of management. The state should be in overall control of the economy, but should be alert to the dangers of over-centralization and managerial remoteness from labour, a point already raised by Crossman in his *New Fabian Essays* (1952). It should strive for efficiency in both the public and private sectors. This gave rise, to the dismay of the left, to the downgrading of nationalization, economic analysis and the class struggle. The revisionists put their emphasis on personal freedom, social harmony and social equality.

Meanwhile in the power struggle within the party the left did not repeat its successes of 1951–2, but the fierceness of the battle is evoked in a speech by Gaitskell at Stalybridge in 1952. He warned of communist infiltration into the constituency parties, and insisted that the Bevanites must be isolated and disciplined. They were a 'group of frustrated journalists'. In the election for the deputy leadership of the party in 1952, Morrison defeated Bevan by 194 votes to 82. Similarly, over the party treasurership in 1954, Gaitskell prevailed over Bevan with a two to one majority, though it was believed that the constituency parties had voted in inverse proportion in favour of Bevan. Bevan himself complained of the oligarchic influence of the great right-wing trade union leaders, but there was no escaping the fact that they had the better understanding of the average and possible Labour voter. Within the parliamentary party, save on some foreign issues, the Bevanites remained a small minority. The issue of German rearmament in particular aroused a great deal of feeling in the party, as well as in the country as a whole. Attlee declared that he would accept it only on conditions that would ensure that the Germans never again became a military threat in Europe. In February 1954 the parliamentary Labour party was only narrowly in favour, and the same was true later in the year at the Trades Union Congress and the annual party conference. That the issue was carried at all owed a great deal to Herbert Morrison in one of his more effective forays into foreign affairs.[5]

Bevan had already resigned from the shadow Cabinet in April 1954 over its attitude to the possible formation of a South-East Asian defence organization. He had denounced this as a colonial plot. German rearmament increased tension within the party in 1954, but the great crisis occurred during the parliamentary debate on 2 March 1955 when Bevan challenged Attlee to state whether he agreed with the government's readiness to accept 'first use' of nuclear weapons in western strategy against Russia. Dissatisfied with his leader's answer, Bevan and some sixty other MPs then abstained on a Labour amendment to government policy, despite a three-line whip. Many on the party's right pressed hard for Bevan's expulsion, denouncing Bevanism as an organized conspiracy to make Bevan party leader. In the end the parliamentary Labour party voted by only 141 to 112 in favour of withdrawing the whip, and many pressed Attlee to protect him from expulsion. The NEC, after complicated talks and man-oeuvres, finally accepted Bevan's apology, but delivered a sharp warning on his future conduct. The episode could not have occurred at a worse time, with the Conservatives preparing for the 1955 election.

Labour differences were hastily patched up. The 1955 manifesto was a cautious document, robbing the left of the emphasis on public ownership which it had managed to reintroduce into party policy since 1951. Even so, the left found itself widely blamed for the party's disastrous showing in the May election. Bevan's own majority in Ebbw Vale fell, and he moved with the air of a Christian enthusiast in a time of religious decline, speaking of a 'sort of [national] spiritual exhaustion, a lethargy of the collective will'. It was the people who were at fault: they would not see the truth. In contrast, an American scholar, not unsympathetic to Labour, could write in 1955: 'Indeed, in a declining age of reason and a dawning era of irrationality and violence, Britain is a last bright symbol of enlightenment.'[6] Britain's political system stood high in western opinion at this time.

As for the 1955 election itself, all were agreed that it was unusually quiet. Gaitskell remarked in the *Socialist Commentary* for July: 'Almost everyone who took part in the Election agrees on one thing – the greater *detachment* of audiences at meetings and of the people generally. Since 1929 . . . I have never known so few people seem to feel themselves really involved.' This atmosphere suited the Conservatives, who in foreign affairs, for instance, had so successfully dispelled fears of trigger-happiness that they could safely argue for the retention of the H-bomb, pending a satisfactory disarmament agreement, without evoking any great alarm or interest. A four-power summit was about to take place, and even German rearmament was no longer a burning issue. At home Labour attacked the cost of living, but whereas the retail price index had risen seventeen points under the Conservatives, weekly earnings had climbed forty points. The number of private cars had increased by 50 per cent; television licences had quadrupled. Rationing was at an end; economies in the welfare state had been marginal; spending on the social services had been allowed to settle at a total which was about two-thirds higher in real terms than in 1938. It was Conservative policy to concentrate on the provision of basic minimum needs, and to encourage individual saving and insurance above that level. The social services should act as a safety net in what was seen as an increasingly mobile society, with expanding opportunities for all able to take advantage of them. The Conservatives claimed to some effect that the socialists were continuing to 'plan' the equal division of 'scarcity', and were clinging to obsolete ideas which were a threat to affluence. The world of haves and have-nots was giving place to one of haves and have-mores. As the most dramatic example of their success they could point to the housing boom.

Not surprisingly the Conservatives increased their majority to fifty-nine, with just under 50 per cent of the vote. Their advance owed much to the dramatic loss of popular faith in Labour, while the Conservatives had clearly lived down their reputation from the 1930s and were now accepted, if with only modest enthusiasm, as the more competent of the two parties. John Strachey remarked about this time that a man asked to name the greatest single achievement of the British Labour party over the past twenty-five years might well have answered the transformation of the British Conservative party. As generalizations go it was not a bad one.

Renewed economic problems, 1955–6

In the spring of 1955 the government and its economic advisers either misread the economic signs, or tended to play down the warnings of impending difficulties. Dow describes government policy at this time as 'neither consistent nor timely'.[7] The dangers of excess demand and imports had been recognized to some extent before the election, and there had been increases in the bank rate and restrictions on credit and hire purchase. On the other hand, the April budget included tax cuts of £150 million, possibly encouraged by what was to prove only a temporary strengthening of sterling. The efficacy of monetary controls continued to be overrated, but it was still difficult to justify the April tax cuts when unemployment was so low and prices were rising. The spurt in capital investment had unfortunately come too late to ensure the continued growth of output necessary both to sustain the expansion of exports and to meet home demand without excessive imports. British steel production, for instance, was not expanding quickly enough to meet the needs of the car manufacturers and some other industries. The booming home market was restrained only from July 1955 with hire purchase adjustments. There were renewed dangers of inflation, and the most serious outbreak of strikes since the war. The first phase of Conservative 'affluence' had been built on inadequate foundations: the price was paid in industrial and export stagnation between 1955 and 1958.

Between 1946 and 1954 the number of working days lost through strikes had never risen above two and a quarter million a year. A rising trend was detectable from the remarkably strike-free year of 1950, but it was only in 1955 that there was a sudden jump to three and three-quarter million days lost. Measurements of this kind, of course, provide only the roughest of guides, but contemporaries were in no doubt as to the changed atmosphere. Theories of economic liberalism and the role of the market were reasserting themselves in the early 1950s, but as Frank Cousins of the Transport and General Workers insisted later: 'If there is to be a free for all, we are part of the all.' It was the railwaymen who really established the precedent for annual wage bargaining, but there were also damaging dock strikes in 1954 and 1955. *The Economist* observed that wages were becoming more a matter of 'social justice rather than mainly a function of customers' demand'. A rash of strikes at the time of the 1955 election may have won votes for the Conservatives, but an increased majority in Parliament did nothing to strengthen the hands of the government when dealing with the unions. Not only were there disputes with management over wages, but within the unions themselves over differentials, jobs and other matters. Increased job security and opportunities meant that there could be less dependence upon the union in many circumstances. The interdependence of industries gave great power even to very small groups of workers. The more relaxed social environment perhaps also had some effect on labour relations. Certainly there was a steady growth in shopfloor bargaining, and a rise in the influence of the shop steward not only with respect to management but to the central union leaders. Unions were less under the influence of a few key individuals. The death of Deakin in 1955 was symbolic of the passing of an era.

On 31 May 1955 a rail strike necessitated the declaration of a state of emergency. This lasted for a fortnight. A partial dock strike dragged on for six weeks with still more injurious effects to the economy. The government thought it detected unease among some union leaders themselves, and attempted a general review of industrial relations. Eden, however, found both sides of industry averse to legislation on official strikes: 'We canvassed the proposal that a secret ballot should be made compulsory before any union took strike action. This had many supporters, but it would be difficult to supervise and would not prevent unofficial strikes.' Even questions of improved arbitration and cooling-off procedures were considered too complex for early action. Eden decided to give preference to 'the battle against inflation'. He hoped through price stability to lessen wage claims.[8] The FBI, however, opposed voluntary price restraint, and pressed strongly for cuts in government spending as the best answer. Its self-confident assertion of the merits of the free market were not fully shared by the British Employers Confederation – this body was more disposed to work with government and unions in broad conformity with postwar trends. Butler's autumn budget won some praise from the FBI but was condemned by the TUC: the government persisted with its cuts in spending on housing, railways, and the power (save nuclear energy) industries. The end of 1955 found Eden disturbed by insufficient saving, by excessive office and factory building, though still hopeful of cooperation with the unions. He concluded that both government and industrialists had been 'captivated by the idea of an "expanding economy". We are right to expand, but now we have done it so that we are bursting at the seams.'[9]

At the end of 1955 a government reshuffle brought in Harold Macmillan as Chancellor of the Exchequer to replace the tiring and somewhat disillusioned R. A. Butler. The Governor of the Bank of England was very pessimistic – the reserves were only just above the danger level of $2,000 million, unemployment in December 1955 was the lowest since the war – and from discussions with other influential figures Macmillan concluded that 'if we were to drift on, we should go on the rocks'.[10] All agreed on the precariousness of the economy: none on a solution. It was no easy matter for Macmillan, as an ardent expansionist, to begin his spell at the Treasury as an advocate of deflation, with thoughts of import controls or changes in the value of sterling as possible emergency measures. The Cabinet was reluctant to accept his deflationary package, the Prime Minister proving very sticky on the end of subsidies on bread and milk. A compromise was finally agreed, but only after Macmillan had threatened resignation to secure most of his points. The bank rate was lifted to 5.5 per cent, allowances on new investment were made less generous (a move later regretted by the Chancellor),[11] and there were various government economies, including cuts in the nationalized industries. Certainly the measures reversed the drain on the reserves, and by the autumn of 1956 the balance of payments showed a modest surplus. Inflation too had slowed. The price was industrial stagnation. The German lead in car exports increased: wages and output there rose roughly in step.

The encouragement of personal savings, of greater industrial efficiency, and of wage and price restraint were also part of the government's economic strategy. Negotiations between government and both sides of industry on the problem of inflation revealed wide gaps between all three. The FBI remained full of complaints concerning government expenditure and union militancy. The British Employers Confederation was more moderate, and both Eden and Macmillan thought that most union leaders basically wished to be helpful, so long as they did not appear to be 'Tory stooges'. The government and industrial associations finally agreed on 'a price plateau' in July 1956, but at the September Trades Union Congress wage restraint was decisively rejected. With the engineering employers predisposed to take a tough line, a new crisis in industrial relations seemed imminent.[12] But first the vulnerability of the economy to external factors was highlighted by the Suez affair.

The Baghdad Pact and Suez, 1955–6

In the approach to the Suez disaster one is conscious both of errors in British policy and of the difficulty of finding realistic alternatives. Given the premises on which policy was based British participation in the Baghdad Pact seemed an obvious move. The 1930 treaty with Iraq was due to expire in 1957, but the RAF in particular believed it vital that they should have access to two important air bases in Iraq. These were expected to play a crucial part in hampering any Soviet military advance in this region. At the same time the British needed to consider the wide-ranging implications of the deepseated rivalry that existed between Egypt and Iraq, now intensified by the socialist republicanism of the former. Iraqi intrigues in Syria in 1954 had disturbed the Egyptians, and intense competition followed between Nuri and Nasser for Arab support. By the beginning of 1955 it was evident that Nuri had been much less successful. The more the British identified themselves with Iraq, the worse their relations with Egypt. The Iraqis, however, were finding other allies in the Middle East, and in the course of 1955 the Baghdad Pact came into existence, embracing Turkey, Iraq, Britain, Pakistan and Iran. Britain had joined on 5 April, and was able to conclude a supplementary agreement with Iraq securing for the RAF the future use of the air bases. The pact was widely condemned throughout the Arab world – critics were active within Iraq itself. The United States, which in 1954 and 1955 was busily strengthening Middle Eastern states which opposed the Soviet Union, nevertheless appeared to recognize the danger of too direct involvement, and did not join the pact. This irritated the British, as did American support for Saudi-Arabia, a country frequently in dispute with the British-protected state of Muscat. Saudi-Arabia, too, despite its monarchical and traditionalist order, was moving into the Egyptian camp.

Harold Macmillan, as Foreign Secretary in October 1955, hoped to persuade the Americans to reduce their aid to Egypt and switch it to Iraq.[13] Nevertheless there first developed a serious Anglo-American bid to improve relations with Nasser. Help was promised in the financing of the critically important Egyptian project, the Aswan High Dam. The British, too, for a while seemed disposed to take a more pro-Arab stance on the question of Israel's frontiers. These western bids for Egyptian favour were not high enough, though it is difficult to see how they could have been raised, nor would success have been assured had they been improved. Arab-Israeli relations were rapidly deteriorating. An Israel that was both more militant and fearful received backing from France, herself increasingly anti-Egyptian because of the support afforded by Cairo to rebels against French rule in Algeria. Nasser may not have been entirely clear in his own mind as to his policy, beyond the elevation of the power of Egypt. There were many potential advantages in his adoption of a strongly neutralist stance in world politics – but there were also dangers if he acted too precipitately. His arms purchases from

Czechoslovakia and his recognition of Communist China injured Egyptian relations with the United States, so that irrespective of British policy Egypt was becoming the focus of much hostility. The British nevertheless added more fuel to the flames by their injudicious attempt to extend the Baghdad Pact to Jordan at the end of 1955 despite its evident unpopularity in much of the Arab world. The attempt to reinforce pro-British elements in Jordan totally misfired. Early in 1956 the young king felt obliged to dismiss the British commander of his forces to strengthen his hand in Jordanian politics. In Britain this was not readily understood, and relations with Egypt deteriorated further. Thus, when the United States withdrew its support from the Aswan Dam project in July 1956, the step (if not its timing) was welcomed in London. There can be no doubt that key figures in the British government were already predisposed to think the worst of Nasser long before he dramatically nationalized the Suez canal on 26 July, and – more dangerously – were predisposed to believe that the removal of Nasser might somehow arrest the decline of British influence in the Middle East.

Despite important gaps in the information concerning the evolution of British policy towards the nationalization of the canal, the main trends and motives seem clear enough. A few details remain obscure, such as the degree of British involvement in the Franco-Israel planning against Egypt. Further clarification would be welcome on the thinking of some ministers, and how far the main body of the Cabinet was bypassed by a narrow circle of colleagues around Eden. Yet, as they stand, the memoirs of Eden and Macmillan are invaluable sources. Macmillan, for instance, makes clear that he regarded the recovery of the canal itself to be an insufficient objective. It was necessary for Britain to seek a friendly Egyptian government and to settle the Israeli question. To Robert Murphy he asserted in August 1956 that unless Britain acted she would become another Netherlands. He clearly believed that Britain's place in the world was at stake: he frequently recalled the failures of appeasement in the 1930s. He was reliving 1938. Eden's mind was also full of parallels with the 1930s, the rise of Mussolini and Hitler, and the failure of appeasement. Similarly, both writers reveal a reluctance to come to terms with American policy. Both were very bitter when the Secretary of State, Dulles, failed to stand by his declaration that Nasser must be made to 'disgorge' the canal. American policy was indeed unfortunately ambivalent, especially in the negotiations in August and September to set up first a Suez Canal Board for the international operation of the canal, and when that failed a users' club to control the canal traffic in conjunction with Egypt. In both instances the United States pulled back from the initial appearance of a strong approach, and in both instances, by its later public stance, it gave the Egyptians every confidence that they could reject the plans without fear of American pressure. This was bad diplomacy, and the only reasonable explanation of Dulles's conduct is that he was desperately trying to buy time in the hope that passions would ultimately cool and enable a compromise to be reached. It would also seem reasonable to suppose that Dulles did not want Nasser to prosper while recognizing that he could not support the tough line the British proposed.[14] Therefore a dangerous ambiguity developed in his policy, not sufficient to mislead those on the British side who were detached enough to see what the American government could or could not do, but a dangerous encouragement to others who were anxious to read what they wanted into American policy. It might have been better for all concerned had Washington pressed consistently for a settlement which the Egyptians might have accepted: as it was, American policy perhaps helped to encourage a British government (which admittedly was only too willing to do so of its own volition) to manoeuvre itself into a position in which an appeal to force could be the only outcome.

The American President was not the cypher many imagined him to be. Eisenhower appreciated that a military operation could involve a long-term expensive commitment, and that it would alienate much Arab opinion. Better to wait, and hope for Arab divisions.[15] This was sensible, though Macmillan argued that Britain could not afford to play it long. Eden was determined to believe that the Americans would at worst remain passively neutral if the British struck, but Sir Pierson Dixon, who found himself unhappily defending British actions at the UN, was convinced that there had been fair warning of American hostility to the use of force.[16] Eden and his colleagues, at the time and since, offered different explanations of and justifications for their policy, but essentially they saw the Suez crisis as the right moment to make a stand against the continuing erosion of British interests in the Middle East. The Prime Minister, for instance, feared the overthrow one by one of Britain's remaining friends in the region by Nasserist intrigues.[17] Had it not been for these wider political aims there might have been room for compromise with the Egyptians over the question of the canal. True, 44 per cent of the canal shares were British owned, some 4,000 British ships used the canal in 1955, and more than half of Britain's oil imports passed through it. But the British government was not interested in discussing the niceties of the legality of Nasser's act in nationalizing what Eden himself described as 'technically an Egyptian company',[18] or questions of compensation, nor was it prepared to wait until Egypt infringed the 1888 convention to keep open the canal to the ships of all countries in all circumstances. With its insistence on some effective form of international control of the canal the British government left Nasser and itself no option but defiance or humiliation.

At the same time one cannot fail to be impressed by the confusion in British thinking and preparation. At the start of the crisis the British had no means of bringing military pressure to bear on Egypt. Some six weeks of cumbrous preparation were necessary. Some thought seems to have been given to the overthrow of Nasser, but none to a successor regime. Vague hopes of a 'friendly' Egyptian government showed only a

ation to turn a blind eye on Anglo-Egyptian relations since ne French grew increasingly impatient with British political ons and changes of military plan. In so far as Britain was drawn into collaboration with Israel from the middle of October, the Israeli Chief of Staff, Moshe Dayan, found it a very uneasy partnership. As he commented in his memoirs, the British were anxious for Israeli action to provide them with a pretext to intervene in such a way that they would not appear to be the aggressors. Of the British Foreign Secretary he wrote : 'His whole demeanour expressed distaste for the place, the company, and the topic.'[19] This reinforces the impression that the British ministers were reluctant – and mediocre – plotters, driven to desperate action by the belief that Britain's future in the Middle East, perhaps indeed her whole future as a great power, was at stake.

With hindsight it is certainly easier to take a less catastrophic view. Nasser lacked the means to be another Hitler or even a Mussolini. Above all, the divisiveness of the Arab world later became more evident, periods of reluctant and partial unity being brought about only by a common threat such as Israel, or by an action such as Suez. But the mood of contemporary Britain must also be considered, especially opinion in the Conservative party. Julian Amery spoke for many when he expressed the hope early in August that British influence would be re-established on 'firm and permanent' foundations in the Middle East. Hitherto the retreat from empire had been accepted without serious protest. Jealousy of the dominant world role played by the United States had been balanced by some gratitude for American support. The nationalization of the canal precipitated something approaching a national sense of outrage, albeit one that did not lead to a consensus as to how the nation should act. Labour took the line that one illegal act did not justify another. What it would have done in office is not clear – it was easy for Labour to moralize from the Opposition benches. Less hypothetical is the fact that the Suez question increasingly divided the nation, and though the polls appear to have moved in the government's favour in November, there was never a convincing majority in favour of the use of force.[20] Among the press *The Times, Spectator* and *Economist* all tended to move against the government, especially once Britain became isolated from many of the maritime states which had originally shown concern over nationalization. *The Daily Express* might complain of the unrepresentativeness of the United Nations, but Britain, France, Israel, Australia and a hesitant New Zealand hardly constituted a representative grouping. Britain's position even within the Commonwealth was weak. Nevertheless the Conservative leadership continued to feel that they were waging a lonely battle for good against evil, a sensation perhaps heightened by the hysterical criticism to which they were often subjected. It was an odd moment in British history, when perceptions of reality were unusually distorted.

Within the Conservative party itself there were some who entertained doubts or reservations. Two members of the government resigned, and there was unease among some who remained. Only a small number of Cabinet ministers were kept fully informed. There was also much concern in the relevant government departments. Lord Mountbatten, the First Sea Lord, was far from happy. If Kirkpatrick, the Permanent Under-Secretary in the Foreign Office, hints in his memoirs at his dismay over the frustration of British policy in 1956, his economic Deputy Under-Secretary, Paul Gore-Booth wrote to him claiming that the 'overwhelming majority of people in the Office felt that our action had been a bad mistake'. Gore-Booth later recalled that a few officials spoke of resignation.[21] There was also said to be little support for Suez among senior Treasury officials.

There now seems no reason to doubt that by the middle of October Eden had despaired of any satisfactory diplomatic solution. The Israeli attack on 28 October 1956 was almost immediately followed by the Anglo-French intervention of 31 October–6 November. Even after months of preparation, and despite the Israeli assault, the British insisted on a methodical amphibious landing, which could only be mounted from Malta, and launched after the Israeli attack. This meant that Anglo-French forces could not begin to seize the canal until 6 November, thus affording opponents of the operation, notably the United States, a precious week of warning during which to prepare counter-action. It would be wrong, however, to regard this delay as the main reason for the operation's failure. Even had a landing been effected earlier, and the whole canal seized before the United Nations could intervene, Britain would still have been vulnerable to American financial pressure. Even if the financial problem had somehow been circumvented, the seizure of the canal would have solved little by itself had Nasser's regime remained in being (as Macmillan and Lord Home, for instance, both recognized).[22] The canal could have been subjected to continuing Egyptian attack, if only by guerrillas, and Britain might have faced the hostility of most of the Arab world: her presence would have been a splendid rallying point for all radicals.

It is not clear what Eden expected to happen if the operation secured the canal. Perhaps he really hoped to trigger off action by the UN, though action more to Britain's taste and susceptible to British influence than proved to be the case. Perhaps he hoped to force the United States to his side. As it was, pressure from other nations, and especially the United States, contributed to the decision to stop on 6 November with the canal only partially captured. Macmillan was influenced by Britain's financial vulnerability – about 15 per cent of the nation's gold and dollar reserves were lost in November, and American support for sterling was dependent on the British abandonment of their objectives in Suez. The divided state of the nation, the unease of some members of the government and of some Conservative backbenchers must also have swayed the Prime Minister. British forces had vacated the canal before the end of the year with none of Britain's objectives attained. Analysis of British policy suggests desperation in both method and mood, a conclusion which surely finds some confirmation in the aggrieved complaint of Macmillan against outsiders with their 'assumption of neutrality based upon superior knowledge and more refined interests which both sides in a fierce controversy find particularly irritating'.[23] In his view, opponents of Eden were 'defeatists'.

The degree to which Suez was a turning point in British postwar history has been much debated. To this there can be no precise answer. Undoubtedly many emerged from the crisis with a new awareness of the limited influence of Britain in world affairs. Radical critics of British society were already active, but Suez gave them more confidence and a wider audience. But in concrete terms it is harder to find lasting results. The continuity in British policies outside Europe is remarkable. The aims remained similar though they were pursued with rather more caution and discretion. Macmillan, the next Prime Minister, was particularly careful to keep in step with the United States. Concessions to nationalist pressures were perhaps more freely granted. Certainly Conservative opponents of colonial concessions sputtered with diminishing effect, and Macmillan was able to accept the resignation of the hitherto influential Lord Salisbury in 1957 (over the return of Archbishop Makarios) without a tremor passing through his ministry. Perhaps the shadow of Suez can be best seen in the trepidation with which Britain intervened in Jordan in 1958, and there might be more than a hint of it in 1961 when Macmillan refused to be put out by Ghana's swing to socialism, arguing that to discontinue British aid for the Volta dam would merely provide further openings for the Soviet Union. Certainly, in contrast to its effect on France, Suez did not significantly influence British attitudes towards the question of European economic cooperation, although it may have sown doubts in some Conservative minds as to the long-term prospects of the Commonwealth when both India and Canada had opposed Britain in the 1956 crisis. Even so, as will be argued later, the withdrawal of South Africa, the collapse of the Central African Federation, Rhodesia, and the adoption of immigration policies by Britain in the early 1960s created a much more obvious watershed in the history of the Commonwealth.

East–West relations, 1955–6

Apart from Suez, which was the biggest single crisis in Anglo-American relations after 1945, there were many lesser differences. The British complained bitterly when the United States refused to lengthen the list of goods which might be sold to Communist China to bring it into line with the strategic embargo on the Soviet Union. In the end the British unilaterally adopted a policy of equalization in May 1957. In deference to the United States, however, Britain did not support the admission of

China to the United Nations until 1961. More serious was the possibility
that Britain might become involved in clashes between America and
China over the future of Formosa and the offshore islands still held by
the Nationalists. A Chinese invasion of Formosa was not likely, but the
offshore island question generated a great deal of international tension
in 1955 and 1958. Macmillan, as Foreign Secretary in 1955, was
reassured to some extent by hints that the Russians were not entirely
satisfied with their relationship with the Chinese, while beneath the
apparent obduracy of the Americans he thought he detected a desire to
be more flexible. His cautious optimism was not misplaced even if he
concluded in the middle of 1955, 'As the summit conference proceeded,
we were to find that the Far East situation . . . was generally felt to be
more dangerous than that in Europe'.[24]

The summit conference in Geneva in July achieved no dramatic
breakthrough in East–West relations. The Berlin, Cuban and lesser
crises lay ahead, but it was one of the main landmarks in a decade of
endeavour by Conservative politicians to lessen the rigours of the Cold
War. In the 1950s the British were almost alone in their search for better
relations with Russia. In the 1960s the main decisions and steps towards
détente were to be taken by others. The significance of these pioneer (or
premature) British efforts in the 1950s is debatable. Did the British, in
fact, do much to kindle hope in the first place, and having done so did
they lay the bare foundations on which others were to build? Or did they
merely add to the confusion in the western camp, and perhaps encourage
Russian hopes of exploiting the contradictions in capitalism? Whatever
its effect, British diplomacy in this period still carried some weight.

There was, in fact, little chance in the 1950s that real progress would
be made towards the easing of tensions in Europe. The western powers
were determined that Germany, or at least West Germany, should be
incorporated in the western alliance. One can only speculate as to the
aims of the Soviet Union, just as one can only speculate as to the
outcome had the two sides been able to agree on a unified, neutralized
Germany. Once the Russians recognized, however, that West Germany
could not be kept out of NATO they made plain their determination that
Germany must remain divided, with the East firmly under Soviet
influence. No solid improvement could take place in East–West
relations until the West was prepared to acknowledge this as a *fait
accompli* for the foreseeable future, and, more important, until the
Soviet Union could feel assured of the viability of East Germany as a
communist ally. This could not take place until its drain of population to
the West had been stopped, and until East Germany itself began to
enjoy material prosperity under a regime that could feel some
confidence in itself. In these developments the building of the Berlin
Wall in 1961 constitutes the critical divide. Only then could West Berlin,
deep in East Germany, cease to be viewed as a destabilizing force. Thus,
irrespective of any positive hopes that the Russians may have
entertained concerning the future of Europe, even from a purely

defensive standpoint there was much that they had to achieve before they could seriously explore the possibilities of *détente* – if that was ever their interest.

If, however, it was premature to think in terms of a major change in East–West relations in the 1950s there was some justification for exploratory talks, provided there were no serious western divisions to encourage a harder line from the Soviet Union. On 15 May 1955 it was possible to sign a treaty putting an end to the occupation of Austria by the forces of the wartime allies, and permitting her emergence as a neutralized state. Russian interest in disarmament was becoming embarrassingly enthusiastic. The general election of May 1955 was one, if not the only stimulus to British interest in top level talks, and Macmillan, the new Foreign Secretary, sought to dispel doubts concerning the utility of a summit conference by suggesting that such a meeting should be designed, not to settle problems, but to inaugurate a long period of negotiations. The British were also well aware of the difficulty of plumbing Soviet motivation: the Soviet decision to sign the Austrian peace treaty had unleashed a great deal of speculation, not least that it was designed to impress the Germans with the advantages of neutrality. The western position remained that of German unity based on free elections and with the right of the reunited nation to choose to ally with NATO. Russia, in return, was offered special security arrangements in central Europe. Such proposals, if seriously meant, were wildly optimistic. Macmillan emerged from the Geneva conference in July 1955 impressed by the Russian fear of Germany, and especially of any connection between a united Germany and NATO. Later, in October, he thought that the Russians might be so determined to hold East Germany that even the offer of a neutralized Germany would not move them.[25] Other suggestions from Eden for the relaxation of East–West tension were equally ineffectual. He was interested in the creation of a demilitarized strip in central Europe, in arms limitation and in arms inspection of specified areas, and in wider disarmament or arms control possibilities. Demilitarization or disengagement did excite continuing interest in the 1950s, notably in Poland. But on the western side opposition hardened with SHAPE viewing disengagement as disadvantageous to the defence of Germany. The West German government feared it might lead to neutralization in central Europe, and the perpetuation of the division of Germany.

The incompatibility between the two sides did not fully emerge until the foreign ministers met in Geneva in October–November 1955, and the discussions developed with an increasing eye to their publicity value. The original 'Geneva spirit' was evaporating. In its place there were only uncertainties. Already there were some western hopes that Russian difficulties with China might make Moscow more amenable in the long run. As it was, Eden believed in the spring of 1956 that the Russians had no plans 'at present' for military aggression against the West. They were likely to put more emphasis on 'economic-propaganda weapons', and therefore NATO strategy should be rethought.[26] Nuclear weapons would provide the main security for western Europe, with conventional arms to provide the main security against local infiltration or intimidation, and to identify a major act of aggression. Other western leaders were generally less optimistic. There was a continuing fear of a revival of Stalinism in Russia. Of only one thing could western ministers feel certain – the solid worth of West Germany within NATO. As Raymond Aron later concluded, the more the governments of both blocs examined the problem of Germany in the 1950s the more they tended to cling to the *status quo*. If they could not be assured of a united Germany that was friendly to them, the more they were prepared to settle for what they had.[27]

The foundation of the European Economic Community

East–West relations, the Middle East, and other aspects of Britain's world role attracted far more British attention and energy than the crucial steps which were being taken at this time in the foundation of the European Economic Community. The British were slow to awaken to the reality of this new challenge. The six ECSC member states began talks in Messina in June 1955, but in so far as British officials paid attention to them it was in the expectation that they would either fail or have only limited economic consequences. Britain became associated with the ECSC in 1955, while Eden was hoping that the WEU would develop into 'a leading authority in the new Europe'. Macmillan continued to interest himself in a confederal approach to the 'unity of Europe'. No great sense of urgency was felt, since France was not expected to feel able to cooperate with her old rival, Germany, without the reassuring presence of the British. The possibility that France and Germany would be able to sink their differences was repeatedly underestimated. The Six themselves provided some false assurance by their own uncertainties. In 1956 they still seemed at times to be looking to the British for a lead. Most of the British Cabinet drew too much comfort from such signs, while those who wished to do more could not fail to note the lack of public interest. Furthermore, according to Sir Philip de Zulueta, one of the Prime Minister's private secretaries, Eden did his best to exclude the Common Market from Cabinet discussion.[28] Eden largely ignored it in his memoirs. The British had even, at the end of 1955, withdrawn their representative, an under-secretary from the Board of Trade, from the Spaak committee set up by the Messina meeting.

The doubts, however, were becoming a little more persistent with the passage of time. If the improbable should happen, the potential of the Six was seen to be enormous. In contrast, the Commonwealth and sterling area, in which the British put so much faith for the maintenance of their position as a world power, appeared to have a much less dynamic future, both politically and economically. Australia, at the 1956 conference, continued to argue for less preference for imports from Britain. Already one-sixth of Britain's trade was with the Six. There was some concern, too, over American interest in the creation of the Community. Thus in 1956 there was gradually evolved a plan which was designed to effect a bridge between the Six and the other members of the OEEC. Macmillan, more enthusiastic than many, hoped that with these proposals the British would be able to seize the commercial leadership of Europe. Broadly it was intended that over a period of about ten years all protective duties on industrial goods would be removed, but each member state should be free to decide its own tariff policy with respect to the rest of the world. The Six, of course, wished to include agricultural and horticultural products, but the British were determined to protect their own and Commonwealth growers. The free trade area would contain none of the supranational elements favoured by some Europeans. Among those who feared that British policy was woefully inadequate in these rapidly changing circumstances was the British ambassador in Paris, Sir Gladwyn Jebb. His warnings became increasingly urgent from December 1956. Yet even he was not an advocate of full British membership, only of more positive alternatives.[29] The British might have exploited the fears of some influential Europeans that the proposed Common Market would possess too many supranational features. In practice Britain was always moving too slowly and halfheartedly. She was always playing into the hands of those such as Paul Spaak who opposed British proposals lest they dissolved the projected community 'like a lump of sugar in a British cup of tea'. The Treaty of Rome, establishing the EEC, was signed on 25 March 1957. For the British this was a development comparable with that of the exclusion of the Habsburg Empire from the Zollverein in the early nineteenth century.

Stagnation and possible recovery, 1957–9

Harold Macmillan succeeded the ailing Eden as Prime Minister in January 1957 at a critical time. Apart from the aftermath of Suez, the implications of which were broadly understood, and the approaching formation of the EEC (whose significance was largely missed), the British economy was stagnating, industrial unrest continued, and much of the national confidence and complacency that had existed at the time of the 1955 election had evaporated. Given the Conservative party's instinct for survival, it was not surprising that it should have soldiered on in office. What was remarkable was that all this should prove the prelude to the great electoral victory of 1959 and the brief era of 'Super-Mac'.

Eden had been a sick man at the time of Suez, and it was soon evident that he could not continue in office. Butler and Macmillan were the only candidates. In political philosophy there was little to choose between them, so that the selection turned on questions of personality and political record. The new leader was chosen, not as a result of systematic soundings of the whole parliamentary party, but mainly of Eden's old Cabinet. Butler, though the younger man, had more experience of the front benches, and was a classic example of the skilled ministerial all-rounder. He was not fully fit in 1957, his performance as Chancellor of the Exchequer appeared less impressive with the passage of time, and he was suspected of hesitancy and ambiguity during the Suez crisis. Indeed, his general sensitivity as a 'political divining rod' was perhaps too marked for him to appear a sufficiently strong leader, especially in the circumstances of 1957. Macmillan's abrupt change of front during the Suez crisis was not held against him: he had at least been decisive and buoyant. From his days as a rebel in the 1930s Macmillan had displayed qualities of élan, nerve and imagination: he could be expected to project a clearer and more vigorous image to the electorate. For people craving a firm lead he was the obvious choice: he attracted support more readily from *all* shades of Tory opinion. He had the support of Churchill. But at the outset he half wondered whether his government could survive more than a few weeks.[30] There was the danger that further concessions to Egypt might precipitate a backbench revolt – Macmillan breathed more easily only from the middle of May when a mere fourteen Tory MPs abstained in a key debate. There were other trials ahead, and always the feeling that time was running out – an election had to be faced before the middle of 1960.

Compared with the concentrated purpose of most western European states, both the Eden Cabinet and its successor were trying to pursue too many objectives simultaneously. Admittedly they were being pulled in different directions by various interest groups. The government dared not push deflation too far and so risk any significant rise in unemployment. It recoiled from a serious stand against wage claims. Cuts in public spending, including defence, were never more than the smallest needed to bring a promise of economic equilibrium: they saved manpower rather than resources into the 1960s. The government was also persuaded that the use of sterling as an international currency must be encouraged, together with London as a great international financial centre and with the large-scale export of British capital, especially to the Commonwealth and sterling area. Justifications were not hard to find for each individual choice of action: justification for the whole ill-assorted package was a different matter. The consequence was that purely internal or external economic problems could have unusually far-reaching effects. Thus in August–September 1957, although Britain was enjoying a modest surplus on current account, a sudden fall of foreign confidence in sterling, only partly related to the strength of sterling itself, could necessitate fresh deflationary measures. Macmillan, writing of his period as Prime Minister, likened economic management to the most delicate of balancing acts. Indeed, Government policy often seemed to have no more will of its own than a ping-pong ball in a game with many players and no rules. Macmillan as Chancellor of the Exchequer had tried to improve the statistical information at the disposal of the Treasury, to escape from a situation in which government was always looking up information in out of date tables. But this, while useful, exaggerated the ability of the government to manipulate what were incompatible economic objectives.

Andrew Shonfield in 1958 and many economists since have argued that the encouragement of the use of sterling as an international currency was a mistake, made worse by the Bank of England's aspiration to make sterling freely convertible. Certainly internal and external economic factors interacted to the long-term disadvantage of Britain. The existence of a vicious circle is clear, if it is not always so clear whether internal economic failings or external pressures were the prime cause of any particular crisis. The reaction of the government in the mid and late 1950s was one of uneasy trimming. International confidence had to be maintained in sterling, great though the cost might be at home, but at the same time for electoral reasons unemployment could not be allowed to rise too high. Furthermore a tough policy on wages could not only alienate opinion at home but, in the event of serious strikes, threaten foreign confidence. Extensive wage concessions, however, added to British costs, reduced the competitiveness of exports, and these together could diminish profits and discourage investment. The permutations in the story are many, but the outcome was almost always the same – certainly there were no happy endings.

The government continued to pursue an uneasy course in 1957. Macmillan in his last days as Chancellor had spoken of the need for a balance of payments surplus of at least £300 million a year to defend sterling and to meet withdrawals from sterling balances. As premier he considered devaluation, deflation or a wage freeze. But defence cuts were the first obvious step. The April budget unwisely gave tax concessions to companies operating abroad but did little to stimulate investment at home. The shipbuilding and engineering employers complained of government weakness in the face of damaging strikes in the spring of 1957, but the Cabinet felt too weak to take a stronger line; it did review its emergency plans when threatened by engineering, rail and power strikes. Only the concession of a court of inquiry narrowly halted on 2 April an escalating strike which threatened to bring out the entire membership of the Confederation of Shipbuilding and Engineering Unions. Hopefully the government set up a Council on Prices, Productivity and Incomes (the Cohen Committee, sometimes called the Three Wise Men) in the middle of the year. Its first report antagonized the TUC by mentioning unemployment as a possible check to wage inflation. The later reports, though more complex, exercised little practical influence. Nigel Nicolson found Macmillan in June 1957 ruminating on the difficulties of explaining to the British public that the nation was living beyond its means.[31] Ironically a speech delivered by the Prime Minister a month later was to go down in history as the 'you've never had it so good' speech whereas Macmillan had thought of it more in terms of 'Is it too good to last?'

The Conservative leadership continued to oppose firmly any idea of legislation to try to curb union powers. Any such move would be fatal to their 'one nation' strategy. Iain Macleod, as Minister of Labour in 1956, doubted the efficacy of secret ballots in preventing strikes. The rank and file, according to his departmental experts, were often more militant than the official leadership. The Cabinet agreed that union reform, if any, must come from the unions themselves and the TUC. Macleod also dismissed ideas of a wage freeze or incomes policy at this time as impractical.[32] Yet positive action of some kind seemed necessary, and for a time the advocates of an economic strategy designed to give priority to price stability began to make headway. The Bank of England urged a high bank rate and cuts in government spending; Lord Robbins spoke out for tighter control of the money supply. Peter Thorneycroft, the Chancellor of the Exchequer, encouraged by two junior ministers, Enoch Powell and Nigel Birch, moved from his earlier cautious optimism to a determined stand against inflation late in 1957. Britain had lost one-fifth of her gold and dollar reserves in less than two months in the summer of 1957. Not everyone agreed that domestic inflation was the main cause of this setback: foreign speculation owed much to major currency movements in Europe. Other members of the sterling area were running deficits, while an incipient recession at home made any further government cuts a serious matter.[33] Nevertheless the bank rate was raised in September 1957 to what was then a sensational 7 per cent, the highest since 1921. Public investment was also held back, and the government endeavoured to ensure that wage increases in the public sector would be offset by economies. The reserves began to recover. Government policy provoked growing Labour and union criticism, but the first and critical test of the Thorneycroft approach occurred within the Cabinet itself at the end of 1957 and in the first days of the New Year.

Thorneycroft's aim was to keep government spending at its existing level with no allowance for inflation. This meant a cut of £153 million in the civil estimates. Departmental ministers responded well, falling only £50 million short of this exacting target. The Chancellor was not satisfied. Macmillan commented on 22 December 1957: 'The Chancellor wants some swingeing cuts in the Welfare State expenditure – more, I fear, than is feasible politically.' Such cuts, he clearly felt, could stimulate wage demands and union militancy. Butler feared rigid adherence to a fixed money total would undermine welfare policies, while Macleod thought that Treasury margins of error in forecasting expenditure made a crisis over £50 million absurd.[34] The subsequent Radcliffe Report of August 1959 on the working of the monetary system appeared to find the Thorneycroft approach oversimplified. A more sophisticated working of the system was necessary in any case, but the report also asserted: 'Monetary measures are part of one general economic policy which includes among its instruments fiscal and monetary measures and direct physical controls.' It added: 'monetary measures cannot alone be relied on to keep in fine balance an economy subject to major strains from both within and without.'[35]

Confronted by a united Cabinet, Thorneycroft (and Powell and Birch) resigned on 6 January 1958. Their isolation in the government, and the apparently trivial sum over which they had resigned, enabled Macmillan to give a demonstration of that 'unflappability' for which he was later to become famed. He departed on a foreign tour the following day with the posts refilled, and with a passing reference to 'these little local difficulties'. But Powell in particular had seen the question as one of principle. A stand was necessary against the remorseless rise in government spending (in fact, as a proportion of the gross national product it had been falling for most of the Conservative period in office up to that time). It was an essential step in the battle for a sound currency. The implications were drastic, and would have entailed a very different Conservative approach to government from that practised since 1951. Although the Cabinet nerved itself to do battle with the London busmen in the summer of 1958 (and won) it was helped by the union's isolation and by public sympathy. The railmen, in contrast, were bought off with a mere 3 per cent wage increase in return for a promise of greater efficiency. Middle-class discontent with the government, as unionized workers and those in the higher managerial and professional posts appeared able to protect themselves so much more effectively against inflation, expressed itself in the Liberal by-election gain of Torrington from the Conservatives in March 1958. This was the first Liberal by-election gain in thirty years. There was ample evidence from other sources of the deep discontent of many of the government's supporters, but such elements could not provide the ministry with the political power to embark on new policies, even had ministers been so minded.

Meanwhile a lively debate was proceeding among economists as to how the government should proceed.[36] It was still possible to believe in 1957–9 that exceptional circumstances were responsible for the nation's difficulties rather than any basic weaknesses. More economists, it is true, were edging towards the idea of an incomes policy as the only means of reconciling price stability, growth and full employment. Others felt that to try to stop inflation would prove more trouble than it was worth. Dr Balogh was seeking an ambitious synthesis of high investment, wage restraint, and social justice, yet with Britain remaining an influential power overseas. He concluded that a short period of high investment (perhaps of a quarter of the national income) should be 'a perfectly simple and attainable remedy', with taxation to contain demand in the short term, and with economic growth to promote price stability in the long run. Professor Paish believed that long-term economic growth was dependent on the creation of some slack in the economy, with an unemployment level of perhaps 10 per cent. Shonfield favoured some sort of exceptional effort, even a five year plan, to transform certain key sections of the economy, such as machine tools, steel and transport, but warned that 'no government will be able to set about the real business of the Plan, which is to release a dynamic movement of production *against* the traditional forces of resistance in the British economy, if its main concern is with the minutiae of social justice in the process.' It would also entail 'the spiritual upheaval of a policy of deliberate retreat from a number of positions of high international prestige, which Britain has traditionally held'.[37] Government policy was much less ambitious.

Thorneycroft's successor as Chancellor of the Exchequer, Heathcoat Amory, was a modest, almost non-party figure. More flexible than Thorneycroft, he continued to restrain the economy for some time. Reflation, when it came, was cautious. The balance of payments improved markedly during the year, helped by successive government squeezes on the economy (so that unemployment was edging up towards 3 per cent by the end of the year) and by a fall in some commodity prices. Sterling was made fully convertible for non-residents at the end of 1958, a victory for the City of London, and it was unfortunate that in all the concern displayed for the development of the sterling area and Commonwealth investment exports remained sluggish, the outcome of stagnant or declining industrial output. Fears both of the loss of foreign confidence and the triggering off of new inflationary pressures at home explain the extreme caution with which reflationary measures were introduced in 1958. In consequence by January 1959 unemployment stood at 620,000, the highest since the war, while the National Institute of Economic and Social Research pointed to the existence of much space capacity. There existed economic and political pressures for a generous budget. Brittan comments: *'The real error of the 1959 Budget is not so much that it gave away too much, but that it came too late'* (his italics).[38] According to Macmillan, the Treasury and the Chancellor were not easily moved from their fears of an inflationary boom. Nevertheless ninepence was finally struck off the standard rate of income tax; tax cuts in all came to a record £300 million. *The Economist* of 11 April had some reservations. It foresaw the possibility of renewed strain on the balance of payments by the autumn. Nevertheless the pace at which the economy grew in 1959 seems to have genuinely taken many people by surprise. The rise in production was about twice as fast as expected.

A blazing summer in 1959 strengthened the new-found optimism. Suddenly there seemed more point in the oft-misquoted remark of the Prime Minister – 'most of our people have never had it so good' – uttered two years earlier on 20 July 1957. The comment was fair enough, given the other warnings in the speech. By the summer of 1959 the public was increasingly impressed by the government's record, whatever the doubts of some economists. Their hour had not yet struck. Net national output had increased by 20 per cent since 1952: earnings by rather more, helped by defence cuts and the improved terms of trade.

Food prices were fairly stable, and prosperity was reflected in the doubling at constant prices of sales of consumer durables. Consumption as a whole had risen by over one-fifth in real terms. The annual wage round was well established. It was described by *The Financial Times* on 4 December 1959 as being as 'rigidly stylized as the classical ballet', while the third report of the Council on Prices, Profits and Incomes concluded that 'at the back of the problem of inflation under full employment is a state of mind'. Questions of comparability between industries and occupations, not of productivity or costs, were uppermost.

British society in the 1950s

David Butler and Richard Rose in their almost contemporary analysis of the 1959 election claimed that 'in the last decade, British society has been changing more than the political parties', and that of the two parties the Conservatives had been more alive than Labour to this transformation.[39] They estimated that British society was now almost equally divided into three parts: the middle and upper classes, the upper working class and the traditional solid working class. Butler and Rose recognized, however, that a great deal of social ambiguity existed among skilled workers and lower paid white collar employees, and habitual and inherited views were often conflicting with changing material circumstances. Unlike some commentators they did not assume that rising incomes automatically led to a more middle-class outlook on society. There were also striking regional differences, the greater growth of new manufacturing industry and of service industries in the south and midlands being mainly responsible for the more extensive social change there. The fortunes of both parties were closely linked with regional fluctuations in affluence and life styles. The gulf between mining towns and English seaside resorts was as wide as ever. Labour remained firmly entrenched in Wales and the north, and was recovering strength in Scotland where the unemployment rate was second only to that in Ulster. Nevertheless, Butler and Rose concluded that the politics of prosperity could be said to have replaced the politics of fair shares and security which had prevailed in the years 1945–51.[40]

Much of the electorate had certainly been exposed to widespread changes in the 1950s. Since 1948 one family in six had moved to new accommodation. In many cases there was movement from old terraced, tenemented and often slum property to new housing estates or to blocks of flats. There was also a great deal of migration from one part of the country to another, especially to the more prosperous parts of the south and midlands. These movements could involve the weakening of family ties and the break-up of long established neighbourhoods. The wider family ties might be weakened by distance, while a sense of neighbourliness might not easily be recreated. It is, of course, important to be wary of exaggerated claims concerning the community spirit in the old slums, but rehousing could bring problems of its own, as well as new opportunities and new horizons. In the same period there was the opening of new vistas through the coming of television (over 70 per cent of the population had sets by 1959) and the spread of car ownership. These, with greater home comforts, encouraged the development of the small-family-centred life. Gaitskell blamed the car in particular for the weakening of group loyalties.

The growth in the employment of married women was facilitated by the availability of labour-saving equipment in the home, and was also stimulated by family demand for increased purchasing power. Hire purchase facilities further extended buying capacity – the hire purchase debt increased by 75 per cent between 1955 and 1959. Juvenile earnings were rising rapidly. Patterns of employment were changing, a real decline occurring in the number of manual jobs while white collar openings increased. Employment in industry levelled off temporarily between 1955 and 1960, and the long-term trend was such that by 1970 the professions and the service industries almost equalled manufacturing as a source of employment. Within manufacturing itself the proportion of non-manual jobs was rising rapidly. The number of children staying on at school beyond the official leaving age almost doubled between 1945 and 1959 (from about 250,000 to 485,000); part-time students at technical colleges also doubled, to 468,000. A new dimension was entering many people's lives with the growing popularity of foreign travel, hitherto a preserve of the well-to-do. Richard Hoggart described working-class life in the 1950s as 'in many respects a good and comely life, one founded on care, affection, a sense of the small group, if not of the individual'.

There was a growing movement to classless leisure activities. Mass production brought similar or identical leisure clothes, consumer goods, even housing to some extent. Supermarkets, the Woolworth, Littlewood, and Marks and Spencer type of store proliferated, catering for a very high proportion of the population. The increased purchasing power of the non-middle classes profoundly affected the commercial world, both in production and distribution. Here were new consumers that were worth cultivation. It was most dramatically expressed in the explosion of what came to be known as the 'pop' world, meeting the growing teenage demand for records and associated equipment, for distinctive clothing, and in time their own shops. On the one hand there was the growing involvement of the better-off workers with building societies, hire-purchase agreements, banks and insurance companies (as distinct from the weekly insurance collector) and similar middle-class institutions. In such circumstances there occurred some separation between these and the poorer sections of the working class. On the other hand significant differences persisted between most salaried staff and wage-earners (however well paid), between those who worked in offices and on the shop floor, between those who enjoyed at least a little choice as to their hours of work and those who had to 'clock-in'.

Rising average incomes of themselves could be a poor guide concerning social change in Britain. Given continuity in work and home, as for instance in the heart of the Yorkshire coalfield, attitudes might change little.[41] The miners' life was tough and unpleasant, with a long heritage of bad industrial relations. Nationalization could not speedily eradicate the belief that change was for the benefit of management; non-manual employees were still distrusted; and what to outsiders appeared to be a narrow and unimaginative outlook on life could be an invaluable protective shell against the rigours of work in the pits. Car ownership was perhaps bringing some broadening of interests, but the uncompromising approach in labour relations persisted. This was not surprising. Significant, too, was a test of the 'embourgeoisement' thesis among well-paid manual workers in the modern industrial town of Luton in the early 1960s.[42] This pointed to the emergence of a new type of worker – one who was then more likely to vote Labour than the average manual worker – rather than of an embryonic middle-class Conservative. For the most part these were people who had deliberately chosen to work in Luton, often moving long distances from their original home to do so, to earn high wages. They took an 'instrumental' view of their work, their firm, their union and indeed their political party. These were means to ends. They provided little satisfaction in themselves, as for example might be found in the work of even some of the more ordinary white-collar employees. In labour relations, the shop-floor and work groups were the centres of interest rather than the union. Promotion often seemed improbable, or undesirable. The workers studied in Luton revealed few middle-class pretensions, yet they appeared to be generally satisfied with society as it was and rarely saw it as one of violently conflicting classes. Such people would be militants, not in the cause of social change or class warfare, but in defence of their own standard of living. Only the craftsmen in Luton displayed more of the characteristics of the so-called 'solidaristic' working class exemplified by miners, steelworkers, or dockers.

A Conservative spokesman declared in 1963: 'Luton is a microcosm of the kind of society we are trying to create.' If so, his party was not anxious to create Conservative voters. At most John Goldthorpe's studies suggested that the workers in question, because of their openness to change, their few cultural prescriptions, their relative lack of class consciousness and their interest in material prosperity, might prove unusually fickle at elections. In so far as middle-class and Conservative affiliations could be discovered among them, these arose usually from family ties with white-collar workers. Residence in middle-class areas had some effect (there was a diminishing tendency to vote Labour), but again the kinship aspect was very important. Where it was not, a conscious middle-class ambition for themselves or their children might be suspected. It was true that ties with white-collar workers were increasing, especially with working wives themselves taking white-collar or white-blouse jobs. The effects of many new pressures were revealed in the New Towns in the 1959 election when support for Labour proved less than most experts anticipated. On the other hand new pressures were at work among the less successful of the traditional middle classes. The routine character of many white-collar jobs was being accentuated by new developments; many white-collar workers were losing status, or were seeing their income differentials erased. This could lead to jealousy of manual workers, or alternatively to interest in the efficacy of well-organized unions.

Talk of a 'swelling middle class' could thus be misleading. people might indeed describe themselves as middle-class without signifying more than residence in a white-collar area or enjoyment of a middle-class income – certainly not middle-class in the sense that the social scientist would wish to use it. The *Economist* exaggerated when it described the New Towns as 'a forcing ground for middle-class values'. One might rather begin to think in terms of a polymorphic middle-income group, a new 'central' class, which embraced, according to one's criteria, one-third or half of the population, straddling the old divide between manual and white-collar worker. Even education was no longer so certain a high road to a middle-class outlook, or to Conservatism in politics. There was still a marked tendency for children to vote as their parents voted. If Britain avoided some of the extremes of European class conflict, the existence of large and long-established industrial communities (from which escape in the past had been exceptional) inhibited social and political flexibility up to the 1950s. Upward social mobility tended to be less in Britain than in many industrialized countries, and the class bias in voting was certainly more marked than in the United States, Australia or Canada. It is true, however, that, given the relatively even balance between Labour and Conservative in Britain, only a small shift of opinion was necessary to remove a government. Merely a change in the balance of abstentions could be significant. What was occurring in the 1950s was not so much a permanent shift to or from any part as the creation of a potentially more unstable central ground for which not only the two main parties would be able to compete, but also the Liberals, and later, in their own countries, the Welsh and Scottish Nationalists.

At the same time, those who commented on the continuing stability and conservatism of British society had much they could still draw on as evidence. The British public remained strongly opposed to the abolition of hanging (only in 1964 was it temporarily stopped by Parliament and then not reintroduced). Parliament was not yet ready to implement the Wolfenden Report of 1957 which recommended the legalization of homosexuality between consenting adults (this was not introduced until 1967). The report was nevertheless an important harbinger of the 1960s, arguing: 'We do not think it proper for the law to concern itself with what a man does in private unless it can be shown to be so contrary to the public good that the law ought to intervene.'

One of the most remarkable breaks with tradition in the 1950s was the introduction of an independent television organization, which ended the monopoly of the BBC. This was the work of a determined minority in Parliament, and was pushed through without great public demand in 1954. The outcome was certainly the provision of more mass consumer-orientated programmes. The BBC, from the war years, had not been insensitive to change, but the existence of a rival, especially one that won so much popularity, probably ensured that in the long run it became more radical and experimental, more responsive to the public mood, and the way was prepared for the satirical and other controversial presentations of the 1960s. Even so the BBC was slow to escape from its essentially middle-class outlook.

During the 1950s it was confidently believed that the problems of poverty were well on the way to solution. Crosland, in *The Future of Socialism* (1956), thought that such primary poverty as remained would go within a decade, given the present rate of economic growth. He accepted that 'secondary' poverty was still acute, and perhaps more intractable, so that more might be required of the social services. But improved social services were not a matter of deep popular concern in 1959. In so far as Labour attracted attention in 1959 with promises of greater welfare benefits, this was lost once welfare was identified with higher taxation. Social workers tended to link poverty with the personal problems of individuals and to emphasize psychological rather than social causes.[43] Better pensions alone seemed to attract voters, and then mainly among the over sixty-fives. Pensioners had suffered badly from inflation down to 1955. Problems of cost deterred the government from positive action. It was reluctant either to increase contributions from the employed – these would weigh heavily on the lower paid – or to increase taxes. In consequence many pensioners were dependent on National Assistance to maintain even the subsistence standard of living defined by the state itself.

The Labour party and the TUC were interested in the question, but also found agreement difficult. Bevan favoured tax-paid pensions; the TUC feared this could mean a return to the means test. Titmuss and some other academics advocated a graduated contributory pension scheme, the final pensions varying according to contributions but with some redistribution in favour or the poorest. Richard Crossman pressed these ideas on the Labour movement. To objections at the 1957 Party Conference that the scheme would perpetuate unequal incomes into retirement Crossman replied that 'it is really for the trade unions to decide whether wages should be equal or unequal and so long as trade unions are prepared to have unequal wages it is a little tough to ask for all pensions to be equal'.[44] Meanwhile the government was preparing its own graduated pension scheme, the National Insurance Act of April 1959, which was to come into effect two years later. This owed much to concern over the prospective increase in the deficit in the National Insurance scheme – it was expected to reach £144 million in 1961. In

1959, too, the government accepted that poverty was no longer a static concept. There was more to life than mere subsistence, and as the prosperity of the nation as a whole rose so the gap between the poorest and those in average circumstances should not be allowed to widen. Poverty was being redefined as an inability to maintain what the majority regarded as decent standards.

Despite the existence of regular employment and rising real incomes for the majority of the population,this still left a sizeable minority who, through illness, incapacity, injury, divorce or separation, were not so fortunate. There were also marked regional variations whose significance was only gradually being appreciated. Unemployment in Northern Ireland, for instance, was running at about three or four times the national average. It was 70 per cent above the norm in Scotland; 65 per cent in Wales, and 45 in the north of England. Average incomes were also lower, though an analysis made in the early 1960s suggested that apart from Northern Ireland these regional disparities were low by world standards. The geographical division of Britain into two nations was also less marked than before the war. Nevertheless, the situation was unsatisfactory, and would deteriorate with the continuing decline in mining, textiles, and shipbuilding. Not only was the industrial plant in such areas becoming more outdated, but there was the general decrepitude of much of the infrastructure – the housing, roads and other services. It was not easy to attract new industries to regions thus deprived, quite apart from the obvious advantages offered by the south and midlands. Employment in Scotland increased by under one per cent between 1953 and 1963 compared with a national average of 9 per cent. About 30,000 Scots were migrating each year. Nearly one-fifth of the population was employed in declining industries.[45] Scotland, since 1945, had badly needed a Secretary of State with the drive and imagination displayed by Tom Johnston during the war.

The momentum imparted to a policy of balanced industrial and population distribution throughout the country by the Barlow Commission and the 1945 Distribution of Industry Act had been lost in the 1950s. The recession of 1958 upset the complacency that had developed concerning the old depressed areas; their vulnerability to cyclical unemployment was again demonstrated. The Distribution of Industry Act of 1958 tried to bring quick and flexible relief on an *ad hoc* district basis, determined by local levels of unemployment. This fire-brigade method had its weaknesses since aid was abruptly cut off once unemployment fell below a certain level, although the local economy might not have been fundamentally strengthened. The Local Employment Act of 1960 suffered from a similar lack of continuity. Merseyside gained some relief with the introduction of vehicle manufacture, as did Scotland, which also shared with Wales a steel project originally destined for the midlands. Redundancies could suddenly hit even prosperous areas, such as Birmingham in 1956. The British Motor Corporation's decision to cut its work force by one-eighth, or 6,000, was unprecedented in the postwar era, and found employers, employees and government ill-prepared. The assumption that no special provisions were now necessary to meet a loss of jobs was challenged even in an 'affluent' region.

Here was an interesting if small example of the upsets being occasioned throughout the country by a rapidly changing industrial technology, in which heavy social costs could be imposed on the redundant, especially the unskilled, and the older worker. Economic growth did not automatically provide answers, even in prosperous areas. It might bypass some regions altogether, leaving decaying industries and urban infrastructure; in others where it occurred it might throw excessive burdens on housing and public services. As for those who lost their livelihoods, or were forced to live in unsatisfactory housing, a cumulative deprivation could develop whose existence was not properly recognized in the 1950s, and whose potential seriousness was even less appreciated. The following decade would recognize the need for 'social growth' as well as economic growth.[46]

The *Socialist Commentary* after the 1959 election published the findings of a survey which suggested that only 17 per cent of the electorate thought the extension of welfare services a sign of a good political party. One hundred years earlier Engels had been fearful of the creation of a British 'bourgeois proletariat'. If this was still a premature fear, a socialist in the later 1950s might yet have repeated his complaint that 'the masses have got damned lethargic after such long prosperity'. It was a lethargy which worried intellectuals and artists as well as left-wing politicians, whether of a revisionist or radical kind. Anthony Hartley argued that there had developed among Britain's leaders in the 1940s and 1950s a hard reasonableness which seemed to lack vision and even to lapse into complacency. At best the conventional intellectual position was mildly reformist, worldly and sceptical. Government was becoming more noted for interference than leadership. Messrs Bogdanor and Skidelsky commented on political science as it was taught in British universities in the 1950s that the concern was with the explanation of government not its improvement.

In the 1950s the political debate remained relatively unexciting. Labour was too divided to provide a clear alternative vision even if many were disposed to listen, which was doubtful. But intellectually life was enlivened by the arrival of the so-called 'angry young men' in the mid-1950s. They shocked, amused, or inspired according to the taste of their readers and audiences. Even among the more conventional their iconoclasm was a welcome novelty. The assaults upon officiousness and pretentiousness delighted some, while for others the main interest lay in the problems of personal identity which afflicted the leading characters in the plays and novels. One had passed from the era of Jude the Obscure to Jude the Uncertain – to a Jude who, having made his way to university, both there and afterwards could find himself engaged in a struggle to understand and to define who or what he was, as well as trying to assert and defend himself in a world of anonymous bureaucrats and managers. In time, as the novelty of the 'angries' began to wear off, some critics complained of their negative attitudes. One literary critic asked of Kingsley Amis, 'What does he like?' In 1965 John Montgomery, though sympathizing with many of the grievances of the young, noted with Dame Edith Sitwell that the 'angries' were remarkable for their despair. They seemed as worn out in some ways as those they criticized.[47]

John Osborne, Amis and the others, however, insisted that their aim was not to provide solutions, it was to expose the snobbery, superficiality, materialism and pettiness which they felt abounded in British life. The so-called 'kitchen sink' writing owed much of its appeal to its frankness and vigour of expression. *The Annual Register* described Osborne's play, *Look Back in Anger* (1956), as 'a vigorous, snarling piece of work. . . . Against the play's omissions had to be set the supreme virtue of vitality. This was the first play since the war to put the point of view of the younger generation at odds with its world.' Osborne's *The Entertainer* followed a year later, while novelists John Wain, Kingsley Amis and Alan Sillitoe also made their impact. The 'angry' movement was at work before Suez, though that crisis may have fortified it by confirming for some the fallibility of the British leadership, suggesting moral bankruptcy to others, or, by revealing the limitations of British power in the world, fuelling their sense of impotence and frustration. To storm the citadels of power in Britain would not be enough – the world, and consequently Britain, would remain much the same. A little later, and sharing much sensitivity concerning the tensions and uncertainties of the period, was Malcolm Bradbury with his *Eating People is Wrong* (1959). He subsequently described the characters in his novel as 'trying to live out the life of personal relations, of decency and goodwill, in a period whose historical and political significance they cannot quite grasp; . . . The characters move through their times with a certain bemused bafflement.'[48]

Yet there were some hopeful signs. It was in 1959, for instance, that Bernard Miles's theatre, The Mermaid, was opened in London, built by voluntary contributions, and designed to provide good and varied drama at a reasonable price. The 'serious' newspapers, especially the Sundays, were gaining in readership. Book sales increased tenfold between 1939 and 1969, with most of the upsurge in new titles being in the realm of non-fiction. 'Do it yourself' or 'Teach yourself' series offered splendid opportunities for people to broaden their skills and knowledge. There was an enormous diversification in leisure activities, with the great majority of people living more varied as well as more comfortable lives. There was no great 'cultural' revolution: it was epicurean and utlitarian in spirit, easily criticized but not so easily improved on.

Chapter 7

The Macmillan era

Labour's internal debates

For Labour the later 1950s would have been a difficult period even without the party's internal troubles, which were in part themselves a reflection of a rapidly changing Britain. How was the party to respond to the undoubted if not universal spread of higher living standards, to the strengthening of those who fitted into the traditional image of neither the middle nor the working classes, to the replacement of fears of capitalism and unemployment by individual problems of identity and fulfilment, to a decline of faith in ideas and ideals: to, in short, a weakening of many of the forces and conditions which had made possible its past successes? How, too, should Labout face a party with a remarkable instinct for survival, and which preserved its buoyancy by jettisoning, amid some protests, those parts of the cargo which were no longer saleable and carrying what (without being strikingly original) had wider consumer appeal?

Although 1955 brought a sort of unity to the Labour party, the inner tensions were only partially papered over. The leadership issue was fairly quickly resolved. Gaitskell first handsomely secured the party treasurership in October 1955 (defeating Bevan by almost five to one), and in December he easily fought off challenges from Bevan and Morrison for the party leadership itself. Gaitskell described himself as a socialist more because of a passion for social justice than for public ownership. Bevan, on the other hand, saw himself as the champion of democratic socialism against bureaucratic middle-class leadership and trade union oligarchs. Despite his official reconciliation with Gaitskell he could still write to his wife in April 1957 of his leader's 'reactionary impulses'. He commented: 'The more I reflect on Gaitskell the more gloomy I become, and the more I dread the ordeal before me if ever he becomes Prime Minister.'[1] The majority of the parliamentary Labour party did not share these views, or only with reservations. Gaitskell's support was inflated by those who found Bevan too authoritarian, and by the absence of a credible candidate just left of centre. In any case at this time the surface unity of the party was less than it appeared, given the growing influence of the left among some trade unions (in 1956 Frank Cousins became leader of the Transport and General Workers' Union). The revisionist-centre-right elements were also active with the publication of Gaitskell's *Socialism and Nationalisation*, John Strachey's

Contemporary Capitalism, and – the most widely praised of all – Crosland's *The Future of Socialism*.

Crosland argued that the world had changed so much that Marxism was no longer relevant. The rich were not only becoming proportionately less rich but political power was no longer in their hands. They were not only retreating in the face of labour, whose strength rested on full employment, but were losing confidence in the old ideas and the old system. Managerial power had replaced that of the owners of capital. Large-scale factory organization had become the crucial feature in the British economy, with little difference existing between ICI and the National Coal Board. Neither private property nor profits menaced the masses: fiscal policies could be relied on to redistribute income in so far as it might be desirable. In industry one should not be fighting yesterday's battles but striving for greater efficiency and competitiveness. A restatement of socialist principles had thus become essential. Socialism was about the elimination of poverty and squalor and the promotion of social equality. The problem was to end social injustice and class antagonism. Income redistribution would be necessary to that end, but also equality of opportunity. The sick, the young and the old posed social as well as economic problems: indeed the social problems were greater than the economic. Labour troubles in high-wage sectors he attributed to feelings among workers that they were undervalued, that social gains had not kept pace with economic gains. The Scandinavian countries demonstrated how more social equality and unity could end or lessen these divisions. Privileges had to be earned through equality of opportunity: leaders would then be less remote. A start could be made through greater egalitarianism in education. 'The school system in Britain remains the most divisive, unjust, and wasteful of all aspects of social inequality.' But he favoured only a gradual introduction of comprehensive education lest educational standards should be endangered. Further nationalization was not automatically ruled out, though postwar experience pointed to many unsolved problems. A fair distribution of wealth was perfectly well attainable in a pluralist society.

All this was stimulating, carefully argued, and backed by many insights, but it is interesting to note how Crosland was misled by the current optimism concerning Britain's economic performance, includding its relation to that of western Europe. He could write: 'I no longer regard questions of growth and efficiency as being, on a long view, of primary importance to socialism. We stand, in Britain, on the threshold of mass abundance.' John Strachey, too, in *The End of Empire* (1959) was equally impressed by the apparent progress of the economy and the decline of poverty. The profit motive, under social control, was a powerfully constructive agent. Radical policies were not necessary in such circumstances, only a watchful promotion of equity (not equality), justice, welfare and democracy. Some in the Labour party were less convinced that problems of economic growth and the removal of poverty were so near solution, and time was to prove them right. Some found Crosland in particular all too optimistic and individualistic. Crosland indeed thought that one could now follow the Webbs' success in inculcating hard work and discipline by putting 'a greater emphasis on private life, on freedom and dissent, on culture, beauty, and even frivolity'.

The Labour party was far from polarized between revisionists and the left. Debate in fact swung to and fro somewhat inconclusively, with public ownership continuing to find a place in the party programme, albeit expressed in vague and somewhat hesitant language. The great battle on this issue was yet to come. Meanwhile Bevan, having returned to the shadow Cabinet in 1955 and gained the party treasurership in 1956, became official spokesman on foreign affairs. Suez did something to bring the party together. Bevan's reputation rose, though in winning new admirers he was in danger of offending old allies. Bevan himself was conscious of the strain. Apart from Suez Gaitskell, like Attlee, was not far removed from the Conservatives on foreign policy. His acceptance of the Eisenhower doctrine in 1957 dismayed Bevan. The case for a strong, pro-western foreign policy was also being put by John Strachey, Kenneth Younger, George Brown and Denis Healey. Questions of power and national interest could not be subordinated to dreams of a 'socialist' or neutralist foreign policy: there could be no weakening of the Atlantic alliance. Bevan was seemingly working for a compromise position, and he was helped by the current interest in 'disengagement' in central Europe, in a unilateral British suspension of H-bomb tests – ideas which the party could safely take up. But there remained the more critical question of British manufacture of nuclear weapons, a matter of the utmost concern to the left.[2] At Brighton in 1957 Bevan opposed a resolution that Britain should renounce their manufacture. This, he argued, was too simple by itself. Britain could not honestly abandon her own programme and simultaneously, not wanting to appear guilty, seem 'to be benefiting by the products of somebody else's guilt'. Nuclear renunciation logically included renunci-ation of Britain's alliances. The result would be, Bevan insisted, to send 'a Foreign Secretary, whoever he may be, naked into the conference chamber'. Unilateralism of this kind he denounced as 'an emotional spasm'. To an appalled friend he wrote privately on 23 October 1957 that his case rested 'upon the argument that if we unilaterally reject the bomb, then we are at the same time rejecting all the alliances and obligations in which this country has become involved, either rightly or wrongly'. In no circumstances could Britain shelter under the thermonuclear weapons of another.

For the old Bevanites these views were a shattering blow. As Michael Foot wrote later in his biography of Bevan, 'Our planet was rocking'. Tories rejoiced openly; Gaitskellites more discreetly. The crisis between Bevan and his old friends is movingly, at times poetically, described by Foot. But in retrospect he came to appreciate Bevan's fear that the party could be damagingly split on the issue, perhaps resulting in another election defeat. Bevan's defence of his position was not entirely convincing, but he had always recognized that one could not treat nuclear weapons in isolation and separate them from the overall strategic context. A reporter close to him during the 1959 election campaign was convinced that Bevan saw the British 'bomb' as an important negotiating card. In general Bevan, like so many of his generation, exaggerated British influence in the world, but he looked forward to a Labour government that might give a lead to easier East–West relations, and find a major role for the Commonwealth, especially through cooperation with India. NATO, however, would remain the major area of British diplomacy, much though one might wish to reshape that alliance. He argued against the alliance's first-use of nuclear weapons. In foreign policy, too, he wished that Gaitskell had taken a more critical view of Anglo-American intervention in Jordan and the Lebanon in 1958.

In home politics Bevan insisted that a more socialist programme was needed to defeat Tory 'affluence', and he feared the establishment of a 'permanently empirical' Labour party. *Tribune* asked in August 1958, 'Does the Labour Party still exist?' But neither Bevan from within the shadow Cabinet nor the left from without could make much impact on Gaitskell. Geoffrey Goodman of the *Daily Herald* thought Bevan during the 1959 campaign a depressed, frustrated and ageing figure, doubting both if the British working class could be stirred into pioneering action and still more if it mattered much either way.[3] While Labour would have fared still worse in 1959 with a more socialist programme, it is easy to see why electoral defeat led to even more bitter internal party strife.

The 1959 election

The Conservative victory in 1959 was not a foregone conclusion. Such a victory seemed improbable in 1957 and during much of 1958. An improving economy, Labour's mistakes and Tory realism were decisive. The Tories were also well led. Shinwell described Macmillan as 'the most astute and able' of Tory peacetime prime ministers, crediting him with a 'delicate blend of adroitness and unscrupulous in-fighting'.[4] He was a skilful parliamentarian, adept at dividing his opponents and uniting his own party, but sufficiently detached to make appreciative notes of the best performances of his opponents. Gaitskell, for instance, he once privately commended for his professional exposition and 'waspish' attacks. On his role in general as Prime Minister Lord Kilmuir contrasted his 'central calmness' with the 'chronic restlessness' of Eden. He had no 'inner cabinet', was accessible to his colleagues, avoided undue interference in departmental affairs while carefully considering all policies in the light of the government's overall strategy and needs.[5] George Mallaby commented: 'For me and many of my friends his compelling charm is that he can feel sensitively, probe deeply, act boldly without ever lapsing into a mood of self-conscious earnestness or unsmiling seriousness.'6 Macmillan had seen war at first hand as an infantry officer in 1914–18. He had seen poverty as the member for Stockton-on-Tees. He was a keen student of history, and though he sometimes drew odd parallels between past and present, and must have bored some foreign statesmen with his liking for historical surveys, his detachment and sense of perspective were usually impressive.

Macmillan has sometimes been criticized for concealing difficulties and for seeking change by indirect or circuitous routes. By his rhetoric and style he helped to divorce the country and his party from unpleasant realities, it was said. Macmillan, however, like Harold Wilson after him, believed that such tactics were often more efficacious – indeed, were often vital for success, given public and party reluctance to face facts. As for his own perception of realities and sense of perspective, he was perhaps too inclined to press for an expansionist approach to economic problems with too little detailed concern for all the implications. He almost certainly dedicated a disproportionate amount of time to foreign and Commonwealth affairs given the long-term course of events for this nation, though at the time he was reasonably successful in making political capital out of his external policies and in maximizing British influence with the limited resources at his disposal.

In 1959 the polls gave Macmillan a clear lead over Gaitskell. Behind the scenes Edward Heath as Chief Whip had done much to hold the party together through and after Suez. Lord Hailsham was a dynamic party chairman with a happy knack at this time of attracting good publicity at party conferences, whether for his sea-bathing or bell-ringing. Best of all for the Conservatives in 1959 was the widespread feeling that the economy was doing well and that even better times were round the corner. A glorious summer completed the sense of wellbeing. Yet the Conservatives might not have won so convincing a victory in October 1959 had it not been for further errors by their opponents. Perhaps 12 per cent of the voters made up their minds during the campaign – a reminder, if taken with the government's earlier unpopularity and by-election defeats, that the remarkable stability among the voters that followed the Second World War was already coming to an end.7 Gaitskell blundered badly on 28 September with his promise of extensive social reform without higher taxes. Too much of the Labour campaign was devoted to topics of no great popular interest, however apposite the reminders that poverty was still widespread and that British economic growth was sluggish by the standards of some other countries. Labour had started from the assumption that it had only to mobilize its traditional supporters – those who had abstained in 1955. The Conservatives in contrast set out to sense the mood of undecided voters, to whom the party was then projected as the party of opportunity and prosperity; the party that had cast aside its old associations with privilege and tradition. The campaign was directed particularly at women voters and better-off manual workers. Labour was much less effective in making its points, though it had, of course, the more difficult task so long as the majority was disposed to believe that Conservative rule had been reasonably successful, and was likely to remain a safer bet than a return to Labour. There was less popular resentment against privilege and wealth than against unions and strikes. Many feared higher taxes under Labour, and perhaps even a check to the nation's rising prosperity. Denis Healey noted the growing gap between the active party workers and the average voter.

The Conservatives in fact lost votes significantly only among those who felt bypassed by the wave of 'affluence': the old-age pensioners and the less prosperous regions such as Scotland. Even in obvious working-class areas in the New Towns and in the south-east and midlands, the Labour vote tended to decline to the advantage of Tories or Liberals. Overall the Conservative vote rose by nearly half million to 13,749,830, marginally their best postwar performance. This gave them an extra twenty-one seats. The Liberals polled well, but were left with six seats as before. Labour's vote declined by 200,000, despite a fairly high poll, and the party returned with 107 seats fewer than the government. Labour's support had fallen by 1.75 million since 1951. A third electoral victory with increased government strength was unprecedented in British parliamentary history, but enthusiasm for Conservative rule should not be exaggerated. The Conservatives had kept their nerve when affairs were going badly: they made the most of their subsequent chances. The mistakes of the Opposition enhanced their credibility. The fact that one-third or more of the electorate in 1959 thought that it mattered little which party was in power (compared with one-fifth in 1951) helped the Conservatives in this election, but if the trend persisted it could tell against them in another. Opinion was becoming more fluid, and this was the real cause of the improvement in the performance of the Liberals. Continuing support for the Conservatives was dependent on continuing faith in their superior competence to govern.

Clause IV and unilateralism

Labour, after this shattering defeat, was not content to lick its wounds. The party fell once more to internal feuding. Gaitskell tried to seize the initiative at the party conference in November 1959, convinced that until Labour altered its image so that it once more appealed to the voters of the centre it could not hope to break the run of Conservative victories. In particular he was convinced that Labour must squarely face the fact that nationalization was a barrier between it and power; that at least some amendment or qualification was necessary of the famous Clause IV of the party constitution, dating from 1918, and with its insistence on the 'common ownership of the means of production, distribution and exchange'. He also believed that Labour must switch its concern from class divisions and class war to class harmony. There were many social problems still to be remedied, but in the quest for a classless society the social dimension was now more important than the economic. Such suggestions, however, provoked a great outcry from many within the party, and not from among the ranks of the left alone. Gaitskell was challenging tradition and instinct as well as ideology, and in so doing he was the initial cause of a two-year struggle during which his own leadership sometimes appeared at risk.

In the eyes of many in the party, who had little sympathy with the left, Gaitskell had acted precipitately, or with downright foolishness. Not even the defeat of 1959, in their view, could justify so direct a challenge. Labour was a creaking coalition and could only survive by living with its contradictions. In the view of Gaitskell and his supporters this was not enough. While the left blamed the electorate for not being more socialist, and insisted that the mountain be educated to come to Mahomet, Gaitskell was more impressed by a mountain of evidence which suggested that Labour was suffering from its 'cloth-cap' image, that it was unduly identified with a section of the community whose numbers were in decline, and was associated with the unions, the militancy of some of whose membership further injured the party's prospects. Douglas Jay even suggested that the party's name be changed to 'Labour and Radical' or 'Labour and Reform'. This was too much for Gaitskell, but in challenging Clause IV at the end of 1959 he could feel that it was the most opportune moment. In the event of failure, with a long period of Conservative rule in prospect, there would be ample time to patch up party differences.

Gaitskell had some initial success. Despite the bitter attacks of the left, the NEC on 13 March 1960 agreed to some additions to Clause IV. It was only growing opposition from some unions which persuaded Gaitskell in the summer that the game was not worth the candle.[8] Even had Gaitskell made no move over Clause IV he would still have had his difficulties with the left, but it seems reasonable to argue that the first issue added to his opponents when a major battle developed in the party over nuclear strategy in 1960–1. There were times when Gaitskell's position as leader seemed in doubt, and it was this – rather than complex and often little understood questions of nuclear strategy – which was really at the heart of the affair. Certainly fears of thermonuclear war were widespread at this time, with the Campaign for Nuclear Disarmament (CND) at the height of its influence. This movement provided a natural outlet for much frustrated idealism in Britain. It drew support from many shades of opinion. Edward Hyams of the *New Statesman* asserted that with the H-bomb man was as much at the mercy of devastating forces as in palaeolithic times. It was understandable that thinking people should try to find alternatives. Support for a unilateral renunciation of nuclear weapons by Britain seems to have varied between one-fifth and one-third of the public in

1960-1, but support faded as CND became increasingly an instrument for political extremists and when rejection of nuclear weapons was associated with the rejection of NATO. What might therefore have been a temporary embarrassment to Gaitskell became a major crisis because of the divided state of the Labour party and the reverberations of the Clause IV issue.[9]

It should have been possible after April 1960, when the government abandoned the Blue Streak missile – the last (nominally) all-British-made nuclear delivery system – for Labour to have rallied behind a new defence philosophy whereby membership of NATO was reconciled with the gradual ending of an independent British nuclear force. Before the battle was over Gaitskell was obliged to make some verbal concessions to his more moderate critics, but it was felt by many observers and participants that had Gaitskell yielded as much earlier he would have bought short-term security as leader of the party at the price of much diminished stature and influence. Thus when the party leadership was defeated at the Scarborough conference in October 1960 by the 'unilateralist' vote (their narrow victory was secured by massive union votes) *The Economist* commented on 8 October that Gaitskell had been fighting for his 'self-respect'. He had been defeated on the central issue of the year. Roy Jenkins claims that there were times following that conference when it seemed by no means certain that Gaitskell would prevail. Yet the latter's base in the parliamentary party was always strong. A challenge for the leadership by a somewhat hesitant Harold Wilson in November 1960 was fought off with a two to one majority. The weakness of the left in Parliament was confirmed in other elections, notably with the choice of George Brown (from the right) as deputy leader. His predecessor, Aneurin Bevan, had died in July. Labour's poor showing in by-elections in 1960 also helped to convince Gaitskell that public support would not be won by a party that was equivocal, or appeared to be too much under the influence of the left, the party conference or the unions. Jenkins saw this as a struggle to determine whether Labour was to be 'a party of power or a party of protest'.

Gaitskell and his allies set out to divide their opponents by insisting that unilateralism led inevitably to a British withdrawal from NATO and to neutralism. The Berlin crisis and the extremism displayed by some of the unilateralists strengthened Gaitskell. Many unilateralists were not neutralists, but some, such as Frank Cousins, were driven into weak debating positions by Gaitskell's tactics. Gaitskell himself conceded that Britain 'as of now' should cease to be a nuclear power, and Labour's defence policy placed increasing emphasis on conventional strength. How this was to be provided was not answered. What mattered was that many unions began to change sides from the spring of 1961 so that at the Blackpool conference in October Gaitskell was assured of virtually a three to one majority in favour of his own (admittedly revised) defence policy. The actual wording however mattered much less than who voted for whose motion.

The economic dilemma, 1959–61

Harold Macmillan in his memoirs once wrote of those 'perplexing and degrading (economic) difficulties' – almost as if 'a great and dominating nation', which he insisted Britain still was, should not be troubled by such material distractions.[10] At the same time he complained of the difficulty of explaining to the public the realities of Britain's economic, strategic and global position. If politicians said too much, people became frightened and resentful; if they said too little, people remained complacent. Politicians and public alike, in twentieth-century Britain, have rarely shown themselves at their best save in the most obvious and desperate crises. Certainly for a generation after 1950 there was a growing tendency for politicians to promise more than they could perform, and for the public to demand more than they were prepared to pay for. Macmillan, in the middle years of his premiership, appeared to reconcile expectations, promises and performance with considerable success, but from 1960 there was a growing feeling that the British economy, and therefore Britain herself, was not so soundly based as most people had recently persuaded themselves. It was not simply that Britain moved into another period of deflation, but that most other western European states appeared to have discovered the secret of faster and stabler growth. Britain was ceasing to be one of the wealthiest states per head of population: she was ceasing to be the wealthiest state in western Europe. EFTA was proving no counterweight to the successful EEC. Britain, having begun to learn to live with American supremacy, was now having to look across the English Channel for something more than art and music and Paris fashions. Above all, ways had to be found to increase her industrial competitiveness.

All comparisons with the EEC member states were discouraging. In the past decade prices and labour costs had risen nearly twice as quickly as in the EEC, with the exception of France. Capital formation as a proportion of the gross national product was much lower in Britain. Where the British gross national product had risen in real terms by about 30 per cent, the average for the EEC states was 80 per cent. True, Britain's industrial performance since the war was a marked improvement over that of the earlier part of the century. British exports had more than doubled in volume since 1938 and they now paid for 90 per cent of the nation's imports compared with a mere two-thirds before the war. As a percentage of the gross national product even Germany rarely exported more. But the spurt in exports was beginning to tail off: Britain now had the lowest annual increase of the leading European industrial states. The trends could no longer be ignored, and there was an understandable growth of interest in the reasons for the success of the continental states. Of particular interest was France where, despite government instability (until the return of de Gaulle in 1958) and a high rate of inflation, rapid growth was taking place. National economic planning and economic growth appeared to be linked in France, though neither in the British Treasury nor among British businessmen was there much enthusiasm for experiments in planning. Nevertheless unease and uncertainty were at least encouraging a new open-mindedness and a greater readiness to consider novel approaches. Academic and newspaper economists busily gave encouragement. Samuel Brittan was later to describe 1960 as the year of the 'great reappraisal'.

The reappraisal, however, was accompanied all too often by the belief that drastic changes were not necessary. A facile optimism developed that faster growth could easily be willed. Professor C. F. Carter offered a salutary warning in the *District Bank Review* of September 1962. Just as doctors could not be expected to provide immortality, so unreasonable hopes could not be placed in the work of economists. The latter could clarify the nature of the choices open to a nation, but the choices would be made by *others*. He insisted that the essence of the British economic problem 'is that the desired purposes cannot simultaneously be attained within the limited area available for manoeuvre'. Later E. E. Hagen and S. F. T. White commented: 'Choice among various economic goals was not contemplated. Rather, new institutions were sought by which the inconsistencies among the goals could be eliminated so that all might be attained.'[11] Britain was trying to reconcile full employment, stable prices, economic growth, the defence of sterling, and a world role. It was a hopelessly over-ambitious task.

From the late 1950s there developed a growing literature which attempted to explain the reasons for Britain's relatively slow growth rate. Government was bombarded with advice from all sides. But there was also disagreement as to how poor the British performance really was: whether more than a marginal improvement was possible or, on the other hand, was necessary. One of the most generally accepted constraints in the British economy, compared with France, Italy and West Germany, was said to be the absence of a large movement of labour from agriculture to industry. Even in the early 1960s one in nine of the German workforce was still employed on the land compared with Britain's one in twenty-seven. The movement from the land was also important in that it provided a degree of mobility of labour that was lacking in Britain – despite migration from old industrial centres in Britain and coloured immigration – and perhaps in some instances a workforce that was more amenable to rapid change. Some economists thought investment in British industry was discouraged by the relative lack of adaptability that was reputed to exist in much of the British workforce, though in general agreement as to the causes of inadequate British investment remained elusive. Heavy overseas investment pointed to the abundance of capital. Recurrent 'stop–go' government economic policies were seen as possible disincentives in that they could breed a long-term feeling of pessimism among British industrialists, but there were those who saw in the current level of investment no more than the continuation of long-established patterns. This led to some speculation that one was dealing with, in some degree at least, deeply ingrained habits of mind.[12] These were to be seen partly in the tendency among British management to 'patch' and use equipment for as long as possible. The only conclusion to emerge with real force around 1960 was the difficulty of assessing the respective contributions of government, management and labour to the current failings in the British economy, not to mention short- and long-term forces.

As far as immediate government was concerned, it has been widely argued that the 1959 budget was too generous, and that of 1960 certainly so. The Chancellor, Heathcoat Amory was a cautious man, but he was persuaded by his Cabinet colleagues in 1960 that a 'neutral' budget would suffice. Amory left office soon afterwards, privately remarking that had he stayed he would have insisted on a higher rate of unemployment or an incomes policy to counter the overheating of the economy.[13] Poor Treasury forecasting may have complicated the government's task, and there was an understandable tendency to delay decisions until the economic trends were clear. This often meant that action was taken too late. The impact of government policy might be felt up to eighteen months later in very different economic conditions. Deflationary measures, when they came in 1960, neither increased unemployment nor exports (though production was checked), and thus further doubt was cast on the adequacy of the instruments with which the government was striving to guide the economy. The Radcliffe Committee had already questioned the current approach to monetary policy, and certainly the 1960 credit restrictions failed to achieve the government's objectives. The search for more varied and subtle instruments was encouraged.

Among British industrialists, too, new thoughts were stirring. Government deflationary measures in 1960 were a sharp reminder, if any were needed, of the interdependence of government and industry. In the case of the large firms at least, the Conservative era so far had meant fewer formal contacts with government than under Labour and, surprising though this might seem, consequently less direct influence on government policy.[14] Business opinion was far from united, but there were those who favoured continuous growth in the expectation that this would lead to greater cost and price stability. If British unit costs could be held in line with those of rival industrial nations, wage demands would be easier to handle. The FBI sponsored 'The Next Five Years Conference' at Brighton in November 1960. One study group produced a careful analysis of the reasons for Britain's slow and unstable growth. Its report attacked past changes in government policy as damaging to investment, and it argued for conscious attempts to assess the growth possibilities in various industries for the next five or more years.

General business interest was not immediately roused, but favourable publicity concerning French indicative planning and growing impatience with 'stop-go' brought converts. Through growth one might be better able to live with full employment and reduce inflation. But first it was necessary to build up long-term confidence. Indicative planning entailed detailed study of likely trends and bottlenecks in the economy over the next five years or so. There must be improved government knowledge of industry and its plans; effective coordination between private and nationalized sectors of the economy; and the avoidance of short-term economic manoeuvres by the government. On the whole business recoiled from planning as such, but there was growing interest among many leading businessmen in closer consultation with the government and in attempts at greater coordination of the economy as a whole. The Iron and Steel Board had been among the first to argue in the 1950s that long-term planning without reference to the expectations of other key sectors of industry was futile. Its third five-year development programme of 1961 was in some ways a pilot scheme for the National Economic Development Council whose work will be examined later.

The Conservative bid for growth

Selwyn Lloyd, the new Chancellor in 1960, brought a healthy touch of scepticism to the Treasury, according to Samuel Brittan. Though lacking any deep knowledge of economics, his instincts were sound. His association with the years of economic crisis from 1960 to 1962 meant that his creative activity was largely overlooked at the time. Certainly much was begun during his stay at 11 Downing Street which will warrant careful examination by some future PhD student.

In March 1961 short-term loans from continental central banks were needed to sustain foreign confidence in sterling; already some overseas sterling area holders were anxious to diversify their reserves in gold and dollars, and there were other warnings of overseas disquiet concerning the British economy. In July 1961 a drastic deflationary package, including a 'pay pause' (directly affecting those in public employment), became necessary. But a straightforward return to the stagnation of 1955–8 was unthinkable. Macmillan failed to interest the Treasury in a floating pound, but it was agreed that the government should try to collaborate with industry in a 'joint examination of the economic prospects of the country stretching five or more years into the future'. A concerted effort should be made to discover 'the essential conditions for realizing potential growth'. The 'pay pause' meant that for the time being there could be no cooperation with the unions, though there were some stirrings of interest from that quarter. Within government itself new moves of importance were taking place. In 1961 came the Plowden Report, partly the product of parliamentary agitation from 1957 against ill-controlled government spending. A select committee in 1958 urged the planning of public expenditure in the light of the expected growth of the economy. Forward expenditure planning was attempted in some departments before Plowden recommended its general introduction.[15] To improve short-term management of the economy the Chancellor was empowered to vary consumer taxes by up to 10 per cent between budgets. In April 1961 there appeared a white paper, *The Financial and Economic Obligations of the Nationalized Industries*, which tried to lay down more positive guidelines concerning the commercial operation of the public sector. The latter had been left confused and demoralized by repeated changes in government policy since nationalization.

Cabinet support was not easily obtained for all these policies. Macmillan exploited the economic crisis of July 1961 to argue that a clear demonstration of forward thinking was politically vital, and was thus able to secure agreement to the establishment of a body designed by the Chancellor to act as a bridge between government and both sides of industry, the National Economic Development Council (NEDC). Union cooperation was only won after some retreat on the 'pay pause', but in March 1962 the first meeting of the NEDC took place. Business interests and the unions both hoped to use the NEDC to increase their influence over government policy and to encourage rapid economic growth. The government did not want a policy-making rival, but an institution through which to communicate with and to guide industry. Some ministers, indeed, had opposed its formation: Treasury officials disliked many features of the new experiment, though the Chancellor saw in the NEDC a supplementary source of advice and information.[16] The future history of the NEDC was chequered, but unlike many of the experiments of the 1960s it at least survived, muddling along and at times providing a useful meeting place for government, unions and employers.

In 1962 the NEDC came out strongly for a 4 per cent growth rate based on over-optimistic estimates and projections. The government's response was hesitant. The Treasury was fearful of premature and too rapid reflation, and not until the summer of 1962 was there general agreement on the worsening recession and declining business confidence. In this context one should not exaggerate the significance of Macmillan's drastic reshaping of the government on 13 July 1962. This included the replacement of Selwyn Lloyd as Chancellor, not because he was an obstacle to reflation but rather because a new face might suggest a more dynamic approach to economic problems. There was a small balance of payments surplus of £90 million in 1962, a fragile basis from which to embark on a policy of growth. The new Chancellor, Reginald Maudling, made it clear in his 1963 budget that he was not trying to achieve growth on the scale and within the specific period proposed by the NEDC (that is, a 4 per cent increase for each year between 1961 and 1966). The government, in any case, was under pressure to reflate, with unemployment reaching 900,000 in February 1963 (a figure admittedly inflated by the severe winter, but with a serious underlying trend). Maudling had already been encouraging exports and investment (by 1963 British investment incentives were said to be among the best in

Europe), and in the 1963 budget it seemed safe to offer more general stimulants. There were tax cuts of £270 million, as well as special grants to some industries and depressed areas. At this time British exports seemed reasonably competitive in price compared with their main rivals, but any large wage increases without improved productivity would be disastrous. The NEDC had also assumed that Britain would enter the EEC in or around 1964. A detailed study of seventeen key industries subsequently revealed that few expected to achieve a 4 per cent growth rate. The government allowed the electricity supply industry to plan its investment on the assumption that the 4 per cent target would be achieved, but in most industries investment was disappointing. It was not surprising, therefore, that the NEDC's hopes of a more rapid growth in the volume of exports than of imports were not realized. Without an incomes policy, too, the domestic demand for British goods and for imports was soon too high. A balance of payments crisis could not be long delayed.[17]

Of Maudling's performance as Chancellor Samuel Brittan concluded that it would be simplistic either to condemn or enthuse. Basically the same might be said of government policy as a whole. In retrospect it appears that the government should have reflated more slowly (but the electoral timetable was against it), or it should have secured more room for manoeuvre in its economic policies. Some economists favoured floating the pound, or devaluation: others suggested a massive mobilization of all reserves to carry sterling through a period of deficit on current account. There was some talk of import controls. Optimism, indeed, was fairly widespread well into 1964, even among economists, though the National Institute of Economic and Social Research was sounding a note of alarm in the spring. The outcome, as we shall see, was as the pessimists predicted.

Meanwhile various ambitious programmes were beginning to gain momentum. Britain's motorways were slowly growing from 8½ miles in 1958 to some 350 in 1965 (though Italy had nearly 1,000 and Germany far more). The Buchanan Report of 1963 was an attempt to grapple with the growing problem of traffic congestion in towns. The rapid spread of car ownership was having profound economic, social and environmental consequences. It was a massive provider of jobs; it conferred great freedom of choice and movement for many, but with its injuries to public transport it added to the problems of others. It encouraged urban sprawl, and could simultaneously cause congestion in the centres of cities during the day and desertion at night. In London the commuter problem was worsened by the boom in office-building from the late-1950s. Macmillan described the capital as a 'great ulcer' sucking in the vitality of the rest of the United Kingdom. More government action also seemed called for as unemployment began to worsen in some of the prewar depressed areas. At the beginning of 1963 unemployment was in excess of 3 per cent in all areas except the southern half of England and Yorkshire. Regional policy from 1958 had been conceived in terms of *ad hoc* emergency operations. From 1962 to 1963 there was mounting emphasis on longer-term efforts. PEP argued in its *Location of Industry* (October 1962) for development areas to provide balanced industrial growth – localities should not be too dependent on one firm or industry. The FBI and the NEDC emphasized that regional growth was dependent on good communications, housing and social amenities, and there had to be some assurance of continuing government aid for as long as might be necessary. Suggestions that it might be productive on the whole to encourage people to move from areas of high unemployment were opposed on grounds of overcrowding in many of the most prosperous regions of the country.

The government, from about 1962, was moving away from its old piecemeal approach: it was more interested in development areas, the creation of natural growth points within regions, and in attacking basic structural problems. It did however recoil from suggestions that some changes in local government might be necessary, many local authorities being deemed too small to make the necessary contribution to the envisaged developments. The government gave special attention early in 1962 to the north-east of England, where unemployment (with the decline of coal and shipbulding) exceeded 7 per cent. So sharp a decline in key industries was threatening the *raison d'être* of whole communities. Lord Hailsham was appointed minister with special responsibility for the north-east. In October 1963 an attempt was made to devise a national approach to regional problems with the replacement of the President of the Board of Trade with a Secretary of State for Industry, Trade and Regional Development. Administration was strengthened both at the centre and in the regions, but it was still difficult to secure the necessary coordination between a number of government departments, not to mention the multiplicity of local authorities. More government aid and incentives were offered to firms moving to areas of high unemployment: there were extra grants to speed slum clearance. The Contracts of Employment Act of 1963 laid down the periods of notice necessary before workers would be dismissed, and the Ministry of Labour took more interest in facilitating the movement of workers from one area to another. Industrial training and retraining at last received some government attention. Postwar interest in this need had soon flagged, but the Industrial Training Act of 1964 laid down that an industrialist must either train his own men or contribute financially to a pool for his branch of industry. Government training centres were increased from thirteen in 1962 to thirty-two by 1966. But there were staff shortages, and even in the mid-1970s there were continuing doubts as to the adequacy of the provision made by the government or by industry itself. British facilities compared very badly with those, for instance, provided in Sweden with a much smaller workforce.

Some of the most ambitious government planning centred on education. Complaints of amateurism were issuing from all sides.

Individuals of genius, backed by solid craftsmanship and obedient clerks, were no longer enough. The potential of all had to be maximized through formal instruction. In fact a considerable expansion had already been effected in education. In 1938 the proportion of the seventeen-year-old age group in full-time education had been a mere 4 per cent: by 1962 this had reached 15 per cent. The number of university students doubled between 1938 and 1960, while there was a fourfold increase in those attending training colleges and colleges of education. Much more, however, was thought necessary, and in October 1963 there appeared the Robbins Report, acclaimed by ministers as 'the most important social document to be produced since the Beveridge Report'. This urged the doubling of university places to 218,000 within ten years, with 319,000 places in higher education as a whole. Given the population bulge, the increasing proportion of teenagers remaining at school and acquiring good qualifications, and the expected employment trends in the professions and among the highly skilled, these recommendations were sound and (with reasonable economic growth) realistic. The Robbins Committee did not neglect technological education. This had received some stimulus in the mid-1950s, including the development of the colleges of advanced technology. The Robbins Report advocated their early elevation to university status. University growth had in fact exceeded expectations by the early 1970s, but with much less success in the education of engineers than had been anticipated.

Other levels of education were also attracting attention. The technically oriented schools promised in 1944 had largely failed to appear, and there was a growing belief that adequate provision was not being made for the average and below average child. The Crowther and Newsom Reports of 1959 and 1963 both favoured raising the school-leaving age to sixteen. The Crowther Report claimed that education 'well down into the modern schools ... pays, always in the long run, and quite often quickly'. Newsom, though recognizing the dangers of 'extending the period of boredom', argued the case for helping less able children. These were, as the title of the report expressly put it, *Half Our Future*. The pattern of employment since the war lent force to such arguments, for of the million or so extra jobs two-thirds had been in technical or clerical grades. The government in consequence planned to raise the school-leaving age to sixteen from 1970–1. Efforts also continued to improve post-school technical training, and to offset the limitations of the apprenticeship system on which so many industries were still dependent despite criticisms of its inadequacies by such bodies as the Anglo-American Productivity teams back in the 1940s.

Bureaucrats and businessmen, scientists and engineers

From the 1960s it was self-evident that for the British economy to flourish one of the basic requirements was effective cooperation

between government and industry, and between certain key professions. Unfortunately this was not easily realizable for a variety of
reasons. There were many subtle and not so subtle obstacles to fruitful
partnership, and such obstacles could indeed occur within what might
loosely be thought of as a single elite group. There was, to begin with, a
much wider gap between government and industry in Britain than in
France, so that French methods and institutions were neither fully
copied nor capable of the same impact in Britain. The NEDC and its
associated bodies lacked the powers of their French models. The
businessmen who were members of such bodies were often too bold and
experimental for the average industrialist in any case, but British
businessmen in general were less amenable to government influence,
and British civil servants ill-fitted and usually indisposed to assume the
role of their French counterparts. Despite the remarkable measure of
control exercised over the economy in the 1940s, the British Civil Service
did not share the French *étatist* outlook. A permanent secretary, Sir
James Dunnett, noted in 1961 that the administrative class of civil
servant tended 'to look at himself rather too exclusively as a man who
advises the Minister on policy . . . and that more mundane tasks such as
formulating and carrying out a road programme are . . . rather below
the dignity of a gentleman'.[18] As far back as 1944 the Report of the
Committee on the Training of Civil Servants had expressed concern as
to whether British bureaucrats were properly prepared for and
organized in their work. The Centre for Administrative studies was set
up in 1963 to improve their training. Lord Hailsham as Minister of
Science began to challenge the tradition for government to try not to
show preference for one firm over another: in the 1960s there was
growing interest in the use of state contracts to encourage business
efficiency. But close bureaucratic-business ties were not easily
established, and the Civil Service was slow to develop managerial and
related skills.

There were problems among businessmen too. Not only did they lack
unity, but their influence in the country was less than many imagined.
True, Anthony Sampson thought one of the features of the 1960s was
the enhanced impact and status of some of their number, but this
highlights earlier weaknesses. Many have commented upon the great
difference between British and American business attitudes and of
attitudes towards businessmen. Americans often felt the social status of
British businessmen to be uncertain; there were doubts as to the social
utility of industry and the legitimacy of profits.[19] British businessmen, it
was also claimed, succumbed too readily to the style, interests and
attitudes of the upper classes (J. P. Nettl was struck by the spread of the
civil service style to the larger business organizations), or, if they failed
to do so, failed also to penetrate the main centres of power. The rugged
entrepreneur of the nineteenth century was out of place: the preference
was for independent and selfless people able to fill any role with
unblemished distinction.

The Civil Service and the universities (not to mention other educational sectors) tended to share the aristocracy's suspicion of 'trade'. Business possessed relatively few representatives from Oxbridge or the leading public schools which should have assured it easy access to the departments of state. The City of London was much better placed in this regard, though in its turn it tended to hold industry at arm's length. Academic criticism of the comparative failings of British businessmen since the late nineteenth century had not been accompanied by many positive efforts to encourage able graduates to enter industry. Industrialists in their turn were often, not surprisingly, suspicious of graduates. Many academics also shared the hostility of the left towards 'capitalism'. The formal education of British managers often compared unfavourably with that of their foreign competitors. In 1966 it was estimated that only one-fifth of Britain's industrial directors had had formal management training. Personnel management was described by H. A. Clegg in the early 1960s as an 'undeveloped profession' despite some progress since 1939. The Institutes of Administration, Labour Management, and Works Managers attracted some students, but the flowering of interest in business schools did not properly develop until the 1960s. Even then industrialists thought some schools too academic, while the schools themselves complained that students reflected the national bias against individual enterprise and competition. Not surprisingly Graham Turner, as late as 1971, was asserting that much of British industry, despite many changes, still retained 'more of the characteristics of the Home Guard than of a professional fighting force: in many of its parts it is poorly equipped and organized, and often indifferently led'.[20] It seems clear that whatever qualifications might be offered to the above generalizations concerning British industrialists, both the image entertained of them by others and their own thinking and conduct made it difficult, if not impossible, for them to emulate their German rivals, who were able to work in an environment of increasingly confident neoliberalism. In Britain herself, business graduates often found greater scope for their skills in American subsidiaries.

The roles and standing of scientists and engineers were also significant. Britain's expenditure on research and development was the highest in western Europe: her standing in scientific research was second only to the United States. But these efforts were not accompanied by rapid economic growth. In part this was a reflection of the lack of sophistication in much British management. But it was also a reflection of prejudices deeply embedded in British society. Science enjoyed more prestige than engineering: within engineering itself there were biases against design and production. Both scientists and engineers were surprisingly limited in their influence over decision-making in industry and government. Leaders in these professions, however, often admitted that too few of their members possessed the breadth of interest, vision and all-round abilities (perhaps sometimes even the inclination) to compete with those trained in the arts and social sciences. The situation was very different in Europe, Japan and the United States. In Britain in the early 1960s few MPs and only 7 per cent of the assistant principals in the Civil Service had scientific or engineering qualifications. The creation of a Minister of Science in 1959 was a welcome sign of new thinking, though even that title reflected the current bias against engineering.

The scientific and engineering professions were themselves the product of a long and complicated history, so that they could not readily respond if and when new expectations were placed in them. The prestige and social standing enjoyed by a profession are bound to influence the calibre of candidates seeking entry to it; they may also influence the material rewards. In 1962 the Education Department of the University of Oxford published a study entitled *Technology and the Sixth Form Boy*. In its sample of opinion the research physicist was placed in status high above the engineer – above, indeed, a company director. The engineer found himself rated above a primary school teacher but below a dentist and chartered accountant. In France and Sweden, in contrast, the engineer was rated at least the equal of the scientist. Sir John Baker, Professor of Engineering at Cambridge, wrote in 1964: 'The fact is that engineering is not attracting anything like its fair share of outstanding talent.'[21] Pure science in the sixth forms was drawing three times as many of the best pupils as engineering. Teachers, the media, and long-standing social prejudices all encouraged this preference. Indeed Baker feared that rapidly expanding educational opportunities had been worsening the situation since 1944, as they left fewer able young people to enter engineering by way of the shop floor. In his presidential address to the British Association for the Advancement of Science on 1 September 1976 he was no more optimistic.

Further biases ensured that atomic energy, electronics, aerospace and defence attracted much the largest proportion of first-class engineers and scientists. Among those to suffer were most educational sectors outside the universities, which in turn affected the training of future generations. In this environment those with undoubted scientific or technological gifts would obviously persevere, but their natural course was to turn to the most advanced openings in research and development whenever possible. Where earlier generations had striven to advance the frontiers of empire, this one strove to advance the frontiers of science and technology. The connection with national interest was sometimes equally tenuous. At the same time one must recognize that industry did not always make the best use of the products of scientific endeavour. There were faults on several sides. As early as 1951 R. L. Meier had argued: 'The present organization of British science, with its strong emphasis upon the fundamental approach, does not contribute much to economic improvement, even though this is one of the principal ends used to justify its further expansion.'[22] In 1952 the British Association for the Advancement of Science set up a committee to inquire into the relationships between science, technology and industry. Its complex findings were published in three volumes by Professors C. F. Carter and B. R. Williams in 1957-9. No simple answers were found.

A firm could not simply graft on scientific and technological progress as 'an optional extra'. A complete range of suitably qualified personnel was usually required, working within the framework of an integrated policy which extended from research and development, through the production processes, and so on to sales and marketing. Even this might be insufficient, since firms were often heavily dependent upon outside suppliers. In the 1950s weaknesses in the steel and machine-tool industries had important repercussions elsewhere. Firms might be hampered by abrupt changes in government economic policies (including 'stop-go'). Restrictive practices might operate among the workforce. Risk capital might not be forthcoming for bold innovations, but some family firms were notoriously reluctant to raise outside capital however much it might be needed, lest this might jeopardize family control of the firm. Managerial conservatism could exist in many forms, and in the case of the famous North British Locomotive Company change came too late, the great manufacturer of steam locomotives for railways all over the world failing to make the transition to diesel and electric traction. On the other hand firms that were too much under the spell of technological progress could prove too adventurous and show too little regard for commercial realities. Industrial success required an all round balance of skills, from conception to final sale. This was powerfully brought out by Dr Ieuan Maddock, chief scientist to the Department of Technology and Industry in 1973. He spoke of Japan's remarkable industrial success despite her small contributions to fundamental engineering knowledge. 'This has been achieved by great attention to the very things we tend to overlook – detail design, quality control, technological marketing and a willingness to adapt to the customer's needs. '[23] British engineers, he thought, put too much emphasis on originality, and paid too little attention to overall costs, probable practical difficulties and commercial appeal.

Britain's use of her scientific and technological personnel was also significant. Even after some reductions, one-fifth of her scientists and engineers were still engaged in defence projects in the early 1960s. Whereas two-thirds of the qualified engineers in France were directly employed in industry, only a little over half of those in Britain were so engaged. A comparison of the employment of both scientists and engineers in Britain with those in the United States found a still lower proportion in industry – only 42 per cent as against 74 per cent. Britain also produced mainly specialist scientists and technologists in a ratio of about four to one, although many held that industry required roughly four generalists to one specialist, so large was the proportion that should be destined for administrative or managerial posts. There were frequent complaints from industry in the 1970s that engineering graduates were often ill-equipped in the arts of communication, and showed too little interest in the commercial aspects of industry. There was less of a deficiency in numbers than in quality and in the relevant mix of skills and attitudes.

Governments were slow to recognize that Britain's limited resources had to be used selectively. There was a tendency to try to find compensation in prestigious scientific and technological successes for fading international political power. The British were also deceptively flattered by their recent successes – when Dounreay could be proclaimed the world's most advanced fast breeder nuclear reactor in 1959, when Rolls Royce were the world leaders in vertical take-off and landing fixed-wing aircraft, when Cockerell's tests of the hovercraft were proceeding well, and when Alastair Pilkington produced the revolutionary 'float-glass' technique. Yet of all these only the last was to enjoy real commercial success in the 1960s, and it is noteworthy that Pilkington's research had been carefully guided by market considerations.

British industry in the early 1960s

The condition of individual British industries is worthy of some consideration at this point. Fortunes varied sharply, with the decline of some being more readily understandable than others. Sadly ominous signs were beginning to develop among some of the front-runners that their health and vigour were not all that they had been. Steel will be examined later in the context of renationalization under Labour in the later 1960s, but it should be noted in passing that not all British users were satisfied with its performance in the 1950s. The machine tools industry had attracted unfavourable comments on many occasions in the past, but it continued to perform below expectations and to be hampered by the lack of standardization in its products. The decline of cotton textiles from 1951 was not surprising, given the attractiveness of this type of industry to developing nations. The British labour force was nearly halved in the 1950s, but it was not until the end of the decade that the government acted against over-capacity. Even then productivity rose more slowly than in most European states.[24]

More surprising was the decline of the British shipbuilding industry. It had few competitors after the war, yet it failed to expand with the enormous growth in the world's shipping from the 1950s. Output fell by over one-third between 1956 and 1964; the labour force by rather less. Less tonnage was completed in 1966 than in 1947, and at 808,000 tons this was only one-twelfth of the world total. True the industry had suffered from steel shortages while the demand for some of the types of ship at which it was most expert (large warships and liners) had declined sharply. Indeed, the age of the passenger liner was rapidly passing, from the late 1950s, with the inauguration of jet air travel. Even the smaller cargo liner offered less scope than the exploding market for tankers and other types of freighter (one could not then foresee the great world surplus in shipbuilding capacity of the mid-1970s). In the context of the late 1950s and early 1960s many British yards, both large and small, appeared conservative, weak in highly qualified personnel, and singularly reluctant to invest. Per capita output, for instance, in the sophisticated Swedish yards was about 50 per cent higher than the British average. High prices and delays in completions added to the uncompetitiveness of British yards. Labour relations were notoriously unsatisfactory. There were too many unions (no less than seventeen on the Clyde, which had the worst strike record in Britain between 1950 and 1956), poor negotiating procedures, and a long history of industrial strife, heavy unemployment, as well as a deep sense of pride in past greatness. Conditions had been and often still were harsh. Memories were long in the close-knit craft communities, especially the fear of unemployment. As a general manager remarked: 'Even if unemployment falls this remains true, because this attitude is bred in the bone.'[25] Few foreign yards experienced such continuity from the past. The seemingly endless (and to outsiders sometimes incomprehensible) demarcation disputes were intimately related to job security. Worse still from the point of view of productivity were the demarcation practices, which caused much wastage of labour and time. But apart from these and other internal drags on the industry it is important to recall its dependence on outside suppliers (in 1954 it was estimated that 54 per cent of shipyard costs arose from outside purchases) so that faults elsewhere in British industry could reduce the competitiveness of British yards.

The British shipping industry also suffered a relative decline. It had been closely identified with the empire, and decolonization found the new states anxious to develop their own companies. In world shipping in general many companies enjoyed advantages denied to the British, but even so the relative stagnation of British mercantile fleets compared with many European competitors is not easily explained. Professor S. G. Sturmey's studies led him to the conclusion that more use of market research, for instance, should have enabled the British to do better than they did. Between 1955 and 1963 Norwegian shipowners added nearly 6.5 million tons to their fleets (the British added a little over 2 million) with no obvious advantages beyond those of their own making. They were readier to use the more economical diesel engined ships and were quicker to appreciate the new trends in world trade. The British were slow to introduce bulk carriers from the late 1950s, and to expand their tanker fleets. They were late in understanding the potential of supertankers and container ships. Managerial conservatism and shortages of qualified staff, both technical and financial, were much in evidence. That with better management much of their former glory could be recaptured was demonstrated by the remarkable revival of British shipping from the late 1960s. In 1973 Britain possessed 10 per cent of the world's shipping, half her tonnage being under five years old, and with net earnings equal to one-third of the nation's private invisible earnings.

Among some of the newer industries Britain's performance was ostensibly more reassuring. Even in 1965, of the world's largest corporations one-ninth had their headquarters in Britain compared with one-seventh for the whole of the EEC. In 1960, outside the communist bloc, Britain possessed the second largest aircraft industry, stood second in the development of computers, was a formidable power in vehicle manufacture, in oil and in chemicals, and in electrical engineering. The highest expectations were placed in British developments in atomic energy for civil use. Yet all was not so healthy as it appeared. In the ten years from 1954, for instance, Britain's share of the world market in chemicals fell from 16 to 12 per cent. World demand had trebled, and West Germany had impressively outrun the British, despite the latter's remarkable advance in the first postwar decade. This momentum had not been fully sustained, with the British proving slow to switch from coal-based to gas- or oil-based chemical technology, and in consequence falling behind in the production of plastics.[26] The chemical industry within the EEC was also achieving great economies of scale. The increased size of the home market was a great incentive, and some chemical developments in Britain were certainly inhibited by the absence of this factor. In the 1950s the economic size of an ICI nylon-polymer plant had increased sevenfold, and for the third generation it was doubling again. When British negotiations to enter the EEC failed in 1963, a new ICI plant was built in Amsterdam to leapfrog the EEC tariff barriers. Continental productivity tended to rise faster, and by the 1960s Britain's chemical imports were rising almost as quickly as her exports. British research as a proportion of turnover had fallen behind that of Germany, but ICI also discovered that much more attention had to be paid to sales and management.[27]

No British exports had risen more in value since 1938 than those of vehicles and planes. The expansion of the vehicle industry had been particularly impressive. Before the war, despite some distinguished luxury products, the car industry had been hampered by too many small firms and by a motor tax policy which discouraged sound engine design. The gradual reduction of the industry to a few main producers (by 1968 there were only four), helped by a sellers' market after the war, had brought an impressive rise in output, productivity and exports. But the important Austin-Morris merger of 1952 (the British Motor Corporation) had not been followed by effective rationalization. British designs left little to stir the imagination outside the sports car field before the work of Sir Alec Issigonis in the 1950s. A credit squeeze was needed to discourage undue concentration on the home market in the mid-1950s, but in general the industry's sales continued to grow at so reassuring a rate that long-term weaknesses in management, investment and salesmanship tended to be obscured. In the commercial field,

Leyland and the diesel engine manufacturers, Gardner and Perkins, performed well. The aircraft industry, however, had been causing concern since the mid-1950s. Throughout the first two postwar decades there was an abundance of ambitious aerospace projects, embracing almost every type of flying machine and missile. But in terms of commercial reward only three aircraft could be counted real successes down to the 1960s (especially in the form of exports). Britain was also a considerable exporter of aero-engines and of aviation electronic equipment, but overall the aircraft industry was beginning to arouse fears in some quarters that more money and resources had been devoted to it than was nationally wise.

Some reference must also be made to the public corporations. These were responsible for all fuel and power (save that directly provided by the oil companies) and much of the transport system. Despite some decentralization under the Conservatives, the government was still in ultimate control of overall financing, so that the investment programmes of the nationalized concerns were often obvious targets in periods of deflation. Prices might be regulated for political purposes, while the nationalized airlines were often required to buy British aircraft with little regard to the competitiveness of such planes. Nevertheless there was growing interest in a more commercially minded approach. In 1956 the Herbert Committee on electrical supply had argued that that industry should be guided by commercial considerations alone – the relevant minister should be responsible for any other decisions. The government's white paper of 1961 on *The Financial and Economic Obligations of the Nationalized Industries* (Cmnd 1337) asserted that the public corporations 'are not, and ought not to be regarded as social services absolved from economic and commercial justification', but it also added that they had 'obligations of a national and non-commercial kind'. The government intended that over a period of years the public corporations should pay an agreed return to the nation, but this was an aim that was more easily stated than achieved.

The railways posed a special problem. With the upsurge in road transport the railways fell increasingly into deficit, and by 1960 it was clear that with current policies (including the 1955 modernization programme) there was no prospect of restoring them to solvency. Railways in many parts of the world were experiencing similar problems. In Britain the operating deficit totalled £67 million in 1960 and was worsening. Operating costs had risen by 300 per cent since 1939, but charges by a mere 50 per cent. The uneconomic nature of many of the rail services and much of the rail network itself was already broadly known. Political constraints were much more important obstacles to change than any deficiencies in the methods of railway accounting. A white paper, *The Reorganization of the Nationalized Transport Undertaking* (Cmnd 1248) appeared in December 1960; early in the new year Richard (later Lord) Beeching of ICI was invited to head the reshaping of the railways. In 1963 a Railways Board, and four other boards, replaced the clumsy structure supervised by the British Transport Commission. The Beeching Report on railway reorganization appeared in March. It avoided social questions – Beeching insisted that social costs should be borne by the community – and set out in stark terms the extent of the reorganization required to eliminate most if not all of the rail deficit by 1970. The capital cost was put at £250 million.

Despite some economies since 1948 it was claimed that half the system was not meeting even the most obvious costs, quite apart from overall operating expenses. The comparable West German railways were estimated to be making about 50 per cent more use of their manpower.[28] The Beeching Report argued that the railways should concentrate upon the work they were best fitted to do, namely inter-city passenger and long-distance freight. Miscellaneous goods services were rightly condemned as uneconomic: much seasonal holiday traffic required the maintenance of capacity that was under-used for the rest of the year. Many branch lines were not commercially viable. Many towns and whole regions suddenly found themselves threatened with the loss of all rail services. At one time it seemed as if no lines would run north or west of Inverness. Wales and the south-west of England were much affected. In the battles to avert closures there were more defeats than victories, though some short scenic stretches were rescued by private steam railway enthusiasts, practitioners of the 'do-it-yourself' cult on the largest scale, and powered too by a national eagerness to indulge in nostalgia. Symbolically the well-known holiday route from Bath to Bournemouth, the old Somerset and Dorset railway, gave way to package holiday flights to Spain and Majorca. Yet much less was achieved than expected, and not merely because the rail system was stabilized at around 11,000 miles rather than the 8,000 envisaged by Beeching. The prospects for freight had been exaggerated. In particular coal movements decreased by over one-third between 1954 and 1970 (the general demand for coal fell, and new coal-fired power stations tended to be built near mines) and few other commodities lent themselves to block train operation. The freightliners attracted less custom than anticipated, frequently outbid by the greater convenience and reliability of road transport. In 1970 the railways' share of freight movements in Britain stood at around 20 per cent or less, dependent on the type of calculation used, while their share of passenger mileage had been halved to 10 per cent between 1957 and 1967. The debate as to what railways the nation needed and could afford was soon resumed.

The other Cinderella among the nationalized industries, coal, had made some notable progress since 1947. Reform had at first been slow: a generation of neglect could not be put right in a few years. New sinkings took ten years to complete; a major pit reconstruction might occupy eight. There were shortages of highly trained personnel, especially among top management. Coal prices were often kept too low by governments fearful of inflation. A satisfactory wage structure was not negotiated until 1955–67. There was little improvement in productivity down to 1957, but over the next ten years it rose from 25 to 36 hundredweights per manshift. A systematic search for new reserves had been rewarded with the discovery of some 10,000 million tons. These developments, however, coincided with a sharp drop in the demand for coal given the convenience and growing cheapness of oil. The Clean Air Act of 1956 meant a steady drop in domestic demand as smoke-free zones spread. Employment in the mines fell dramatically from 700,000 in 1957 to 419,000 in 1967 and 264,000 by 1973.

The Central Electricity Generating Board was much criticized when the severe winter of 1962–3 (the worst since 1881) brought power cuts in the face of an unexpected 18 per cent increase in consumption. Demand, however, was not easily forecast: new stations took time to build, nor was it easy to make design decisions in a time of rapid technical change and when faced by the competing attractions of coal, oil and nuclear energy. The Suez crisis had been a stimulant to interest in nuclear power, and in 1957 the Board was aiming at the generation of 40 per cent of Britain's electricity by nuclear stations by 1970. But in 1960 policy changed again as oil became unexpectedly plentiful and cheap. Many practical difficulties were also being encountered with the nuclear programme. The building effort was spread too thinly among three consortia, whose own expertise was limited compared with the two American giants in this field. There was a continuing debate as to the best type of nuclear station, and there were many technical problems as scientists and engineers operated at and beyond the boundaries of existing knowledge. Thus although Britain was producing more electricity with nuclear power than any other western state in the early 1960s (though only about 4 per cent of Britain's electricity came from nuclear stations), this did not lead to rapid expansion at home or to foreign orders. In 1971, 70 per cent of the nation's electricity came from coal, and 20 per cent from oil. Hydro-electric development in the north of Scotland, though small by national standards, had brought many advantages to that region. Both there and for rural areas through the British Isles electricity was doing much to raise agricultural pro-ductivity (this was rising at a rate of about 5 per cent a year between 1956 and 1964). In particular, the labour-intensive task of milking was revolutionized.

One of the most unexpected developments was the beginning of the revival of the gas industry. In the 1950s it had seemed doomed to steady decline in the face of the convenience and versatility of electricity. Its prospects were transformed first by the use of naptha, a by-product from oil-refining, and later of natural gas. The first North Sea discoveries opportunely occurred in 1959, with Britain's first gas strike coming in 1965. Underground pipelines transformed the supply system so that gas rapidly began to lose its Victorian image and to re-emerge as one of the most efficient energy suppliers of the later twentieth century.

British industry thus presented a very mixed picture at the beginning of the 1960s. With the passage of time it has become clearer that in many sectors rapid change and adaptability were not to be expected – old habits and ways of thought were too deeply rooted. The British industrial experience was longer and deeper than that of most of western Europe, and was not offset to the same degree by the dislocation following the Second World War. Little has been said in this section on the problem of labour, though this was a vital dimension, and will receive more detailed treatment later. At the same time it is worth noting that labour from the land on the continent was often more flexible or amenable than British workers with generations of industrial experience, often of the harshest kind, behind them. The point should also be stressed that compared with other English-speaking countries fewer workers in Britain had serious expectations of promotion and of rising in the world. Henry Pelling in his *America and the British Left* (1956) was only one who stressed that Britain's stratified society hindered economic progress since it maintained so wide a gulf between men and management. These conditions all favoured a basically conservative trade union movement, more concerned with short-term advantages, and contributing to a situation in which labour was often used inefficiently and in which unit costs of production rose too rapidly compared with key rivals.

The contrast with some European states might be taken further. West Germany possessed many advantages denied to Britain in the 1950s: larger labour reserves, a smaller defence burden, no international role for its currency, no illusions of world status, while defeat and a horror of inflation (to mention no more distant historical experiences) made for a degree of discipline and purposefulness that was lacking in Britain. With success came more national unanimity, so that there occurred an interesting drawing together in political philosophy of the two main political parties. There was less friction between capital and labour, and between industry and the state. There were consistent efforts by the state to devise tax and economic policies that were conducive to economic growth and were not diverted to problems such as income redistribution, tax equitability, or defence of an international currency. With France the problem is different and perhaps more difficult. C. T. Sandford and others have thrown doubts on the efficacy of French planning. Interestingly the French were beginning to modify their approach even as the British looked to them for some guidance. But the British did not seek the same intimacy between state and industry in any case. The French also enjoyed the advantages of an economy that was less exposed to international pressures. When serious difficulties impended in 1958, the French devalued. They had also made use of import controls. Although they too had had their imperial distractions, they were able to concentrate on their economic problems with fewer conflicting priorities than the British. Governments in Britain had done much less than in Germany or France to encourage industry or to remove impediments to growth. If there is no single economic strategy for growth, both Germany and France had stumbled across answers, and had stuck to them.

Chapter 8

Britain and world affairs, 1957-63

The EEC and EFTA

Macmillan's premiership was the last period when Britain was clearly ranked at number three in world affairs. Even the formation of the EEC had not yet resulted in an obvious decline in Britain's influence or in her special relationship with the United States. Macmillan, however, appreciated that this was likely in the long run, and hence much of his time was devoted to the task of trying to reconcile Britain's relations with the Commonwealth, the United States and the EEC.

The Six signed the treaty in Rome on 25 March 1957 which created the European Economic Community. Within a transitional period of from twelve to fifteen years the erection of a common external tariff and the progressive abolition of all internal barriers were envisaged, supplemented by the gradual abolition of impediments to the free movement of persons, capital and services inside the Community. There was to be a common agricultural policy, and many other possibilities for coordination and cooperation existed. Macmillan saw there was a real danger of the Common Market coming into being but with no free trade area to follow. Unfortunately France, having won very satisfactory terms for her colonial empire within the EEC, and also deeply resentful towards Britain over Suez, was not very helpful. Macmillan found Chancellor Adenauer ostensibly more sympathetic in May, and was assured that the creation of the EEC would be followed by the establishment of a free trade area. In October the Council of the OEEC agreed that detailed negotiations should begin for the creation of such an area. But 1957 remained a troublesome year for the new Prime Minister, with the Conservative party proving strongly isolationist both towards the United States and Europe. There was a growing danger that the EEC would take effective form before there was any guarantee of the existence of the free trade area. Macmillan was so impressed by the European urge for political unity that he was even prepared to give some sort of political gloss to the free trade area. But he was also noting rather ominously in the middle of the year, if with undue optimism concerning Britain's strength:

We must not be bullied by the activities of the Six. We could, if we were driven to it, fight their movement if it were to take the form of anything that was prejudicial to our interests. Economically, with the Common-

*wealth and other friends, including the Scandinavians, we could stand
aside from a narrow Common Market. We also have some politico-
military weapons.*[1]

These 'politico-military weapons' were less strong than he imagined.
Britain's new defence policy, from 1957, already involved cuts in the
British conventional contribution to NATO. This pleased neither the
Europeans nor the Americans, especially at a time when NATO
planners were becoming disillusioned with the potential of tactical
nuclear weapons and were once again looking to increased conventional capabilities to provide an adequate spectrum of deterrence in
Europe. Nevertheless, it was vital that British defence spending should
be cut. The envisaged economies were still expected to leave Britain
with a defence budget that would absorb 7 per cent of the gross domestic
product in 1962. On the other hand, to have cut or eliminated the British
nuclear programme would not have led to an appreciable strengthening
of Britain's conventional contribution to NATO.

Britain was also at a disadvantage compared with France in the
competition for West German favour. If de Gaulle needed time to
consolidate his position in France, the British could not turn this
interlude to their advantage as they were unable to give West Germany
strong support from November 1958 when the Berlin question was
reopened by the Soviet Union. Macmillan at that time believed, not
least because of British public opinion, that a flexible negotiating stance
was necessary. This did not satisfy Konrad Adenauer, who found de
Gaulle's position on Berlin much more gratifying. The French and
Germans also had a greater mutual interest in the development of the
EEC than in any hypothetical relationships with Britain. De Gaulle was
able to trade opposition to Britain's free trade proposals for support of
Adenauer over Berlin.[2]

In these circumstances Britain's successful thermonuclear test in May
1957 was mainly of value in the context of Anglo-American relations.
Already the American desire to station intermediate-range ballistic
missiles in Britain had been strengthening Macmillan's hand here, and
now a British H-bomb persuaded the Americans to offer close
cooperation in the development of nuclear weapons and delivery
systems in return for a growing integration of British strategic nuclear
forces with their own. When the Russians successfully launched the
world's first manmade satellite in October 1957, thereby demonstrating
an apparent lead over the Americans in ballistic missiles, the
consequent American alarm further enhanced Britain's importance in
American strategic thinking. In the long run this may not have been so
advantageous, since it encouraged the British to attach more value to
their nuclear force than it properly deserved. But with the French
aspiring to create their own nuclear capability, and with the British
strategic nuclear force so well advanced by 1957, Macmillan's
determination to exploit it as an asset is understandable. For some

years, indeed, there seemed no reason to doubt its contribution to Britain's standing as a great power. In 1960 Britain drew even closer to the United States. The British ballistic missile, Blue Streak, was cancelled. Instead Britain was to purchase an American bomber-launched missile, Skybolt, which would prolong the service life of the RAF's V-bomber force, and this in time might be followed by the British development of a submarine nuclear deterrent, based on the American Polaris system.[3] Meantime the British provided the Americans with a Polaris submarine base in the Holy Loch in the Firth of Clyde.

Britain's bargaining position with respect to the EEC, however, continued to deteriorate. Her one chance might have been the continuing political weakness of France, but de Gaulle's re-emergence steadily eliminated that possibility. As it was, in the 1957–8 negotiations for a free trade area, Britain found the rest of the OEEC in favour of the position of the Six on agriculture.[4] Concessions had to be offered on this point, though still with some safeguards for the Commonwealth. Yet detailed discussion of a free trade area by an intergovernmental ministerial committee under the chairmanship of Reginald Maudling in 1958 made little progress. The French insisted on a common external tariff, where the British desired exceptions. France's partners would have preferred to square the circle, but not at any price. When it came to a choice they could not fail to be swayed by the fact that the EEC existed, and that tangible benefits from that institution were imminent. This weighed heavily with the West Germans in particular. Their own lack of self-confidence left them vulnerable to the influence of de Gaulle. He did not wish to expose French industry to any more formidable competitors. Commonwealth preference and British agricultural policies provided cheaper food in Britain, and this helped to reduce the wage costs of British manufacturers. In November 1958 the French felt sufficiently assured of German support (and with the Six as a whole anxious to implement the first 10 per cent reduction in their tariffs on 1 January 1959) to bring the free trade area talks to an end. Nor was this outcome displeasing to the Americans. The envisaged free trade area had none of the political advantages promised by the EEC to offset its expected economic drawbacks.

The free trade area negotiations were not a total loss from the British point of view. Interest had been mobilized in Britain in the possibility of new courses. The considerable measure of mutual interests which existed between the British, Scandinavians, Austrians and Swiss had been confirmed. British farming interests had no cause to oppose ideas for a free trade area which excluded agriculture. Industrialists, who had been divided at first, became more responsive as fears concerning the future adequacy of Commonwealth markets developed, and as they foresaw a threat to other markets from the creation of the EEC. The FBI became a strong advocate of the European Free Trade Area (EFTA). The TUC was also in favour, so that the British government was well placed to enter into talks with the five states mentioned above, and later with Portugal. Between December 1958 and January 1960 the foundations of EFTA were laid, the Stockholm convention being signed on 4 January, and coming into effect on 3 May. EFTA, however, was no more than a trading device. A British minister commented that its primary purpose was to enable Britain to reach agreement with the EEC countries. It was expected that the elimination of industrial tariffs and quotas would be achieved among the 'outer seven' by 1970, but little more than this seemed to be envisaged. Indeed, EFTA provided Britain with minimal advantages, since few tariff barriers existed with her new partners. More trade was carried on between EFTA and the EEC than within EFTA itself. At best it was a halfway house for Britain, but it could also be asked whether it was a halfway house to anywhere. EFTA strengthened the French case that Britain's interests in Europe were narrowly commercial. The United States was unsympathetic. Not surprisingly, even as EFTA came into being in 1960, so British attention was once more being attracted to the EEC.

Macmillan and the Soviet Union

In the meantime, Macmillan's efforts to ease East–West relations had been redoubled only to encounter a disastrous setback at the Paris summit meeting of May 1960. In the 1950s few western states shared the British readiness to talk with the Russians. The British were the first to welcome the Russian leaders to their soil (in 1956). Traditional British pragmatism was at work. But they also had more incentives. Domestic political considerations played a major part, with the Prime Minister showing great anxiety lest Labour should draw political advantage from any appearance of inflexibility on the part of the western powers. Despite their retention of office for thirteen years, the Tories rarely felt secure. If foreign policy usually had little influence in elections (though the Tories did not forget the supposed impact of the warmongering insinuations in the 1951 campaign) there was always the possibility that it might prove a major issue in the struggle for the centre, where Macmillan still detected remnants of old Liberal and nonconformist traditions. Thus in 1957 he feared for a time that Bevan might try to make the H-bomb 'the great grappling point' against the government, or that this weapon, in conjunction with American bases in Britain, or memories of Suez, might sway crucial middle-of-the-road voters against his party.[5] Later he was troubled by Labour's interest in central European disengagement, and perhaps too by Asian disquiet over the arms race in general. He complained of an orgy of defeatism in the British press in December 1957: 'It is raining umbrellas!'[6]

Such thoughts help to account for Macmillan's persistent interest in these years in the nature and extent of Soviet ambitions and the possibility of realistic compromises. To this end he was prepared to consider a variety of moves to test Russian intentions and to demonstrate to British opinion that the responsibility for the continuing East–West tension did not lie with his government. A personal visit to Russia had great attractions. It might form a step in the negotiating process. Even if the attempt failed, it would help to strengthen public morale against a Russia which had been shown to be unresponsive. He was by no means sanguine as to the outcome. August 1958 found him speculating whether Khrushchev was a megalomaniac – could he be another Hitler? Persisting fears of communist intrigues in the Middle East had been reinforced by the unexpected revolution in Iraq in July, and by the political instability in Jordan and Lebanon. Khrushchev had blown hot and cold, adding to the sense of crisis. Then in November came the Russian demands that four-power control of Berlin be brought to an end, that West Berlin be reconstituted as a demilitarized 'free city', and that over questions of access the western powers should deal with East Germany and no longer with the Soviet Union. If these demands were not met within six months, the Russians threatened to make a unilateral agreement with East Germany. Russia was also denouncing the remilitarization of West Germany. Macmillan noted the specious attractiveness of Russian proposals to create two Germanies, each outside the European alliance system. Such an outcome would be greatly to the military advantage of the Russians.

Macmillan visited Russia (21 February to 3 March 1959) with very mixed feelings, though at least with the satisfaction that the Labour party was apparently put out by his trip. He was subjected to the full force of Khrushchev's varied and sometimes extraordinary personality. The Soviet leader used every device to try to separate Britain from her other allies, and to impress on Macmillan Russia's determination to conclude a peace treaty with East Germany in the near future. It was not easy to divine Khrushchev's real intentions at this stage, though Macmillan returned not without some hope as to the future. Certainly he remained convinced that the West must not lose the initiative. A summit was vital to prevent any worsening of the situation, or , if that was too pessimistic a view, to avoid a position in which the West was outmanoeuvred and left as a helpless onlooker while Khrushchev concluded a separate peace treaty with East Germany. He insisted that the West must negotiate over realities and not forms – he was, for instance, convinced that the West could and would not fight over whether Russian or East German agents controlled the access routes to Berlin. Nor was the American position entirely rigid, whatever the surface appearance.[7] Similarly, while disengagement in central Europe was not practicable, Macmillan concluded that some modest forms of arms limitation and inspection should not be ignored. Again his memoirs reveal his anxiety to satisfy British public opinion, and it is interesting that when, in the summer of 1959, Russo-American relations suddenly eased and made possible Khrushchev's September visit to the United States for bilateral talks, there was some concern lest this should be popularly viewed as a snub to the British.[8] As it was, the government was able to claim some credit for the apparent progress towards a summit conference in the general election campaign in the autumn of 1959, and any public disquiet over East–West relations or nuclear tests and the arms race was too small to influence the outcome.

The summit conference was finally agreed for May 1960, with the four leaders meeting in Paris. This was the conference that never was. It broke up immediately with bitter recriminations over an American spy plane which had been shot down over the Soviet Union. It is unlikely that any way forward would have been found at that time – only the Berlin Wall and the Cuban missile crisis would persuade enough statesmen that the *status quo* could not be seriously challenged. The British thus had to content themselves in East–West relations with closer trading, scientific and cultural contacts. Perhaps these would make the Russians 'more agreeable' in the long term.

First bid to enter the EEC

The failure of the Paris summit may have helped to increase the government's interest in the EEC, but many other considerations were already pressing it in that direction. Macmillan's memoirs make the evolution of his own thinking clear. On 22 October 1959 he remarked: 'The question is how to live with the Common Market economically and turn its political effects into channels harmless to us.'[9] He contemplated some form of British association, and hoped to win concessions for British trade from de Gaulle by supporting his ambition to join the ranks of the great powers – that is, to share in something akin to the Anglo-American special relationship. This could not be allowed to grow into an 'inner directorate' since this would offend Britain's other European allies.[10] Indeed, the British had to be very wary lest efforts to manoeuvre themselves into the EEC left them more isolated than before. All too often they found themselves making cosmetic overtures, such as vague proposals to Germany in 1960 for more cooperation in the face of the Soviet Union, which earned them little or no good will. Meanwhile, as tariff cuts proceeded ahead of schedule within the EEC, time was beginning to run out. On 9 July 1960 Macmillan admitted that Britain faced the awkward choice of a decreasingly sympathetic America and a proud powerful 'Empire of Charlemagne' on the one hand (that is, if Britain stayed out of the EEC), or entry at the expense of EFTA, the Commonwealth and British agriculture on the other. December 1960 found him musing:

We are harassed with countless problems – the narrow knife-edge on which our own economy is balanced; the difficult task of changing an Empire into a Commonwealth . . . ; the uncertainty about our relations with the new economic, and perhaps political, state which is being created by the Six . . . ; and the uncertainty of American policies towards us – treated now as just another country, now as an ally in a special and unique category.[11]

Even so the British still underestimated de Gaulle's fears of their connections with the Commonwealth and the United States. For de Gaulle, it was essential that France and Europe should not be dissolved in a wider Atlantic system. Lord Gladwyn himself later admitted that he had failed to appreciate the general's determination that France should lead Europe as a third force in world affairs. His own view in the early 1960s was that if Britain failed to secure entry she risked absorption by the United States or Russia.

The political case for British membership of the EEC was recognized and emphasized in the conclusions of a committee of senior civil servants drawn from the relevant ministries and set up early in 1960 to review Britain's relations with Europe. A strong united Europe including Britain, was desirable. The committee thought the economic arguments for British entry more evenly balanced, though membership was expected to be a spur to British industrial efficiency. The new joint Permanent Secretary to the Treasury, Sir Frank Lee (late of the Board of Trade), was much more insistent on this point, arguing that British industry had for far too long been feather-bedded by Commonwealth and sterling area markets. Many academic analysts took the same view. Not surprisingly the initial FBI reaction had been to think of safeguards. The EEC was also thought to be too ambitious within itself, and too restrictionist with respect to the rest of the world. By 1960, however, many large British firms were becoming more interested, if only because they increasingly feared the advantages which their European rivals might gain as the EEC developed. Its home market of 170 million alone gave British industrialists pause for thought. The FBI retained its reserve until 1962 by which time most business interests, including cotton textiles (which saw in the common external tariff a defence against cheap imports from the Commonwealth) had swung over. The union movement was divided, with Bill Carron of the AEU and Sam Watson of the miners among the supporters of entry. The NUGMW was very interested in the EEC's economic potential. But the opponents were also strong, and with the anti-Market case tending to prevail within the Labour party – especially on the basis of the expected current terms for entry – the TUC opted for a fence-sitting position.

Within the Labour party there was strong support for entry from Roy Jenkins and George Brown. Hugh Gaitskell at first seemed mildly sympathetic, but he swung to opposition in the autumn of 1962, perhaps from disappointment over the envisaged terms as well as in response to a renewed threat to party unity if an unequivocal policy were adopted one way or the other. Not all the left wing opposed entry, but the Victory for Socialism group left no-one in any doubt as to their hostility. Some in the party argued that the EEC would increase the division in Europe between East and West and there was not a little feeling that ties with the Commonwealth would be endangered. Gaitskell himself was very sympathetic to this argument. William Pickles, in a vigorous pamphlet – *Not With Europe: the political case for staying out* (Fabian International Bureau 1962) – opposed the EEC as undemocratic though his references to the Commonwealth prompted the historian Max Beloff to dismiss him as a romantic. Jenkins put the concern of some of his colleagues for the Commonwealth in perspective on 2 August 1961:

If by 1970 we are still a sluggish, crisis-ridden nation unable to provide substantial resources of development capital to the Commonwealth, whatever sentimental arguments the Commonwealth may produce during the months of negotiations, they will turn their backs on us far more than if they find that by being in Europe we are economically prosperous and dynamic and able to offer them the economic leadership which to some extent they need.

But there were reservations the other way too. As Wilson observed on 25 July 1960: 'If a middle-aged, portly man seeks to join a bunch of athletes lapping round a track, it may make him more athletic, or alternatively, he may drop dead or, at best, retire panting from the track.' Unrealistic arguments were to be found in both camps. Sir Arthur Bryant in his *A Choice for Destiny; Commonwealth and Common Market* (1962) included an outdated emphasis upon kinship and the 'British' race. Pro-Marketeers were often guilty of exaggerating the amount of influence Britain was likely to exert should she gain entry.

Nevertheless in the confused current of opinion in 1961 and 1962 the trends were unmistakably in favour of the EEC. Apart from the Labour party, Lord Avon was the only notable political opponent. Of the main interest groups, the most serious and sustained opposition came from agriculture, with the National Farmers Union insisting that as little change as possible should take place in Britain's current agricultural policies. If the TUC was hesitant, pro-Market sentiments were in the ascendant in most of the influential groups in Britain. This was reflected by the press where the movement in favour, which had been led by the *Guardian, Observer* and *News Chronicle*, was soon followed by the *Daily Mail, Mirror* and *Herald*. If *The Times* was equivocal only the Beaverbrook press, the *Daily Worker* and the *New Statesman* were staunchly opposed. In so far as opinion polls offer guidance, it would seem that despite the low rating of the government, by September 1962 those in favour of entry outnumbered opponents by some 50 per cent, though 'don't knows' constituted nearly a quarter of the respondents.

These movements of opinion undoubtedly facilitated Macmillan's task of handling his own party. There were divisions and uncertainties, even in the Cabinet, well into 1962. But as early as June 1960 the possibility was mooted that Britain might join Euratom and the European Coal and Steel Community. In the parliamentary debate of

25 July the Foreign Secretary emphasized British inseparability from Europe: 'outside Europe we could not fulfil our complete role in the world.' Changes in Cabinet personnel, especially in the great reshuffle of July 1962, enabled Macmillan to strengthen the pro-Marketeers. In 1961 both Macmillan and some of his colleagues became all the more convinced of the need to make a bid for entry as they familiarized themselves with the thinking of the new American president, John F. Kennedy. Only within the EEC was Britain likely to maintain her current influence in Washington, while the Americans further hoped that with Britain as a member the EEC might become more outward-looking. The British, of course, had no desire to act as an American agent, but in any calculation of the promotion of British interests in the Atlantic world it was hard to avoid the conclusion that the nation's influence was bound to diminish save as a member of the EEC.

Additional urgency was imparted to British decision-making by the knowledge that the Six were making more rapid progress than expected towards a customs union and a common agricultural policy, and in 1961 there was even discussion of increasing political cooperation. Some Conservatives were now beginning to detect domestic policy attractions in a bid for entry. They believed that the EEC could provide the party with a new and exciting issue in home politics at a time when it badly needed to refurbish its image. The modernization of the British economy might possibly be tackled more easily and productively within the context of the broader issue of entry to the EEC. Managerial lethargy, restrictive practices, tariffs and the agricultural support system might all prove more amenable in this context. Nevertheless Harold Macmillan, mindful of the fate of Peel, felt it necessary to proceed with the utmost caution. Among his leading colleagues Butler in particular had many reservations on behalf of agriculture and the Commonwealth. For Macmillan himself the Commonwealth was also a sensitive point. Where he felt with many of his ministers that some compromise might be necessary on agriculture in the last resort, the Commonwealth was more difficult. The latter, so Macmillan noted, presented problems that were political, economic, but above all emotional. To a great extent the EEC was still seen rather as an addition to Britain's relations with the Commonwealth, and indeed with the United States, than as an alternative.

Apart from domestic considerations, delicate negotiations were necessary with Britain's partners in EFTA and with members of the Commonwealth. Soundings in June–July 1961 found Australia and New Zealand especially hostile, but the Cabinet felt able to announce its decision to apply for membership on 31 July. The decision had in effect been taken in April, when it was agreed that whatever the short term economic price, the losses in general would be much greater in the long run if Britain remained outside. Nevertheless the state of feeling in the Cabinet, the Conservative party and the country as a whole persuaded the Prime Minister to proceed with care. He may have hoped that such tactics might also improve Britain's bargaining position by persuading the Six that Britain was not over-eager for entry. If so he miscalculated, for the host of reservations on behalf of British agriculture, the Commonwealth and EFTA played into the hands of de Gaulle, who strengthened his position with every delay, and exploited each British hesitation to support his argument that Britain was insufficiently European. The other Five were also less disposed to give special treatment to the British than the latter fondly imagined. The position of the Labour party created doubts in Europe as to whether Macmillan could in fact carry the country with him. There seemed a real possibility that the Conservatives would lose the next election: how then would the ensuing government stand towards Europe? In domestic politics, however, the hostility of the majority of the Labour party could be turned to advantage by Macmillan, as few Conservative MPs would oppose his policies to the extent of playing into the hands of the Opposition.

At the annual conference of the Conservative party in October 1961 a motion supporting the conditional application for entry was over-whelmingly passed in contrast to the earlier Labour party conference. There the emphasis had been on opposition to entry save on the most stringent terms which would include retention of the freedom to use 'public ownership as a means to social progress in Britain'. Duncan Sandys as Minister for Commonwealth Relations strove to still Conservative fears for the future of the Commonwealth by arguing that there was no incompatibility between it and the EEC; indeed membership should increase Britain's ability to play a more useful role in the Commonwealth. But most members of the Commonwealth remained sceptical and particularly at the conference in September 1962 they continued to press their objections. New Zealand had a special cause to fear for her economy, with over half her foreign sales going to Britain. On the other hand most members were finding increasingly diversified markets for their products, even if the EEC did not as yet appear to offer the same openings for their trade as it did for Britain. Macmillan claimed that, taking the conference as a whole, objections to the EEC were couched nearly as often in political as in economic terms. Nor could the Commonwealth states offer a viable economic alternative to the long-term potential of the EEC. The hitherto hesitant Butler had already become a convert in August, arguing that Britain could not let slip so big an opportunity to increase her wealth and strength.

Serious negotiations could not begin between Britain and the Six until after the completion within the EEC of plans for a common agricultural policy. This was an important development leaving the British less room to bargain over the future of their own farmers. Heath's promise of October 1961 that he would seek a long transition period could no longer be met. Farming fears were demonstrated in November 1962 when the Conservatives lost South Dorset through the intervention of an anti-Common Market candidate. The NFU continued to argue that the common agricultural policy would give British farmers less than the current Exchequer grants, which, at £270 million a year, provided about three-quarters of their net income. Some analysts, however, believed that the efficiency of the average British farmer – he was about twice as productive as his EEC counterpart – should ensure a prosperous future. As for the expected rise in food prices for the consumer, these might average only 10 per cent over a possible transition period of six years, not a heavy addition to the cost of living index, especially if real incomes rose. Macmillan was perhaps right to believe that at the last the farming community would prove neither united nor decisive in its opposition to the EEC. Nevertheless the agricultural question may have caused some Cabinet divisions even at the end of 1962, and certainly the lack of Cabinet unity on the EEC discussions as a whole added to the delays in 1962. These also meant that Macmillan and Heath could not pursue the one tactic that their friends in Europe believed would ensure success, namely a bold initiative in favour of entry which would leave most of the detailed negotiation to a later stage. Macmillan persisted in his hopes that de Gaulle's opposition on economic grounds might be bought off with Anglo-French cooperation in foreign and defence policies. De Gaulle, for instance, opposed any federal tendencies in the EEC, and here British support might be attractive. In fact, de Gaulle was convinced he could control the EEC unaided, and that a British presence would add to his difficulties. On defence, too, Britain had little to offer, unless she was prepared to engage in full-scale nuclear cooperation with France. Again its attractiveness to de Gaulle remains uncertain. There would have been problems with Washington. A French proposal for a joint venture to build an isotope separation plant had already been vetoed by the Americans.[12] Anglo-French nuclear cooperation must have ended Britain's profitable nuclear partnership with the United States. At the end of 1962 the British secured American help with the development of a nuclear submarine Polaris force on the most favourable terms. To have turned to France and forfeited such an apparent bargain would have been a great leap in the dark, especially at a time when Macmillan felt in need of a diplomatic coup to boost his prestige within his party. It is unlikely in any case that this Anglo-American agreement did other than confirm de Gaulle in his existing doubts as to Britain's readiness to reduce her currency to 'the modest status of a simple English pound', and to 'moor herself to the Continent'. At the Rambouillet meetings of 15–16 December 1962 with de Gaulle, that is before the Polaris agreement at Nassau, Macmillan claimed that he found the General's attitude 'very intransigent', giving little hope for the future.[13]

There is no need to follow the 1962–3 negotiations in detail. The main difficulties arose over Britain's quest for a long transition period during which subsidies would continue to be paid to British farmers, and over the question of Commonwealth exports to Britain, especially of food from New Zealand. The Six, and notably France, were insistent that

Britain should raise the price of food as soon as possible, and similarly institute levies on imported food. Britain would be required to discriminate against many existing trading partners, including those within the Commonwealth. Edward Heath led the British negotiators with a technical skill that was widely applauded, and he was able to win some concessions for Commonwealth interests by August 1962. But the special problem of temperate foodstuffs, notably from New Zealand, remained, as these competed directly with many EEC products. Some compromise on British agricultural interests did not appear impossible by the end of the year, and there were many on the British side, including Macmillan, who argued that it was the approaching success of the negotiations which precipitated de Gaulle's veto on 14 January 1963. Dr Walter Hallstein, the EEC Commission's President, more guardedly remarked: 'It could not fairly be said that they had failed on technical grounds, or that they were already on the verge of success.'[14] The question of temperate foodstuffs was still unresolved. But there was certainly no reason to suppose that British entry would prove unworkable, and there was widespread dismay among the Five (although some West German ambivalence was evident) when the news broke of the General's veto. The outcome was decided in January 1963 by the incompatibility of French and British interests, notably, but not exclusively, as they were interpreted by de Gaulle, and by the inability of the Five to risk a breach with France. De Gaulle had consolidated his position in France by the plebiscite and elections of October–November 1962, and he was able to rely on Adenauer, despite divided opinions in West Germany.

De Gaulle's veto was an immense blow to Macmillan. He commented: 'All our policies at home and abroad are in ruins.' He could see no alternative to the EEC. If a Commonwealth free trade association were possible it would have developed long ago.[15] Through entry to the EEC he had hoped to find a solution to Britain's faltering economy and world position, and to provide a much needed boost to his party's fortunes. Yet – outside the Conservative leadership – few of his countrymen shared his dismay. The opinion polls revealed again and again the fickleness and superficiality of public feeling on the EEC which for most people remained a mysterious entity sometimes vaguely menacing, sometimes vaguely hopeful. It was not a major issue in the 1964 election campaign. Only the Liberals positively favoured entry, though both Labour and Conservatives promised to seek links with Europe that were consistent with Britain's Commonwealth ties. Office in fact soon persuaded key Labour figures that a different set of priorities was necessary if Britain was to remain a *major* power. Gaitskell had declared in 1962 that Britain could not abandon one thousand years of history. The passage of time suggested that one thousand years of history were abandoning Britain.

Middle East and Commonwealth problems, 1957–63

After Suez the British continued to make concessions when confronted by sufficiently strong nationalist pressures, but the most general impression in Britain was not usually one of retreat so much as of a progression from the role of protector and trustee to that of senior partner. Continued participation in the sterling area by ex-dependent territories, the negotiation of new defence treaties and the maintenance of British bases all served to strengthen the belief of many from both the left and right, however different their standpoint, that Britain still had a major part to play in Afro-Asian affairs. From 1957 to 1964 Britain appeared to enjoy remarkable success in ending colonial relationships without breaking all other ties in the process. Great satisfaction could be felt in the early experience of independence of both Ghana (1957) and Nigeria (1960). The British performance seemed singularly impressive compared with that of France or Belgium. Even where serious problems arose, the course of events encouraged rather than discouraged the sense of commitment.

The Cypriot question, it is true, found Greece and Turkey near to war at the end of 1963. The Zurich agreement of February 1959, which gave Cyprus independence in 1960, was ingenious but unworkable. In the long run only partition and the separation of the two peoples gave any promise of peace. This was not yet feasible. For the British the 1959 agreements were a welcome escape from four years of violence and fiendishly complicated negotiations with Athens and Ankara as well as the Cypriots. The British, once they had decided that self-government in some form would have to be conceded, tried various expedients. But terms that satisfied the Greeks did not satisfy the Turks, and vice versa. The British, for their part, by 1957, were anxious only to secure sovereign bases in Cyprus and could afford to be flexible on political issues. In the end it was fear of uncontrollable communal violence on the island that prompted the Greek and Turkish governments to agree to Cypriot independence, with special safeguards for the Turkish minority. Cyprus became independent in August 1960 and joined the Commonwealth a year later.

Although the emergency in Malaya did not end until 1960, Malaya became independent in August 1957. In October 1957 she entered into a defence agreement with Britain and this was complemented by the continued banking of her considerable foreign exchange surplus in London. The defence agreement which accompanied the grant of self-government to Singapore in 1959 was more extensive, since it allowed Britain to use bases on the island to meet SEATO as well as local Commonwealth commitments. Ceylon in 1956, Jordan in 1957 and Iraq in 1958 withdrew British base rights in their territories, but – with more recourse to air transport and with the use of Cyprus, Aden, Kenya and Singapore – British strategy was little affected. The Duncan Sandys defence review of 1957 in any case put more emphasis on mobile air and sea forces, the manpower cuts making possible the end of National Service by 1962. There were, it is true, a few critics of this strategy, and Macmillan thought it wise to set up an interdepartmental committee to review Britain's world position over the next ten years. It did not report until 1960, and then apparently in an inconclusive compromise statement.[16] The committee suffered from a division into those with a European and those with a global bias. The Foreign Office, the Colonial Office, the Commonwealth Relations Office and the service departments all had differing approaches and priorities. It was consequently easier to drift and make adjustments according to the needs of the moment rather than to try to devise any grand design. The course of events meanwhile seemed to strengthen those who favoured a global role.

The battle for influence was continuing in the Middle East between the great powers, the local states themselves, and often the factions within these states. American fears that the Suez debacle would be followed by communist gains precipitated the Eisenhower Doctrine in January 1957. Aid was offered to all who feared aggression from any nation controlled by international communism. The British welcomed this move, though there were fears later in the year that the United States might over-react to an apparent threat of a communist takeover in Syria. When anti-communist groups in Syria turned to Egypt for support early in 1958 the resultant United Arab Republic intensified the rivalries among Middle Eastern states. Iraq and Jordan drew together, but in July 1958 the pro-British regime in Iraq was overthrown. The political affiliations of Iraq's new leaders were uncertain, and communist influences could not be ruled out. The political situation in Jordan, rarely stable at the best of times, deteriorated, with the Foreign Office believing that it had ample evidence of attempts at outside subversion.[17] The Lebanon had been in a state of political and religious turmoil for some months, events there being followed with great concern in Washington. The position of the West in the Middle East seemed seriously at risk. Yet the British and American governments reacted more out of desperation than conviction. To let matters drift seemed more dangerous than to intervene, especially when faced by requests for help from King Hussein and the President of the Lebanon. Macmillan was careful to keep in step with the United States – indeed the British operation would not have been feasible without American help – and he encountered only half-hearted criticisms from the Labour party. The Soviet Union was less concerned once it was clear that no Anglo-American move against Iraq was intended. Oddly enough, in a rather blundering fashion, the limited intervention helped to cool tempers and apprehensions. Lebanon and Jordan discovered some stability, and complications soon developed in the relations between Iraq, Egypt and Syria.

In 1961 the British-protected sheikhdom of Kuwait became independent, though with a new defence treaty with Britain. Macmillan had recently described Kuwait as the key to the economic life of Britain. It then possessed about 20 per cent of the world's proven oil reserves; it supplied some 40 per cent of Britain's oil needs. In addition, the Kuwaiti Oil Company was half-owned by British Petroleum, and a large proportion of the foreign earnings of Kuwait was banked in London. It was hard to imagine any place outside the British Isles which was of more economic importance to Britain at that time. In the summer of 1961 the unpredictable General Kassim of Iraq reasserted his country's traditional claim to the sheikhdom. Kuwait was highly vulnerable and if Britain were to act effectively she had to do so in advance of any move by Iraq. Forces began to arrive in July. The political situation was also favourable since other Arab states did not look with sympathy on Kassim's ambitions. The threat of crisis speedily disappeared. The British action was probably wise in the circumstances, but this episode, with the effective British intervention against mutineers early in 1964 in the newly independent states of Kenya, Uganda and Tanganyika, at the request of their governments, encouraged the belief that Britain could and should maintain a policing capability East of Suez. Many influential figures, both in and out of government, and of many political shades, were attracted by this prospect. In the early 1960s plans were maturing for the expensive re-equipment of Britain's armed forces to continue this role in the face of the increasingly sophisticated arms at the disposal of possible opponents.

The political geography of the territories bordering the Indian Ocean was being transformed much more quickly than had been anticipated. In the early 1960s serious communist incursions into the region seemed possible, either independently or in association with the nationalists in Indonesia and in the Arab world. Sukarno of Indonesia, Kassim of Iraq and Nasser of Egypt also posed threats in their own right. Yet, apart from Kuwait in 1961, it was East and Central Africa that most concerned the British between 1959 and 1963. The complacency which had begun to return to British policy-makers from 1955, as the Mau Mau threat in Kenya was brought under control, was rudely shaken in 1959. Only in January of that year the Colonial Secretary and the three colonial governors of Kenya, Uganda and Tanganyika had tentatively agreed that they should work to independence for these territories no sooner than the early 1970s. Michael Blundell, leader of the moderate whites in Kenya, thought the envisaged time-scale should make possible the creation of a genuine multiracial state.[18] These plans were soon shattered. First came the coroner's inquest on the deaths of eleven Mau Mau detainees in the Hola prison camp. Brutal treatment at the hands of their warders was the cause. There were further shocks to the nation's conscience when the Devlin Commission reported in July that African opposition to the Central African Federation was widespread in Nyasaland, and that the proclamation of a state of emergency in February had resulted in the creation, 'temporarily, no doubt', of a police state. Emergencies had also been declared in both Rhodesias.

Understandably, therefore, liberal and pragmatic opinion in Britain became increasingly uneasy in the course of 1959. It could no longer be assumed that the British had time on their side in the process of decolonization.

As early as May 1959 Blundell was surprised to find the Conservative Bow Group's views on Kenya more akin to those of Labour's left wing, with one man one vote as an early essential. Macmillan himself appreciated the need for new approaches, given the new trends of opinion within his own party, the Opposition and the country as a whole. He evidently feared that any future colonial emergency which entailed serious bloodshed would find opinion in Britain seriously divided. To Eisenhower in August 1959 he expressed the fear: 'We have our Algerias coming to us – Kenya and Central Africa.' He saw the colonial impulse weakening in other European countries; Britain could not afford to be last in the process of decolonization. He was impressed, too, by the arguments of one colonial governor, who thought that though many colonies were unprepared for independence any attempt to rule them for another fifteen or twenty years would have to be undertaken against the most capable of the local people.[19] At least with independence the popular leaders would learn more about government than they would in prison. Macmillan, however, hoped to do more than run before the storm. He warned Monckton that if the Central African Federation failed, so too would the multiracial experiment in Kenya. He was trying to avert a 'maelstrom of trouble' in Africa, but in saving the Europeans Britain could not resort to the policies of South Africa.[20] With the 1959 election victory behind him Macmillan appointed a new Colonial Secretary in the person of Iain Macleod, a clear indication of his determination to seize the initiative and prevent his government being forced into an untenable position.

Macleod himself agreed that although speedy action was dangerous, a slower pace would be more dangerous still. So convinced was he of this that he was prepared on occasion to move more quickly than his advisers wished. At least in Uganda and Tanganyika there was no significant white presence, so that the acceleration of independence there posed problems of an essentially technical kind – the provision of an adequate administrative cadre. The Tanganyikan leader, Julius Nyerere, had himself in the 1950s been asking for independence only inside a generation, and for some time he thought in terms of a close partnership with Britain. Tanganyika became independent in 1961; Uganda (delayed a little by internal disunity) followed in 1962. Kenya with its sizeable white minority, the shadow of Mau Mau, and tribal rivalries, was more difficult. The white settlers had many friends, especially in the Conservative party, as Macmillan noted a little uneasily at the beginning of 1961.[21] Tom Mboya, a leading Kenyan nationalist, wrote later:

I have had the impression about several Colonial Secretaries . . . that

*they would have come forward with more positive programmes, but
hesitated because of their own back-benchers. Colonial issues only
became hot matters in the House of Commons when settlers went over
and spoke to Tory back-benchers, and then the Ministers were
subjected to heavy pressure. It became evident that the face of East and
Central Africa depended more on the atmosphere inside the Conservative Party than on any logical analysis of the African case as such.
. . . The number of contradictions – the way British Somaliland was
handed independence almost overnight, the way the Wild Committee
provided a liberal franchise for Uganda, a country almost without
settlers – shows that the only consistent factor in the Conservatives'
colonial policy was a yielding to the greatest pressure.*[22]

Indeed, Macleod's efforts to hasten colonial independence brought him
many enemies in his party in the early 1960s. He was consequently
under something of a political cloud in 1963 during the struggle for the
succession to Macmillan. Mboya, on the other hand, paid tribute to his
tactical skill during the highly complex talks over the future of Kenya.
Blundell, though disappointed in the early 1960s to find Macleod more
radical than he then thought wise, later commended him for the
soundness of his judgement. Macleod's biographer, Nigel Fisher, rated
him the best Colonial Secretary since Joseph Chamberlain. Certainly
none had created so much stir, though Macmillan's part in the
accelerated decolonization must not be forgotten.

The passage of Kenya to complete independence was not completed
until the end of December 1963 (Macleod moved to another office in
1961). It was a difficult business. The British remained suspicious of the
most powerful Kenyan figure, Jomo Kenyatta. He was suspected of
extremist sympathies. But the divisions among the Kenyans themselves
were formidable, and the British found it easier to work with the Kenya
African Democratic Union than with Kenyatta's Kenya African
National Union. The ascendancy of the latter only became clear in 1963,
and following independence, apart from the unfortunate affair of the
army mutiny, Kenya achieved more political stability and maturity
under Kenyatta than had been anticipated. Difficulties later arose over
the large Asian minority, but white farmers were either bought out or
settled under their new African rulers.

Conservative sympathies for white settlers also complicated the
government's task in its handling of the Central African Federation,
sympathies that were fully exploited by the federation's formidable
premier, Sir Roy Welensky. By 1959 the Labour party was prepared to
accept the right of any member territory to secede from the federation
should a majority of its people so decide. It was no longer possible to
ignore the strength of African hostility throughout the federation. Both
Macmillan and Lord Home had serious doubts as to its viability in the
spring of 1959. The British government still preferred the federal
solution, and as late as 1962 it was looking for something that might be

salvaged. In 1959 it set up the Monckton commission in the hope, according to Butler, that it would be able to reassure 'Church and the middle-of-the-road opinion at home' that the dominant white minority's interpretation of multiracialism and partnership was becoming more generous, and so dissuade Labour from any firm commitment to dissolve the federation. Macmillan, as we have already seen, was anxious to keep his options open as far as possible. According to Monckton the Premier discussed the question of secession with him during the Commission's inquiries, although supporters of the federation insisted that secession was not included in the remit of the Commission. In fact this issue could not be ignored. The Commission wished to make constructive proposals, but given the state of black and white opinion it could only have recourse to what Monckton described as 'desperate optimism'.[23] It argued that while secession was not possible under the present constitution, this could be reviewed by the British Parliament. The possibility of secession might induce Africans to give the federation a further trial. Other reforms were proposed which might make federation more acceptable to African opinion. When the federal leaders met with British ministers in Lancaster House in December 1960 to demand independence they were firmly told that this was dependent on the creation of governments in the three territories which the Africans would support. But the white determination to cling to power had been strengthened, if that were possible, by recent events in the Congo. The abrupt Belgian withdrawal from that colony had been followed by horrific violence and confusion. It left the British government torn between the dangers of clinging too long to power in a colony and surrendering it too soon.

Parallel with discussions over the future of the federation were complicated negotiations on the constitutional future of each of the three territories. There was a bitter struggle for the ear of the British government between Welensky (with many supporters within the Conservative party) and Kenneth Kaunda's United National Independence party as to who should control Northern Rhodesia. In February 1961 Welensky even made preparations to resist by force any British attempt at armed intervention. One wonders if this threat influenced thinking in Whitehall at all during the later Rhodesian crisis of 1965.[24] The government wavered unhappily at first, but swung steadily towards UNIP from 1962. A conference which produced the 1961 constitution for Southern Rhodesia failed to win African assent. The black nationalists feared that such a constitution, once approved, would be used by Rhodesian whites to secure independence; with independence the whites would be able to act as they saw fit. The Africans insisted on a formula that would provide ultimately for majority rule. In March 1962 R. A. Butler was appointed to a specially created office of Central African affairs to try to resolve these problems, and also to try to relieve the tensions that had developed within the Conservative party. Nyasaland and Northern Rhodesia were allowed to secede, the federation expiring at the end of 1963, and these two territories on becoming independent in 1964 took the names of Malawi and Zambia. Welensky complained bitterly in his memoirs of a British lack of will. His ideas included the formation of an African equivalent of the Baghdad Pact, or CENTO, to resist the spread of communism. It is difficult to imagine any step more likely to facilitate the spread of communist influence. Indeed, the unpalatable truth that Welensky had to face was that there was no good reason for continuing British support of the federation. As Macmillan later reflected:

Had I then realised, or had indeed any of us realised, the almost revolutionary way in which the situation would develop and the rapid growth of African Nationalism throughout the whole African continent, I think I should have opposed the putting together of three countries so opposite in their character and so different in their history.[25]

Harry Franklin concludes, 'The tragedy of federation is that its white Rhodesian architects created the very thing which they wished to avoid, African self-government, with greater speed and with more bitterness than would have accompanied its growth without federation.'[26] It is true that one must accept the difficulty of foreseeing the future. Lord Malvern, the federation's first premier, claimed in 1962 that he had once thought it impossible to produce 'an advanced African'. But the contemporary doubts and hesitations of the British Labour party (and others) over the creation of the federation are worth a thought beside the Conservative predisposition to ignore warnings of impending conflict.

The Conservative leadership was rapidly shedding imperial illusions by 1960. A speech by Macmillan in the Chamber of the old Cape Colony Parliament in South Africa on 3 February 1960 attracted great attention. His prime concern had been to remind South Africans that no nation could live in isolation, and that much as each member of the Commonwealth must respect each other's sovereignty, 'in this shrinking world in which we live today the internal policies of one nation may have effects outside it'. It was thus necessary to say, ' "Mind your own business, but mind how it affects my business, too." ' The sentence, however, which mainly caught the world's eye was more sweeping. 'The wind of change is blowing through this continent, and, whether we like it or not, this growth of national consciousness is a political fact.'

Macmillan's hope that South Africa's membership of the Commonwealth might be preserved, somehow or other, soon became another victim of the 'wind of change'. Less than seven weeks after his speech, 83 Africans were killed and about 350 wounded, mostly as the result of an incident outside a police station at Sharpeville. This strengthened the campaign at the United Nations against South Africa's racialist policies, and it was only with difficulty that a crisis was averted within the Commonwealth in 1960. But South Africa's determination to become a republic gave new opening to her critics since this act had to be endorsed by the rest of the Commonwealth if South Africa were to remain a member. The British government continued to argue that more pressure could be exerted on South Africa while she remained within the Commonwealth, but discussions at the Prime Ministers' Conference in March 1961 resulted in the withdrawal of South Africa. The latter retained her existing economic and defence ties with Britain. The economic links were of great importance to Britain – about half her trade with the African continent at that time was with South Africa. The latter's departure meanwhile brought no relief to Commonwealth racial divisions.

In Britain herself, in 1961–2, there were two important developments. Legislation was passed to control the flow of immigrants into Britain, a necessary measure given the social and political implications of the growing coloured communities. But it damaged Britain's position as the cultural centre of the Commonwealth, and accorded ill with ideals of multi-racialism. Secondly, Britain's move towards the European Economic Community understandably dismayed many members of the Commonwealth for political and economic reasons. It is true that the negotiations revealed how seriously the British government still considered its Commonwealth commitments, while de Gaulle's veto prompted some reconsideration of the Commonwealth's potential, but that exploration, mainly conducted by the succeeding Wilson government, tended only to underline its diminishing relevance to British interests.

The interest of the Labour party in the Commonwealth at this time was quite marked. Bevan had hoped for close cooperation with India, Ghana, Australia and New Zealand in particular – Britain's influence alone was too limited.[27] Gaitskell welcomed the departure of South Africa as a positive gain for an institution that stood for racial equality, political freedom, self-government and economic cooperation. Some of his party, indeed, saw the Commonwealth as a potential internationalist and socialist force in world politics. Great hopes were entertained of a partnership with India, while Canada appeared in a more progressive light following her response to the Suez crisis. Such thinking was reflected in the work of Derek Ingram and Guy Arnold who published respectively in 1960 and 1964 *Partners in Adventure* and *Towards Peace and a Multiracial Commonwealth*. If Labour's opposition to entry into the EEC rested much more on domestic British considerations than on concern for Commonwealth interests, the latter was still given much prominence in the programme which Labour was putting before the electorate in the run-up of the 1964 election. Much interest was displayed in Britain's relations with the Third World and the United Nations, and this extended in some instances to a policing role and the containment of communism. Denis Healey argued in February 1964 that mobile peace-keeping forces would be the most likely British military requirement from the later 1960s.

The government, and some independent commentators too, were showing great interest in such possibilities, and both in foreign and defence policies an intensification in British activities East of Suez can be detected during this period. The Kuwait crisis of 1961, the Sino-Indian war of 1962, the crisis in Laos, the intensification of the civil war in South Vietnam, Indonesian opposition to the formation of Malaysia, all encouraged this trend. Subsequent generations will not easily understand how a nation whose economic situation was far from healthy could have persisted so lightheartedly with long-term commitments East of Suez, especially in view of the expensive re-equipment of the navy and air force which this would entail over the next ten or fifteen years. Admittedly a rapid withdrawal from these regions would have been irresponsible and impractical, but Britain tried to choose a more positive course. It was as if, denied success in Europe, she was seeking compensation elsewhere, intent on proving her continuing greatness. The anodyne outcome of the review undertaken by the Future Policy Committee of 1958–60 has already been noted. The Foreign Office was more accustomed to working closely with the defence ministries than with the Treasury; insufficient attention was paid to economic issues in the conduct of 'high policy', so that in practice the sterling area, a global role, close relations with the United States and the guarded pursuit of a liberal internationalist economic order were all accepted as natural with insufficient counting of the costs.

The 'special relationship' in the early 1960s

De Gaulle's veto in January 1963 made it all the more important that Britain should be able to maintain her 'special relationship' with the United States. One of the ways in which this could be done was through the maintenance of her role East of Suez. Much as the Americans had been disappointed by Britain's failure to enter the EEC they still welcomed a partner in some of their activities outside Europe. British politicians grasped at this opportunity to exert influence or at least to gain a hearing in Washington. In time it perhaps became the main *raison d'être* for British policies in the East. The reality of the special relationship had also been dramatically demonstrated by the Nassau Polaris agreement of December 1962. Its closeness was demonstrated in other ways.

Despite the age gap, Macmillan established a good working relationship with the new American President, John F. Kennedy. Some of the self-confident technocrats in the Kennedy entourage were less impressed. They found the British old-fashioned, Macmillan himself weak and emotional. Macmillan was inclined to exaggerate the ability of Britain to act as a worldly-wise yet cultivated Greece to America's Rome. Personal diplomacy has severe limitations, as Lord Salisbury emphasized in the late-nineteenth century when tempering the enthusiasm of some supporters of Anglo-American partnership in those days. But Kennedy certainly gave the impression of paying due respect to Macmillan's views. David Ormsby-Gore, the British ambassador in Washington, was a friend of the Kennedy family, and this also facilitated communication between the two governments. Anglo-American relations were never again to be so close, and if the two governments did not always see eye to eye it is reasonable to argue that the intimate dialogue maintained between them was at least to the short-term benefit of all concerned. These were extraordinary years in East–West relations, the Cuban missile crisis of 1962 (the most dangerous postwar incident) being followed by some relaxation in tension in 1963 with the negotiation of the test ban treaty. Berlin and a worsening situation in South-East Asia likewise demanded much attention.

From 1960 Macmillan possessed a Foreign Secretary in Lord Home who was not averse to occasional plain speaking in public, supplemented by some flair for diplomacy behind closed doors. He was, at times, too critical of the United Nations for some tastes, and too interested in stability for the sake of stability in Africa. Yet he also worked to reduce East–West tension, and to bring Communist China within the United Nations. He did useful work in the Laotian crisis of 1961 where recent American encouragement of the formation of a right-wing regime had turned into a disastrous failure. Laotian neutralists had joined the communist Pathet Lao, and with support from China these forces were threatening to defeat all America's allies in that country. Given the disturbed situation in South Vietnam and fears of a 'domino' effect through South-East Asia, fears that were not confined to Washington, a dangerous escalation of the crisis seemed possible. British influence was limited, with India carrying more weight with Russia in favour of a compromise. Kennedy, too, was disposed to be conciliatory. Yet it was salutory for Ormsby-Gore in February 1961 to speak out bluntly concerning the bad impression made by the Americans in giving aid to crooked, right-wing gangs in Asia.[28] Some Anglo-American military movements in Thailand were deemed necessary in 1962, but gradual progress was made towards a new, if temporary, compromise on the governance of Laos. One crisis at least had been eased.

The British similarly strove to reduce the tension over Berlin, where East–West relations deteriorated sharply in the second half of 1961. The meeting of Kennedy and Khrushchev in Vienna in June had not been a success, and the building of the Berlin Wall in August was followed by Soviet nuclear tests in the autumn. American military strength in Germany was increased, and Britain was asked to send two extra brigades. Britain, however, was facing both an economic crisis and a general over-commitment of her armed forces. The Kuwait crisis was in progress. There were also divisions in the Cabinet. The service of 9,000 conscripts was prolonged, and an extra division was prepared for despatch to Germany if necessary. But in general little encouragement was given to America's desire to build up NATO's conventional forces to such a strength that a non-nuclear resistance could be offered to any Russian aggression for a period at least sufficient 'to force a pause'. There was also some feeling in Washington that British readiness to negotiate on Berlin in 1961 encouraged Russian obduracy. At the same time much Anglo-American diplomatic cooperation proved possible.[29] There was no question of demolishing the Wall, and Kennedy himself was anxious to negotiate at an opportune moment. The Russian attitude became more flexible from November, and another (brief) breathing space had been won.

The greatest of the postwar crises had yet to be overcome. In the autumn f 1962 Russian missile sites were discovered in Cuba. Despite much speculation no truly satisfactory explanation of Russian motivation has yet been provided. It is not surprising therefore that at the time it was suspected that the Cuban bases were no more than the first move in a more elaborate strategy. A renewed Berlin crisis was among the possibilities. Many in Britain found it hard to understand American concern when so many American missiles and bombers similarly menaced the Soviet Union. This ignored the peculiar circumstances of this case – above all the sensitivity of most Americans on the question of Cuba, an island which was then felt to fall as naturally within the American sphere as Finland within that of Russia. Reason or morality count for little in such circumstances, as the British had demonstrated over Suez. Furthermore, Kennedy had been assured by the Russians that no offensive missiles would be emplaced in Cuba. In these circumstances there was little that the British could do. Yet Kennedy chose to consult Macmillan and Ormsby-Gore at some length during the crisis. In general it would be an exaggeration to speak of British 'influence'. The British were given more opportunity to express their views than might have been expected: they may have contributed a little to the larger pool of ideas, but only because of the openmindedness of the American President. He perhaps welcomed the opportunity to view the crisis from a non-American perspective.

The Cuban crisis, like the Berlin Wall, was a demonstration of the realities of contemporary power politics, and from which the statesmen of the world for a time seemed to learn the appropriate lessons. As if as an earnest of their intention to behave with more restraint in the future, good progress was soon being recorded in the nuclear test ban negotiations which the British had been promoting to little effect since the late 1950s. The Russians accepted the principle of inspection and the main problem in the first half of 1963 was to encourage an adequate response from the United States. Kennedy was later to thank Macmillan for his persistence in the question, and if Britain could not claim credit for decisions which the super-powers alone could make (in the end no amount of British dexterity could bring agreement on inspection and therefore underground tests were excluded from the agreement) moderates in both countries were not strong or self-confident enough not to welcome an intermediary. The partial test ban treaty of 5 August 1963 was perhaps a mixed blessing for Britain. Professor Northedge persuasively argues that it helped to foster British illusions concerning their place in the world.[30] If at the time it seemed a powerful vindication of British possession of their own nuclear force, the occasions when Britain would be able to sit at the top table were running out. Nor did a new Prime Minister's emphasis on Britain's 'independent' deterrent make much impact on the electorate in the general election of 1964. His opponent tended to give the opposite impression – that Britain's days as a nuclear power might well be numbered. By an effective sleight of hand, however, he both united his party and left open the possibility of the retention of the nuclear force for at least another generation. Majority opinion in Britain was content to leave such matters to the experts.

Chapter 9

The transition from Conservative to Labour, 1962-6

From Macmillan to Home

The replacement of seven Cabinet and nine other ministers on 12–13 July 1962 transformed Macmillan in popular parlance from his by then tarnished image of 'Supermac' to that of 'Mac the Knife'. So many dismissals inevitably caused much bitterness, and the strain on Macmillan is reflected in his memoirs. The Prime Minister later explained his action chiefly by reference to his anxiety to launch an incomes policy and to his belief that Selwyn Lloyd was past his best as Chancellor of the Exchequer. It was, however, above all the action of a politician who felt that only drastic measures would save his party at the next general election and that the national interest demanded a bold dash for growth and innovation. By-election defeats, popular resentment over the pay pause, a jaded atmosphere inside and outside the government after nearly eleven years of Conservative rule were the features of the day, though it was some consolation to Macmillan that the Liberals rather than Labour were the main beneficiaries in the first half of 1962. The Liberals were dismissed by the premier as 'purely opportunist' – they stood for nothing and therefore constituted no permanent threat to the ministry.

Much more thought had to be devoted to the economy. The economic rules of the 1950s no longer seemed to apply. Deflation had failed to check wage demands sufficiently. The 'guiding light' of 2.5 per cent was almost immediately broken by the dockers in May 1962 with an increase of 9 per cent. If the general situation in 1962 was little better than in the previous year the economy was nevertheless facing a new phenomenon in which output was static or in decline while inflation continued. In the early summer of 1962 Macmillan devoted a great deal of thought to these matters. He noted on 12 June: 'Roy Harrod thinks the economy is on the decline and should be expanded, but without increasing wages (which merely increases costs). There seemed no answer to *how* this was to be done.'[1]

The premier complained of unimaginativeness in the Treasury. He found only some ministers interested in an incomes policy, and a Cabinet of 24 May 1962 had been hopelessly divided on the subject. Macmillan continued to believe that an incomes policy should form part of an ambitious and comprehensive strategy designed to relieve the economic problems of the country.[2] An incomes policy was needed to remove the unfairness between the public and private sectors – one could not keep hammering the nurses! Yet he was reluctant to seek statutory powers on wages, and hoped that it might be possible to sell a programme of restraint as part of an overall policy of economic growth and social justice. The National Incomes Commission, for instance, might be used to report on 'claims of special importance'. Indeed, 'an open air cure' might be found through a public analysis and debate concerning the problems. This would take time and Macmillan could not forget that his ministry had barely two years to run. His moves to enter the EEC might, if successful, provide one electoral asset, but in the early summer of 1962 he was also impressed by the possible value of a younger team of Cabinet ministers. He had to regain public faith in the progressive outlook of his government.

It was not easy to do this. In January 1963 the EEC gambit failed, and soon after the ministry was rocked by the Profumo affair when a minister admitted lying to the House of Commons concerning his relations with a Miss Christine Keeler. There was some talk of a security risk. Macmillan was a little unlucky, but also a little unsure in his handling of the matter. Britain was still uneasily poised between the moral conventions of the post-Victorian era and the so-called 'permissive' society of the 1960s. The political importance of this 'affair', however, was only marginal, and much more to the point was the continuing pessimism among the public as to the country's future wealth and strength. Arthur Koestler edited the dramatically titled *Suicide of a Nation?* This appeared in 1963, and there were various publications of the *What's wrong . . .?* variety. Parliament, industry, the unions – little escaped the critics. Anthony Crosland wrote of a 'middle-aged conservatism, parochial and complacent', settling over the country. Younger leaders, true professionals, these became the popular panacea. Meritocracy should replace what Koestler had dubbed 'rule by mediocracy'. Popular discontent, which had at first expressed itself as Liberal protest votes, reaching a peak in the Liberals' capture of Orpington in March 1962, at last began to work to the advantage of Labour. In 1963 and for much of 1964 the polls put Labour well ahead.

Nevertheless, as the economy began to pick up in 1963, so, slowly, one can detect a Conservative revival. The party itself showed resilience. As was stated in *The Political Quarterly* in 1961:

If a guiding principle must be looked for it is simply the assumption that the Conservative Party ought to govern and will govern even though there be no other principle to guide it when in power, or to dictate its pattern of revival when it goes through the rare, unnatural but at the same time calcining process of electoral defeat.[3]

Robert Rhodes James in 1972 also described the party as natural rulers whose success was based on their faith in themselves and in their fitness to rule: they were a party that stood for flexibility and realism in a country where the vast majority were not dogmatists. Professor

Grainger in his *Character and Style in English Politics* noted the surprise of some more thoughtful Conservatives at their continuing success in the twentieth century, especially from the 1930s when so many forces favoured the left, including much of the language of political science and still more of sociology. Thus it was 'only because of *reliable performance* that a party which has so long persisted in giving authority to an inner circle within a class can continue to expect to have the business of government confided to it by a mass electorate'.[4] Certainly the party had had a remarkable run of success since 1900. It had spent almost three-quarters of the period in office, by itself or in coalition. Yet enough has surely been said in previous pages to show how fortune had favoured the party in, for instance, the 1950s, and how serious were the doubts of its more sensitive leaders concerning their real hold on the electorate.

The Bow Group, founded in 1951 as a sort of Conservative Fabian Society, and acting since then as a research and discussion body, felt that the party was still not adapting itself quickly enough to the conditions of the second half of the twentieth century. The group's journal, *Crossbow*, in its enthusiasm for modernization, was impatient with old debates about classes, the role of the state, or illusions concerning British greatness. Growth, efficiency, success, these should be the aims. As for the state, the only question was not whether it had a role, but what kind of role it should play. In fact the party's new-found enthusiasm for 'planned growth' encountered few significant critics. Enoch Powell was already actively opposed, but many businessmen had become at least partial converts. So strong was the return to the emphasis on the role of the state that public expenditure by 1963 once again absorbed about 41 per cent of the gross national product (as in 1951, and this time with much less devoted to defence) compared with the lowest postwar proportion of 36 per cent in 1958.

This flexibility and determination to hold on to power helps to explain the capacity of the Conservative party to survive the major political crisis that accompanied the resignation of Harold Macmillan in the autumn of 1963, and under the somewhat improbable leadership (in the context of the early 1960s) of an ex-member of the House of Lords, to come close to victory in the 1964 election. What was seen by many as yet another triumph for the old 'inner circle' within the party was nevertheless accompanied by an impressive revival of Conservative fortunes. Macmillan, following the Profumo affair, had been rated the most unpopular Prime Minister since Chamberlain in 1940. He had lost his worldly image and suddenly appeared shy and out of touch. Inwardly, too, he had his doubts. Some younger ministers were looking for a new leader, but were divided among themselves as to the succession. Macmillan claims that it was only on 7 October 1963 that he finally decided to soldier on until after the next election. Twenty-four hours later he was in hospital facing an operation which he wrongly anticipated would require too long a period of convalescence to enable him to remain in office. The leadership question had come to a head just as the party was assembling for the Blackpool Conference. The timing could hardly have been more unfortunate, and the Prime Minister decided to exercise a close watch over the selection of his successor from his hospital bed. Had it not been for recent legislation, the Peerage Act of 1963 (brought about in particular by the determination of Anthony Wedgwood Benn that he should not be forced to succeed his father in the Lords), Macmillan believed that Butler would have become premier. But now that peers could disclaim their titles (this seemed only fair in itself and logical after the institution of life peerages in 1958), Lord Hailsham made a bold bid for the leadership. It was too bold for many of his cabinet colleagues and Conservative MPs, whatever the enthusiasm of many of the constituency rank and file. Even so Butler (and Maudling) did not make much impact at the party conference, and it was in the highly improbable surroundings of Blackpool that the aristocratic fourteenth Earl of Home began to emerge as the most promising candidate.

Home had had a useful if unremarkable career before 1960. He had served under Neville Chamberlain, but any shades of Munich had been easily cast aside, especially when he had subsequently shown himself a critic of rapid decolonization (especially under Macleod) and as broadly satisfactory to the right wing of the party on foreign policy. In 1960 Macmillan had defied recent political convention by making Home Foreign Secretary, the first peer to hold that post since Lord Halifax in 1940. The appointment was generally criticized, even ridiculed, but within a year *The Times* reversed itself to rate Home one of the most successful ministers in the government. Home was popular in the Foreign Office – the best since Bevin according to some officials. He had a reputation both for plain speaking and common sense.

Macmillan organized a poll of the Cabinet, peers, MPs, and the executive committee of the National Union. He claimed in his memoirs that he was surprised to find Home the preponderant first choice. Not a few in the party were dismayed and critical. Macleod thought nine in a Cabinet of twenty favoured Butler with eleven opposing Home. Yet Lord Dilhorne spoke of an overwhelming consensus for Home. The Chief Whip, Martin Redmayne, insisted that all four groups consulted preferred Home, though there was only a narrow majority among MPs. Much probably depended on the weight given to the degree of opposition voiced against each candidate. Here Home certainly stood to gain. Significantly the Conservatives never used this system to choose a leader again. Once the choice was known, on 18 October, Hailsham, Maudling, Macleod and Powell all rallied behind Butler. Further support seemed possible, and both Macmillan and Home recognized that the latter might be unable to form a government. Within twenty-four hours, however, Butler had given way, putting party unity ahead of personal ambition. In the end only Macleod and Powell held aloof, Macleod protesting against the continuing dominance of the 'magic circle of old Etonians'. Many outside Conservative ranks shared this feeling, and found it hard to understand the bias against Butler. For too many Conservatives, however, Butler was insufficiently right-wing, too subtle, or perhaps too indecisive.

The new Prime Minister renounced his peerage to become Sir Alec Douglas Home. He correctly reminded the leader of the Opposition that the latter was, in a way, as much the fourteenth Mr Wilson as he himself had been a fourteenth earl – neither had been able to choose his father. 'Are we to say that all men are equal except peers?' Nevertheless Sir Alec found it hard to escape from his past, partly from his own manner, but mainly because so many were determined that he should not be allowed to do so. A lighthearted remark that he did his 'sums with matchsticks' unfortunately misfired, while the promise of a 'donation' to pensioners was a bad slip. Television was not kind to him, and it had now become the crucial medium of communication with the electorate. Nor was Home's expertise in and preference for foreign affairs an asset at a time when the nation was absorbed in domestic questions. Yet the Conservatives came closer to victory in the election of October 1964 than they could ever have dared to hope under any leader in 1963. How much they did so because of or despite Home is not readily assessed. What is clear is that Home was never entirely at his ease as leader of the Conservatives. He blossomed as an elder statesman once he had relinquished the leadership.

Home's ministry followed basically the policies already initiated by Macmillan. It did pass one controversial piece of legislation, the abolition of resale price maintenance. This was designed to increase competition in the retail trade, and it was undertaken very much at the behest of Edward Heath, the Secretary of State for Industry, Trade and Regional Development, despite the opposition from within the party and despite its unpopularity among small traders, one of the traditional bastions of the Conservatives. The Act affected about 40 per cent of consumer spending: it encouraged and was assisted by the spread of supermarkets. It was at least one blow against rising prices.

The shadow of the next election dominated this shortlived government. Home's two predecessors as premier had enjoyed some freedom of choice concerning election dates. He had virtually none. There was little chance of victory in the first half of 1964, a time when the Chancellor of the Exchequer would have preferred an election on the ground that it would be easier to take corrective measures over the balance of payments in the autumn, should that prove necessary.[5] The budget of April 1964 increased taxation by £100 million, which according to *The Economist* of 18 April was only a quarter of the sum required to slow national growth from 6 to 4 per cent, as was the Chancellor's intention. 'Many people are already complaining that this budget was too lenient.' True precision was, of course, impossible, but with an anticipated balance of payments deficit there was something to be said for *The Economist*'s argument that a rather tougher budget would have been salutary psychologically. The Opposition, however, was unsure what line to adopt, while Brittan recorded that even some very senior Treasury administrators were fearful of any move that would revive business fears of 'stop-go'. Some thought the economy likely to slow down of its own accord in any case.[6] The true scale of the balance of payments difficulties was not appreciated until the summer of 1964. Obviously had there been a spring election, and the return of a government with a working majority, corrective measures could have been taken more easily and perhaps to better effect. Nevertheless Brittan concludes that the crucial question in 1964 was not the handling of the economy that year by the Chancellor so much as the whole economic strategy that had been developing since 1962. Once this strategy had been adopted its only chance of success lay in the readiness to adopt exceptional measures to carry it through, of which the most obvious would have been devaluation or import restrictions. To this one might add that it would have been more reassuring in the longer term had the government shown some interest in reducing the burdens borne by the British economy, such as in overseas defence spending, the international role of sterling, foreign investment, and through a more selective approach to government spending at home. Fundamental changes of this type could not be implemented quickly, but it was disturbing to witness the lighthearted way in which the government assumed new commitments in the early 1960s and failed to re-examine old ones. In this perspective an earlier election in 1964, even with a decisive result in favour of either party, might only have marginally improved the situation and merely postponed the day of reckoning.

The revival of Labour

The close-fought battle that restored Labour to power is worthy of careful examination. Chance and negative considerations determined the outcome quite as much as any renewed popular faith in Labour, yet, as in 1951, given so narrow a margin of victory, even small contributions by the winning party were significant. Labour's fortunes in the early 1960s had varied dramatically. After the 1959 election, as we have seen, it was almost as if a large proportion of the party, both right and left, were bent on political suicide. Labour's weakness was reflected in Liberal strength up to 1962, so much so that for a time the Liberals had hopes of the formation of a new radical party or of some realignment of the left-centre forces in British politics. Alternatively an election deadlock between the two main parties might leave the Liberals in a position of critical importance. The British electoral system, however, continued to discriminate against the Liberals, giving them no chance to prove themselves more than a useful ginger group.

The successful battle against unilateralism greatly enhanced Gait-skell's standing as a politician: this and other Labour feuds had also impressed many in the party with the perils of disunity. The evidence of the polls was clear, and in Gaitskell's last months as leader the Liberal challenge faded and Labour's recovery seemed assured. The divisive question of entry into Europe in 1962-3 was handled with some skill. Gaitskell's death in January 1963 might have reopened serious rifts in the party, but there existed no obvious candidates around whom a new battle of the left versus the rest could consolidate. Support of the left for Harold Wilson did not preclude his drawing from other elements in the party. The remaining Labour MPs were at first divided in their support between George Brown and James Callaghan. Wilson secured a lead on the first ballot and won on the final vote by 144 to 103 against George Brown. The party had elected a leader who, though ostensibly left of centre, and with less direct support than Gaitskell, could in fact bridge party differences more easily than one with more commitments. For some time to come Wilson was in the happy position of making decisions which the left would not readily have accepted from another (they could accept them from him as necessary preliminaries in a long-term campaign) while the rest of the party welcomed them as victories for what they conceived to be realistic democratic socialism. Only in time did doubts develop as to the direction in which Wilson was leading the party. Some wondered whether he was leading it anywhere.

Wilson was probably better equipped than Gaitskell to consolidate party unity and to appeal to the broad spectrum of political opinion from left to right. Certainly he won more popular support according to the polls. He was not afraid to use the word socialism, but skilfully linked it with the modernization of the economy. He clearly understood the muddled thinking but deep feeling that permeated much of the Labour party. A little insight into the rank and file can be gathered from a 1961 study of the determining influences in the lives of 110 MPs.[7] The best-remembered author was Shaw, followed by H. G. Wells and G. D. H. Cole, and only then by Marx. Among recent books, whose impact seemed limited, those of Galbraith, Crosland and Strachey were most mentioned. Of early personal influences Keir Hardie and Lloyd George were the chief figures, the latter for his political style, not his politics. These findings suggest a party moved more by instinct than by theory.

Wilson had long been cast as a future power in the Labour party. He had proved himself both as a civil servant and minister by his early thirties, but it was only in Opposition that he really developed as a debater. He was critical of capitalism for its inefficiency and failings rather than on grounds of principle. He described himself as 'a British Socialist', by which he meant the rejection of 'dead Marxian generalisations about the proletariat . . . (as well as) aristocratic patronisings about "the people" '. Although Wilson had resigned at the same time as Bevan in 1951, he had been careful to argue his case on pragmatic grounds, and he entered the shadow Cabinet when Bevan resigned in 1954. Wilson's connections with the left of the party consequently remained ambiguous, with a mixed appearance of fortuitousness and expediency. From 1955 he distinguished himself several times as a politician who was more concerned with healing party wounds than debating over the finer points of political theory. As a politician he still had much to learn in 1963, but whatever his future mistakes he was sustained by remarkable resilience and tactical fertility. His critics, and they were many, revealed as much of their own limitations in the course of their attacks as they did of his weaknesses.

In terms of a party programme various ideas were beginning to form in the early 1960s. The renewed national interest in planning fitted in well with the party's predilections. There was also growing emphasis in Labour thinking on science and technology, and it was not difficult to blend these with planning and a greater role for the state in the economy. A NEC document published in 1963, *Labour and the Scientific Revolution*, could be read by the left as denoting new interest in public ownership and initiative, and by the centre and right as a pragmatic bid for modernization. Crossman applauded this bridging of party differences with science-based socialism to make men masters of technological change. Editorials in *The New Statesman* took the same line, enthusiastically acclaiming scepticism, science and reason as the high road to socialism. Vernon Bogdanor thought much of the party's enthusiasm for science mere sloganizing,[8] and Crossman later confided in his diary that the party had only 'very half-baked plans' for most of its objectives.[9] It was not difficult, in fact, to attract attention with vague general statements as to how Britain's problems could be solved. In 1958 J. K. Galbraith had attracted much attention with his attack on public squalor amid private affluence. Labour in turn made much of democratic planning for the public good. The decay of the welfare state, capital investment and industrial development, it was asserted, all must be reversed. More regional and urban development was required, plus an expansion of public transport, youth and education services. Conservative activity in these fields was already considerable, but did not reassure opinion in the way that Conservative 'affluence' had won votes in 1959.

Labour, following its 1959 defeat, had paid more attention to research into the composition of the electorate. The work of Mark Abrams in the early 1960s appeared to discredit the earlier Labour belief that its main problem was to mobilize its traditional supporters – with their full support victory would be assured, or nearly so. Abrams concluded that the solid Labour vote might constitute no more than 35 per cent of the electorate. If the Conservative vote was smaller, Labour strategists clearly had to pay more attention to the uncommitted or 'target voters'. It was found that these tended to sympathize with the Conservatives on defence and nationalization, but to look to Labour on housing, education and welfare. The uncommitted were unmoved by political ideologies, but were critical of 'stop–go' and were looking for strong leadership to promote economic efficiency and growth. As the election drew near Labour concentrated its main energies on the target voters in marginal constituencies. Certainly it succeeded in winning an unusual amount of middle-class support in the 1964 elections, though working-class backing fell away a little.[10]

The 1964 election

If Labour's programme in 1964 really contained nothing very new, Wilson contrived to make it sound so. Ministries of Technology and of Economic Affairs were promised to spearhead a second British industrial revolution. The revisionist social democrat parties in Scandinavia and West Germany could be cited as successful undoctrinaire examples of modern socialism. Labour's programme was well received by the press. Even forward-looking industrialists who were interested in 'planned growth' appeared to feel that a Labour government would not necessarily prove unacceptable. The Conservatives remained on the defensive, and presented a rather tired look after thirteen years in office. *The Sunday Times* commented on their 'Old Guard' appearance. The party tended to rely on memories of the 1930s, with warnings of possible setbacks under Labour rule. The Prime Minister showed a misguided faith in public interest in the so-called 'independent' deterrent. The government hoped for a quiet election, and on the whole fought a less professional and competent campaign than Labour.

There were almost four million new voters compared with 1959: nearly half the electorate had been put on the register since 1945. Britain was more affluent in 1964 than five years earlier, but expectations were rising faster. In 1955 and 1959 electors tended to compare conditions with austerity under Labour; in 1964 they tended to ask why things were not getting better even faster. Furthermore, although the public mood is not easily measured, it would seem that where critics and rebels had found it difficult to dent the contentment and conventional outlook of the majority for much of the 1950s, they now had a more receptive audience. There was less deference, more impatience, more insistence on quick results. If there were any new gods they were those of reorganization and rationalization, of efficiency, professionalism and youthful aggressiveness. There was emerging 'an autonomous and militant youth culture'. Jobs on the whole were not difficult to find for the young: if many were unattractive, one could often change. The younger generations were thus more self-confident, less respectful, and better placed than their predecessors to spend money on leisure and luxuries. There were many who were quick to exploit this comparative affluence, and there thus began to emerge the 'swinging London' of the 1960s, from 'pop singers' to young fashion designers. Superficially it was an age of youthful classlessness and colour.

Anthony Sampson, between the 1962 and 1965 editions of his

Anatomy of Britain, commented that in only three years an era had ended – the world wars and empire seemed to belong to a past age. Almost everyone was anti-establishment. 'Reverence and stuffiness are out of fashion', he concluded. Satire and impudence were weakened only by exhaustion from the frenzy of energy devoted to them in 1963. Christopher Booker went further and argued that the years 1963–4 were a divide between those who, like the 'angries', however sensational, had still been interested in real life, and those who now sought 'a kind of faery world where nothing seemed really to matter'.[11] The fantasy world of radio's *Goon Show* in the 1950s gave place to the cruder iconoclasm of *That Was The Week That Was* (1962) on television, while in print *Private Eye* from 1961 developed new dimensions in investigation and criticism. Yet one should beware of appearances. As Norman Shrapnel commented in *The Guardian* of 7 January 1963: 'The current satire cult has bitten home all right, rather in the way that a blunt hatchet might sink into a log of soft wood. . . . It changes nothing. Nobody – and this is the crucial point – expects it to change anything.' Macmillan professed himself mildly amused by some of the attacks. He was more troubled by the increasingly cynical mood of the public as a whole, especially of the young and the better educated among them. If President Kennedy embodied for him much that was hopeful in the emerging new world, there was another side he did not like or understand.

If politicians soon learned how to handle the most aggressive of television interviewers, the general effect of the satire, irreverence and cynicism was to lessen such mystique as still surrounded individuals and institutions. Even royalty was not immune, and had indeed been exposed to attack since 1957 in ways unknown since the nineteenth century. In general, however, the monarchy proved flexible and resilient while yet retaining more mystique and majesty than the last of the European royal houses. The Duke of Edinburgh introduced enlivening touches of humour and abrasiveness. Meanwhile there was no great 'cause' to distract from the cults of satire, youth and novelty. CND was in decline, and Vietnam was yet to come. In the early 1960s the Young Socialists made some impact, but if they imparted vigour to sections of the Labour party, their political thinking and activities were often liabilities. The many-shaded left, indeed, was divided over the basic trends in mixed economies of the British kind. Some complained that working class and intellectuals alike were becoming the willing slaves of technological society, and were ensnared by its comforts. Others believed that any equilibrium within such a society could not last; destabilizing forces must in time open the door to drastic change. Moderate socialists welcomed this society as one in which gradual, non-revolutionary social progress could be achieved.

Britain, in practice, did not fit easily into any of these categories: the improvement in living standards, though widespread, was not universal; the improvement, though appreciable, was not sufficient to generate either the inertia feared by some, such as Herbert Marcuse, or the degree of restraint and unselfishness demanded by moderate reformers to complete the orderly transformation of society. There were sharp regional differences, and there were also large pockets of poverty even in the most affluent areas; high rents in such areas could be especially damaging. Crosland in *The Conservative Enemy* (1962) showed more awareness of poverty than in his previous work. If the growing comprehensiveness of welfare provision helps to explain why weekly allowances under National Assistance had almost doubled since 1949 – also the sharp increase in the number of pensioners – there was no room for complacency on this issue. Labour could win votes here, or at least encourage abstentions among former Conservative supporters.

Housing had also become a major issue once more. Increases in population and internal migration account for the acute shortages of housing in some areas. In the later 1950s there had been some contraction in local authority building. The Rent Act of 1957 failed to stop the decay of much privately rented property, and it was only in 1964 that the government provided a large-scale stimulus to council and housing society building with a new Housing Act. This came too late to recapture for the Conservatives the good reputation they had previously enjoyed in this field. But the election did not merely centre around obvious hardships. Labour had to make an appeal to those whose life style was improving and who were anxious that this should continue to be the case. Eighty-five per cent of the population now had television; over 50 per cent had washing machines; about 44 per cent were home-owners. Holidays abroad were no longer the preserve of the well-to-do; 7.5 million cars crowded the roads. Prosperity of a sort was reflected in the rise of the hire purchase debt from £369 million in 1957 to £900 million in 1964. Apart from the rising earnings of many manual workers, the balance of employment was also changing, with manual jobs between 1951 and 1966 remaining static at a little below 14.5 million and with a small shift in favour of the skilled and semi-skilled within that figure. In contrast white collar employment increased by 2.5 million to nearly 9.5 million. Less than half the population, it seemed, thought of themselves unequivocally as working-class, and more than a quarter of the electorate in any case voted outside their own class (by academic definition). Detailed studies of the electorate by Butler and Stokes[12] between 1963 and 1966 found only about two-thirds of the sample thought of themselves in class terms and under half expressed very strong attachment to a party. Gallup polls discovered that up to half the people in their samples could see little difference between the two main parties (only one-third had thought thus in 1959).[13] In the circumstances of 1964 this could only help Labour, if merely in the sense that it facilitated abstentions to the detriment of the Conservatives.

Although the 1964 election aroused much interest, one of its most significant features was the relatively low poll. The victors, Labour, secured 10,000 fewer votes than in 1959, and only a marginally higher share of the poll. The Conservative suffered the biggest drop in postwar support by either party – almost one and three-quarter million votes. Liberal strength interestingly increased – a sure sign of hesitancy on the part of the electorate. There was an unusual number of regional variations, and overall no decisive swing to Labour occurred. The latter finished with a meagre four-seat majority over all other parties, and a lead of only 200,000 votes over the Conservatives. Labour appeared to win mainly through a loss of confidence in the former government, helped by its projection of itself as a united party with flexible and forward looking views concerning the future of Britain. It was to Labour's advantage where it merely persuaded former Conservatives that they could safely abstain.

There was another new dimension to the 1964 election: the question of coloured immigration, mainly from the West Indies, Pakistan and India. No accurate estimates existed of the number of non-white people living in Britain (800,000 was a popular figure) but the actual numbers were less important than the spreading belief that coloured immigrants were adding to the housing shortage, were a burden on the welfare services, and were competing for jobs. The first legislative controls on immigration from the Commonwealth had been instituted in 1962 The impact of this issue on the 1964 election is by no means certain, but it may account for three Conservative gains in the west midlands (these took place against the national electoral swing).

Labour and the 1964 economic crisis

The election of 1964 was placed in its proper international perspective when the announcement of the results was dwarfed by the first Chinese nuclear test (16 October) and the fall of Khrushchev (15 October). The new government, however, quickly demonstrated that in its approach neither to foreign nor to domestic affairs was it any more ready than the previous administration to take a hard and critical look at the realities of the nation's situation, or at least to accept the full implications of any such study. In so far as it took steps to relieve the problems, it took at least as many if not more to worsen them. Whether a larger majority, and the prospect of a longer spell in office would have encouraged more realism must remain speculative, but certainly the probability of another election in the near future encouraged the pursuit of short-term advantages.

No party had tried to govern with so small a majority (the first and second Labour ministries had been in special positions as minority governments). At one stage its majority was reduced to a single member. In the middle of 1965 the Liberal leader, Joseph Grimond, spoke of a possible deal with Labour – a move which antagonized some of his colleagues and which Wilson ignored. Coalition or political arrangements were unthinkable to the party after the trauma of 1931, and indeed after its experience of dependence on Liberal votes in 1924 and again from 1929. Labour must govern alone or return to Opposition. Nor could it merely act as a caretaker government; this would not have been tolerated by the party rank and file. There must be movement towards a more 'socialist' society however much members might disagree on their definition of socialism. Nor would it have been wise electorally. Labour could not afford a revival of the political atmosphere of the 1950s when the Conservatives had flourished as the party with the reputation for greater competence, nor could it risk forfeiting its claim to be the more effective party of reform and modernization. Its victory in 1964 had been based essentially on popular disillusionment with the Conservatives, but on so narrow a margin that it was government on approval.

For many of those eighteen months of precarious survival between the elections of October 1964 and March 1966 the government was in grave danger of losing popular favour simply on the grounds of doubts as to its competence to govern. In economic policy it at first appeared highly accident prone, however much this was cushioned by a considerable public readiness to believe that the fundamental economic crisis had been the responsibility of the previous government. The new Cabinet was desperately short of experienced ministers. Only Wilson himself had been in the Cabinet; only two of his team had had senior ministerial experience, one of whom, Patrick Gordon-Walker, was lost to the government as Foreign Secretary when he failed to win a seat either in the general election or at a by-election in January 1965. Nevertheless his ministry contained several figures of great promise: George Brown, temperamental but uniquely thrusting and imaginative; James Callaghan, not at his best at the Treasury though clearly blessed with a tough and shrewd political mind beneath a usually relaxed and amiable exterior; and Barbara Castle who, if too volatile for the very highest posts, proved the outstanding woman politician of the postwar era before Margaret Thatcher and Shirley Williams. Roy Jenkins and Denis Healey were also successful ministers if sometimes lacking a sureness of touch in the rough and tumble of politics. Meanwhile in 1964-6 the slender majority acted as valuable cement in a party so prone to internal divisions, though it also meant that two Labour back-benchers were able to frustrate the government's first bid to nationalize steel: the critical parliamentary debate took place on 6 May 1965. The personal strains and tensions were also considerable, and George Wigg thought the toll of office in these circumstances diminished the Prime Minister's capacity to take and act on decisions.

There has been much debate over the seriousness of the economic crisis inherited by Labour in October 1964 and the degree to which it was worsened by the errors of the Wilson ministry. Samuel Brittan's conclusion, however, seems eminently reasonable:

One of the few near-certainties of recent history is that if Mr Maudling

*had remained Chancellor, he would have had to face the same choice
between devaluation and relying solely on a much more deflationary
internal policy, which confronted the Labour Government.*[14]

Maudling had in fact made preparations for the introduction, if
necessary, of import controls and other defensive measures. From the
middle of September 1964 the signs of a major balance of payments
crisis were increasingly evident, and a deficit of £700 million or more
was expected. A week after the election Maudling conceded in *The
Sunday Times* that 'the time may now have come to introduce import
quotas, surcharges or export subsidies'.[15]

The government's most pressing aim should have been the
maintenance of foreign confidence to avert a run on sterling. Long-term
policies might give some hope for the future, but only if sensible short-
term measures provided a foundation. Various options were to hand
concerning the balance of payments deficit, of which the most attractive
theoretically was devaluation. With hindsight many, including ministers, have joined such contemporary advocates of that solution
as the chairman of the EEC Monetary Committee and the OECD's
Secretary-General. Not all economists, however, were then of that
opinion. There was disagreement as to the price competitiveness of
British exports and how quickly resources could be switched to take
advantage of openings provided by devaluation. Much would also have
depended upon the reaction of other states – how many and which
would have devalued as well. It would have been a blow to the holders of
sterling, and would have been bitterly opposed by the United States.
Indeed George Brown believed in 1964 that with American aid the
British economy could quickly be restored to health. Wilson, according
to his memoirs,[16] saw more difficulties through devaluation than
opportunities at that time. If he described these more in economic than
political terms, it was the latter which should have given him most cause
for thought. As Andrew Graham and Wilfred Beckerman argue: 'Those
who assert the pound sterling should have been devalued in 1964 know
their economics but not their politics.'[17] Always there was Labour's
slender majority and the need for another election. Devaluation might
have been presented as an inevitable consequence of Conservative
'mismanagement', but such a gambit would have been highly
unpredictable in its consequences. Devaluation could still have been
seen as weakness by the electorate, especially once its costs were
appreciated. It would have been hard to maintain the government's
'tough' and 'dynamic' image. It may be doubted whether the ministry,
even with a large majority, would have ventured on devaluation in 1964.
Among many opponents would have been the Treasury, and also the
City with its concern for the international role of sterling.[18]

It is still difficult with the evidence to hand to decide how far the
government's first moves arose out of over-confidence that it could
avoid both devaluation and deflation, or out of fear for the political

consequences if it chose either. The picture drawn in the Crossman diaries[19] suggests both, though with a heavy bias in favour of initial innocence and euphoria. Callaghan (the Chancellor of the Exchequer) and sometimes the Prime Minister showed more caution. The seriousness of the economic situation did not strike Crossman himself until 22 November. The government was under constant pressure from backbenchers to raise old age pensions. Crossman notes the recurrent preoccupation with the policies needed to win the next election. This obsession was unfortunate. None of the government's promises to modernize the economy had much bearing on the immediate economic crisis. An untried ministry had to win foreign confidence, yet it envisaged increased public expenditure despite a balance of payments deficit of what then seemed alarming proportions.

From the outset decisions and events interacted with damaging results. Wilson rejected import quotas as too blunt an instrument – based on his earlier experience at the Board of Trade. Instead a 15 per cent import surcharge (save on food and raw materials) was introduced without due regard for Britain's international obligations. On 11 November a mini-budget announced both higher taxes and welfare benefits. There were vague references to capital gains and corporation taxes. All these steps were bad for business and foreign confidence, if understandable in the light of Labour's philosophy. The deflationary elements in the budget were obscured, and subsequent government moves were slow to reverse first impressions. The bank rate was raised in vain on 23 November. Within the government and Labour party there were suspicions that the City of London might be feeding the fears of foreign investors and speculators, and indeed before the end of the year the gloom and defeatism of the City had earned rebukes from both *The Sunday Telegraph* and *The Sunday Times*. Crossman, however, accepted in a diary entry of 12 December that the ministry's policies were in part to blame, and Wilson later accepted that the Cabinet for too long was guilty of underestimating the impact of speculators on sterling.[20] Yet lessons were not readily learned, and even in 1966–8 the government continued to experience the utmost difficulty in viewing the economy through the eyes of nervous foreign holders of sterling. Much of the value of the Macmillan, Wilson and Crossman records lies in their revelation of the time and nervous energy devoted by politicians to the parliamentary-electoral battle rather than to what the simple layman might think would be the main concerns of government.

By the last weeks of 1964 there was a disturbing and damaging lack of confidence in the relations of the Cabinet with the Governor of the Bank of England, Lord Cromer. The latter pressed for massive public expenditure cuts, especially when a rise in the bank rate on 23 November achieved nothing. The Prime Minister asked whether foreign speculators should be allowed to overrule the British electorate and insist on Tory measures under a Labour government. The Governor might have talked of the difficulty of implementing Labour measures in a western world with a largely 'Tory' outlook. But faced by a premier who now threatened another election (or a floating pound) Lord Cromer turned to the Central Bankers and was able to raise a three billion dollar loan on the 25th. The situation was momentarily stabilized though at the cost of the largest 'rescue' operation yet attempted by international and other bankers. The government had already damaged that disposition of some at least in the City and business to view the election of a Labour government with an open mind.

There was even little real substance in one of the government's much vaunted triumphs at the end of year when George Brown secured a Joint Declaration of Intent on prices, profits, incomes and productivity from leaders of both employers and employees. The dream of constructive cooperation in these matters between government and both sides of industry soon faded. Disappointments also followed the creation of the Department of Economic Affairs under George Brown. Such strength as it possessed was due to its ebullient Minister, but it was fatally crippled from the outset by persistent economic crises which guaranteed the age-old dominance of the Treasury. Wilson himself saw the DEA and Treasury as complementary, but this, too, was unreal, for the Treasury could not concentrate on short-term and financial problems to the exclusion of long-term questions and physical resources. These were too much bound up with the balance of payments and domestic demand. The result was overlapping responsibilities and much uncreative tension between the two, with the Prime Minister arbitrating or deciding in the last resort. In time Brown's energies were mainly concentrated on incomes policy and not on economic planning. Douglas Jay in the *Political Quarterly* for 1968 believed that in so far as an effective economic overlord had ever existed, this had been confined to the period when Cripps had been able to combine those powers with the office of Chancellor of the Exchequer. He had been further assisted by his personal influence over some other departmental ministers. The DEA was a haphazard creation, but this was only an incidental cause of its failure.

The 1966 election

The government's popularity was at a low ebb for much of 1965. The economic breathing space won at the end of 1964 was shortlived, a poor set of trade figures announced in May 1965 triggering off another run on sterling. On 27 July the government was obliged to make a number of economies. It also introduced tighter credit and further aid to exports. Even so in the summer of 1965 Washington expressed doubts whether more aid would be forthcoming from the Central Banks unless Britain had more than a voluntary incomes policy. In British industry as a whole wage costs per unit of output had long been rising faster than among her main rivals. George Woodcock of the TUC warned Brown in December 1964 that he must not expect too much from the unions concerning wage restraint under the Declaration of Intent. As Labour had found with its foreign policy and the Soviet Union from 1945, so now it discovered in its relations with the unions over wages, left cannot necessarily deal with left. A government white paper, *Machinery of a Prices and Incomes Policy* (Cmnd 2577) of February 1965, was followed in April by the institution of the National Board for Prices and Incomes under the chairmanship of a Conservative politician, Aubrey Jones. This replaced the NIC. The NBPI itself lacked teeth, having only the powers of a royal commission, yet being expected to deal with low wages, pay differentials, and productivity deals – all within the confines of a new pay 'norm' of 3 or 3.5 per cent. The outcome, not surprisingly, was disappointing. Between October 1964 and July 1966 hourly earnings rose more than twice as fast as output per man hour and well ahead of the intended 'norm', and ahead too of retail prices.

The Prime Minister was among the critics of British unions, and not only on the question of wage claims. He had been impressed by the strategy of some American labour leaders, such as Walter Reuther of the American Automobile Workers whose approach included the idea that unions must be prepared to try and force inefficient firms to modernise themselves, and so be in a position to pay higher wages. Reuther even had his own efficiency experts. Wilson was highly critical of the outdated rule-books of many British unions, and of the persistence of restrictive practices. The AEU rule-book, he later insisted, should be consigned to an 'industrial museum'. Some union leaders shared his concern, including over the dangers of a wages free-for-all. Confused bargaining between George Brown and the TUC early in September 1965 led the latter to institute an incomes policy committee which was to be informed of all wage claims by affiliated unions. The committee could do no more than discuss wage claims with union leaders. Union leaders who feared that inflation could lead to independent government action, unemployment or damage to the social services had also to be wary lest they were outflanked by militants if they spoke too strongly in favour of wage restraint. Moderates argued for loyalty to a 'workers' government'. Meantime inflation hit hard at those without strong unions to protect them. In July 1965 it was estimated that up to a quarter of a million families, although the father was employed, were living below the National Assistance minimum. Indeed, some economists argued that the relative cheapness of much British labour encouraged its wasteful use by employers, but such arguments were of academic interest in the mid-1960s when the government feared for the competitiveness of British goods abroad. But it was not easy to check the accumulated momentum of years in which expectations had constantly risen. Efforts to help the lower paid or to encourage productivity could provoke disputes over traditional wage differentials. Professor V. L. Allen commented that unions had taken on the competitive nature of their environment: if they were to maximize their returns they had to play the market by what they thought the market would bear even if, in consequence, they competed with each other in a wasteful, self-defeating struggle.

The government, not surprisingly, in addition to the TUC's vetting scheme, intended to proceed with its own plans for statutory powers on wages and prices in the longer term, and the promise was a necessary prerequisite for the additional aid supplied to Britain by the Central Banks on 10 September. For the time being the speculators against sterling were beaten back, but with over three million votes being cast on 8 September at the TUC conference against the proposals both of Brown and Woodcock it was evident that difficulties would soon recur. Cecil King, the press magnate, recorded on 18 February 1966 that Harold Wilson was talking of the need for an early election to secure the passage of the envisaged 'early warning' legislation without which the government's prices and incomes policy would remain ineffective.[21]

September 1965 also saw the publication of the government's National Plan, the fruit of much labour by the DEA. The Plan envisaged a growth rate of 3.8 per cent per year for the period 1964–70. It was not a sophisticated econometric exercise, and relied heavily on the replies from firms as to their probable courses of action in the light of the government's promise of a 25 per cent expansion of the economy over the rest of the decade. Its basic figures, indeed, were 'political' rather than economic in that they were calculations of what the government hoped would happen, and that through projections of this kind firms would be inspired to take appropriate action. Among the drawbacks of the Plan, according to Brittan, was the encouragement it gave to the delusion that alternatives existed to a radical effort to get to grips with the nation's balance of payments problems. The NEDC, it is true, showed some interest in the possibility of an altered exchange rate to encourage exports, but the Plan referred only to cuts in government and private spending overseas, and made much of the hope of a steady rise in exports. More attention should in fact have been given to the actual outcome of the 1963 projections by the NEDC in which exports, the production of steel, coal and motor vehicles had all fallen below expectations, whereas imports had exceeded them. Frank Brechling and J. N. Wolfe had commented most perceptively early in 1965 on the outcome of the previous government's bid for growth. Too rapid a cyclical upswing could create bottlenecks and structural maladjustments. 'These cause a lengthening of delivery dates and a rise in prices which, in turn, encourage imports and discourage exports. . . . One might also conjecture that some of the increase in imports induced by domestic bottlenecks is irreversible.'[22]

The Plan, indeed, was obsolete before it was published, given the government's earlier deflationary moves: these entailed changes in the business calculations used by the DEA. Subsequent economic crises and government changes of policy from 1966 removed any remnants of life. Its failure was implicitly acknowledged by the government when its successor, *The Task Ahead* (1969), proved no more than a cautious discussion document. But the full extent of the nation's economic difficulties did not become clear until after the election of March 1966. For the time being the ministry was able to cling to a neutral economic policy, real incomes were rising, and there was little unemployment. World trade was growing so rapidly that rising unit costs in British industry for the time being were of less consequence than usual. Wilson's cautious handling of the Rhodesian crisis reassured the public, and the government's standing with voters generally improved. In the early months of 1966 all the psephological omens were favourable. Wilson therefore set 31 March 1966 as the date for the election. Crossman thought it none too soon as fresh economic problems seemed imminent.[23] The timing of the election found the Conservatives ill-placed to fight. They were still trying to regain momentum after the setbacks experienced since 1961.

The Conservatives were far from united as to future policies. If this might be concealed in an election campaign, it nevertheless contributed to the feeling of many Tories that victory was improbable. At one extreme were those who believed that no radical departure from the policies of the Macmillan era was necessary. But the main pacemakers in the party were those who argued for radical change and reappraisal. Edward Heath as chairman of the Advisory Committee on Policy soon had thirty policy groups at work. Their labours resulted in the policy document, *Putting Britain Right Ahead*, which was approved by the party conference in October 1965. Market research was undertaken to gain a clearer picture of the electorate, and to try to find out how to present the party and its programme in the best light to the voters. There was also the question of the party leadership. After the 1964 general election Home had set up an inquiry into ways in which the leader might be elected. It was no longer enough that a Conservative leader should 'emerge'. By February 1965 it was agreed that there should be a straight vote by MPs.

Home's position at first seemed secure. But he did not distinguish himself as leader of the Opposition whereas Heath was making a name for himself as a debater on economic questions, a field in which the Prime Minister was much feared by the Opposition. Pressures for a change consequently mounted, and Home stepped down. The election took place in July, and was contested by Heath, Maudling and Powell, the latter standing so that strong supporters of the 'free market' might make their presence felt. Maudling's association with the 1964 deficit damaged his chances. It was even suggested that his election might not be well received by foreign bankers. Even so he polled 133 votes against Heath's 150. Powell received 15 votes. Heath's margin of victory was thus fairly narrow. Nor did he prove as effective a leader against Wilson as had been anticipated. He showed less skill than Macmillan in searching out and exploiting the divisions of the party opposite. He was not without problems within his own party, where the Rhodesian issue found the Monday Club and Lord Salisbury ranged against Sir Edward Boyle and the anti-Smith Tories. The Conservatives were badly divided over the government's decision to impose an oil embargo on Rhodesia. When this was debated in the Commons on 21 December 1965, Julian Amery and forty-seven other Conservatives voted against the government, thirty-one voted in support, all in defiance of Heath's desire to abstain. Earlier, at the party conference in Brighton in October, Powell had caused consternation among many Conservatives when he questioned the long-term value of Britain's bases East of Suez. He argued realistically that in time the Asian states must themselves establish their own local balances of power. Home was given his first opportunity to display his gifts as an elder statesman when he intervened later to explain that the Conservatives in office would allow no political vacuum to develop in the East that might menace western interests. But he also declared on 26 April 1966 that he expected Britain's role East of Suez to be mainly that of an air-sea power in the future.

A significant gap separated the views of Heath and Powell on the degree to which the principles of the free market should be accepted. Heath was less concerned with theory: his prime concern was with efficiency in pursuit of which a flexible attitude to the role of the state was necessary. He advocated lower direct taxation, trade union reform including the establishment of industrial courts with legal powers, a new approach to the social services with more assistance being given to those who were mainly in need, and with more of the burden of the services being directly placed on employers (this might also lead to a more efficient use of labour). In general he wanted to see more emphasis placed on competition and incentives. Many Conservatives now saw their party's policies before 1964 as too paternalistic and as contributing factors to the sluggish British way of life. *Putting Britain Right Ahead* publicized the swing away from the Conservatism of the 1950s, but the party was far from united on these matters. There was no complete rejection of national economic planning. The hardening of feeling against incomes policies was not universal, and in the 1966 election manifesto, *Action Not Words*, emphasis on competition was toned down when research among the electorate discovered an adverse reaction to the more extreme proposals.[24]

The party's image among the general public remained largely the one fashioned by the last few years in office. It was a party that many thought to be stuffy, stagnant, out-of-date and upper-class. It was still associated with the pay pause, unemployment, and the neglect of the educational and social services. Labour's slogan, 'You *Know* Labour Government Works', received more credence than the government's performance strictly deserved. Heath's popularity, according to a poll in February 1966, stood below that of Home and far below that of Harold Wilson. The Conservatives could do little more than hope that their new programme – their most direct challenge to Labour since 1945 – would begin the long process of educating the public into new modes of thought and interest. In fact the Conservatives, in the whole Heath era from 1965 to 1975, never showed themselves particularly adept at capturing the imagination of the public. Managerial efficiency in industry and government was not an attractive subject in itself, imperative though it was, while drastic modernization could hurt many people from trade unionists to small shopkeepers and businessmen. In their bid for the votes of the people of the centre the Conservatives were continually reminded of their heterogeneous composition, including those who might be described as 'the gearbox of an increasingly technological society' and others who felt themselves its victims. Iain Macleod noted in 1965 that it was one thing to proclaim efficiency, but what of the inefficient and the failures in life? He might also have added, what of those who were more interested in stability than in change?

The Conservatives proved vulnerable during the 1966 election campaign to the charges that their programme would entail 'union-breaking', 'dear food' (through the proposed ending of food subsidies), and the revival of the 'means-test state'. No other issues attracted persistent attention, though Heath and his colleagues might have derived some academic satisfaction from the fact that their analysis of the state of the economy was soon shown to have been much more accurate than that provided by the government. The election itself ended on a low note with the smallest relative turnout of voters since 1945. Labour just managed to top 13 million for the first time since 1951, an improvement of 800,000 on 1964, and representing almost 48 per cent of the votes cast. The Conservative vote fell by 600,000 (to 42 per cent), and the Liberal vote even more. Various tests of opinion by the pollsters suggested that enthusiasm for Labour was fairly circumspect, but disillusionment with the other two parties was still more evident. The outcome for the Liberals was especially disappointing since less than a year before they had held high hopes of at last recovering a position of real influence in British politics. They now faced another four or five years in the shadows. In January 1967 Grimond resigned the leadership. The Conservatives were half-resigned to defeat before the results were known, though their worst result since 1945 was not an encouraging start to their bid for a long-term recovery. Labour was continuing to attract the younger voters, and had perhaps won a majority of the female vote; if so, this was for the first time. The nightmare days of a tiny majority were over with 363 victorious Labour candidates about to return to Westminster. In fact new and worse nightmares awaited them.

Withdrawal on all fronts

Deflation, 1966–7

Labour's electoral victory in 1966 was almost its only cause for satisfaction in the later 1960s before its own illusory political recovery early in 1970, based on a temporary strengthening of the British economy. Both at home and abroad the Wilson government suffered one blow after another to its ambitious hopes. Finally not even severe deflationary packages could ward off devaluation at the end of 1967, while these same economic constraints remorselessly compelled a reluctant ministry to abandon its pretensions to maintain a world role for Britain. A bid to join the EEC was also defeated by de Gaulle. It was a dismal record after the great expectations and grand promises of 1964. Labour charges of thirteen wasted years under the Conservatives from 1951 were beginning to rebound.

The government was in trouble from the moment of its electoral victory in 1966. The Treasury pressed hard for a deflationary budget, but Wilson, Callaghan and Brown were dismayed by the prospect of an immediate retreat from their election assurances concerning the state of the economy. A new tax, the selective employment tax, appeared to provide some cover for the discomfited ministers. It was presented by the Chancellor of the Exchequer as an instrument to discriminate in favour of manufacturing as opposed to the service industries. Scarce labour, it was argued, would be pushed into manufacturing where it was most needed. It would be a useful weapon in the battle for growth. Nevertheless there was a deflationary motive behind it also: it seemed an ingenious alternative to obviously harsher measures. In practice its brief life (until ended by the next Conservative government) was a controversial one. Certainly it failed as a deflationary measure in 1966. The seamen's strike (which began on 16 May and lasted until July) and the publication at the end of June of a bad set of trade figures for the first quarter brought a new collapse in foreign confidence.

On 3 July the Cabinet lost its Minister of Technology, Frank Cousins. He resigned when the Cabinet persisted with a Bill requiring advance notice of wage and price increases. If necessary their implementation would be postponed while their merits were investigated by the Prices and Incomes Board. Cousins argued that strong price controls would force firms to control their wages. The rest of the Cabinet thought this impractical. Cousins's resignation carried government and unions further apart as the run on sterling was accelerating. The drain was not checked when the bank rate was raised to 7 per cent on 14 July. The government was at last being driven to accept that overriding priority had to be given to righting the balance of payments. In such circumstances some ministers at last began to consider the possibility of devaluation. George Brown states in his memoirs that he had been slowly changing his mind since 1964. His advisers in the DEA had been arguing for some time that the National Plan was unattainable so long as Britain tried to defend sterling at $2.80.[1] By July 1966 the government could no longer pretend that by any ingenious strategy it was possible to reconcile the current high level of public spending and general level of demand in Britain when output was rising by a mere 2 per cent a year – and there were signs that this rise was tending to level off. Unemployment was low and still falling. A sharp increase in exports was indispensable, but could not be forthcoming without some cut in home consumption or such a cut in the value of sterling as to make exporting highly profitable. Imports had to be discouraged either by suppressing home demand or by devaluation. Brown preferred devaluation to a massive deflationary package. Other ministers reluctantly began to see that one or the other was inescapable. According to Richard Crossman, Wilson's economic advisers, Kaldor and Balogh, had been urging devaluation since July 1965. A year later he thought nearly all the government advisers in favour of floating sterling. He and Crosland favoured devaluation or a floating pound, and the Chancellor himself appeared to show some interest.[2] The Prime Minister, however, once he was sufficiently impressed by the Chancellor that a decisive choice must be made one way or the other, chose deflation, and this was agreed at a critical Cabinet meeting on 19 July. At the same time it appears that Wilson offered some assurances that future consideration would be given to the circumstances in which some new approach to the exchange rate might be attempted. George Brown remained bitterly critical, and talked of resignation. Colleagues reminded him of the damage that would result to the government and perhaps to the economy. Brown stayed, but he was so dismayed by the Cabinet's decision that he was able to insist on a switch of offices with Michael Stewart, the Foreign Secretary, soon afterwards.

The government's cuts of July 1966 were the harshest since 1949, and soon brought about a rise in unemployment. Any lingering hopes in the National Plan were destroyed. The cuts marked the end of the expectation of politicians of both parties, and of many businessmen and academics, that through some element of indicative planning the British economy could be quickly and dramatically reinvigorated. Emergency measures announced on 20 July included decreased bank lending, hire purchase and building restrictions, increased taxes, government cuts, and a £50 foreign travel allowance. A six-months standstill on prices and wages was announced, to be followed by six months of severe restraint. Wilson countered trade union protests with warnings that the alternative was still more stringent deflation, though some relief for the lower paid was promised. By the end of July Britain was more heavily in debt than ever, though the Bank of England was working skilfully with the Federal Reserve Bank of New York and others to persuade speculators that Britain could still raise any loans needed to avoid devaluation. Public opinion, however, swung swiftly against the government, and as early as 14 July Plaid Cymru had captured Carmarthen from Labour in a by-election. The nation found what consolation it could in England's victory in the World Cup on 30 July.

In this situation Labour fears of a 'bankers' ramp, easily developed. A great electoral victory was being robbed of its power. In fact the motivation of the speculators and others was narrowly economic, and was based on technical judgements concerning the parity of the pound, the balance of payments, and the state of the economy. Sir Leslie O'Brien, Governor of the Bank of England from 1966, and others, had reason to wonder whether Britain's ability to borrow so heavily was truly in her interest, since it encouraged only halfhearted measures in response to each crisis.[3] Might it not be said that the foreign bankers, in their concern for the maintenance of the current parity of sterling, were being too kind? If there was a political dimension in the affair it sprang from government policy. Wilson's arguments against devaluation significantly included the need to work with the United States. The Crossman diaries are full of suggestions that in this period the Anglo-American relationship was one of the greatest determinants of Wilson's policy; sterling, Vietnam, the British presence East of Suez, Rhodesia, British influence in Washington were all part of a complicated package. In particular devaluation might have damaged the dollar and injured what standing Britain still enjoyed in Washington.[4] Thus, although there certainly existed many fewer arguments against devaluation in June–July 1966 than in November 1964, the psychological and political obstacles were still considerable. It should have been clear, however, that these political pretensions in world affairs were no longer realistic. In so far as sterling was defended for political reasons for another sixteen months it was wasted effort. This was probably the greatest single mistake of the Wilson ministries, and one for which the Prime Minister himself would appear to have been particularly responsible.

The summer of 1966 was one of profound disappointment for all who were deeply interested in politics and economics. Lord Robbins in the House of Lords on 28 July attacked intellectuals for fostering the belief in 'growth without discipline, stable prices with unrestricted demand, over-full employment without inflation and balance-of-payments difficulties. With the war in Vietnam also arousing fierce criticism, Britain was moving into an atmosphere in which the revolt against authority, established practices and ideas could swiftly gather further momentum. Indeed affluence and technology would be denounced by some as false gods. Widespread disillusionment with two governments within two or three years meant that there could be no steady swing back to the Conservatives as after 1947. The young tended to move further left, or to leave conventional politics altogether. In Scotland and Wales the nationalists provided an obvious outlet. By the autumn both unemployment and short-time working were increasing as the government measures began to bite. The tax bill alone had been increased by some £800 million to try to divert more goods abroad. Government references to overmanning and the need for more productivity provoked the trade union leader, Jack Jones, to comment: 'The Government got the productivity and the workers got the sack.' Unfortunately for the government, there was not even enough of the former, so that the hopes at the beginning of 1967 that the nation's deficit on current account was being rectified once again proved illusory.

The 1967 budget was basically neutral, though with government spending continuing to rise the inflationary pressures were still strong. Yet unemployment reached its highest figure for twenty-seven years in July 1967. Trade union protests both against unemployment and the continuing government efforts to restrain wages increased, while there was much restlessness and discontent within the parliamentary Labour party. The massive majority in the Commons inevitably gave backbenchers more freedom of action. Furthermore, most of the new intake were middle-class professionals, full of ideas, and less amenable to discipline than the average trade union member. The Prime Minister later commented on their unusually independent character. He also found them hard to categorize, their place in the political spectrum varying from issue to issue. Many shared a common impatience with parliamentary procedures. The government was thus singularly ill-placed. Any appearance of an improvement in the nation's economic situation would trigger off pressures for a policy of reflation, the effect of which must have been a new balance of payments crisis. If the economic situation worsened, further deflation was politically un-thinkable. The Middle Eastern war and the dock strike in the summer of 1967, though obviously damaging could not have been of decisive importance in these circumstances. In fact the British economy was already in trouble before the Arab–Israeli war closed the Suez canal. *The National Institute Economic Review* of February 1968 concluded that in the previous year 'the underlying performance . . . was rather weaker than usual'. The government was not forced into devaluation by bad luck. It is difficult to see how devaluation could have been avoided – if not in November 1967, then a little later. Nevertheless, before the economic crisis at the end of the year is examined, it is desirable that a survey should be made of British relations with the rest of the world in this period.

The Wilson government and Anglo–American relations

Although Britain was to be one of the initial signatories of the Nuclear Non-Proliferation Treaty of 1968, she was rapidly ceasing to enjoy an automatic right to join in the deliberations of Russia and the United States. As their relations tended to ease so they stood in less need of an intermediary, especially one whose claim to a special position above all other second-class powers could no longer be justified in material terms. Labour's hopes of a great expansion of British trade with Russia and eastern Europe were also disappointed. There was some unspectacular progress with Romania, both in trade and certain other contacts. Romania ended the jamming of BBC broadcasts in 1964, while Britain lent some discreet support to that country's bid for greater independence within the eastern bloc, especially after the Czech crisis of 1968. But in 1970 the eastern states as a whole were involved in no more than 4 per cent of Britain's trade.[5]

British relations with the United States became much less intimate, contrary to the desires of the Wilson government. Its leading ministers appreciated that without considerable American backing Britain's pretensions as a world power would have little meaning. For them, when they took office, any significant retreat from Britain's global role was unthinkable. The party's equivocal stand on Britain as a nuclear power was soon dropped. The Nassau Polaris agreement was not renegotiated, though only four, not five submarines were built. For a time Britain was troubled by American efforts to establish some kind of European mixed-manned nuclear force, but in 1967 this was dropped in favour of new nuclear planning arrangements within NATO. It might have been expected that de Gaulle's growing separation both from the United States and from NATO would have enhanced British influence, but economic and social needs cut into British defence forces, which were overstretched by world commitments until the end of the decade. Britain became more active in NATO only from 1968, following the decision to abandon the East of Suez role, but in so doing drew closer to her European allies rather than to the United States with its Vietnam preoccupations.

The American struggle against communism in Vietnam caused the British government many embarrassments, and was one of the main causes of the weakening relationship. The Wilson ministry inherited their predecessor's fear of the spread of communism in South-East Asia. In December 1962 Macmillan and Kennedy had agreed that Communist China seemed to be emerging as the main threat to world peace. The war between India and China in 1962 was followed by some Labour interest in a new defence relationship with India, possibly including a nuclear dimension. But India's next dispute was with Pakistan (which left Britain an embarrassed spectator on the sidelines), while American conduct in Vietnam by 1965 was provoking the criticism of many more than the habitual British critics of the United

States. The Americans, in their determination to prevent a communist victory in South Vietnam, found themselves increasingly obliged to intervene directly given the failings and divisions of the anti-communist forces in that country. In 1965 the United States began to bomb North Vietnam – which was assisting the communists in the south – as it began to resort to almost any means to stem the communist tide. There was growing talk in Britain (and elsewhere) of American aggression and of American support of a reactionary regime against a people wishing to be free. As early as March 1965 Crossman recorded the growing concern of many Labour MPs, and he wondered if the issue might not prove as divisive and damaging to the Wilson ministry as had the Korean War to Attlee in 1951.[6] The Cabinet, to some extent, accepted that a communist takeover in South Vietnam might menace other states in South-East Asia, but over and above that it recognized that Vietnam could not be separated from other issues in Britain's complex relationship with the United States. Some measure of British support for American policy in Vietnam was necessary in view of the current dependence of the British economy on American financial support. Subsequent British efforts to exert economic pressure on Rhodesia also required American backing, and so too to some extent did their presence East of Suez. In December 1964 the British had secured something of a *quid pro quo* when President Johnson had agreed on the importance of both countries' military efforts 'in support of the legitimate governments in South-East Asia, particularly in Malaysia and South Vietnam'. The United States had not initially looked with much favour on British support of Malaysia in its dispute with Indonesia.

In practice over Vietnam Wilson had to trim uneasily between American and party pressures. He wrote later of an attempt by the Foreign Office in March 1965 'to get me to take a much more committed pro-American line on bombing in Vietnam. I refused.'[7] Generalized support for American policy was maintained, coupled with criticism of some particular actions. Wilson's recurrent efforts to mediate between the United States and North Vietnam were in part designed to satisfy his own party, and there could be no question of meeting the American desire that some British forces should be sent to South Vietnam. These balancing tactics were not wholly effective. The Canadian premier noted President Johnson's annoyance with British policy in April 1965, and there were many subsequent sharp complaints.[8] At home, too, the government was under fire. One singularly ill-fated attempt at mediation arose out of a Commonwealth conference in June 1965, though it may have helped ease the Prime Minister through meetings where several participants were determined to put pressure on him over the future of Rhodesia. There was another major effort in the winter of 1966–7 in conjunction with the Soviet Union to try to arrange a cessation of American bombing of the North and further reinforcement of the South in return for a secret ending of infiltration of forces into the

South by Hanoi. The Permanent Under-Secretary in the Foreign Office, Gore-Booth, thought the Russians genuinely interested, but there was a last minute change of heart by Washington. He doubts, however, and it would seem with good reason, whether any real progress could have been made towards a cease-fire in Vietnam at that stage.[9] Vietnam was the scene of too desperate a struggle to be resolved by diplomatic ingenuity.

The increasing coolness in Anglo–American relations over Vietnam was for some time cushioned by the American interest in British policy in the Middle East and the Indian Ocean. The Americans had no wish to establish a significant military presence of their own in these areas, and they welcomed a continuing British presence. Indeed, Sir Philip de Zulueta believed that the main external pressure on the British to remain East of Suez by the 1960s came from Washington – much more so than from British business interests.[10] Crossman recorded the Defence Minister's assessment of American policy on 11 December 1964:

Healey replied that what they wanted us to do was not to maintain huge bases but to keep a foothold in Hong Kong, Malaya, the Persian Gulf, to enable us to do things for the alliance which they can't do. They think our forces are much more useful to the alliance outside Europe than in Germany.[11]

The Americans were showing some interest in the joint development of Indian Ocean island bases, if this would ease Britain's defence problems, for while at this stage the Wilson government required no prompting to stay East of Suez, the costs were considerable, and the turmoil in Aden was a reminder that the local peoples might not always welcome a British presence.

The east of Suez debate

The early years of the Wilson ministry were marked by several sweeping claims concerning Britain's world role and interests even if there was an intended element of rhetoric in the Prime Minister's assertion of 10 July 1965 that 'our frontiers are on the Himalayas and in the standard of living of the people of India'. At the same time, from the early 1960s, there was the beginning of a debate, extending to official circles, as to how much longer Britain could or should maintain bases, or even a military presence, in the East. There was a tendency to rely more heavily on air and seaborne forces, and perhaps in time to depend mainly on bases in Australia, South Africa, and among the islands of the Indian Ocean. The Conservative ministries before Wilson were concerned about costs. Terence O'Neill found Douglas Home in May 1964 speculating on the value of foreign bases, and even wondering whether chances had been missed to make friends with Egypt.[12] The Foreign

Office was thinking on similar lines, but Britain and Egypt were still cast as rivals in southern Arabia as the British struggled to retain their surviving toeholds in the Middle East. With the loss of facilities in Kenya (as that country moved to independence in 1963) the British turned to Aden. In 1962–3 the colony of Aden was attached to the British protected sheikhdoms of the hinterland. Anti-British forces, however, were already gathering strength in Aden, and in 1962 a revolution took place in the Yemen. The Egyptians supported the anti-royalist forces in the ensuing civil war. Macmillan hoped for a royalist victory, though he felt some embarrassment at backing 'reactionary and really rather outmoded régimes'.[13] He saw a republican victory in the Yemen as only the prelude to a general collapse in the British position in Aden and perhaps in the Gulf.

Unrest continued to mount in the federation. The Wilson ministry at first explored the possibilities of a new political settlement. In February 1966 it decided to evacuate the base within two years. It hoped to disengage leaving an independent South Arabian federation that would prove friendly to Britain. The federated sheikhs vainly begged for promises of continuing British military support, but it seems unlikely that the federation would have survived for long, even with British backing. As it was, despite British military operations into 1967, the power of the sheikhs rapidly disintegrated, and the radical nationalists were able to set up their own independent state of South Yemen at the end of the year. The closing of the Suez canal and the defeat of Egypt in the Six Day War with Israel in 1967 meant, however, that British interests were not damaged by the outcome. Egypt was henceforward too preoccupied with the recovery of the canal to pursue an active policy in the Arabian peninsula, and some slow progress could at last be made towards a better Anglo-Egyptian relationship.

When the British decided to pull out of Aden it was not at first intended to leave the Gulf as well. Circumstances soon pointed to a different conclusion. Important as the devaluation crisis was at the end of 1967 in speeding an almost total withdrawal from East of Suez, the Six Day War in the summer had already demonstrated the inability of British forces in the Middle East to prevent the interruption of oil supplies. British forces could operate effectively only where the local political situation permitted them to do so. Indeed, their presence could be counterproductive: they could provide a focal point for local discontents. British oil interests seemed best protected by the acumen of the companies, and by the skills and services which they could offer the Arabs. As far as the political stability of the area was concerned, this would depend increasingly on local circumstances, and especially on the growing strength of Saudi-Arabia and Iran.

Further east a large, and in this case successful, military operation was also followed by an early evacuation. In September 1963 the federation of Malaysia, made up of Malaya, Singapore, Sabah (ex-British Borneo) and Sarawak came into being with British encouragement. The federation concluded a defence agreement with Britain. A mutually profitable relationship was anticipated. Unfortunately differences between the Chinese of Singapore and the Malays worsened, and in 1965 Singapore left the federation. More serious were the efforts of Sukarno of Indonesia to destroy the federation *in toto*.[14] His motivation was complex. The uncertainties of these years must be recalled, with nationalist aspiration running high, with fears of neo-colonialism easily aroused, and with Communist China emerging as a new but unknown quantity in Asian affairs. The government of Sukarno was anxious to consolidate its influence in the region. Its use of force against the federation, however, remained hesitant: merely a modest level of infiltration across the borders. A large British military presence also acted as a deterrent to any escalation of the conflict. British land units were actively engaged in Borneo, and the Indonesian probing operations were skilfully contained, partly by well-calculated military responses, but also through the inability of the Indonesians to enlist any significant support within Malaysia itself. At times it seemed as if the campaign would drag on indefinitely. The cost to the British Exchequer was considerable. Patience and restraint were finally rewarded in 1965-6 when internal dissension in Indonesia brought about a change of regime and a gradual restoration of peace.

'Confrontation' with Indonesia did much to awaken the Cabinet to the dangers of open-ended commitments east of Suez. Crossman's impression of 14 February 1966 was that the Defence Committee favoured the evacuation of Singapore by 1970 and the maintenance of only a limited British role in the East in the future.[15] The Prime Minister, however, was reluctant to act precipitately and was concerned too for his relations with the United States. He had also to think of Britain's Commonwealth partners in the East. Even so 'confrontation' was less a demonstration of Commonwealth cooperation than might be imagined, for both Australia and New Zealand sent aid only when they were convinced of American support should Indonesia prove too strong for the British to handle. Britain's military presence east of Suez had already become a matter of debate at home, with Powell as Conservative shadow Minister of Defence joining Labour and Liberal critics in 1965. Among leading defence analysts, Alastair Buchan thought Britain should withdraw within the next five or ten years. Backbench Labour unrest was evident on the subject in 1966, and in the course of that year and the early months of 1967 the government decided to evacuate Singapore by the mid-1970s. Mobile forces were to be retained to intervene in an emergency.

There were attacks from both sides of the House of Commons on this halfway solution. Paul Gore-Booth testifies to the tension within the government itself. There were persistent fears within the Foreign Office lest defence cuts should prove so extensive as to necessitate the repudiation of political commitments. The main theme in policy-making was, 'as ever, finance', and the conflict between foreign, defence and financial considerations caused 'moments of great bitterness which endured until 1968'.[16] Nevertheless it must be emphasized that the long-term defence projections inherited by the Wilson government were unrealistic. There was little that could be done to reduce commitments before 1966. What was disturbing was the Cabinet's tendency to make long-term cuts in the strength of the armed forces without making sufficient adjustments to the nation's commitments. Consequently it was fortunate that they were compelled to face stark realities by the economic crisis from November 1967. Only then did they make a firm decision to abandon the Persian Gulf and Singapore by 1971 and to give up any specific capability for military operations east of Suez. Small forces would continue to operate and train in the area, and larger units might be sent according to circumstances. George Brown, the Foreign Secretary, continued to argue that insufficient time had been allowed for the rundown, while the conversion of both Wilson and Healey, the Defence Minister, to this conclusion had been slow and hesitant. Yet any other decision would have been heavily dependent on good luck for Britain to have escaped the embarrassment of military failure or renewed burdens in defence expenditure. Good fortune, as it happened, accompanied and facilitated the withdrawal.

There was sharp criticism of the decision from Washington, Australia, New Zealand, Singapore, some Arab sheikhdoms and from many Conservatives. Coupled with American resentment over British policy on Vietnam, the decision to pull back from east of Suez greatly reduced Britain's standing in Washington. Conservative talk, while in opposition, of modifying the withdrawal lessened with the approach of the 1970 election, and in practice the Heath government carried through Labour's intentions with only marginal alterations. From the later 1960s as Britain made further bids to join the EEC it was vital that her defence policy should be increasingly centred on Europe. Given American distractions in Vietnam, and the development of renewed doubts in Europe as to how firmly the United States would continue to commit itself to NATO, not to mention the growing strength of the Soviet Union and the fears prompted by its intervention in Czechoslovakia in 1968 and more generally in the Mediterranean, Britain had good cause to give priority to her European commitments. Defence cuts might afford some relief to Britain's ailing economy, and they were also politically vital in the winter of 1967–8 if Wilson was to win acceptance from his Cabinet and party of the other measures that were deemed necessary to follow the devaluation of sterling. As the Prime Minister later commented: 'There was no guarantee that we could get a package of the required scale through the Cabinet, let alone through the Parliamentary party.'[17] Defence cuts came first in his statement to the Commons on 16 January 1968. Champions of Britain as a world power were dismayed, but the heavens east of Suez did not fall when the British props were removed – others were already bearing the burden.

African crises and the Commonwealth

Events in Africa were also demonstrating the passing of Britain as an imperial power. With the collapse of the Central African Federation in 1963, white-settler hopes were concentrated on Southern Rhodesia, which was already self-governing. Independence was demanded in March 1963, but the British government was not satisfied that the 1961 constitution gave adequate protection to Africans. Ultimate majority rule was not assured. Macmillan observed that to grant independence in these circumstances would offend 'all progressives and even moderate opinion' in Britain. Yet to refuse independence would not help the Africans, and would force the white Rhodesians into 'the hands of South Africa'. He appreciated that a British failure to help the Africans would offend most of the Commonwealth, but Britain had 'no physical power' in Southern Rhodesia, only a '*legal* position and some *moral* influence'. He concluded that if the whites seized independence unlawfully they must be treated as rebels, but he envisaged no more than economic sanctions.[18] His successor, Home, made no further progress, and although his biographer, Kenneth Young, argues that the Conservatives were more flexible than Labour concerning the 'principles' designed to safeguard African rights, it is by no means certain that a Conservative electoral victory in 1964 would have made much difference to the final outcome. Britain had never yet conceded independence to a territory with so restricted a franchise, and in October 1964 the Home government was not satisfied that the Rhodesians were prepared to make a sufficiently representative test of African opinion concerning independence under the 1961 constitution.

The advent of a Labour government in Britain certainly hardened white Rhodesian opinion under the leadership of Ian Smith, and increased the pressure for a unilateral declaration of independence. In March 1965 Wilson perhaps unwisely made it explicit that his government would not use force, save in the event of a collapse of law and order. This facilitated the declaration of UDI on 11 November 1965. Some critics have argued that Wilson should have been prepared to use force, and that an immediate intervention in the event of UDI would not have been effectively resisted. Intervention in landlocked Rhodesia would not have been a simple operation at the best of times, and in 1965 British forces were heavily committed elsewhere. Instant success would have been vital. Still more important were the political objections. Wilson had a minute majority: a military clash with the white Rhodesians would have been very unpoplar, and must have favoured the Conservatives electorally. Whatever Wilson's often frantic manoeuvring failed to achieve, it met his political needs in Britain, broadly satisfying public opinion, and creating a situation in which Conservative differences over Rhodesia came into full prominence.[19] But though feelings ran high among some politicians, most of the public would gladly have washed their hands of the whole affair.

The Wilson Cabinet therefore chose to continue negotiations where possible, and gradually stepped up the economic pressure on Rhodesia in the hope that this would bring concessions. At times the government appeared to be wildly optimistic as to the potency of sanctions, but it had to show confidence in its own measures, and some gestures were necessary to reassure black Africa. When fully implemented there were still many loopholes in the economic blockade, notably those provided by South Africa and by Portuguese Africa. The first Commonwealth conference to be held outside London was summoned by Nigeria for January 1966 on the Rhodesian issue. The Canadian premier noted Harold Wilson's manoeuvres to buy time with limited economic sanctions with considerable admiration. Crossman for one doubted their efficacy.[20]

Britain did not demand of Salisbury the institution of one man, one vote, or majority rule as prerequisites for legal independence – only guarantees of 'uninterrupted progress to majority rule'. Various safeguards for the African population were required, but these fell short of those demanded by black African states. The terms which Wilson offered to Ian Smith in 1966 and 1968 were widely condemned as too generous to the white Rhodesians. On both occasions they were rejected. It is possible, though not probable, that they might have been accepted from a Conservative government. In December 1966 it was proposed that a Royal Commission should determine whether the terms were acceptable to the people of Rhodesia, an interesting interpretation of the fifth of the six principles agreed with Commonwealth prime ministers that there should be an appropriate test of Rhodesian opinion concerning any settlement. In November 1971, when a Conservative government reached an agreement with Smith, the terms were referred to the black Rhodesians by means of a commission of inquiry. This reported majority black opposition, and the agreement collapsed.

In the meantime, although Wilson's measures had seemingly inflicted little injury on the white Rhodesians, they had saved Britain from permanent embarrassment in her relations either with the black African states (only two had broken off diplomatic relations) or with South Africa (where Britain had major economic interests). Fears for the British economy and of disquiet among the British public if the crisis deepened account for the strong Cabinet support for Wilson's bid for a settlement with Ian Smith in December 1966.[21] By 1969 the steam was going out of the debate with the African states. The Commonwealth had been damaged but not destroyed by the issue. African demands on Britain, however, had done much to diminish support among the British public for the Commonwealth as constituted in the 1960s. As for the future of Rhodesia itself, this was to be resolved by the collapse of the Portuguese colonial empire, the new-found strength of the Africans, and the consequent reactions of the Americans, the South Africans and the British in the mid-1970s. In September 1976 there began a new bid to find an agreed road to majority rule.

It may well be that, apart from Rhodesia, the last serious crisis to affect a Commonwealth country and particularly concern Britain was the civil war in Nigeria between 1967 and 1970. Nigeria had been troubled with tribal rivalries from its inception as an independent state. These became increasingly serious in the mid-1960s, and in May 1967 Lieutenant-Colonel Odumegwu Ojukwu proclaimed the independence of the Ibo eastern region under the name of Biafra. Civil war followed. Wilson later described this war as becoming for a time the main foreign preoccupation of his government, absorbing much time and energy.[22] In 1968 it overshadowed Vietnam. The British involvement was reluctant, and was prompted above all by the fear from August 1967 of Russia emerging as the main ally of the federal government. British interest in Nigerian oil meant that Britain could not lightly stand aside in the face of a possible Russian-backed reconquest of the oil-producing regions. Britain was drawing 10 per cent of her oil from Nigeria before the civil war (a valuable source when supplies from the Middle East were not always predictable). British investments totalled some £200 million. The British could draw some comfort from the fact that only four African states favoured Biafra. Most feared that a successful assertion of independence by Biafra might encourage other centrifugal forces. Britain therefore continued to supply arms, though not bombs or aircraft, until the war ended in a federal victory in January 1970. The government persisted despite virulent criticism from many shades of opinion in Britain. It was vindicated by the outcome, not least by the moderation of the federal forces in their moment of victory despite widespread and wild prophecies of genocide.

In general the Commonwealth dimension in Labour's overseas policies had been disappointing. Comparatively little had resulted from hopes of revived trading contacts. Canada, notwithstanding some flurries of interest, was too firmly fixed within the American economic orbit. Australia was anxious to protect her own industries and was establishing important links with Japan. The potential of most other Commonwealth markets was very limited. Between 1962 and 1966 the Commonwealth's share of British exports fell from 31 to 26 per cent (in the later 1950s the Commonwealth had taken about 40 per cent). Similarly, where 20 per cent of exports from Commonwealth countries had gone to Britain in 1962, this had fallen to 12 per cent by 1969. Nigeria, whose exports had occasioned Britain so much concern in the negotiations for entry to the EEC in 1962, achieved a form of associate membership with the Community in 1966; British exports to Nigeria thereafter encountered more competition. Malaysia in the same year ended preferential treatment for about one-fifth of her imports from Britain. Throughout the Commonwealth many of the older trading patterns were becoming obsolete. Japan had become Australia's best customer, while the main growth areas for British exports were the United States, Europe and the Middle East. Within the Commonwealth or sterling area there were significant increases in British sales only to

Canada, Australia, New Zealand and some parts of Africa. The main direction of British foreign investment in the 1960s was towards Europe, the United States, South Africa and (inside the Commonwealth) Australia and New Zealand. British net earnings from foreign investment outside the sterling area had nearly overtaken those from within by 1969; in 1963 earnings within the sterling area had been twice as large. Developing countries within the Commonwealth required levels of aid far beyond the capacity of Britain; India and Pakistan, for instance, were each securing up to 90 per cent of their needs from non-British sources.[23] Thus the soul-searching over economic ties with the Commonwealth which had accompanied the first British application to enter the EEC progressively lessened as the decade wore on.

The Commonwealth, it is true, continued to attract sympathy of a rather nebulous kind in Britain for some time to come. Attacks on the Commonwealth, notably by 'A. Conservative' in *The Times* of 2 April 1964, and by Dean Acheson in 1962, provoked a considerable outcry. Pride forbade acceptance that the Commonwealth had become 'a gigantic farce', or that the special relationship with the United States of Britain as head of the Commonwealth was, as Acheson claimed, 'about to be played out'. Throughout the 1960s opinion polls continued to show more feeling for the Commonwealth – though chiefly for the white members – than for the United States or western Europe. But it was also significant that interest declined with the age of the respondents. Circumstances also tended to lessen such interest as there was. Rhodesia, coloured immigration and persistent economic problems all worked against those who had hoped that Britain might continue to provide political leadership and economic aid. Those who had looked for a closer relationship with India were particularly disappointed. The Russians emerged as the peacemaker following the war between India and Pakistan in 1965. Indeed, Cecil King believed that Russia's successful mediation at Tashkent in January 1966 did much to make Harold Wilson more European-minded.

Yet the Commonwealth persisted even if the material advantages in this 'concert of convenience' were largely at an end. Lester Pearson, a leading Canadian politician of the period, remarked that it was easier to describe what the Commonwealth was not rather than what it was. He concluded that although there was no constitutional or legal relationship yet there was a distinctive social, perhaps family relationship.[24] In the end, of course, even the Cheshire cat's grin disappeared. The Commonwealth had not quite reached that state in the mid-1970s.

Labour and the EEC

Harold Wilson, before 1965, had not found much to say in favour of the EEC. The possibility of some sort of link was not excluded, but in opposition it was not difficult to believe that alternative solutions could be found by imaginative leadership. Office forcibly brought home to the new Prime Minister just how limited Britain's options were in the real world and just how quickly those options were contracting. Wilson's conversion was not immediate. At first he explored the possibility of some bridge-building between EFTA and the EEC, and this was discussed at an EFTA conference in Vienna in May 1965. Troubled by the tariff threat posed by the EEC, Wilson next considered the possibility of British association with the EEC under article 238 of the Treaty of Rome, or the creation of some loose free trade arrangement. Neither seemed very promising. Those close to Wilson give somewhat different accounts of his subsequent evolution, their interpretations often being coloured by their own feelings for or against. Crossman's diaries suggest growing Cabinet interest from the beginning of 1966, though there was much recognition that de Gaulle was unlikely to agree and that the British economy would have to be strengthened. Crossman thought George Brown more impressed by the difficulties in private than he professed in public. The Prime Minister was moving in favour of entry, provided the terms were right. He seemed swayed by the conviction that Britain would face more problems outside the EEC than inside it. Cooperation with the United States was proving very costly, notably through Britain's contribution East of Suez, while the need to keep partly in step with Washington over Vietnam was annoying many in the party.[25] If the government made little reference to the issue in the general election in March 1966, the Queen's Speech immediately afterwards indicated a disposition to pursue the matter further.

The main supporters of entry in the Cabinet were Roy Jenkins, George Brown and Anthony Crosland. Michael Stewart had also swung over following his appointment as Foreign Secretary in 1965. Those who did not oppose the Common Market on principle could not fail to be increasingly impressed by the difficulties already noted in Britain's relations with the United States, by the costs and disappointments attending Commonwealth relationships, and by the need to combat the disillusionment concerning the state and future of the British economy which was becoming endemic from the summer of 1966. Opposition to entry from various groups and interests in Britain seemed likely to be less influential than in 1961–2. Agriculture and some sections of industry would still pose problems, but the newly formed Confederation of British Industry was actively in favour, while an opinion poll in July 1966 recorded three-quarters of those to express an opinion favouring entry. The parliamentary support of the Liberals and most Conservatives was assured. There were, of course, strong opponents in the Labour party (and in the Cabinet), but these would prove of little moment given a satisfactory response from the EEC itself.

The fact that the dramatic rise in British exports to the EEC was levelling off in the mid-1960s strengthened rather than weakened the case for entry. The market in Europe was still growing rapidly, but Britain was not sharing proportionately in this expansion, partly because of deficiencies in her own industries, and partly because of non-membership. Entry to the EEC of itself would not cure Britain's economic problems – British industry had to be revitalized. But without entry the problems seemed likely to prove as great, if not greater. As the Common Market boosted the efficiency of its member states' industries, so they would compete more effectively against British industry elsewhere. The huge costs of advanced technology also pointed to large, assured home markets and in some cases to international partnership. The strength and scale of some American corporations and the spread of their activities to Britain and Europe suggested that in some instances European partnership might be necessary for the survival of some home industries. The Prime Minister showed great interest in 'a new technological community to pool within Europe the enormous technological inventiveness' of its peoples to increase European independence and competitiveness in the world. There was a risk, he insisted, that Europe might sink into a condition of 'industrial helotry' if American business continued to expand unchecked. Perhaps he was mainly intent here upon appealing to the anti-American fears and prejudices of de Gaulle and in demonstrating the new extent of Britain's European sympathies. Certainly the British government took little action to constrain the activities of American multinational companies in Britain – on the whole their presence was welcomed – while efforts at scientific and industrial cooperation with European states were to experience a very chequered history. In general the European fears of American multinational companies lessened over the next few years, while in Britain both Rolls Royce and Hawker Siddeley demonstrated that even in the peculiarly American field of aerospace one could bridge the Atlantic as well as the English Channel.

An important meeting of the Cabinet took place at Chequers on 22 October 1966. Denis Healey was ready to propose an approximate terminal date for Britain's presence East of Suez, though there was no question as yet of a final decision.[26] Since the election George Thomson, as Chancellor of the Duchy of Lancaster, had been given special responsibility for European affairs, while George Brown had been chairing a committee to report on the social and economic implications of entry to the EEC. Wilson thought the committee's reports, with other information, had greatly strengthened the case for entry. Apart from the positive aspects, there was the realization that the longer Britain's entry was delayed the more serious the political and economic decisions that might be taken in her absence. Nevertheless the Cabinet still felt that the economic pros and cons of entry were narrowly balanced. There would be losses as well as gains, not least the ending of cheap food imports into Britain. Brown and Stewart, indeed, favoured entry mainly on political grounds. The Cabinet remained divided on the question of entry, but agreed on 22 October that Wilson and Brown should tour the capitals of the Six, which they did early in 1967.

Intensive studies of the economic implications of entry continued.

Many of these were not susceptible to precise measurement, though there seemed good reason to suppose that entry would raise food prices by between 10 and 14 per cent. The implementation of the Common Agricultural Policy since the first British application added to the problems of entry. This policy was mainly designed to benefit food exporting countries such as France, and Britain, if admitted, might find herself shouldering an extra balance of payments burden of some £200 million. British cereal producers were expected to benefit from entry, but farmers who were dependent on cheap imported feeding stuffs were likely to suffer. The smaller livestock and dairy farmers, especially of the north and west, would require a satisfactory transition period. There also appeared to be a need for some controls in the movement of private investment capital to Europe lest an uncontrolled drain to other parts of the world should occur by way of Europe. Crossman thought most ministers foresaw a hard time for Britain during her first three or four years of EEC membership, but the leading Marketeers 'all now feel that the attempt to have a socialist national plan for the British Isles keeps us balanced on such a terribly tight rope that it has really got to be abandoned and that of course is the main reason for entry into the Market'. Wilson also hoped that entry would stimulate private investment in Britain.[27]

The decision to make a formal application for entry to the EEC was taken by the Cabinet on 2 May. Crossman estimated that ten ministers were truly in favour, seven were critical or hostile, and six, including himself, were possible supporters. In his case he thought the attempt must be made if only to prepare the ground for a Little England alternative.[28] Callaghan (a 'maybe') told the Commons on 6 May how office had impressed him with the influence of 'international forums' and the extent to which the autonomy of nations had diminished. If he emphasized the many economic and political imponderables associated with entry, he seemed disposed to accept that, with the right terms, membership was the best option open to Britain. Yet even as the Cabinet made its move public support for the EEC began to falter. There was the tangible fear of higher food prices: more intangible fears concerning 'rule by foreigners' easily developed. Above all there was the current disillusionment with the Labour government. The local elections in the spring of 1967 had been a disaster for Labour. Parliamentary support for entry to the EEC was strong, though careful management of the Labour party was necessary, with perhaps one hundred MPs opposing or feeling unease over the proposed step. The House of Commons vote on 10 May nevertheless gave the government an overwhelming majority – 488 votes to 62. Thirty-five Labour members voted against entry, and about fifty abstained.

Among the Six the Benelux states and Italy were strongly in favour of British entry, though even they were troubled by the problems that might be occasioned by the membership of a country with both a fragile economy and a reserve currency. By article 108 of the Treaty of Rome,

each state was expected to help any member that was suffering from balance of payments difficulties. The West Germans were somewhat equivocal. Ruled by an uneasy coalition they still lacked the political confidence appropriate to their economic strength. Little sympathy could be expected from France. De Gaulle made dampening remarks to the effect that Britain needed to achieve a 'profound economic and political transformation'. He had told George Brown in private in December 1966 that he already had enough trouble protecting French interests in the EEC as it was currently constituted. Later he refused to rise to Wilson's bait that France might soon need Britain to maintain a balance against West Germany. He was unimpressed by other attempts by Wilson to demonstrate how rapidly Britain was moving from the American orbit towards Europe. Britain had helped to defeat the American plans to provide West Germany with a limited nuclear role. There was no question of modernizing the British nuclear submarine force with American Poseidon missiles. But de Gaulle still professed to see Britain as essentially an Atlantic power. In any case Britain and France were far apart on NATO and the United Nations, while de Gaulle was to support the breakaway state of Biafra and to pursue an independent pro-Arab policy in the 1967 Middle Eastern crisis.

The Middle Eastern war of 1967 highlighted British political and economic weaknesses. Before the Six Day War broke out on 5 June Wilson had attempted to take a positive line to maintain the freedom of movement of shipping through the Straits of Tiran. These had been closed to Israeli vessels by the Egyptian reoccupation of Sharm-el-Sheikh. British proposals of international action had not been well supported elsewhere. In the war itself the Israelis swept to conclusive victories. In August the American and Russian leaders met at Glassboro. Britain, in what had once been a region where she had exercised the main if not the only voice, was left to sponsor an ineffectual resolution in the Security Council in November. The war, as has already been noted, had damaging effects on the British economy and sterling. Though not the sole cause of the devaluation crisis in November, the war had been another reminder of Britain's extreme vulnerability. The Brussels Commission, when favouring the start of negotiations on British entry in September, had insisted that Britain must achieve a durable equilibrium in her economy and balance of payments. Major adjustments would be necessary over the international role of sterling. The EEC *Opinion on the Applications for Membership from the United Kingdom, Ireland, Denmark and Norway* (1967) noted how Britain, more than any other state, experienced 'recurrent conflict . . . between achievement of a growth rate comparable to the annual average attained over a period of several years in most other industrialised countries and the need to balance external payments'. Faster growth repeatedly brought payments problems, and this necessitated severe restraint and the virtual end of growth. The difficulties seemingly stemmed

from defects in the distribution of productive resources (inadequate and misdirected investment, numerous obstacles to improvement of productivity, the pattern of employment, the tax system) or from the economic, monetary and financial burdens inherited from the second world war and the country's international position in the postwar world.[29]

It was an apt summing up of the consequences for Britain of her extraordinary impact upon and involvement in world affairs since the eighteenth century.

In the best of circumstances it is clear that Britain would have found no easy way into the EEC in 1967. As it was de Gaulle interposed a second veto on 27 November. Despite assertions that Britain was economically too weak to join the Common Market at that time, his main motivation was political. The British government refused to take 'non' for an answer, and spoke of continuing talks with the 'Five'. Yet de Gaulle's position at the end of 1967 seemed invulnerable, save for his own ultimate mortality. The best that Britain could do was to show patience, cooperate with the Six (or as many of them as would allow her to do so) and strengthen her economy.

Chapter 11

Industrial reorganization and industrial relations

Labour's first moves

Despite the overall failure of Labour's hopes in economic policy, it is still useful to look at the government's efforts to assist certain industries or sectors of the economy, and at their consequences. In so far as progress was made, and even in so far as plans for new developments existed in 1964, the Wilson ministry was much indebted to its predecessors. If Labour was more directly interventionist and discriminatory in its treatment of firms, yet the Conservatives had moved a long way by 1964 from their neutralist stance of the 1950s. They had initiated an impressive range of inquiries: Rochdale (ports), Buchanan (town traffic), Jenkins (company law), Molony (consumer protection), Crowther, Newsom and Robbins (education), Trend (civil research) and Pilkington (broadcasting). A formidable body of information was to hand, or was about to become so. To these Labour added much of its own, including the Fulton inquiry (its reports were published in 1968) into the Civil Service as part of an attempt to introduce more expertise and professional management into its highest ranks.

Professor Brian Chapman likened the Civil Service in 1963 to a 'closed corporation', little influenced by the community at large. Richard Rose later described Whitehall as too much influenced by English university education which prized 'the critical intelligence, rather than the mind skilled at constructing things'. [1] Some civil servants themselves accepted that in general they were happier in the realms of politics than of management. Lord Armstrong, even after some implementation of the Fulton proposals, thought that the Civil Service needed to develop two arms, one for the managerial role as well as that for policy-making. There were repeated references to the French civil service, whose star personnel had received more professional or vocational training, and who had gained more direct experience of industry before being assigned to top posts in that field. Yet it would be wrong to see the British Civil Service as wholly static in character or conduct from 1945. Fulton underestimated the degree of change that had already occurred in some departments, while its own proposals did not bring about an overnight revolution. A Civil Service College was established, and more flexibility of promotion within the Service was allowed to try to weaken the old dominance of the administrative class by Oxbridge Arts graduates. Preference was not given, as Fulton proposed, to 'relevant' university degrees, though there was a tenfold increase in the number of government economists between 1964 and 1974. But despite the changes, and the rise of more people with unconventional backgrounds to the top, the complaints persisted in the mid-1970s that, although the managerial role of the Civil Service was increasing, its strength still lay in political, policy-making and monitoring roles.

One of the key weaknesses of some seemingly attractive government proposals was the difficulty encountered in finding suitable personnel for their implementation. The aspirations of the government included the improvement of managerial techniques both in industry and in its own departments, the application of more commercial tests to research and development, and the diversion of more effort at government research establishments to civil purposes. In theory it also seemed possible for the state to increase industrial efficiency or to encourage the manufacture of certain products by discriminatory use of the great purchasing power of the public sector of the economy, as well as by special financial inducements or development contracts. Later (from 1966) more direct state action was to be taken through the new Industrial Reorganization Corporation. In practice, however, government departments and agencies often found that involvement brought new problems. State assistance could encourage industrial dependence upon the state; it could discourage initiative, and, by slowing decision-making processes, act as a drag rather than as a spur. Often the state lacked all the necessary information for intelligent intervention, so that the relationship with industry, instead of being creative and stimulating, could degenerate into something very different.

There were gains and losses from the many-sided activities of the Wilson government. Building on the work of the early 1960s, it had some success in identifying bottlenecks and deficiencies in the economy, and sometimes, as we shall see, it was able to put remedies in train. The 1965 Redundancy Payments Act provided graduated redundancy payments according to a worker's length of service. It was hoped that this might facilitate labour mobility and supplement the rough and ready union approach to redundancies of 'last in, first out'. Both the National Plan and the Devlin Report (August 1965) showed awareness of the need to transform Britain's docks. Many of these were notoriously inefficient and strike-prone. Dock labour was employed by no less than 1,500 firms, many of which were too small. Three-quarters of the dockers were still employed on a 'casual' basis. Many employers lacked a sense of social responsibility towards their workers; many dockers were notoriously militant. Unofficial strikes abounded. Some British exporters saw the rundown state of the docks as the biggest single bottleneck in the drive for more exports. The 1966 Docks and Harbours Bill reduced the number of private employers and sought to provide more regular employment and better conditions for the dockers. In the longer term the government hoped to nationalize the docks, but it fell from power in 1970 before this could be attempted. This was reserved for a later ministry.

In other fields of transport the government continued with the motorway programme. Eight hundred miles had been completed by 1971. Passenger-car mileage had by then increased sixfold since 1950, and accounted for nearly 80 per cent of all passenger mileage in Britain. Labour stabilized the rail system at around 11,000 (Beeching had recommended 8,000). British Rail's capital debts were cut by the government from £1,562 million to £365 million, and a policy of deliberate subsidy for uneconomic services was instituted. But the ambitious Transport Act of 1968, at that time the longest Act in modern British history, which set up the National Freight Corporation to control all traffic starting or finishing by road in the nationalized system, and to encourage the use of rail transport whenever this was most economic and efficient, was not seriously implemented even by Labour itself before 1970. The attempt to create an integrated internal freight system remained a dream. Limited areas of success within the nationalized transport system were swamped by the early reappearance of huge rail deficits from 1971, despite the subsidies. British rail revenue fell in real terms by a quarter between 1963 and 1973. By 1975 it carried only about 18 per cent of the nation's internal freight, and 8 per cent of the passengers. By the standards of most continental railways it was still heavily overstaffed.

A bid to renationalize steel was frustrated under the first Wilson administration, but the huge majority won at the 1966 election removed most obstacles. Even so some ministers still favoured a compromise. Crossman thought the measure 'irrelevant'.[2] The necessary legislation was, however, duly carried, and in 1967 the British Steel Corporation was duly established. In July it took control of 90 per cent of the nation's steel-making capacity, organizing the industry into four groups. Its heritage was a mixed one. There were too many small concerns by the standards of the mid-1960s. Many of the furnaces were ill-sited in view of the nation's heavy dependence on imported ores, while the ports themselves could not handle the largest of the new ore carriers. Even so according to some estimates its net output per head was above the national average for industry in 1963, whereas the ensuing record of the British Steel Corporation between 1967 and 1976 was very disappointing. If it was hampered by government price controls and other forms of intervention, its investment programmes were not rewarded with commensurate increases in productivity down to 1975, and by European standards in the early 1970s it was seriously overmanned. In general, though some nationalized industries performed more creditably, the government even in the mid-1970s seemed no nearer a satisfactory working relationship with public corporations.

In the private sectors of industry the government was much concerned by the vulnerability of many firms to foreign competition, both at home and abroad, and among its solutions were the formation of larger (and, it was hoped, more efficient) companies, plus the diversion of resources from defence and other less profitable sectors to export and import-saving industries. It was a matter of concern that although Britain was devoting more of her gross national product to research and development than her European or Japanese rivals, this was not reflected in the economic growth table. One survey of scientific papers published in 1965–71 estimated that Britain stood second only to the United States in the world and first in mathematics and systematic biology. Wilson had declared before the 1964 election that if one word could define socialism it should be the word 'science'. But what if science and technology in Britain were unduly concentrated on defence and on the aerospace industry in which Britain repeatedly failed to compete effectively with the Americans? The government's scientific adviser, Sir Solly Zuckerman, calculated that defence was absorbing about one-fifth of the nation's scientists and engineers employed in research and development, and about two-fifths of the national expenditure upon the same.[3] It was estimated that the aerospace industry took nearly 40 per cent of the nation's expenditure on research and development and yet supplied no more than 4 per cent of the nation's exports. The respective percentages in the engineering and electrical industries were 17 per cent (of national expenditure) and 25 per cent (exports).[4] Britain was getting better value for money from research and development in vehicles than in aircraft, yet compared with key rivals it was providing too few highly qualified personnel in such industries as vehicles, various forms of engineering, and chemicals. As late as 1972 it was estimated that 87 per cent of the Department of Trade and Industry's spending on civil industrial research and development was being concentrated in only four main areas, aircraft, space, nuclear and computer technology. Japan and Germany in particular resisted the lure of the aircraft industry. Japan devoted a very high proportion of its scientific and technological personnel to the appraisal of new developments with their commercial potential firmly in mind.

In Britain even in 1976 high technology was being described as the 'last refuge of the enthusiastic nationalist',[5] while three years earlier Lord Rothschild as head of the Central Policy Review Staff, and with high technology very much in mind, had insisted that Britain must abandon illusions of Victorian greatness. At a Research and Development Society symposium in London in April 1976 Dr Mark Abrams, director of the survey unit of the SSRC argued that Britain had to think essentially in terms of producing for those markets which were more likely to expand. The great task was to ensure that British research and development were applied to the creation or improvement of products for those markets. Professor Harry G. Johnson, a former member of the British Council on Science Policy, went so far as to say in 1975 that the best argument he could see for not cutting expenditure on pure science very far (and it was not a very hopeful one) was that there might be more economic benefit from it than had so far been established.[6] One must be careful in the face of temporary disillusionment or passing changes of fashion, but these reactions in the early and mid-1970s are interesting comments on what Labour did and did not do. It is also evident that in the realm of aerospace, although they achieved some useful redeployment of resources, the economics of that industry continued to be distorted by the continuance of Concorde. N. K. Gardiner in a report for the Department of Industry in February 1976, *The Economics of Industrial Subsidies*, concluded that the net effect of aerospace launching aid from 1945 to 1974 had been a loss in national welfare. He estimated that at 1974 prices over £1,500 million of government money had been invested since the war in civil aerospace for a return to the taxpayer of under £150 million. But Concorde had then absorbed about £700 million of that sum, while civil aerospace earnings in exports and in import-saving totalled some £8 billion. Given some overlap between civil and defence needs, the final balance sheet is not easily drawn up.

Britain and aerospace

Labour from 1964 made a determined attempt to reduce the proportion of the nation's scientific and technological resources devoted to defence and aerospace. The Conservatives had belatedly tried to rationalize the aircraft industry from 1959 by reducing it to five main units. Much thought had been given to earlier errors whereby too many aircraft projects had been attempted. It was seen that the relationship between government and aircraft firms had left much to be desired. But these good intentions had been upset by a proliferation of new projects in the early 1960s, essentially Concorde and three advanced military aircraft. Not only were the long-term costs of the projects underestimated, but too little attention was given to their probable sales appeal among foreign purchasers. The unexpected costs and short production runs of many aircraft before 1960 should have alerted the government to such perils. But the British continued to build to their own particular and usually ambitious specifications, so inflating costs and reducing foreign sales appeal. In 1957 Sir Roy Fedden, a distinguished aeronautical engineer, complained that British air policy suffered from 'delusions of grandeur'. Mary Goldring of *The Economist* offered early warnings concerning the doubtful commercial prospects of *Concorde*.

Costs, of course, are notoriously difficult to calculate on the borders of known technology. The same is true of economic judgements in the context of defence policy. But in the early 1960s policy-makers should have looked more critically at the costs of a long-term major British presence East of Suez for which new generations both of ships and aircraft were required. Labour, from 1964, tried to prune the costs of such a presence, but were slow to challenge the assumptions on which policy was based. Labour might also have cancelled *Concorde* had it not been for the compensation clauses which the French could invoke.

Instead they drastically revised the aircraft programme for the RAF, cancelling in particular and in the midst of a great outcry the highly sophisticated TSR-2. Close questioning in 1967 by the Committee of Public Accounts suggested that this project had been ill-conceived from the start. Costs had been grossly underestimated; neither government nor contractors possessed adequate financial control procedures. Both main contractors were in the process of internal reorganization following recent mergers. Too many technological breakthroughs were attempted simultaneously. A Conservative spokesman broadly accepted this criticism in the Commons on 7 March 1968.

British activities in aerospace were also subjected to detailed scrutiny by the Plowden and Elstub Committees in 1965 and 1969. Both were sharply critical of government and the aircraft firms. Government departments were too often guilty of sudden changes of policy and of ill-informed intervention within the aircraft industry. The aircraft firms were found to be lagging in modern managerial techniques by comparison not only with the Americans but also with, for instance, the French company, Sud Aviation. The average American firm possessed much more capital per employee; it also made much better use of it. True, much of the American two- or threefold advantage in productivity stemmed from the large home market which ensured longer production runs. Rolls Royce was further handicapped against Amerian rivals by the fact that it was producing more engine types from more limited resources. A government-assisted merger with Bristol Siddeley still left the combined firms' resources overstretched. Not surprisingly the Plowden Report of December 1965 concluded that the industry should not overcommit itself, and should aim to build aircraft with good market prospects outside Britain. More market research was vital. In 1966 it was estimated that to recover the costs of an advanced plane, at least 250 had to be sold; for an advanced engine, 1,600. The tremendous advantage possessed by American firms is underlined in the simple fact that in 1961 American airlines carried rather more than half the world's air traffic: western European airlines combined carried only one-fifth. But even with their chances of long production runs American companies still found the building of advanced airliners a very hazardous business.

In the circumstances a growth of British interest in international aircraft projects in the 1960s is understandable. Such schemes, however, were not easy to arrange. National jealousies and ambitions, as well as many technical problems, had to be overcome. The advantages of large assured markets and of shared development costs could be offset at least in part by higher overall costs. The permanent support of a partner could not always be guaranteed, and there could be disagreements over aircraft specifications. Aircraft manufacture was a highly unstable and unpredictable business, both for civil and military purposes. Since 1950 there had been many and abrupt changes of policy concerning the type and number of aircraft required by the RAF. The civil airlines were exposed to sharply changing patterns of demand. A good aircraft could easily arrive on the market at the wrong time. Multinational projects therefore did not guarantee success or an easy way forward. The ultimate technical success of *Concorde* still left huge questionmarks against the vast costs and manner of its development. Two collaborative military projects, despite false starts and many ensuing difficulties, were more soundly conceived. If by 1970 the aircraft industry still appeared to be imposing excessive burdens on the British economy in relation to its returns, the Wilson ministry had had some success, especially in the military field in correcting the extravagance of the early 1960s. The export record had also improved. But the next government also inherited its share of problems.

Government and industry

To carry through the modernization of British industry great hopes were placed in the new Ministry of Technology (1964) and the Industrial Reorganization Corporation (1966).[7] New legislation included the Science and Technology Act (1965), the Shipbuilding Industry Act (1967) and the Industrial Expansion Act (1968). The government unfortunately gave the impression that rapid modernization was possible. The effect of government help was often weakened by its hastiness and by doubts as to how long and in what form it would continue. Too often there was energy without depth of understanding. The IRC in particular provoked very different responses from industry. Some welcomed its help and expertise; others found it interfering, superficial and pretentious. Its interest in increasing exports from certain key industries and in increasing their competitiveness was theoretically sound, but it perhaps too readily assumed that larger companies were one of the best remedies.

Britain, by western European standards, was not short of large firms in the later 1960s. Many mergers and takeovers were already occurring, or would have occurred in some fashion, for good or ill, without the good offices of the IRC. By 1969 about 60 per cent of those employed in the private manufacturing sector were working for firms with over 1,000 employees, and with over £10 million in investment capital. Firms were sometimes acquired to protect 'sleeping giants' from unwelcome competition. Takeovers could also result in asset-stripping. Business-men might sometimes complain that mergers were best left to market forces, but the motivation in such circumstances was often sadly negative. By accident or intent mergers could perpetuate mediocrity by reducing competition. Organizational complexity could delay new investment. A union of firms might still leave undersized separate factories within the organization, or increases in productivity were achieved merely by closing down the most inefficient plant and by shedding labour. For a variety of reasons investment, efficiency and profitability might not be basically improved, and in some cases problems of management and organization might have been drastically increased. The researches of Kenneth D. George and T. S. Ward in the early 1970s into large firms in Britain and western Europe led them to the conclusion that the case for bigness in industry was far from proven. The government in the later 1960s had acted on the basis of little information and analysis, and by 1970 the IRC was more concerned with productivity and exports than mergers.

Fear of American competition had undoubtedly influenced both the British government and industry in favour of some mergers at that time. There was growing awareness of the expanding activities of American multinational corporations in Britain and in western Europe, with both perceptive and alarmist reactions to their performance and potential. In general their efficiency by comparison with British firms was impressive, and therefore at least some of the reorganization of British industry must be seen as a response to this challenge. Nevertheless it should be noted in passing that the government had to bear many other considerations in mind when assessing the impact of foreign-owned companies operating in Britain upon the economy as a whole. Britain as the world's second largest foreign investor (over one-sixth of the total) could not lightly, even if she had been so minded, have obstructed foreign investment in Britain. If the ratio narrowed in the course of the 1960s, Britain was still investing more abroad than others were in Britain. Indeed, it was being anxiously debated in the 1960s whether Britain was wise to invest so much abroad, and the Wilson ministry intervened sufficiently to ensure that by 1969 such investment was no longer a major strain on the balance of payments, as it had been in 1964. In its turn the effect on the balance of payments of foreign-owned companies was also a complicated one. Their contribution to the British economy as exporters and import-savers had to be weighed against their remissions to parent companies. There were fears that international companies might add to the scale of speculation against sterling in periods of economic crisis, but it appeared that in 1967 American subsidiaries took precautions of a very limited kind against devaluation. The government was more troubled by the 'gnomes' of Zurich than by IBM.

On the whole Britain had occasion to welcome foreign investment as a stimulating and expanding force in the economy. There was concern only when American investment appeared to threaten vital or promising industries, such as computers or vehicles. Indeed with respect to the latter there was more concern, especially in the 1970s, whenever the scale of operations of Ford, General Motors or Chrysler in Britain seemed endangered. Rather, British governments were concerned with maintaining the viability of the remnants of the British-owned car industry against their and other competition. Hence the creation of the enormous British Leyland concern. When Labour fell from office in 1970 the question of controls on foreign firms operating in Britain was being explored, but less out of a sense of alarm than through recognition that here was an important new dimension in the economy. American-owned firms were responsible for about 10 per cent of manufacturing sales in Britain by 1970 (including over half the cars and tractors, 80 per cent of the washing machines, and 40 per cent of the computers). The American invasion, however, was slowing as the economic problems of the United States increased, and as low returns diminished the attractiveness of investment in many British industries.

Ostensibly the case for the IRC's creation of British Leyland in January 1968 was a good one. As it was the sales of its various components in 1967–8 were only one-eighth those of the American giant, General Motors. Among its European competitors at that time, Volkswagenwerke sold more, Fiat nearly as much, and the Renault concern about half. British Motor Holdings, made up primarily of the old Austin and Morris firms, was obviously ailing, while the Leyland concern, mainly a producer of commercial vehicles, had a successful record in domestic organization and in foreign sales. Chrysler had just purchased the British Rootes car firm, so that over half of British vehicle production was under American control. BMH had to be revitalized, and the IRC looked to Leyland to do the job. The merger was assisted by an IRC loan of £25 million, and government intervention may have speeded the operation by about a year. The outcome was singularly disappointing, the new assemblage adding to the problems of Leyland rather than reducing those of the BMH complex. In the mid-1970s there were still sixty separate plants scattered about the country, lacking a common identity, generally suffering from under-investment and from poor use of existing plant. Labour relations were poor in some plants, with a great feeling of remoteness from management, especially in the old Morris works. Wage questions were handled by over 240 bargaining units. By 1975 the financial situation had become so bad that massive government aid was needed, and British Leyland became 95 per cent state-owned. By that time its fixed assets per man and its labour productivity were the lowest of the main car producers in Britain.

Not that the American subsidiaries in Britain were that much better. In December 1975 the Central Policy Review Staff reported its findings on the British car industry. It claimed that continental productivity (based on a comparison of the use of similar equipment to produce similar cars) was about twice as high as in Britain. In the manufacture of car engines it was about 50 per cent higher. Overall the British car industry compared unfavourably with its main European rivals in fixed assets per man employed. These weaknesses were sharply underlined by the changed position of Britain among the car producers of the world. In 1955 Britain had been responsible for a quarter of car production outside the United States; in 1974 this had fallen to a mere 10 per cent. In 1965 British car manufacturers held 95 per cent of the domestic car market: by 1974 this had fallen to 65 per cent. In commercial vehicle production the British record was much better, while sales of vehicle components were still more impressive.

Other industries which felt the rationalizing hands of the IRC or some other government agency in the 1960s were the manufacturers of electrical equipment, the shipyards and the machine tool industry. In shipbulding the aim was to create integrated companies in each major area, while government aid was also used to try to buy out restrictive practices among the unions. Special government action was used to try to save shipbuilding on the Upper Clyde, but a major crisis was postponed for only a few years. For the manufacture of electrical equipment a vast new company was formed in 1968 from GEC and English Electric. Elliott Automation – a company with ideas in excess of its resources – had already been merged with English Electric. Electrical engineering, like chemicals, was an industry in which Britain was falling behind West Germany in research, development and investment, and where there was a much lower turnover per employee. Imports of sophisticated manufactured goods were rising more quickly than British exports of the same, and in 1975 it was estimated that despite all the government, business and academic interest and activity from the early 1960s, British increases in productivity for each unit of new investment from 1963 were only about half the west European average. Concentrated and intelligent effort could bring rewards, however, as was demonstrated in the Ransome and Marles-Hoffman-Pollard amalgamation to strengthen British ball-bearing production. Productivity was raised by 20 per cent within two years.

Action was also desperately required in the machine-tool industry. Both in the late 1930s and in the early 1950s British armament programmes had been embarrassed by weaknesses in this industry, and yet the early 1960s still found Britain importing more and more sophisticated machine tools. Germany was once again a leader in this field. This was an industry in which quality and reliable delivery dates mattered more than price. Sophisticated skills of many kinds were required, yet the Mitchell inquiry in 1960 found only twenty-three graduate scientists and engineers in British firms. A series of mergers in 1965-7 brought into being Staveley Industries, one of the largest machine-tool manufacturers in Europe. The Ministry of Technology provided some finance to help tide the industry as a whole over the adverse periods of cyclical demand to which this industry was notoriously subject, but the sharp mid-1970s recession again occasioned major problems. The industry was denied the steady growth it so badly needed. The 1975 order level was the lowest for twenty years, and the skilled work force had declined from 90,000 to 63,000.

Considerable aid was also given to the computer industry to try to keep it in the race against American competition. Unfortunately the British International Computers and Tabulators were too slow in following the all-powerful American IBM into the replacement of the punched-card machines with transistorized computers. With the merger of ICT, English Electric and Plessey to form IC (Holdings) Ltd, Britain created the fourth largest computer organization in the world, and the largest in Europe. Yet it was still a dwarf beside IBM. Britain did remain ahead of Germany in computers, and also in textile machinery. Electrical engineering and office machinery exports did well in the 1960s, but in engineering in general the British performance remained below that of their main rivals. Foreign tariffs and quotas posed some problems, but many firms lacked sales sophistication and supplied only indifferent after-sales services. Too few firms were giving sufficient strength and status to their staff in these departments, possibly a relic from the old days when British export dominance required much less sales support. British engineers often appeared biased against employment in marketing, yet in machine tools, chemicals and computers, an ability to understand and even anticipate the problems and needs of customers was vital. Once again it was possible to see at work that deeply rooted British weakness whereby there was often no adequate synthesis of skills and understanding throughout the industrial process from research to the sale of the final product. American subsidiaries were frequently though not invariably more successful in this respect. Again, however, the built-in advantage of the enormous home market of the parent companies was important. This seemed to stand out in the case of Ferranti, whose semi-conductors' expertise was scarcely inferior to American rivals, but who lacked an adequate domestic demand. On the other hand Birmingham Sound Reproducers succeeded in breaking out of a small home market into a highly competitive world with an inspired design, sound production engineering, and an emphasis on simplicity and efficiency. It broke through many of the oft-mentioned obstacles to enterprise in Britain.[8]

One of the most revealing studies of British industrial performance was provided by R. W. Bacon and W. A. Eltis in 1974. British and American use of machinery was compared. Little difference was found in the service life of machine tools – in some respects the advantage lay with the British. Comparisons of investment and wages as a whole failed to reveal why in 1969 the average American worker was producing three times as much as his British counterpart. So large a gap could be explained only by more intensive use of machinery in America and/or by lower manning ratios, reinforced by longer production runs for the vast home market. In specific industries, such as aerospace and computers, there were clear advantages in equipment, and there was a greater concentration of American output in sectors where capital intensity was comparatively high. The Americans were also well in the lead in the use of numerically controlled machine tools, possibly, according to Bacon and Eltis, the most important technological development since 1945. Britain was also behind Europe in the use of such equipment. But while there were these technical and capital advantages in certain sectors of American industry, what also stood out were American advantages in management, marketing, and in the more efficient use of capital and labour. British awareness of their deficiencies in these fields was reflected, for instance, in the efforts in the 1960s to reduce labour restrictive practices, to provide more places in retraining centres (there were still only 9,000 in 1969), and to strengthen courses in business management.

Among the varied efforts of the government to help British industry was aid to smaller firms that had hitherto been daunted by the problems of trying to compete in foreign markets. Highly controversial, however, was the Industrial Expansion Bill of 1968 which would have empowered the government to buy shares in private industry. This was feared by many businessmen as possible backdoor nationalization. Criticism of the Bill was so formidable that in the end the ministry sought no more than the power to provide 'risk' capital to assist in research and development, and in industrial rationalization. This retreat annoyed some of the government's left-wing supporters, who also complained that the IRC was too conservative and cautious in its treatment of industry. It was propping up, not replacing private enterprise. Critics on the other side of the political spectrum complained that the government was too often propping up inefficient enterprises and that through this action it was slowing the growth of the economy as a whole. They argued, too, that in so far as new government policies assisted industry, taxes and regulations offset the gains. Clearly the government achieved little beside its original hopes. Setbacks to the economy as a whole diminished the value of its more constructive moves, and loss of office in 1970 meant the abolition of the IRC and other changes of policy. The wisdom or otherwise of many measures is not easy to establish in such circumstances.

Regional policy and local government reform

Regional policy also caused dissension and disappointment.[9] There was the continuing debate as to the respective merits of taking plant to the workers or encouraging the unemployed to move to areas of high activity. Over and above this there was the dramatic emergence of a new political dimension: the enormous growth of the nationalist parties in Scotland and Wales in the later 1960s. Expenditure on all regions rose eightfold between 1964 and 1968 to £250 million, but, as the Red Queen told Alice, it took an awful lot of running merely to stay in the same place. The 1966 Industrial Development Act set up new development areas to embrace most of Scotland and Wales, the north and Furness, Merseyside, and the south west of England. This represented about 40 per cent of the land area of Great Britain and about 20 per cent of the population. Other extensions followed. This was the most ambitious attempt at regional planning yet, making possible the introduction of the growth-point principle as proposed, for instance, in the 1961 Toothill Report on the Scottish economy or the 1963 Central Scotland

Plan (Cmnd 2188) in the hope that aid and relief could be transmuted into sustained economic expansion. Universities assisted in regional research to try to identify problems and indicate likely trends. Sudden emergencies had still to be catered for, such as in the winter of 1967 when special action was required in the Rhondda Valley to combat an unemployment level that had risen to three times the national average. Pit closures were a major cause of unemployment problems in many areas.

Government action on behalf of the development areas took various forms, including the building of advance factories, increased investment grants and special loans. The Regional Employment Premium from September 1967 provided manufacturers in development areas with £1.50 weekly for each employee. There were many pitfalls. Labour of the right kind was not always readily available even in areas of high unemployment. Healthy regional development required a good variety of firms and jobs, plus the necessary supporting services. Wales remained short of the sort of posts to which those with good educational qualifications might reasonably aspire. But it was also being slowly recognized in the 1960s that the development areas were not the only ones which required special treatment. Overcrowding had also to be tackled in the south-east and in the west midlands. The whole region from the Wash to east Dorset and spreading out from the London conurbation required careful study. Certain areas, on the other hand, seemed ripe for increased urbanization, such as Humberside, Severnside and Tayside. The sharp fall in the birth-rate (and therefore in population projections) was not then foreseen, nor the blight that was beginning to creep into some of the affluent areas themselves. The Hunt Committee did report in 1969 on the problems of the so-called 'intermediate areas' which included parts of Yorkshire, Humberside, Derbyshire, north-east Lancashire, south-east Wales, Leith and Plymouth. For these the government decided on 24 April 1969 to provide 25 per cent grants for factory building and 75 per cent grants for clearing derelict land, as well as assistance in retraining and in improving the infrastructure.

By 1970, in the light of various calculations, the relative positions of the regions seemed much the same. In terms of unemployment the position of the north had markedly deteriorated. Unemployment was still high in Scotland, but had improved in relation to the national average since 1959. Without the regional aid, of course, the position would have been much worse, unless, of course, there had been a massive migration to the areas of full employment with the consequent strains on housing and services in those communities. One unlooked-for consequence of intensified regional activities was the attention it directed to the inadequacies of the current system of local government. In particular the personnel of the regional economic planning councils and planning boards, established to provide effective machinery for regional economic planning within the framework of Labour's National

Plan, complained of the lack of expertise in local government. The smaller authorities lacked financial and other resources. Efforts to think on regional lines constantly fell foul of the patchwork of local authorities and local rivalries. The distinction between town and country, too, was becoming less real, as more urban workers commuted from the country, and country dwellers in general became more dependent on urban services. The land hunger of some big cities could only be met by ending their rivalry with rural neighbours. The increasing scale of many local services pointed to larger units; the ideal minimum unit for each police force was estimated at around a quarter of a million. The vexed question of local government, which had occasionally excited interest since 1945, thus at last came to the fore. Separate Royal Commissions for England and Wales, and for Scotland, set up in 1966, were able to take the first real steps towards the reorganization of local government since 1888.[10]

The Wheatley Commission for Scotland in fact caused delays, since a two-tier system had been devised by the Scottish Office in June 1963. Nine regional councils finally emerged in 1975. The Redcliffe Maud Commission for England and Wales saw a diluted version of its proposals implemented by a Conservative government between 1972 and 1974. The Heath government showed considerable respect for traditional county boundaries, and some critics doubted whether the reorganized had been radical enough to bridge rural–urban divisions, and to provide effective authorities which could resist the growing power of the central government. But the mid-1970s were also preoccupied with plans for devolution in Scotland and Wales. Even if Scotland and Wales proceeded no further than devolution, this might radically alter local government in those components of the United Kingdom, and might even have consequences in England. Certainly the reorganization in local government left many questions unanswered, and many complaints concerning its character and adequacy, and still more its cost to ratepayers.

Devaluation

No matter what new ventures the Wilson ministries attempted, they were never free for any length of time from threats to the balance of payments and to sterling. Ambitious schemes turned to dust or at best were left unfinished as foreign confidence in the strength of the British economy declined. Manoeuvre as the Cabinet did to try to avert devaluation, it was at last driven into a corner and forced to admit defeat. The Treasury, indeed, had begun to consider devaluation even before the autumn crisis of 1967. It had been disturbed by the probable adverse effects on the balance of payments, at least in the short run, if Britain were to succeed in its 1967 application to join the EEC. It doubted the ability of the British economy to meet the expected obligations within the EEC at the current exchange rates. The Prime Minister had been informed of this conclusion 'in unusually categorical terms' shortly before the formal decision to apply for membership. 'But once devaluation became thinkable in one context, it became thinkable in another. The application to join the EEC was thus the real origin of the Treasury's change of attitude towards the $2.80 parity.'[11]

The application may even have increased speculation against sterling in expectation of ultimate devaluation. The Prime Minister remained staunchly opposed, though the Chancellor thought that both he and Wilson would accept a 10 or 15 per cent devaluation as a condition of entry to the EEC.[12] Otherwise the government must be shown to have no other option. Callaghan, in January 1968, defended the failure to devalue in the spring of 1967 on the ground that the current forecasts 'were not showing a situation that would have enabled us to justify devaluation to other observers', and were even in some respects encouraging.[13] Michael Artis of the NIESR later agreed that the forecasts had been 'misleading'.[14] Callaghan also argued that devaluation before the Middle Eastern war would not, in any case, have eased Britain's economic position during it: there could have been a second 'forced devaluation'. Critics, with hindsight, are inclined to settle on May–July 1966 as the great missed opportunity for devaluation, though on purely economic grounds it would not have come amiss at any time from 1961. Sterling, however, continued to be seen as one of the few remaining ties in the Commonwealth; it formed a key part of the special relationship with the United States; British prestige as well as supposed material interests were bound up with sterling. Reginald Maudling commented in 1967 that as Chancellor he had never been able to make up his mind whether sterling's world role was 'a privilege rather than a handicap'. Sterling's world roles discouraged thoughts of devaluation.[15]

If devaluation was hastened by the effects of the Middle Eastern war of 1967, and the national dock strike of September–October, the long-term trends in British exports and imports suggest that it could not have been long delayed. Profit margins on British exports were being badly squeezed: British prices were often uncompetitive. There was no prospect of any developments at home, such as increased investment and falling unit costs, relieving this situation. Yet, according to Harold Wilson, the Governor of the Bank of England still opposed devaluation, except perhaps in the context of entry to the EEC.[16] By 4 November, however, rumours of devaluation were spreading rapidly, and an increase in the bank rate on the 9th had no effect. Wilson was beginning to have his first doubts, though at first he was inclined to a floating pound as the best solution. International uncertainties were increasing, and it remained to be seen how many other states might devalue. The Cabinet was coming to accept devaluation as inevitable,[17] although on 11 November the central bankers appeared to be evenly divided. But for Britain to be supported by yet more foreign loans would mean further domestic deflation and a stronger prices and incomes policy. From the government's point of view this would mean 'sacrificing the unemployed to the bankers'. The decision to devalue, with the accompanying cuts in public spending and the imposition of credit restrictions, was worked out between 13 and 16 November. Devaluation was announced on the 18th. A standby credit of $1.4 billion was still required from the IMF, and this necessitated a Letter of Intent from the Chancellor on 23 November concerning cuts in spending in Britain.

The resultant deflationary package still fell short of the estimates made by the Treasury, and soon proved woefully inadequate. A balance of payments surplus of £500 million was required by 1969, and this would entail a transfer of resources from the home market of about £1 billion. Government hesitations allowed a massive consumer boom to take place before the 1968 budget, and in December 1967 there was yet another run on sterling, and talk of another devaluation. A new Chancellor, Roy Jenkins, inherited a situation in which there was less freedom for manoeuvre than at any time since 1951. At the turn of the year the Cabinet again tried to agree on the measures needed to make devaluation work and to swing Britain back into balance within a year or so. Resignations from the Cabinet seemed more than likely, though in that game the one resignation the government could not afford was that of the new Chancellor. The atmosphere was electric, relations between ministers also having been recently damaged by a dispute over the resumption of arms sales to South Africa (advocates of a resumption being finally defeated).[18] Of the Cabinet wrangles over the January cuts Wilson commented: 'It was the only time in six years that colleagues seemed to be keeping their own tally (of cabinet voting).'[19] In the end only Lord Longford resigned.

The overall package was expected to save £716 million over two years, and included a delay in the raising of the school-leaving age, the imposition of prescription charges, and the decision to hasten the retreat from East of Suez. The left was not satisfied that the arms cuts had gone as far as they might, but they were sufficient to avert a major revolt over the other economies. Only twenty-six Labour backbenchers abstained on the main motion. But the sense of disillusionment was profound. No section of the party had escaped disappointments in the failures of most aspects of government policy since 1964. Nor did devaluation and the January cuts promise an early end to the nation's problems. In fact the turnround in the balance of payments took longer than expected, and there were further crises before foreign confidence in the British economy was reasonably well established. World liquidity problems, the growing speculation in gold, and fears of a devaluation of the dollar provided an international economic environment in which only the strongest economies could move with some confidence.

An international currency crisis in March 1968 brought a new flight from sterling and fears of another devaluation. At the request of

Washington, Wilson, working with only two colleagues, proclaimed a bank holiday to ease the general situation. In protest at the failure to consult with more colleagues George Brown resigned. This time the break with the premier was not mended. Jenkins's budget of 19 March 1968 was praised for its elegance and coherence, but it was also a harsh affair, entailing tax increases of the order of nearly £1 billion in a full year. On the international front the institution of the two-tier gold system in the same month temporarily relieved the world liquidity crisis. But the general pressure on sterling continued, with withdrawals from balances proceeding so rapidly that over half the credit provided by the central bankers in the last two years had been used before June 1968. Overseas sterling area members were diversifying their reserves, and the scramble from sterling was only halted in the autumn by a complicated international agreement whereby holders of sterling balances agreed to retain a certain portion of their reserves in sterling in return for protection against further devaluation of the pound. The Bank for International Settlements in Basle, backed by twelve central banks, provided a $2 billion loan to Britain for up to five years to support the arrangement. Britain's official liabilities to foreign governments, central banks and international organizations had risen since 1962 from £4.6 billion to nearly £8 billion. Britain had the largest government foreign debt per head of population, and, according to Susan Strange, Britain was, 'in effect, the ward of the developed countries of the non-Communist world'.[20]

The government suffered severely at the hands of the electorate for these economic setbacks. In March 1968 there were three Conservative by-election gains, and in the May local elections Labour fared badly at the hands of the Conservatives and the nationalists. There was press speculation about the future of the Prime Minister, and about possible successors. There was talk of a coalition government. Strains were growing within the Labour party. The new Prices and Incomes Bill was introduced in May 1968 and there were over thirty Labour abstentions on the second reading. Twenty-three voted against in July, but no disciplinary action was possible, given the state of party feeling. In September the incomes policy was voted down by over seven to one by the TUC, and by nearly five to one at the Blackpool Party Conference. Yet with the relaxation in the wages 'freeze' a scramble for higher earnings was taking place, with average earnings rising about twice as fast as the government had hoped. Imports continued to run at a higher level than was desirable, while the growth in exports owed much to the spurt in world trade as a whole. As Roy Jenkins frankly admitted in 1969: 'We were floated up more by the buoyancy of world trade than by our own efforts.'

In such circumstances sterling was easily damaged. Speculation concerning the future value of the franc and mark injured sterling in November 1968. An international conference was needed in Bonn to paper over the cracks, and there was a further dose of deflation within

Britain, coupled with the introduction of an import deposit scheme designed to discourage imports. Alarmist rumours of a government crisis on 5 December hit the pound, and gave rise to what was known as 'mad Friday'. The editor of the *Guardian* and at least one Swiss banker suspected that British 'gnomes' might have been at work.[21] A wave of strikes early in 1969 made a poor start to another year and April found the Chancellor adding to the nation's tax bill and privately turning his mind to the possibility of floating sterling in the autumn if the situation seemed no brighter. In May further credits were required from the IMF, and a second Letter of Intent promised adjustments to the British economy to hasten a balance of payments surplus. In the course of 1969 the Chancellor for the first time looked to severe restraint of the money supply as another instrument with which to try to cut domestic demand. Michael Artis writes of a major change in the official view of monetary policy: 'This conversion not only related to the pressure from the International Monetary Fund but probably also represented a sense of despair at the apparent failure – up to then – of the standard weapons of economic management to produce "the goods" (a balance of payments surplus).'[22] There was a final speculative flurry in August 1969, but at long last the combination of massive deflation in Britain, devaluation and the buoyancy of world trade was carrying Britain firmly into surplus for the first time since 1963, and on such a scale as to satisfy even the most sceptical speculator.

Britain, however, achieved a growth of 8 per cent in the volume of her exports in 1969 against a rise of only 2 per cent in the volume of imports by a diversion rather than an increase in output. The rise in unemployment reflected this state of affairs, as did the stagnant level of investment save in manufacturing. The return to a surplus in the balance of payments thus did little to offset the generally disappointing performance of the British economy in the 1960s by the standards of other industrialized nations. For most of the decade world trade had grown very rapidly, but Britain had usually lacked the industrial capacity to take advantage of it save by exercising extreme restraint at home. But restraint on this scale discouraged new investment: the profitability of most industries was low, and a decade which had opened with both main political parties confident that they could revitalize British industry closed with the solutions seemingly as distant as they had ever been, if not more so.

Industrial relations

The Wilson government made one other great (and again unsuccessful) effort to carry at least part of Britain into the second half of the twentieth century. The desperate bid to 'modernize' labour relations in 1968–9 was largely prompted by the Cabinet's need to impress foreign opinion by its determination to make devaluation work and to end the balance of payments deficit.[23] There was a similar need to regain public confidence in Britain with a display of strong government. But over and above this it was impossible to feel complacent concerning the general trends in labour relations in this country in the course of the 1960s. The accelerating wages scramble whenever the government relaxed the controls on earnings was but one aspect of the growing power of unions and indeed of shop floor workers. Britain had seemed only moderately strike-prone by international standards in the 1950s, but there had been less room for complacency as the next decade lengthened. In 1965 the Wilson ministry had set up the Donovan Royal Commission on Trade Unions and Employers, and its report of June 1968 confirmed many of the worst fears. The report stressed the growing frequency with which formal machinery was being bypassed in industrial negotiations. The result was mounting confusion and disorder.

The unions themselves had not been wholly inactive or unconcerned. In 1962 the TUC was finally persuaded by George Woodcock to examine trade union organization. Although the number of unions had been much reduced since 1900, there were still nearly 700 of them, not all affiliated to the TUC. In the car industry Ford found themselves dealing with twenty unions whereas Vauxhall negotiated with only two. The situation was especially complex in shipbuilding, but fears for the future of that industry in the 1960s encouraged reorganization. By 1968 the number of unions had been cut to about 530, with notable new alliances such as the Amalgamated Society of Boilermakers, Shipwrights, Blacksmiths and Structural Workers, the Engineers and Foundry Workers, and the Electricians and Plumbers. The eleven largest unions embraced almost 60 per cent of the membership. But tentative references to industrial unionism only persuaded British unionists that this was impossible or undesirable. British union men had done much to establish such unions in Germany after the war, but there they had been working in exceptional circumstances and with almost a blank sheet. In Sweden, with a smaller workforce and with a much shorter and simpler history of industrial relations than Britain, it had still taken thirty years to complete the grand reorganization. Rapid change was not to be expected in Britain. Unions jealously guarded their autonomy against the TUC and other unions.

Mere size was no answer. Large unions often found themselves losing contact with and control over the rank and file. One of the features of the postwar era, powered by full employment, had been the rise of the local shop steward and of workshop bargaining. Union subscriptions had been falling in value, so that unions often found it difficult to recruit and pay the staff they needed at a time when it was vital that their expertise in many fields should have been improving. Wage differentials, and variations in pay between regions and between different firms in the same industry plagued industrial relations. In some industries, such as the car industry, highly complicated wage systems provided fertile grounds for dispute. One set of wage negotiations could set off a chain reaction through a whole plant or a whole industry. A strike by even a handful of discontented workers could often cause far-reaching disruption. By the early 1960s, too, strikes were occurring with increasing frequency over questions other than wage claims. Strikes over 'other working arrangements, rules and discipline' quickly doubled to about one-third of the total. Particularly vulnerable were the car firms, and among them the car assembly plans. But within this industry, as within others, generalizations can be dangerous. Some firms were more strike-prone than others: the anti-union history of Morris Motors perhaps helps to explain the continuing militancy at Cowley. Workers with a long history of quiescence might suddenly explode as a result of dramatic gains in earnings by comparable workers in another firm. As inflation became accepted as a fact of life the tendency to try to outpace it was understandable. Furthermore, in any comparison with West German workers, the greater legal and formal safeguards enjoyed by the latter should be borne in mind. In Britain, the worker looked instinctively to his union or shop steward.

The government's dismay over the rise of shop floor wage bargaining was a little ironic given its own encouragement of productivity deals, which of course required that type of approach. Incomes policy had been circumvented in other ways, so that the Prices and Incomes Board concluded that its effect between 1965 and 1968 had been to reduce incomes by no more than one per cent a year (though even that was the equivalent of a saving of £100 million in imports or 100,000 unemployed). The Donovan Commission was especially impressed by the prevalence of unofficial strikes – they represented about 95 per cent of the total in recent years. The majority of its members, however, opposed reform through government legislation and legal coercion. Working and wage agreements, it was contended, were too vague and complicated to be enforceable by law. Reform must primarily be the task of industry itself, though with assistance from a proposed industrial relations commission (with advisory powers alone). In time the Donovan Commission expected new institutions, rules and conventions to emerge that would ease current problems. This seemed defeatist to many, but it was in fact a sensible recognition that the influence and aspirations of workers could not be abruptly changed, whatever the practice in other countries. Old habits died hard, and in Britain the law had played an unusually small part in labour relations, or when it had, it had usually appeared as a threat to workers' interests. As for the possibility of rapid change by other means, the experience of ICI between 1965 and 1972 was to demonstrate the need for patience and still more patience. Only after several false starts was some progress made towards a new structure of labour relations in that company, and one which belatedly reflected the new confidence and aspirations of the workers. The contrast between Vauxhall and Ford was a further demonstration of what could be achieved by sensitive management and a responsive union movement over a period of years. The better labour relations record of Vauxhall was perpetuated when both Vauxhall and Ford established factories on Merseyside. Ronald Dore in an important comparison of British and Japanese labour relations noted that those in Britain had been instituted in the free market context of the nineteenth century, Japan's in the much more regulated society from 1945. Students of labour relations in Britain ignored its long history at their peril.

There was an obvious deterioration in Britain's strike record in 1968. Past concessions to the government by moderate union leaders had tended to weaken their influence. Warnings that a wages scramble would delay reflation, tax cuts, and an expansion of the social services made less and less impact. As its incomes policy crumbled, so the government's standing in the country as a whole continued to fall. Towards the end of 1968 *The Times* and *Daily Mirror* both pressed for a coalition: a Gallup Poll recorded only 30 per cent support for Labour. The Conservatives threatened to seize the initiative with their *Fair Deal at Work*, published in April 1968. Its proposals for the reform of industrial relations attracted much attention, and Labour had cause to fear that union militancy would work in favour of their opponents at the next election if left unchecked. Mrs Barbara Castle as Secretary of State for Employment and Productivity was determined to save the unions from themselves, and had been persuaded by November 1968 that some strengthening of government powers over the unions was unavoidable. Talks with the TUC and CBI on the Donovan Report found some union leaders critical even of its modest proposals. There was no consensus within the Cabinet, though those in favour of action could find much to support their arguments by reference to the need to regain both foreign and domestic confidence.[24] The Chancellor was badly in need of a measure of this kind to reassure the IMF. The government's *In Place of Strife* (Cmnd 3888) was published on 17 January 1969, 'penal clauses' appearing in only three of its twenty-seven proposals, some of which would have strengthened workers' rights in industry. A Commission on Industrial Relations was proposed, plus an Industrial Board, to provide an institutional framework for the modernization of labour relations. These, in conjunction with the Secretary of State for Employment, would be concerned also with the prevention of inter-union disputes. Recourse might be had to fines, as, for instance, if workers refused to agree to a twenty-eight day 'cooling-off' period in the case of an unconstitutional strike. Fines might be employed to back up orders for a ballot before a strike which could constitute a serious threat to the public interest. Initial hopes that legislation on these lines would not provoke a crisis among the unions or in the Labour movement as a whole were soon disappointed. Over fifty MPs began openly to show their opposition; others had doubts, and within the Cabinet James Callaghan was known to be hostile. His opposition resulted in a serious personal rift with the Prime Minister.

The government's legislative proposals were announced by the

Chancellor in his budget speech of 15 April 1969 – clearly it was hoped to impress foreign opinion. The strike ballot proposal was dropped, but provision was made for the use of fines in the last resort in inter-union and unoffocial disputes. The TUC bitterly opposed fines with their 'taint of criminality', but agreed to Wilson's offer to discuss any alternative propositions they might care to make. It was a testing time for the acting General Secretary of the TUC, Victor Feather (he did not properly succeed Woodcock until September). On the one hand he was fighting to protect the traditional rights of the unions, but on the other he saw the need for a constructive response. The unions possessed great powers in this struggle, not least their dominant financial contribution to the Labour party. They were supported by a majority on the NEC, and there were moves by some Labour MPs to unseat Wilson from the premiership. The unions, however, could not ignore the damage that might be inflicted on Labour by an entirely negative response on their part. The Conservatives would benefit electorally. In May, therefore, the General Council of the TUC produced its *Programme for Action* which, while insisting on no government sanctions, promised some action against inter-union disputes. Any union which refused to accept the decision of the General Council in such a matter could be suspended and if necessary expelled from the TUC. A special meeting of the TUC in June produced overwhelming support for this small concession – but nothing more. A meeting of the Cabinet on 17 June suggested that a majority of ministers now either opposed the Bill or entertained strong reservations. The Chief Whip reported that more than half the parliamentary party was opposed. Indeed, had MPs been able to rally behind one figure, the Prime Minister might have fallen. Roy Jenkins concluded that it was too late in any case to secure the passage of the Bill. A final meeting of Wilson and Barbara Castle with the TUC took place on 18 June at which they were able to secure only one more marginal concession. It was a delicate meeting, with Hugh Scanlon of the AEU warning that his national committee might well retract the concessions already made if the government continued to press. Other unions declared that no decisions would be workable without the backing of the AEU. The government was therefore able to gain no more from the TUC than a 'clarification' of Rule 11 concerning the TUC's right to intervene in disputes that menaced the jobs of other workers who were not directly involved. Again the TUC finally agreed to suspend a refractory union.

Harold Wilson claimed in his memoirs that the unions had moved forward forty years in one month. Feather later thought that in the ensuing year the TUC might have saved the nation approaching 3 million strike days. The tangible gains were in fact of dubious value at best. Of most significance was the discovery of some formula which could begin a healing process between the parliamentary party and the unions, and within the parliamentary party itself. The argument that the Cabinet had once again muffed an opportunity to carry forward a useful reform is doubtful in the extreme. The rights and wrongs of the intentions of the Prime Minister and Barbara Castle need not detain us here, but it is clear that they could have proceeded further only at their own political peril and that of the Labour movement. It is surprising that they were prepared to go as far as they did.

Chapter 12

The United Kingdom at the end of the sixties

Northern Ireland

British complacency had been dented in many ways since the mid-1950s, but the nation was still ill-prepared for the spectacle of part of the United Kingdom becoming a constant prey to bomb attacks, to violence and counter-violence of all kinds, to the internment of citizens without trial, and to the use of the armed forces in an internal political dispute. The Irish question which had for so long troubled British politics had been thankfully forgotten since the 1920s. A few remembered Northern Ireland as a place where the police wore revolvers, the Irish Republican Army occasionally caught the headlines, while a remarkable number of Irish appeared to spend more time in Britain than in their homelands. The neutrality of Eire had been resented during the Second World War, though the Dublin government had chosen wisely and had conducted its foreign policy with a fair measure of skill. In April 1949 Eire became a republic and left the Commonwealth, but continued to act as a reservoir of labour (mostly unskilled) for the United Kingdom. Most of its food exports went to the same destination, and over half its trade was with Britain. The inhabitants of the two states enjoyed reciprocal rights of citizenship. Dublin protested when Whitehall, in recognizing the republic, added that any change in the status of Northern Ireland could only be by act of the latter's parliament at Stormont.

It was a well established convention, challenged occasionally by a few Labour MPs, that Westminster did not interfere in the affairs of the North. There was some vague and ineffectual awareness that the Catholic minority in the province did not receive equal treatment with the Protestants.' This seemed of less consequence when, in the mid-1960s the Northern Ireland government with Terence O'Neill as prime minister, and with some union and middle-class support, both launched a modest reform programme in the province; and began seeking closer relations with the South.[1] On 5 August 1966, however, O'Neill warned Wilson that a period of consolidation would be needed in the province in view of the hostile reactions from the more extreme Protestants. But pressure for reform was also growing among the Catholics, and in February 1967 the Catholic Civil Rights movement was founded. Whitehall pressed O'Neill to make further concessions, especially to meet Catholic complaints of discrimination in local elections and in housing. O'Neill's efforts to respond encountered only more discontent on both sides. His reforms were a threat to all extremists. The discontented perhaps needed no outside encouragement, but the late-1960s also witnessed serious disturbances in the United States over Negro rights and Vietnam, student unrest was widespread, and there were major riots in Paris in 1968. Violence flared in Londonderry on 5 October 1968. Wilson urged O'Neill to hasten parliamentary reform, but the British government, in recognition of the threat to O'Neill from his own party, was soon preparing contingency plans for various forms of British intervention. Unionist party divisions finally forced O'Neill's resignation on 28 April 1969. Britain was a step nearer direct involvement under the powers provided by the Government of Ireland Act of 1920.

The new Ulster Cabinet did not abandon the reform programme, but it could no more arrest the train of events than O'Neill before it. On 12 August the Protestant Apprentice Boys march in Londonderry precipitated more violence, and on the 14th the Ulster government was forced to ask for British military assistance. Whitehall was determined not to become directly involved without corresponding political influence. It could not afford to appear simply as the defender of the Protestant Ascendancy. By the Downing Street Declaration of 19 August the Ulster government promised to take the fullest possible account of British views of the rights and status of *all* Northern Ireland's citizens. Whitehall began to exercise a general oversight though not direct control over Ulster's affairs. For the time being British intervention was generally welcomed by the Catholics, while British information suggested that the IRA was a weak, divided and unimportant organization at that stage.

Important evidence of the state of opinion in Northern Ireland at this time is provided by a detailed survey conducted in 1968 among some 1,300 citizens of the province.[2] Only 13 per cent of the Catholics interviewed admitted to support for the most extreme measures to end Partition, though no more than 30 per cent seemed prepared to accept its continuance. If three-quarters of the Protestants seemed disposed to make some concessions and to seek closer relations with the South, half were prepared to defend Protestant control of Ulster by any means. Most Catholics described their nationality as 'Irish', and almost as many Protestants felt that Northern Ireland was very different from England. Indeed Professor Moody argued in *The Ulster Question, 1603–1973* that Protestant Ulster was more than an outlying part of British society, while Catholic Ulster was not indistinguishable from the rest of Catholic Ireland. The British had great difficulty in comprehending the nature of the Ulster question and for a long time exaggerated the possibilities of a reasonable compromise. O'Neill thought James Callaghan exceptional among British politicians in his efforts to grasp the special Ulster dimensions, and the terrible force of phrases, dates and historical episodes (reaching back to Cromwell and beyond) which had no meaning to the British.[3] In addition, although the province had experienced some economic advance in recent years, its unemployment rate was well above the national average. In 1968–9 it was over 7 per cent, with the rate among Catholics being three times as high as that for Protestants. There were disproportionate numbers of Catholics among the lower paid and those with poor educational qualifications. Over 90 per cent of the important Harland and Wolff shipyard was Protestant, only 6 per cent of the senior civil servants were Catholic, and only 11 per cent of the Royal Ulster Constabulary. The Cameron Commission of 1969 found clear evidence of gerrymandering in some local elections, and nowhere else in the western world were Catholics so much excluded from positions of influence. The great majority of Catholics were convinced that they were the victims of discrimination.

Given the history of Ireland and the current condition of Ulster there was reason to doubt whether any scale of reform could win sufficient Catholic acceptance of partition. Equally there was little prospect that sufficient Protestants would agree either to radical reforms or to approaches to Eire (where clerical influences over the Dublin government were much feared) which would begin to erase the border. Lord Salisbury had asked in 1873, 'Is it just conceivable that there is no remedy that we can apply to the Irish hatred of ourselves . . . there is no precedent in our history or any other, to teach us that political measures can conjure away hereditary antipathies which are fed by constant agitation?' Nevertheless the British government from 1969 had to hope that a determined reform programme might yet save the day. Through the reform of local government voting, the creation of fair electoral districts, a centralized system of housing allocation, a body to handle complaints of discrimination, the disarming of the police and the disbanding of the B Specials (an auxiliary force seen by Catholics as one of the most hated agencies of Protestant power) it was hoped that Catholic discontents might be appeased. More impartial police and security forces were envisaged.

Yet concessions to one side provoked trouble from the other. Protestant riots accompanied the disbandment of the B Specials in October 1969. The first half of 1970 saw the rise of a new Protestant challenger to the Unionist party in the person of the Rev. Ian Paisley, who won his way to Westminster in the general election of June 1970. On the other side the formation of the Social Democratic Labour Party failed to arrest the increase in violence among the Catholics, in part in self-defence against the extreme Protestants. The IRA itself had split into the ultra-militant Provisionals and the more cautious (Marxist) Officials. Catholic opinion was by the spring of 1970 ceasing to regard the British army as their defenders against the Protestants. The reasoned dialogue that the British government, mainly through the person of James Callaghan, had tried to promote, was losing ground. The first Catholic clash with the army occurred in west Belfast on 2–3 April.

Religion and 'permissiveness'

While 'Catholic' and 'Protestant' battled with each other in Northern Ireland most religious denominations in the rest of the United Kingdom continued to lose influence. It is true that well into the 1950s most churches could claim some increase in active membership – as for instance represented in the number of Easter communicants. But thereafter only the Catholics and some fundamentalist sects continued to grow. The Society of Friends remained stable: for the rest, including the Salvation Army, there was an unmistakable decline in active membership. Interest in the ecumenical movement was as much a sign of weakness as of vigour. Sundry attempts at radically new presentations of religion had little lasting effect. John Robinson, bishop of Woolwich, made an interesting attempt in *Honest to God* (1963) to find a replacement for the concept of God as 'an old man in the sky' and to face the challenge of changing ideas on morality. Some three-quarters of a million copies of the book were sold in the 1960s, but it is doubtful if it greatly influenced the thinking of many people. Most churches continued to lose their old central social position, notably in education but also in other aspects of people's lives. The church was no longer as it had been in Victorian times, 'the moral health department, an office for the good administration of souls' as the Frenchman Hippolyte Taine described it.

Morals were being viewed increasingly as a matter for individual choice. With the secularization of education and thought, with the growth of new welfare, advice and psychological services, and with religion largely ceasing to be identified with social and political differences, the status and influence of the clergy could not fail to decline. The continuance of Catholic schools, the demands placed by Catholicism on its membership, its appeal to potential converts through its less compromising character and greater evocation of mystery, help to account for its greater success. But it, too, was helped by the presence of so many Irish workers in Britain, a community within a community. The long-standing Catholic–Protestant differences in Glasgow sometimes cast an ominous shadow. In politics there were still a few remaining links between the Liberals and nonconformity in, for instance, the extreme south-west of England. Nonconformity was also linked with Labour and Plaid Cymru in Wales. The percentage of church weddings fell significantly in Britain from the mid-1950s until they represented only about two-thirds of the total. On the other hand the percentage rose in Ulster to around 95 per cent. Yet it would be premature to describe the British as an essentially secular people. Well-presented religious programmes on television enjoyed considerable success. The majority of people seemed as reluctant to disavow any sort of belief as to attend church.

Some found it tempting to link the spectacular rise in crime and of the so-called 'permissive' society with the decline in religion. Christie

Davies, in *Permissive Britain*, put the matter rather differently, asking which in the overall perspective of history seemed the more in need of explanation, the permissive or the puritanical societies. One of the features of the twentieth century was the swing from a moralistic view of life to more pragmatic and functional attitudes. The debate on capital punishment in 1948 had centred mainly on the moral aspect: by the 1960s the main question was its efficacy as a deterrent. It was finally abolished in 1969. The Divorce Reform Act of 1969 eliminated, from 1971, the necessity for a matrimonial offence before a marriage could be dissolved. The test to be applied was whether a marriage had irretrievably broken down. The number of divorces more than doubled in the early 1970s, but marriage and the idea of the family unit as the norm remained as strong as ever. The strength of the family was reflected in the National Children's Bureau survey of 14,000 sixteen-year-olds in 1974.[4] This gave an impression of great continuity in attitudes from generation to generation. If nearly 10 per cent had been in trouble with the law, and many showed poor motivation in their school-work, this rebelliousness on the whole did not extend to any widespread interest in breaking from traditional family concepts. A more permissive attitude to sex had certainly been accompanied by an increase in the proportion of illegitimate births in the 1960s. But instability in family life had also been affected by the growth of employment among mothers of young children. The percentage of working mothers overall had grown from 26 per cent in 1961 to 40 per cent in 1971.

Functionalism was also evident in the changing attitudes to birth control. The Family Planning Association had begun life under another name in 1930, but widespread interest in systematic birth control developed only in the 1960s. In addition the controversial Abortion Bill was passed in 1967. The British birth-rate fell sharply from the later 1960s. In 1947 it had been 20.7 per thousand: by 1975 it had fallen to 12.4. Indeed, with migration, the population of the United Kingdom fell slightly in 1974–5. There was a great relaxation in the censorship of books, films and the theatre, but this gave rise to serious debate, on functional and other grounds, as to how far this relaxation was responsible for a rise in crimes of violence and sex. Though academic research produced somewhat ambivalent conclusions, there was no room for complacency. Between 1951 and 1972 cases of burglary, robbery and fraud known to the police tripled; cases of wounding and assault increased ten times; motoring offences increased nearly fourfold. The most dramatic rise in crime took place among the under twenty-ones. Dangerous drug offences doubled between 1969 and 1972. There was a general rise in alcoholism from 1945. Such developments were common to the whole industrialized world, with Britain suffering less than some. The Committee on Children and Young Persons had concluded as early as 1960 that the upsurge in crime, at first popularly attributed to the Second World War, was related to the whole course of material change and cultural evolution (or confusion) in the twentieth century. 'It is not always so clearly recognized what a complete change there has been in social and personal relationships (between classes, between the sexes and between individuals) and also in the basic assumptions which regulate behaviour.'

The 29th Congress of the International Psycho-Analytical Association in 1975 devoted itself to the study of the implications for itself of social change. Concerning the decline in commonly accepted values it was agreed that this was increasing the psychological problems of many people and adding to the numbers who were turning to psycho-analysts for help. In another age such problems, in so far as they had existed, would have fallen more naturally to priests and ministers of religion. The speed of change was also remarkable. Soon after the war Geoffrey Gorer had made a study of British society and one of his key questions had been the fate of the aggression that had for so long marked British life. He commented on the remarkably restrained behaviour of football crowds. Less than a generation later he would have had no need to pose such a question. In a more general view of British society, *Paris–Match* commented in 1972 that the English had finally escaped after two centuries from 'puritanical morality and industrial assiduity'. Yet the English 'swinging' image of the 1960s did not long endure. Research by the British Tourist Authority in 1976 suggested that the average Frenchman's view of the English was still very much that of a reserved and conservative people.

Immigration and discrimination

The question of coloured immigration first began to attract attention around 1953, though the real start of migration from the West Indies to Britain can be dated from the arrival of the *Empire Windrush* with 492 persons, many of them ex-servicemen, in June 1948. These early immigrants very strongly saw themselves as 'British subjects', yet sensing resentment at their coming they also asked, 'Is it because we are coloured?' Britain was rapidly assimilating large numbers of European refugees from Nazi or communist regimes in the 1940s, and given the postwar labour shortage and the large-scale emigration to the Commonwealth the British government was anxious to recruit foreign labour. The Royal Commission on the Population thought in June 1949 that 140,000 young immigrants a year might be needed, though anxiety was also expressed that the race and religion of the migrants should facilitate intermarriage with the host population. Continuing labour shortages, however, diminished concern on these counts, and in any case under British law any Commonwealth citizen was permitted to settle permanently and enjoy full rights. The number of coloured immigrants (still estimated to be well under 100,000) did not attract ministerial attention before 1954. A tentative bill on controls was drafted in 1955 and Macmillan showed interest in such a possibility again in 1957. Apart from critics of immigration on racilist grounds there were MPs, trade unionists, and civil servants in the Home Office who foresaw growing practical problems. But the Colonial Office and Commonwealth Relations Office were anxious to avoid difficulties with the West Indies and India. The government remained inactive, though some churches and unofficial bodies and individuals began to take active steps to try to promote the interests of the coloured population. The Institute of Race Relations was set up in 1958.

In August of the same year occurred the first race riots. The government was negotiating with India, Pakistan and the West Indies in the hope that they would impose long-term controls. Some ministers were anxious to do nothing to damage the Commonwealth, but in 1960 the number of immigrants rose sharply. The Cabinet had agreed on legislation by May 1961, but knowledge that such legislation was imminent produced an even greater influx. In the first ten months of 1961 some 113,000 arrived from the West Indies and the Indian subcontinent. The Immigration Bill was published on 1 November 1961. It introduced a quota system for ordinary immigrants, with vouchers for those with special skills or with actual jobs. A poll at the end of the month suggested that the bill enjoyed 90 per cent popular support. Nevertheless there was a fierce battle in the Commons. The bill was widely condemned as a concession to racial prejudice, and among the strongest opponents were Hugh Gaitskell and *The Times*. It passed its third reading by 277 votes to 170 on 27 February 1962 (the large number of abstentions is interesting). The bill certainly boosted immigrant entry in 1961–2; it may have encouraged permanent settlement by Indians and Pakistanis especially who might otherwise have sought only temporary employment. With hindsight it might be argued that the government should, at an earlier date, have followed the practice of West Germany in particular and admitted workers from abroad on a temporary basis, and made special housing and welfare provision for them during their stay. But this would have been unthinkable in the context of the Commonwealth and of Britain's special place in it during the 1950s. In the case of some immigrants Britain owed a special debt for their part in the war effort. As it was, by the early 1960s, the weight of past events and ideas, current illusions concerning the Commonwealth, and significant failures of imagination had saddled many of the poorer communities in Britain, as well as many of the immigrants themselves, with a host of problems.

Well before the 1964 election Labour had come to accept the need for some controls on immigration, though it hoped to achieve this through cooperation with certain Commonwealth countries. In February 1965, however, the Wilson ministry itself had to tighten the restrictions on the entry of unskilled workers (polls suggested at least 80 per cent of the British people thought too many immigrants had already been admitted). The government tried to balance these restraints with more positive moves against discrimination. The Conservatives had already set up the Commonwealth Immigrants Advisory Council in 1962. Labour published its rather tepid Race Relations Bill in April 1965 which set out to prohibit racial discrimination in public places, and introduced penalties against incitement to racial hatred. A Race Relations Board was set up in 1966, though with the emphasis on conciliation rather than punishment in the case of proven discrimination. The Conservatives, too, were showing interest in policies of integration, and the racial issue did not figure prominently in the 1966 election. But the battles against discrimination and for integration were not to be won by vaguely professed good intentions. Liverpool had had long experience of coloured communities and was a practical demonstration as to how discrimination could become institutionalized. The churches in general proved too middle-class and remote from West Indian experience. West Indian church-going dropped sharply by comparison with practice in the Caribbean, and they often turned to small churches of their own creation, mostly Pentecostal in doctrine. Those from the Indian subcontinent were still more disposed to cling to their own ways, while the West Indians found themselves largely driven back into their own communities.

Apart from the great contribution of Commonwealth doctors to the National Health Service, especially in the hospitals, the great majority of immigrants were poor, unskilled or with only limited skills. These were obliged to concentrate in poor areas and to take a limited range of jobs, notably in transport, the more menial jobs in the hospitals, and in west midland factories. In 1961 about one-third of the immigrants were concentrated in the Greater London area, especially in the boroughs of Lambeth, Paddington and Kensington. A further 7 per cent were in Birmingham. The areas of greatest immigrant concentration were often poorly served in housing, schools, medical and other facilities. Immigrant poverty and the desperate need to save encouraged overcrowding. Unfamiliar cooking smells, exuberant West Indian celebrations, and other miscellaneous differences could create friction with the local population as well as more profound fears over jobs, property values, mixed marriages, and intangibles that could not be properly articulated. Schools often felt special strains, despite efforts to confine immigrant children in any one institution to one-third of the register at most. In Bradford there were many Pakistani children whose parents knew little or no English. In 1976 only about half the Asian-born adult immigrants in Britain could speak English reasonably well. For the children of immigrants there were cultural clashes but often, worse, a sense of rejection by the country and society in which they had lived all or most of their lives. The disillusionment and frustrations of so many of this second generation would perhaps prove the greatest problem of all. Special government aid in housing and services for areas with large immigrant communities grew in the later 1960s, but a faltering economy posed a double threat in that it would increasingly restrict the aid which could be offered and in the greater vulnerability of the coloured population to unemployment.

The Home Office under Roy Jenkins in 1966–7 strove to achieve a balance between conflicting pressures and interests. Jenkins declared on 23 May 1966: 'I define integration, therefore, not as a flattening process of assimilation but as equal opportunity, accompanied by cultural diversity, in an atmosphere of mutual tolerance.' This was sensitive and intelligent. But he also added realistically that immigrant entry must be determined by the absorptive capacity of the country, 'the social factor being for the moment, I believe, more restrictive than the economic'. Uncertainty as to the numbers of immigrants already in the country, exaggerated fears as to their birth-rate, and expectations of a flood of dependants joining those already here created a volatile atmosphere which easily exploded when Asians with British passports began to arrive from Kenya, fleeing from prejudice and pressures in that country. Many more were expected to follow from East Africa as a whole. New government legislation to control entry appeared in February 1968, and a stiffer bill against discrimination was introduced at the same time. Protection was extended to employment and housing. Discrimination, however, was so varied and hard to define that the amount actually tackled was no more than the proverbial tip of the iceberg. Studies published in 1974 and 1976, for instance, found ample evidence of continuing discrimination of all kinds.

Formalized opposition to coloured immigrants at first made little progress. The National Front was formed in 1966, but the first real opportunity for public opinion to express itself with dramatic force on the subject did not occur until Enoch Powell's Birmingham speech of 20 April 1968. Parliament was discussing the new Race Relations Bill, and Edward Heath was hoping to overcome divisions within his party on this subject with a 'reasoned amendment'. Basically, however, the two front benches wished to maintain a reasonable measure of quiet cooperation and consensus on the issue. Powell had shown independence on other occasions, but never so starkly as now. His concern over the racial issue was of fairly recent origin. He had once been a great enthusiast for empire, but as one who prided himself on his rigorous pursuit of logic it was not surprising that, when he found Britain rejected in India and Africa, he should finally have insisted on the right of the British to reject the alien peoples among themselves. Powell, in his Birmingham speech, warned that in the light of his projections of the growth of the non-white population in Britain – there could be over five million by the year 2000 – the English might become 'strangers in their own country'. He declared: 'Like the Romans, I seem to see "the River Tiber flowing with much blood".' Even so strong an advocate of the end of coloured immigration as Gerald Nabarro, a pugnacious Conservative backbencher, thought the speech 'unnecessarily theatrical, lurid and unrestrained'. Nevertheless it evoked remarkable sympathy

and interest in the country. Gallup found three-quarters of those polled
in favour and only 15 per cent against. On the other hand about two-
thirds favoured some legislation against racial discrimination: more,
however, opposed the current government bill than supported it.

Powell continued to attract as much attention as any British
politician, though he was assisted by a lemming-like rush by the media
in search of controversial copy. Nevertheless the race question played
only a small part in the 1970 election. Powell was dismissed instantly by
Heath from the shadow Cabinet following his Birmingham speech, and
the racial issue was kept out of the mainstream of British political
discussion. The racial dimension within British society helped to lessen
interest in the Commonwealth – certainly in the non-white Commonwealth – and even to strengthen prejudices against it. Immigration
restrictions caused occasional friction with visitors from Australia and
New Zealand. Britain's place at the centre of the Commonwealth
continued to decline. At home the racial dimension threatened to create
long term and explosive problems.[5] By 1975 immigrants totalled over 3
per cent of the population.

Social reform

One of Labour's most emphatic promises in the 1964 and 1966 elections
had been a radical improvement in the social services, with special aid to
the least well-off members of the community. Expenditure rose sharply;
the social services secured a higher share of the gross national product
than ever before. Yet Professor Victor George commented that the
'performance of the Wilson Labour government in the 1960s was
certainly worse with regard to social reform than that of the Attlee
government in the 1940s.[6] As early as 1967 Peter Townsend was
complaining that the reform measures were no more than 'hot
compresses on an ailing body politic'. Britain's overall performance in
social welfare ranked below that generally achieved within the EEC.
There were obviously grounds for complaint and disappointment, but
at the same time it had to be remembered that the Wilson ministries were
struggling with recurrent economic crises and slow growth. Britain
could afford to spend less freely than West Germany or France. In
addition there was a steady rise in the numbers and proportion of the
population who were too young or too old to work. By the end of the
decade pensioners represented about 15 per cent of the population. In
1941 the ratio of children and pensioners to the working population had
stood at 488 to 1,000; in 1969 the ratio was 655 to 1,000. Much of the
greater expenditure was thus absorbed by rising numbers. In these
circumstances the plight of the poor could only have been relieved by a
radical redistribution of wealth. Many sociologists inclined to or
strongly favoured this solution. Some suggestions on these lines were so
facile as to ignore the competing claims of investment and defence:

others showed more awareness of the difficulties, and justified the radical nature of their arguments with the comment that through extreme proposals one might attract attention and more response, however limited. For those in daily contact with deprivation the dilemma could be acute. Drastic remedies, however impractical, could appear the only way forward.

As the decade progressed, so official inquiries and those of influential academics such as Peter Townsend, Richard Titmuss and Brian Abel-Smith dispelled the complacency of the 1950s that poverty was being steadily eroded. Estimates varied as to the numbers involved, and as to what constituted unacceptable levels of poverty. It had become official policy from 1959 that as average living standards rose, so too should those of the poorest in the community. A government survey in 1966 concluded that 166,000 families, embracing some half million children, were living below the official subsistence level because of the low wages of the father. As an employed person he had no claim on supplementary benefits. Another 20,000 families were affected by the 'wage stop' whereby the unemployed father was not entitled to full supplementary benefit since this would have raised his income above what he could expect to earn if fully employed. It was estimated that 75,000 families were not claiming benefits to which they were entitled, and 65,000 were dependent upon the mother's earnings to rise above the minimum standard. The Department of Health and Social Security published estimates for 1972 that there existed some 1.25 million families with incomes below the basic supplementary benefit level despite the efforts of governments in recent years to fill gaps in the system. Pensioner households were particularly vulnerable, and represented 60 per cent of the above-mentioned total. It was also calculated that since 1948 governments had been hard put to raise the basic pension above 30 per cent of the average manual wage – often it had fallen below that percentage.

Poverty, it was evident, was not being steadily confined to the incorrigible or incompetent. Educational and employment opportunities had not increased significantly for the poorest; insufficient attention had been paid to the effects of rapid industrial change, with the consequent loss of jobs, the obsolescence of certain skills, and the fall in demand for unskilled labour. The cumulative effect of generations of poverty had been underestimated, together with the continuing stigmas that were attached to poverty, and the accompanying sense of rejection and failure. Professor Titmuss argued in 1966 for policies of social as well as economic growth; for positive discrimination in favour of the deprived (he argued that since 1948 the better-off had gained more from the improved social services than the poor).[7] Various groups were also becoming active to plead the case of the underprivileged, the disabled and handicapped. Over a million people suffered from permanent injuries, illnesses or deformities. The partly disabled, for instance, although able to undertake many forms of work, suffered from an unemployment rate of 14 per cent in 1971. In these circumstances there was great scope for such organizations as the Disablement Income Group (set up in 1965), the Child Poverty Action Group, and Age Concern. Housing for the poor was provided by Shelter. Deprivation took so many forms that voluntary action had a major role to play despite the growth of state provision. Fatherless families were especially exposed to poverty: much had still to be done in the struggle for equal rights for women in the provision of social security. Some, indeed, were coming to argue that the struggle on behalf of the underprivileged should take more positive and direct forms, with homelessness, for instance, being combated by 'squatting' in unoccupied buildings. This developed from 1969, and in some areas gained a neasure of local authority acquiescence. Paternalism, it was said, was bad in itself and bad for the poor. Self-help and self-organization were encouraged as steps on the road to self-confidence and self-betterment.

The motivation of those involved in work of this kind was mixed. Some were moved by deep hostility towards the existing political and social order, but even those who were less radically inclined often found government policy half-hearted if not heartless. Certainly the government's approach to social policy could be governed by more than simple welfare considerations. Thus the National Insurance Act of 1966 introduced wage-related unemployment and sickness benefits, a move chosen against the preference of some ministers for increased family allowances and supplementary benefits as being cheaper and having the added advantage of possibly encouraging mobility of labour. Nevertheless one of the first steps of the Wilson government had been to set up the Seebohm Committee to 'review the organization of responsibilities of the local authority personal social services in England and Wales'. This reported in 1968. It insisted that not only was there need for improved provision but also for the systematic reorganization of the services provided by the local authorities. These had grown up haphazardly over the years, with many overlapping responsibilities and a great want of coordination. The Local Authority Social Services Act was passed in 1970 (separate provision had been made for Scotland in 1969). Greater attention was being paid to the prevention and cure of problems before families became irretrievably 'broken', while in the 1970s there was to be an extensive elaboration of personal social services of all kinds before development was upset by the economic crisis in the middle of the decade. In 1966 the National Assistance Board was merged with the Ministry of Pensions to become the Ministry of Social Security, in part to try to remove the stigma that was attached to National Assistance. Supplementary benefits were no longer so described: people's entitlement to such benefits was publicized, yet it was still found that not all those eligible applied.

By the late 1960s a new approach to pensions was needed. With the growing numbers of retired people, with the current contributory system and the government's reluctance to throw too much of the burden on the taxpayer, the problem of providing adequate pensions was growing. Nearly 30 per cent of all pensioners were in need of supplementation. Far more so than in much of western Europe retirement in Britain meant passage to second-class citizenship. The government white paper on superannuation published in January 1969 (Cmnd 3883) noted:

The present annual cost of retirement pensions alone is over £1,500 million, which is the equivalent of 5s 3d on the standard rate of income tax. Even if it were remotely realistic to consider a transfer of this order from contributions to taxation, the Government would still think it wrong. . . . People do not want to be given pensions and benefits: they want to earn them by contributions.

The same document estimated that state and private occupational schemes for retirement covered about half of the working population of 23 million. Despite their growth (private coverage had doubled to 8 million since 1955) it was estimated 'on present trends that even by the turn of the century about a third of retirement pensioner households will still have no occupational pension at all'. The government made an ambitious and complicated attempt to provide adequate pensions for all under the direction of Richard Crossman, the minister with overall responsibility for the social services. The 1970 election (and the government's defeat) intervened before the necessary legislation could be carried.

Housing attracted much attention in the search for a strategy to break the 'cycle of deprivation' as well as for more general reasons. The problems varied sharply from area to area. Glasgow continued to suffer from the worst overcrowding of any major city in Europe. Nearly two-fifths of the nation's housing stock dated from before 1919, and up to 200,000 homes were becoming unfit with the passage of each year. A revolution was occurring with the decreasing availability of privately rented accommodation. In 1947 this sector had provided well over half of all housing; by 1966 it provided less than a quarter (though around 37 per cent in London); by 1975, the figure was down to 16 per cent. There had been a great increase in local authority housing, but this did not easily meet the needs of the young or those moving from town to town. The growth in owner-occupation had been still more remarkable, the proportion rising from barely a quarter after the war to about one-half by 1970. In the 1950s incomes had risen faster than house prices on average. The trend to home-ownership once established, it proceeded very much under its own momentum in the 1960s. It was an attractive investment, and a pleasure in its own right. Gross advances from building societies rose from £544 million in 1961 to £3,649 million in 1972, or more than twice as fast as the rise in individual house prices. Housing completions of all kinds reached a postwar peak between 1964 and 1968 at around 400,000 a year, but thereafter rising costs and the general state of the economy brought a decline. Completions were down to a quarter of a million by 1974.

A vast improvement in the housing of the majority of the population could thus be recorded since the war. Impressive progress was made in the 1960s in the modernization of old property, and according to one estimate the percentage lacking basic amenities was halved to 16 per cent in the course of the decade. Certainly the overall housing situation in Britain appeared to be much more satisfactory than in France. Nevertheless no less than 100,000 were reported to be homeless in 1975. The decay of old property and the increasing difficulty of finding the funds to refurbish or to build new left housing as a major ongoing problem. State and local authority aid was not always directed to those most in need, though there was some implementation in the 1970s of the Seebohm Report's 1968 recommendation that housing policy must take account of family needs whether in municipally or privately rented accommodation. Needy tenants of both kinds began to receive financial help with high rents. The Wilson government also made some small provision for poorer house purchasers. Rising costs of new construction, recognition of the sometimes damaging social and economic consequences of pulling down old housing in the centres of cities in favour of estate developments around the periphery, were also leading to rather more emphasis on the rehabilitation of older property. Other aspects of postwar housing policy were causing concern. By the early 1970s there was growing criticism of the great multistorey tower blocks of flats. There had been too little analysis of the social and psychological effects of 'high-rise' living. For the architects the tower blocks had been exciting challenges; for planners they had saved space. The planners had had great scope since 1945. They had had many successes, but by the early 1970s there were grave fears that people had been too readily cleared from city centres, that old property had been too readily bulldozed into the ground in favour of building schemes whose skylines and outward appearance were more impressive than the sort of life that could be led within them. Advances in material comfort had not necessarily been accompanied by the preservation of neighbourliness and a sense of community.

Developments in education

One of the proudest boasts of the Wilson ministry was that it had succeeded in raising national expenditure on education above that on defence. The great expansion in education was already under way when Labour took office in 1964, notably in higher education. In fact between 1957–8 and 1968–9 expenditure on education in real terms rose faster than the gross national product, consumer spending, or spending on the National Health Service. Indeed, by 1965 expenditure upon education had already doubled in real terms since 1948. The distribution between its various components had also shifted dramatically. Primary education, once the largest element, had absorbed 37 per cent in 1948; its share had fallen to a little over a quarter. University, further and adult education had risen to almost as much by 1965. Secondary education now had the largest share with 32 per cent. Where only 7 per cent of seventeen-year-olds had been at school in 1950, this proportion had risen to 12 per cent by 1962 and to 20 per cent by 1970. School-leavers with two or more A-levels more than trebled between 1955 and 1972. The number of universities doubled in the 1960s and the students doubled with them. The rise in the numbers attending on a full- or part-time basis at other adult or further educational institutions was equally or even more impressive. In 1970 the interesting experiment of the Open University was launched in an attempt to provide higher education outside the confines of specific qualifications for entry and attendance for three or four years in a particular institution.

Widespread confidence existed in the 1960s concerning the great cultural, social and economic rewards to be anticipated from this general increase in educational provision at all levels. The following decade saw much more scepticism. The expansion of higher education was allowed to gather momentum well into the 1970s without sufficient regard for the state of the economy, the balance between the more academic and vocational subjects, and the motivation of all with the necessary ability to undertake such studies. Applications for entry to many courses began to falter while planners were still drawing upward curves on their graphs. They were restrained, it seemed, only by the economic crisis of the mid-1970s and by a sudden awareness of the falling birth-rate. A considerable expansion of higher education was undoubtedly needed in the 1960s. It was important that certain essentially vocational courses be given university or degree status, without which they could never be more than second-class citizens. It was also true that the economy could absorb many more arts and social science graduates, especially if they emerged blessed with a sense of reality and a readiness to adapt, as well as with good critical minds. What failed to occur was a satisfactory balance in numbers and quality between arts, science and engineering graduates. In particular too few good students were attracted to engineering. Furthermore pure research received too much emphasis in scientific-technological studies, absorbing more than its share of what first-class talent there was. Meanwhile the arts and social sciences flourished (in most subjects, though less so in languages and economics). Given the nature of British society the direction of students into certain fields of study was unthinkable. Nevertheless those to whom the expansion of higher education had been entrusted since the early 1960s had often acted in a euphoric and over-optimistic manner (the British aerospace policy-makers were not unique). They had paid too little attention to the many and long-established biases in British society against the more mundane areas of industry and commerce.

There was disappointment, too, that more working-class children had not succeeded in reaching university. Although numbers rose, the proportion of students from the homes of manual workers did not rise significantly above the pre-existing figure of about 25 per cent (indeed in Scotland the expansion resulted in a decline in the proportion of such students to around the national average). Yet in some ways it was perhaps more surprising that so many from manual backgrounds managed to graduate. Despite the massive postwar expansion in the grammar schools, these had continued to be dominated by the middle classes. Of the threefold division in secondary schooling Professor Halsey commented in 1961 that the system confirmed rather than created an individual's social status; the tripartite system, or 'tri-partheid', was an obstacle to the promotion of talent. The state grammar schools themselves continued to be overshadowed by the various public, independent and direct grant schools. Whereas only 7 per cent of fourteen-year-olds in England and Wales attended such schools, at eighteen they provided about one-third of the university intake (according to an estimate for 1967). Reaction to this situation explains the determined efforts in the later 1960s to transform secondary education by the use of the comprehensive school.

Labour's conversion to comprehensive education had been slow and uncertain. Its Minister of Education in January 1965 ws still talking somewhat vaguely of his hope that within five years comprehensives would become the 'normal pattern' for secondary education. Harold Wilson, with many others in the Labour party, was a grammar school product. These were not readily persuaded that the grammar schools had failed as instruments for social mobility. Gaitskell had talked vaguely of 'grammar school education for all'. Experiments had been proceeding in comprehensive education since the war in London and the midlands, but only about one-sixth of local authorities had shown much interest. Among parents, the eleven-plus examination for entry to the grammar schools caused many anxious hours, but there was no great public demand for radical educational experimentation. The Conservatives disliked comprehensive schooling, but did not oppose local developments. They confidently claimed that prosperity would narrow the diferences between the grammar and 'modern' schools. There were, however, wide regional variations in the provision of grammar school places – the national average was one-fifth. In working-class areas children tended to leave school at the earliest opportunity in any case (twice the proportion of children stayed on at school in London after the age of sixteen as in the north of England). Some secondary modern schools were preparing pupils for the General Certificate of Education, but overall received far fewer resources to devote to each child than the grammar schools.

Labour's sudden drive to introduce comprehensive education from 1965 may have been influenced by fear of an electoral defeat in the not too distant future and by the need to conciliate certain pressure groups within the party. Pressure was brought to bear on local councils that were hesitant over or hostile to comprehensive developments, and in July 1965 the Ministry of Education issued Circular 10/65 which laid down the intended pattern for comprehensive education. Up to six types of school were initially recognized, to allow for organizational problems. Basically the government demanded that schools should either cater for all pupils over the age of eleven or be fitted into a two-tier structure whereby children changed schools at thirteen, fourteen or sixteen, in the last instance proceeding to sixth form colleges. By the end of 1969 in England and Wales, out of 163 local educational authorities, 129 had either implemented comprehensive schemes, or had had their proposals accepted by the government. Only eight authorities had refused to submit schemes. There was a more than tenfold increase in the number of comprehensive schools in England and Wales in the 1960s, mainly after 1965. By 1970 they were catering for about one million pupils or about one-third of the secondary school population. Another important development, the Certificate of Secondary Education, was introduced in 1965 for less able pupils.

It would be premature to attempt any firm verdicts on comprehensive education within barely ten years of its first serious introduction. The quality of schools continued to vary sharply from area to area. Local authorities continued to vary among themselves. There could, for instance, be fivefold differences in book allowances. The poorer areas, even when given greater resources, could not always attract good teachers, or retain them for any length of time. Many schools continued to stream their pupils. But the performance of the new schools was difficult to judge in an age when so much else was in a state of flux. By the end of the decade there were growing complaints of falling educational standards, in particular of a decline in the basic skills in numeracy and literacy. But it was premature to lay these at the door of the comprehensive schools, especially when attitudes to life in general had become so much more relaxed compared with the immediately preceding generations. What might be said was that the comprehensive experiment was introduced in haste with limited resources (not least in personnel in many subjects). It was yet another example of that widespread faith in the 1960s that Britain's problems could be easily diagnosed and effective solutions speedily provided. There was over-confidence in new teaching methods, in new approaches to education and too great an eagerness to act on the basis of too little research.

One tentative research conclusion, however, which received growing support in the 1970s was the difficulty of countering by any educational system or methods the imprint made upon a child in its first five years of life by its family and the community around it, not to mention their continuing influence. This was brought out most forcefully in the National Child Development Study of the fortunes of 17,000 children born in 1958. Subsequent studies showed a 'marked and consistent relationship between the occupation status ("social class") of the children's fathers and most aspects of the children's behaviour, development and ability'.[8] Over half the children with unskilled fathers were below average in general knowledge; they were more likely to be poor readers; they fell below average in most respects, including health. Support to such conclusions came from other sources, including research in the United States. The president of the British Psychological society, Professor Jack Tizard, argued emphatically in July 1976 that intelligence was largely settled by the age of five, though a poor or good environment thereafter could raise or lower the IQ to some extent. If such conclusions were true there was still scope for the schools, though experts were divided as to whether more could be done in socially mixed classes (as often promised though not necessarily offered under the comprehensive system) or alternatively through a concentration of resources on schools in deprived areas. The unexpected drop in the birth-rate was providing the educationalists by the 1970s with a little room for manoeuvre at a time when the economic crisis might have bitten still more deeply into their resources.

Debates on education were much coloured by political considerations. Education was a vital instrument in the hands of those who wished either to change society radically or to preserve the essentials of the existing order. The return of a Conservative government in 1970 meant the relaxation until 1974 of the pressure on local authorities to introduce comprehensive schools. On the other hand there were those who wished to end the independent sector in education or somehow merge it with the state system. No progress was made in this direction in these years – indeed, parental concern over uncertainties and experimentation within state schools perhaps gave added strength to the fee-paying schools. But there were also debates which were more narrowly educational in content, such as the degree of specialization which should be promoted in the upper schools, or whether science and mathematics should be incorporated into the 'very framework of daily thought' of the most dedicated arts pupils. Teaching methods provoked much controversy, especially in primary schools, with the Plowden Committee of 1967 encouraging the use of 'informal' teaching to stimulate the curiosity and imagination of young children. The researches conducted by Neville Bennett in Lancashire and Cumbria among ten- and eleven-year-olds in the early 1970s, however, suggested that the more formal methods still had much to commend them.

In any reference to increased opportunities for people from all walks of life one must be careful not to underestimate the obstacles that faced even the most determined and talented from among the poorer classes. These often lived in areas where school was no more than an interlude between play in the back streets and unskilled employment. A 1968 analysis concluded that 96 per cent of working-class children had left full-time education by the age of seventeen: the average middle-class child was nearly thirty times as likely to be still at school. Promotion was becoming more dependent on school and other educational qualifications. Advancement in engineering by way of apprenticeships and the shop floor was less frequent. From 1971 the chartered engineer needed a degree or its equivalent, and educational standards were being raised in many other careers. Overall there was a continuing swing in the economy in favour of white collar or white blouse jobs. True, many of these were of a very routine kind, and much of the upsurge in non-manual employment took the form of female labour. Nevertheless the number of white collar jobs had doubled to 9.5 million between 1931 and 1966 alone, whereas manual jobs had actually fallen by 377,000. Unskilled jobs had declined by one-third; skilled and semiskilled had increased a little. Skilled and white collar employment together represented over 60 per cent of the total by 1966 compared with under half in 1931. These changing social patterns were reflected in the parliamentary Labour party. By 1970 the Wilson Cabinet contained only three of working-class origin: over half the party had had a university education. What had once been essentially a working-class party now drew barely a quarter of its strength from those roots.

The opposition and Edward Heath

Between 1966 and 1970 Labour lost no less than fifteen by-elections, an unprecedented series of defeats for a government since the war. Given the misfortunes of the country, economy and government since 1966 these losses were hardly surprising. Nevertheless the apparent recovery in the economy after 1968 and the relaxation in restraints on wages brought a sudden revival of Labour in the spring of 1970. The evidence of the polls was backed by the results in the May local elections, so that at that time few doubted (whether in or out of the Labour party) the wisdom of the Prime Minister in deciding on a June election. That Labour should then have so unexpectedly lost that election would seem to support the case of those who argue that the electorate had become increasingly volatile, and that no great weight need be attached to the patient efforts of the Conservative party to rethink their policies in the later 1960s and to re-establish their credibility with the electorate. One qualification is necessary. The very earnestness of the opposition's preparation for a return to office under Edward Heath, which initially seemed to make so limited an impact on the voters, was perhaps of real value at the height of the election campaign when a bad set of trade figures triggered off old memories of the recurrent balance of payments problems under Labour. This sudden scare invested Heath's pro-gramme with a credibility and relevance which he and his colleagues had hitherto been unable to impart to it.

The custom of allocating specific policy areas to certain opposition figures in a formalized manner dates from 1955. Older parliamentary hands such as Macmillan and Morrison had lamented the new rigidity, but as policy-making became more complex, and television increased the need to avoid confusion as to the capacity in which opposition members were speaking, so the new system had certain practical advantages. In 1955 Attlee had also been swayed by the need to increase party discipline, given his problems with the Bevanites. Powell's 'rebellion' in 1968 perhaps owed something to his feeling of being unduly constrained as a 'shadow minister on defence'. Heath, by temperament, favoured the shadow minister approach, with the detailed preparation of policies in anticipation of a return to office. If these preparations were less complete than was claimed, they became an essential part of the new Conservative image; indeed efficiency itself became an ideological aim. Heath as a politician rarely exuded warmth, or shone as an orator. He was at his best at the conference table, or deep in the affairs of state. Other sides of his personality emerged in his qualities as a musician and yachtsman. His temperament and style would have been more at home in mid-Victorian politics (if not necessarily with Palmerston or Disraeli). But in the 1960s he appeared too often to many people, so *The New Statesman* put it, as 'a walking, talking Blue Book'. This, however, should be read more as a criticism of the age, than of Edward Heath.

The Conservative revival after 1947 was helped by the widespread impatience with state controls and rationing. In the later 1960s there was no comparable movement against state interventionism in the economy. This had its critics, but it did not strike deep chords among those whom the Conservatives sought to woo. There was no comparable recovery of support among the young. True, efforts to revitalize constituency organizations left the Conservatives with a much greater lead than usual over Labour in this respect by 1970. The Conservatives continued to suffer from internal divisions over Rhodesia, race relations, planning, incomes policy, and education. The right wing, strengthened by the formation of the Monday Club in 1961, was increasingly active, but it failed to find either a real leader or even a consensus within itself on major issues. Powell, who might have filled that slot on race relations and the championship of the free market, was out of step with some on the EEC, or in his disbelief in the utility of nuclear deterrence in western Europe, or in his opposition to a British role East of Suez, or his refusal to support capital punishment. Meanwhile Reginald Maudling and others doubted the wisdom of an unequivocal party stand against an incomes policy.

The Conservative party appeared more right-wing in philosophy in the late-1960s than it truly was, partly because of its chosen style, partly through its need to satisfy its varied right wing, and partly as a result of simplistic political debate. Wilson strove to give the Tories as right wing an image as possible. The clashes were also highly personalized (which the media encouraged), with both parties recklessly giving hostages to fortune. Nevertheless Heath and his colleagues were not content to follow the methods and thinking of Macmillan and the main Conservative leaders before 1964 with their concern to deprive Labour of the centre ground. In particular they were determined to grasp the nettle of union power with an Industrial Relations Bill, and to find means to reduce the burden of taxation on the most enterprising elements in the population. A more competitive and, they hoped in consequence, a more efficient and generally prosperous society would result. Government itself needed reform (Heath had been impressed by French governmental expertise during the 1962 EEC negotiations), though not with the object of increasing its role in society. The state had its duties, but with respect to industry its great responsibility was to remove impediments to industrial growth and efficiency. As Heath had asserted in 1966: 'It is the job of Government to help industry overcome problems and to help modern capitalism to work. . . . our task is to remove the obstructions . . . to enterprise and competition in our business world.' Industry must be freed from government meddling; it should learn to stand on its own feet again (without government subsidies); it should be enterprising, with profit as a necessary and legitimate end. This fell short of Powell's vision of the free market economy, but it also seemed to recoil from Conservative inter-ventionism of the early 1960s. Through faster growth the current welfare services would be preserved, despite higher rewards for individuals, but their future expansion would be on a more selective basis, designed to help those most in need.

Inquiry in fact demonstrated that it would be very difficult to cut government spending. To offset the somewhat hasty promise to end the selective employment tax (which was raising some £600 million by 1970) the value added tax (VAT) had to be substituted. Although this would bring Britain into line with her possible EEC partners, and promised to be a simple and flexible means of raising money from the government's point of view, its effect might also be inflationary. In general the Conservatives, if returned to office, were more likely to find themselves redistributing rather than cutting the tax load, and in so far as this hit wage-earners in strong unions a further acceleration in wage claims could be envisaged. But the long-term dependence of real incomes on investments and incentives was not easily explained, and the Tories in the late-1960s had the more pressing task of trying to win sufficient 'target' voters to restore themselves to power. The volatility of the electorate was one asset. This was especially true of the young, and of skilled manual workers outside large unionized industries. Target voters were deeply interested in better housing and in economic growth, but were otherwise little interested in politics. For the Conservatives to win they had to draw about half their support from manual workers and their wives. The decline in class feeling already noted, and the belief of perhaps half the electorate that there was little difference between the two main parties, could this time work in favour of the Conservatives, as the party no longer so directly associated with the failures of government.

The Scottish and Welsh nationalists

Scottish and Welsh nationalism had never been entirely submerged, even if they had found their strongest expression on great sporting occasions. English experience of the self-confidence of most Scots outside Scotland left them ill-acquainted with the sense of neglect at the hands of a remote government felt by many Scots still in Scotland. The English rarely pretended to understand the Welsh save as a people with a passion for singing and rugby and who occasionally produced individuals with the volcanic talents of a Lloyd George, Aneurin Bevan or Dylan Thomas. In the late-1940s there had been an upsurge of Scottish feeling, but this had died down in the 'affluent' 1950s, and where expectations had been disappointed in Scotland this had then worked to the advantage of the Labour party from 1959. Had disillusionment with Labour not set in so quickly after 1966, the Conservatives might in time have regained the remarkable strength they had temporarily enjoyed in the mid-1950s. In Wales the Liberals might have benefited. But events were not only telescoped; they coincided with the re-emergence or emergence of many nation states. Canada had its troubles in Quebec. If some of the new small states seemed born to trouble, in Europe Austria, Norway and Denmark displayed a capacity for managing their affairs that most states might envy. Not that the first upsurge in support for the Welsh and Scottish nationalist parties was to be thought of primarily in terms of a bid for independence. The motivation was mixed, even confused. Many felt they could vote for the nationalists against Labour when they would never have dreamed of voting Conservative. But the element of national pride was also strong; there was a growing determination that the people of Wales and Scotland should have a greater say in the running of the affairs of their countries. Many people throughout Britain were trying to find suitable instruments through which to express their hopes and frustrations. In the nationalist parties the Scots and Welsh had unusually effective vehicles.

Despite vast increases in regional expenditure in Scotland in the 1960s, employment tended to decline faster than new jobs could be created. The spread of light industries did not always provide employment for the kind of labour that was available, or proved suitable for women rather than men. Not all types of industry were attracted to Scotland, despite the many inducements. Transport costs were a serious deterrent in many instances, though once again American subsidiaries showed more imagination and drive than some of their British counterparts. But Scotland's investment needs were enormous, especially on Clydeside where about two-fifths of the workforce was concentrated, and where the decline in shipbulding was also destroying a wide range of dependent industries. Coal and textiles were also contracting. Employment in mining fell from 85,000 to under 29,000 in 1971, though the closure of inefficient pits brought an impressive rise in productivity. The steel industry was also being modernized, at the expense of more jobs. Trends in the Scottish economy were not easily measured, short-term movements creating contradictory impressions. But for the period 1964–73 it appeared that the Scottish gross national product had grown at an average of 2.8 per cent per year, or slightly more than the British average. The employment level in Scotland was then running nearer to the national average, as were average earnings. Clearly regional aid had had some impact, and it was only in the early 1970s that North Sea oil began to make an impact on the Scottish economy. Some 60,000 jobs had been created by 1976, but only 15 per cent of these were in the great problem area, Clydeside. One estimate placed its investment needs as high as £10,000 million, and there were other areas with similar problems in relation to their size. The Highlands and Islands Development Board was set up in 1965 to try to tackle the problems of one-sixth of the land area of Britain. Again some progress was made before the oil boom – indeed the latter threatened some centres with the burdens of over-expansion – but in the winter of 1975–6 unemployment in the Highlands was still above the average for Scotland.

Such was the general environment in which the Scottish National Party made their dramatic advance from 1967. The party's progress was often erratic, and in 1974 Labour was still able to hold off their challenge in Clydeside. Yet it was in the burgh of Hamilton, not far from Glasgow, that the SNP in November 1967 gained their first seat in Westminster since 1945. Hamilton was the second safest Labour seat in Scotland. This was followed by a 30 per cent vote for the SNP in the ensuing municipal elections. The SNP was unable to sustain this level of success into 1969–70, but they had prompted both main parties (with some help from Plaid Cymru in Wales) to begin to explore the possibility of devolution. In March 1970 a Conservative constitutional committee headed by Sir Alec Douglas-Home reported in favour of an elected Scottish assembly with limited powers. The government itself had set up a Royal Commission on the Constitution whose task included a review of the whole problem of centralization in Britain. This Commission, chaired first by Lord Crowther and then by Lord Kilbrandon, reported in October 1973 (Cmnd 5460). The majority favoured the creation of elected Scottish (and Welsh) assemblies, though with the retention of a veto by Westminster. A minority report also favoured the creation of five English regional assemblies. Although the SNP vote in the 1970 election was less impressive than at one time had seemed likely (Hamilton was lost and a single seat won), an opinion poll suggested that two-thirds of the people of Scotland favoured a separate parliament. The fortunes of the SNP were soon boosted by the development of North Sea oil and by continuing disillusionment with the management of British and Scottish affairs in Westminster by Conservative or Labour. Thus what had started in the late-1960s as very much of a protest vote, on the lines of earlier Liberal by-election successes in England, was becoming a much more permanent and potent force in the early 1970s.

Meanwhile Wales had been given her own Secretary of State by the incoming Wilson administration in 1964. But Welsh economic discontents were reinforced by a cultural revival which, though far from embracing the majority of the people, was of great significance. There had been a dramatic decline in the percentage of Welsh speakers in the twentieth century – from 60 per cent in 1891 to 20 per cent according to the census of 1971. Efforts to preserve and cultivate the Welsh language in the 1960s sometimes became so extreme as to prove counter-productive. Some actions by young enthusiasts in the Welsh Language Society were viewed by Plaid Cymru as a threat to its electoral advance. Owen Edwards of BBC Wales declared at the national Eisteddfod in 1969: 'I should like to delete three ugly words which have become fashionable to use these days – Bradwr (traitor), Taeog (serf), and Cynffonnwr (sycophant).[9] The Welsh Language Society was much affected by the restless youth and student movements of the late 1960s. But Plaid Cymru faced the more practical problems of trying to extend its appeal from traditional Welsh-speaking and strongly nonconformist rural areas – where cultural concerns were backed up by fears of English holiday-cottage buyers and of the drowning of yet more Welsh valleys to provide reservoirs for the insatiable English cities – to industrial Wales with very different grievances and desires.

Although Plaid Cymru's president, Gwynfor Evans, won Carmarthen in July 1966, his party's later advance was not on the whole comparable with that of the SNP down to 1974. Nevertheless the upsurge of Welsh nationalism was having some effect. In the late-1960s there was extra provision on television and radio for Welsh speakers and Welsh interests, while legislation in 1967 gave equal validity to the Welsh language with English in Wales. Concessions such as these, as well as those mentioned in the Scottish context, indicated the degree to which the nationalists were introducing a new dimension into British politics. Even so, the 1970 general election showed no marked departure from previous patterns in Wales or Scotland. The SNP doubled its vote, but only by more than doubling the number of its candidates. It lost the deposits of two-thirds of its sixty-five candidates, and did well only in north-eastern Scotland and in the Highlands. Its sole victory was in the Western Isles. Eleven per cent of the Scottish poll, however, would have seemed much more impressive had it not been for its recent phenomenal successes. Plaid Cymru lost Carmarthen, and two-thirds of its candidates also forfeited their deposits.

The 1970 election

Labour's renewed popularity in the spring of 1970 took many people by surprise, but still more were astounded by the Conservative electoral triumph in June. Harold Wilson's standing among the public had remained remarkably high despite bitter press criticism and the many setbacks which the nation had experienced under his leadership. He triumphantly rode out unrest and intrigues in his own party, and criticisms that his was too presidential a style of premiership and also that his government lacked any central and long-term direction. That he should have been acutely suspicious of the media was not perhaps surprising given the barrage of attacks to which he had been subjected. He was, of course, paying the penalty for having aroused too great expectations down to 1966. He had himself been guilty of too much optimism on many counts. He had been oddly inflexible on some issues, such as the defence of sterling at \$2.80 or over Britain's world role, yet in general he was seen as a leader too much given to hasty short-term manoeuvres and improvization. The views of the pundits and the politicians around him nevertheless left public opinion little affected, and Wilson's standing in the polls continued to run ahead of that of Edward Heath.

The government had succeeded at long last in righting the balance of payments only at the cost of extreme deflationary measures. Unemployment had been creeping up since 1966 to what, by the standards of the first postwar generation, was the high figure of 2.5 per cent. The retail price index had risen by 5 per cent in 1969 and by almost as much in the first half of 1970. Prices had risen by more than one-fifth since 1966, and total retail consumer expenditure by very little more at constant prices. The number of strikes was increasing. Improvements to the social services had taken place at the expense of increased taxes for many and had fallen below the expectations of others. There was little in the government's foreign policy to impress the public. Unnoticed by the public were ominous trends such as the steady erosion of the competitive edge provided to British exports by devaluation. There was in fact little to suggest that the government had made real progress in the solution of Britain's underlying economic weaknesses. One of its main successes was largely accidental – the retreat of Britain from a world role – though there had been a marked improvement in the management of the nation's armed forces.

Labour's electoral tactics in 1970 were largely defensive. Its constituency parties were strong neither in organization nor enthusiasm after the disappointments inflicted on the rank and file from 1966. Party membership had declined from the second postwar peak of 1965, itself below the 1957 record. There was even a fall (from 58 per cent in the mid-1960s to under 54 per cent in 1968) of trade union members affiliated to the party. Even Labour's hold on the traditional working-class areas seemed to be weakening. The party was failing to attract the radical young, who tended to move off to join socialist parties of various hues on the extreme left, or to concern themselves with direct industrial or social action. Moves on behalf of 'squatters' or other underprivileged sections of society were common. The introduction of votes for eighteen-year-olds in 1969 did not, as expected, help Labour. This lack of enthusiasm was critical when there were probably more basic Labour supporters than Conservatives in Britain.

The Conservative campaign was dogged rather than inspired. As the period 1970–4 was to indicate, the party was short of leaders adept at communication with the public. The death of Iain Macleod soon after the election was a sad loss. No front bench since the war had been so weak in this field. The prominence enjoyed by Enoch Powell, was a reflection of this deficiency. The electorate in 1970 was mainly interested in inflation and the state of the economy, so that Conservative attacks on Labour's failures rather than emphasis on their own programme had more impact, especially when an untypical set of trade figures published shortly before polling day played into their hands. The complacency which had lately restored Labour's fortunes was rudely and perhaps decisively shattered. The question of the EEC did not loom significantly, and Powell's assaults both on that and on immigration were weakened by his exaggerations. Some Conservatives indeed thought that Powell had cost the party three seats, though others pointed to the slightly above average swing to the party in the west midlands (Powell's home base). A higher than average national swing also deprived Labour of Clapham where a distinguished West Indian doctor was their candidate. If Powell was the most notable critic of his own party, there were many right-wingers who found Heath's approach too technocratic, too much concerned with economic growth, and too little concerned with the rights of the individual. Some wished to take a similar line to Powell on immigration, or to attack the permissive society with tougher measures against criminals and more emphasis on law and order. Differing shades of emphasis within the party, however, were of little consequence as more people took fright at the possibility of renewed economic difficulties under another Labour government.

Despite a relatively low poll (72 per cent) the Conservatives secured more votes than Labour in 1966, and a lead of no less than one million in the 1970 election itself. The swing against the Wilson government was the largest since the war. The Liberals did less well than in 1964 or 1966, a sure sign of the strength of the movement against the government. There was certainly none of the hesitancy over a change of ministry that was shown in 1964, though the Conservatives' victory was less impressive than those of 1955 and 1959. The reasons for their victory were as much negative as positive, but at least they were once again seen as the more competent party. Thus, to the consternation of most people, the next session of Parliament opened with a new Prime Minister, and with 330 Conservatives facing 287 somewhat bemused Labour MPs.

Chapter 13

The Heath government

Return to office

Edward Heath had won a great personal victory in 1970, and he entered office giving every appearance that he believed that by firm leadership the British people could be imbued with a new sense of purpose. Less than four years later he departed from Downing Street having reversed some of his basic policies, and with the electorate in a state of considerable confusion and dismay. His premiership bore some resemblances to the reign of the eighteenth-century Habsburg, Joseph II. There was growing discussion by 1973–4 as to how far or even whether Britain was still governable. The old debate over the possibility of the Prime Minister enjoying excessive powers was giving place to speculation as to where power truly lay. In the 1960s pundits had debated what was wrong with Britain and had canvassed many solutions. In the 1970s there was more scepticism as to the possibility of solutions even if one could agree on the diagnosis. Economists were taking much more account of social conflict and power relationships; rationality in what ostensibly were economic choices could not necessarily be assumed.[1] Eric Roll noted as early as 1973 in his *History of Economic Thought* that economists had become over-confident in the mid-1960s and economics too mechanistic as a discipline. Britain had been second only to the United States in the western world in the development of economic theory, yet the British economy seemed to gain relatively little from this intellectual brilliance. The followers of the American economist Milton Friedman, with his monetarist theories, took less account of the political and social dimensions, though it was perhaps only the shock of the economic and political crises in Britain in the mid-1970s that turned so many towards the study of monetary policy. Severe restraint of the money supply despite heavy unemployment was not readily thinkable before one had looked into the inflationary abyss, with all its possible consequences, in the mid-1970s. When union leaders themselves recoiled, new thinking became possible.

During the election campaign Edward Heath had warned of impending economic difficulties. The *National Institute Economic Review* for February 1971 remarked that, apart from the improvement to the balance of payments, the year 1970 had 'proved conspicuously unsuccessful in other respects . . . accelerating price rises, a wage inflation of virtually unparalleled intensity, and a declining pressure of demand'.[2] The government at first chose only cautious reflation, partly because official forecasts were too optimistic, and partly because of the fear of too rapid growth with all its inflationary and balance of payments problems. New considerations began to weigh more heavily from 1971, when unemployment continued to rise. The Conservative leaders in any case were convinced that persistent slow growth would intensify the nation's problems. Inflation itself could be aggravated as those in employment strove to use their bargaining power to keep ahead of rising prices. Constricted resources would slow efforts to improve housing, education and welfare services. Brendon Sewill, who was special assistant to the Chancellor of the Exchequer from 1970 to 1974, recalls the government's anxiety to avoid the compromise policies of the 1960s. It hoped to achieve rapid growth by entry to the EEC, through tax reform and tax cuts, and by a new approach to industrial relations. 'The strategy was no less than an attempt to change the whole attitude of mind of the British people to create a more dynamic, thrusting, "go-getting" economy on the American or German model';[3] If the details were different, the mood was very similar to that of Labour in 1964.

It is important to resist the influence of hindsight. The oil crisis of the mid-1970s could not reasonably have been foreseen in 1971. Even the dramatic rise in the price of primary commodities was not then in sight. The immediate worries on the international stage were the size of the American balance of payments deficit, problems of international liquidity, and whether Britain would gain entry to the EEC. British competitiveness in world markets had to be maintained – for real success it had to be improved. This would require high and intelligent investment at home (which was bound up with expected rates of profitability) and a slowing down of inflation. The government had no faith in any incomes policy as a weapon against inflation: the outcome was friction, frustration, anomalies and inflexibility. Yet wage restraint was vital, at least in the initial stages of its bid for growth. Discussions with unions leaders, however, proved totally unproductive. As for investment incentives, experience of the efficacy of Labour's investment grant system since 1966 had been mixed. These could be used to give priority to firms moving into less prosperous regions, to sectors of industry that were expected to help the balance of payments, or to companies whose expansionist potential was limited by current low profitability. The Conservatives argued that the scheme involved high expenditure out of proportion to its return. They disliked the idea of aiding firms whether or not they were making profits, and believed that tax allowances, by increasing current liquidity, would be more effectual. In practice, for various reasons, manufacturing investment fell away.[4] If Labour had been too inclined to meddle with industry, and to subsidise or prop up sectors of the economy with dubious prospects of growth or even of survival, the Conservatives switched too abruptly to policies in which firms were expected to stand on their own feet. The new Minister of Technology, John Davies, asserted in October 1970, 'I will not bolster up or bail out companies where I can see no end to the process of propping them up.' This fell short of the hopes of *laissez-faire* purists, but it represented a sharp turn away from the policy of the previous government.

The Heath government abolished the Industrial Reorganization Corporation and the Prices and Incomes Board to accord with the new atmosphere of greater freedom and initiative. Both moves were somewhat precipitate, and the government had to resort to new institutions at a later stage. It underestimated both the difficulties of inducing industry to invest and of restraining the rise in incomes. As we shall see it also exaggerated its ability to restrict the powers of the unions. The ministry's aims and strategy were bold, but a cautious approach gave even less prospect of success. Without growth unemployment would not be reduced, or if reduced it would only be at the expense of national competitiveness. The level of unemployment that might restrain wage demands then appeared to be far beyond what was politically tolerable. Growth gave the best prospect of ultimately reducing unit costs, and of providing the greater rewards that would offset any unpopularity that might be generated by changes in policy on taxation, the social services or industrial relations. Nor could the ministry afford to linger. The benefits of its policies had to be clearly felt in good time for the next election. It was, according to its lights, acting with the best interests of the nation at heart. Had it succeeded, however uneven the distribution of the final rewards, the size of the national cake for distribution between the social services, wages and incomes would have been much enlarged. But for success the government needed the correct responses from industry and the unions, and also a favourable international environment over which Britain's influence was now very small indeed. But the government's vulnerability was highlighted from the outset by the rapidly worsening strike record at home. If 1970 was bad, 1971 was even worse. The situation was worse than at any time since 1926.

A resolution at the Labour Party Conference in the autumn of 1970 which argued the need for an incomes policy was defeated by only 300,000 votes, but with the weight of the TGWU, led by Jack Jones, and Hugh Scanlon's AUEFW thrown against it the trend in union ranks was clear. The Labour party itself was still recovering from the shock of the election defeat, and was disposed to think that militancy of all kinds should be discouraged. Elections to the parliamentary committee of the Labour party and the National Executive Committee favoured the centre and the right. Roy Jenkins was decisively elected deputy leader. But party morale as a whole was low, and the leadership's overall standing had been weakened by defeat, as well as by the disappointments of office. The Conservative government's insistence on the Industrial Relations Bill provided the party with an obvious cause to fight, and drew it closer to the strongest unions. The party also agreed to drop all further ideas on an incomes policy or union legislation. The search for positive policies was more difficult – and divisive. Eric Heffer, for the left, complained that the late Wilson ministry had been essentially 'Gaitskellite', and that the revisionists continued to dominate the party. The left, he complained had failed to back its theoretical insights with practical programmes, so leaving the field to the pragmatists. Crossman more bluntly had commented long before that the real division in the Labour party lay between 'practical policy and emotional protest'. Certainly the party faced the continuing dilemma of how to please the unions, party workers and the electorate simultaneously.

Into Europe

The most important achievement of the Heath ministry, in the sense of an aim being consciously pursued, was its successful negotiation of British entry into the EEC. This was a fitting climax to Heath's pioneering if abortive efforts under Macmillan in 1962. At the same time it must be recognized that a Labour victory in 1970 would probably have had much the same outcome, might well have been attended by less controversy, and not been followed by the feeling of insecurity which attended British membership from 1973 until the 1975 referendum put the matter, in the foreseeable future, beyond doubt. In many ways the average British citizen found the question of the Common Market remote, complex and boring, with a hint of menace in its vague promise of change. Even for the experts it was an extraordinarily difficult matter; Uwe Kitzinger commented: '. . . one would have had to be a constitutional lawyer and an agricultural economist, a diplomat and an international monetary expert, a lobby correspondent and a social security specialist to understand it all.'[5] It was often easier to pick out the disadvantages. The price of food was expected to rise, if by an uncertain amount. There was some feeling that the middle classes were more likely to gain while the working classes would lose. The one real constant was the speed with which public opinion changed on the issue, with little reference to the merits of the case.

Certainly the 1967 veto by de Gaulle gave time in which new doubts could develop, and for opposition forces to gather strength. The Common Market Safeguards Campaign was launched at the end of 1969 with Douglas Jay as chairman. Its members included twenty-two Conservative MPs and thirty-eight Labour. Notable politicians included Barbara Castle, Ian Mikardo and Peter Shore: there were Jack Jones and Hugh Scanlon from the unions. Other opponents of the EEC included the Keep Britain Out group, and the Anti-Common Market League. The TUC was moving from a position of tepid support in 1969 to one of opposition by 1971. The change of government was influential here, though there were also increasing fears of a diminution in British control over the economy, a possible rise in the influence of international companies, and a general strengthening of capitalist forces. In general the strangest bedfellows began to align themselves for or against the EEC. The leaders of the main British churches were mostly in favour, though there were some fears of a 'Catholic' Europe among the more extreme Protestants, especially in Ulster. The cautious support of the Church of Scotland reflected the considerable measure of suspicion entertained by Scots towards the EEC. Anti-Market feeling tended to be strongest among the older and poorer sections of society, the staunchest nationalists or those who had not yet despaired of the Commonwealth connection, and generally among those who were the strongest supporters of radical social change. Internationalists were divided, depending on whether they saw the EEC as a step towards or away from the sort of international order which they favoured.

Opponents of the EEC were encouraged by a government white paper published in February 1970 and by the conclusions of a meeting of Anglo–American economists at Ditchley Park in the middle of June. The latter were doubtful concerning the economic advantages of entry unless protectionism again became a feature of the world economy. The white paper was more optimistic on this count, but estimated that the nation's balance of payments might be adversely affected to the extent of £100 million or even £1,000 million by the end of the decade. Food prices might rise by a quarter. The ambiguity of the white paper may have been influenced by Cabinet divisions. On the other hand conditions in western Europe were at last beginning to move more in Britain's favour. The sympathetic Willy Brandt had become the West German Chancellor in September 1969, and his country was now sufficiently self-confident to act more independently of France in foreign policy. De Gaulle had been greatly weakened by the French strikes and riots of 1968: the franc, the key to so much of his past success, was more vulnerable; the Soviet invasion of Czechoslovakia in 1968 reminded the west Europeans of their continuing dependence on the United States at a time when American foreign policy appeared rather less predictable. De Gaulle may have been reviewing his own strategy, but in April 1969 he resigned, having at last experienced a defeat in a referendum. For the EEC this was a great opportunity to escape from the stagnation which had beset it since 1967. Under pressure from France, it was at first preoccupied with the resolution of major problems in agricultural policy; these were settled in April 1970. Talks with Britain were due to open on 30 June.

It is significant that despite the change in government in Britain there was no delay. The new chief British delegate, Anthony Barber, was said to have made virtually the speech prepared by his predecessor, George Thomson, in Dundee during the election campaign. The new government, however, possessed a more dedicated Europeanist in its Prime Minister – certainly one who was more direct in his methods than Harold Wilson. There was a marginal addition to British military strength East of Suez (over and above that envisaged by Labour) as the five-power Commonwealth defence arrangement covering Malaysia and Singapore took shape in 1971. But at the Commonwealth conference in Singapore in January 1971 Heath demonstrated his determination to pursue an independent line even if the issue, the British right to sell arms to South Africa, was not particularly well chosen. Britain's lack of influence in Washington was becoming more evident with the passage of time. There was no place for Britain as an intermediary in Russo-American relations, and in 1971 the United States moved suddenly to ease its relations with Communist China. At least the degree of Anglo–American separation made it easier for Britain to refuse to act as an American agent in the Middle Eastern war of 1973. Given British dependence on Arab oil, the Foreign Office needed as much room for manoeuvre as possible and could not afford to spare much sympathy for Israel.

For a government convinced that Britain must try to exert significant political and economic influence in the world the only way forward lay in entry to the EEC. Every further delay before entry meant that yet more crucial decisions as to the Market's future character would be taken without reference to British interests. In stark power terms, whereas Britain had enjoyed a gross national product of $47 billion in 1950 against only $75 billion for the future 'Six', by 1970 the respective figures were $121 billion as against $485 billion, with the gap widening all the time.[6] Serious discussions began between the EEC and Britain in September 1970. If West Germany was now more sympathetic to the British case, the French were still reserved, understandably championing their own interests, and, as their partners understood, also making the front running in the defence of existing common EEC interests against the British with their special claims. There was first of all the financial problem. Uwe Kitzinger summed up the situation:

One could argue that the EEC raised the bulk of its funds from those countries that were the big importers (of industrial goods no less than farm products) from outside the Community; and it then spent the bulk of its funds in those countries which were the largest producers of foodstuffs.[7]

Britain would be hard hit, being almost as large an importer as West Germany, yet with her smaller farm sector she would pay more than the richer West Germans mainly for the benefit of the French, who also enjoyed a higher per capita income. Furthermore, although Britain's balance of payments was satisfactory in 1971, future difficulties seemed all too probable, so that at least a satisfactory transition period before Britain paid her full share was essential.

France also wanted an immediate acceptance of the Common Agricultural Policy whereas the British again required an adequate transition period. In the spring of 1971 the French raised the question of sterling balances: these should be scaled down. They also expressed concern at the privileged position of the London capital market. At the end of March 1971 there was much pessimism among British negotiators as to French intentions. There were fears that Paris might once again be working for a failure of the talks. Meanwhile support for entry was falling in Britain, stimulated by Labour's divisions and the government's falling popularity. Secret and detailed Anglo-French talks, however, were preparing the way for a meeting in Paris on 20–21 May 1971 between Edward Heath and the French President, M. Pompidou. The British could also count on some assistance from the other members of the EEC. Willy Brandt's *Ostpolitik* resulted in treaties with Russia, Poland and East Germany by the end of 1970, and – with the strength of the West German economy – was a clear indication to the French that their days of ascendancy within the EEC were at an end. If the French could no longer dominate the EEC of the Six there was less objection to its enlargement. Indeed, in some circumstances a revamped *entente cordiale* might not be without its uses. The British seemed likely to share the French bias against majority voting. The French had also to recognize that the continued exclusion of Britain would only antagonize their partners and impede the further development of the EEC. Britain's image, though tarnished in economic matters, was still that of a stable and just democracy. Britain would improve the balance within the EEC. France no longer had reason to fear her American or Commonwealth connections or interests. Britain's relative weakness might even be advantageous, especially from the French point of view. Weakness would make her less assertive. It was not then anticipated that her weakness might become a liability.[8]

The terms that were finally hammered out in 1971 for British entry were by no means generous. Transitional periods of up to six years were negotiated before the common external tariff, the Common Agricultural Policy, and contributions to the Community budget were fully applied to Britain. There were also transitional arrangements to meet the special problems of New Zealand dairy products and Commonwealth sugar producers. The expected results of these agreements were profoundly altered by the combination of the dramatic rise in food and oil prices, the world recession of the mid-1970s, and the growing weaknesses in the British economy. The same fate befell a rather vague British promise, demanded in particular by the French, that the sterling balances should be steadily run down following British entry. The British in their turn found their new partners' readiness to cooperate in the regulation of their currencies in international crises to be of much less consequence than was promised on paper. References to progress towards monetary union were no more than pious hopes. The terms of entry in these circumstances were much less important than the fact.

Nevertheless the terms and the decision to enter had still to be ratified by the British Parliament: indeed, as it happened, by the British people as well in a unique referendum. The government launched a vigorous campaign in favour of entry, notably in its white paper of July 1971 (Cmnd 4715). It could rely on the great majority of leading newspapers for support. A new ally was the NFU which in 1971 began to see possibilities of a greater expansion of British agriculture inside rather than outside the EEC. It was also impressed by the dependence of agriculture on the state of the British economy as a whole; if that were expected to gain from entry so too should the farmers. But in general it was the opponents of entry who were gaining in strength at this time, notably through their advances in the Labour party and in the unions. For a time in the summer of 1971 the position of Harold Wilson appeared to be in jeopardy until he moved closer to those who opposed entry on the terms negotiated by the Heath government. The NEC voted in July by sixteen votes to six for a stand on these lines. This was overwhelmingly supported by the Brighton Party Conference in October, though a motion calling for the withdrawal of Britain's application for entry secured only two million votes. Fortunately for the government the pro-Market faction in the Labour party led by Roy Jenkins was not overawed.

There were difficulties, too, within the Conservative party, with thirty or so MPs firmly opposed to entry, and some whose vote was uncertain. Thus the government, with only 326 seats in the Commons, required the support of other parties to ensure a parliamentary majority in favour of entry. A free vote, finally conceded by the government on 18 October 1971, made it easier for Labour's pro-Marketeers to give their support. They had to defy the labour whips to do so. In the key vote of 28 October, sixty-nine Labour MPs voted for entry, and twenty more abstained. Thirty-nine Conservatives and Ulster Unionists voted against, and two abstained. The final vote of 356 against 244 stood in disappointing contrast to the Commons vote of 1967 (488 to 62) from the point of view of the pro-Marketeers. The vote was also memorable for the fact that no less than 131 MPs had voted against their own parties, a unique event in British parliamentary history since May 1940 and the fall of Neville Chamberlain. The Lords voted by 451 to 58 for entry, notable figures among the opponents including Lords Balogh, Shinwell, Strang and Wigg.

The parliamentary battle was by no means over, and much of 1972 was devoted to the passage of enacting legislation. In Britain, international treaties were not necessarily part of domestic law: the treaty of accession therefore had to be backed by suitable parliamentary legislation. The highly complex implications of the treaty were finally reduced to a twelve clause bill. Its passage was one of the hardest fought in the whole history of Parliament. In this struggle Liberal support and Labour abstentions were often crucial. There were 104 divisions, many with majorities below double figures and one being as low as four. The bill was not ready for the royal assent until 17 October 1972. But the Labour party also suffered from the strain. Strong opponents of the EEC brought great pressure to bear on Jenkins and his followers. Harold Wilson tried both to maintain party unity and to keep his options open concerning Britain's future relations with the EEC. But internal pressures in the party by October 1972 forced him to put great emphasis on the renegotiation of certain clauses in the treaty of accession if and when Labour returned to office. Should such renegotiation fail, he appeared to envisage a long period of repeated negotiation before either Britain or her EEC partners finally decided that separation was unavoidable. Lord George-Brown and George Thomson continued to insist that a Wilson government (re-elected in 1970) would have been glad to accept the terms secured under Heath, but given the explosive state of the Labour party there was much to be said (in terms of party politics) for the trimming position adopted on the future of the EEC by Wilson, Callaghan, Healey and Crosland. In the last resort perhaps only the promise of a national referendum, or some other test of public opinion, had enabled Wilson to hold his ground and yet preserve party unity. Acceptance of the idea of a referendum by the shadow Cabinet, however, precipitated the resignation on 10 April 1972 of Roy Jenkins as deputy leader, and also of George Thomson and Harold Lever. These resignations made it easier for Jenkins and his companions to abstain during key votes on the EEC, while the dissension within the Labour party lowered its standing in the country at a time when the government's popular position was weak.

The treaty of accession had been formally signed in Brussels on 22 January 1972, and came into operation a year later. But the attitude of the majority of the Labour party ensured that at least another election had to be fought before there could be a real air of permanence about Britain's membership. A Conservative victory in the election of February 1974 might have put the issue beyond doubt. Harold Wilson, however, had first to head a minority Labour government and then complete the process of renegotiation after a second election in 1974 with only the slenderest of majorities. A weak political position, plus preoccupation with renegotiation and preparations for the referendum, made it difficult for the new government to grapple with the nation's critical economic plight. But the question of Britain and the EEC had to be resolved once and for all, whatever the intervening costs. Renegotiation was a necessary political exercise for the Labour party, especially the Cabinet, though it is doubtful whether it brought changes of any real consequence in the terms of British membership. As it was it failed to unite the Labour party although a majority of ministers now declared themselves in favour. Above all, Harold Wilson, Roy Jenkins, James Callaghan and Denis Healey were finally united: no other names in the Labour party carried so much weight among the electorate as a

Some Conservatives opposed entry, and the Welsh and Scottish nationalist parties committed themselves against the EEC. Opponents of membership in 1975 were able to argue that two and a half years within the EEC had brought no obvious benefits for Britain while no less than one-third of the country's massive trade deficit of £6.6 billion in 1974 was with the Community. Beyond this the case of the anti-Marketeers was less impressive. The Commonwealth's share of British trade continued to fall, and those who continued to argue that case, with an emotive reference in one instance to 'British farmers' in the antipodes, lacked only the monocle of Joseph Chamberlain in their reversion to Britain at the turn of the century. In 1975 most Commonwealth countries, if with varying degrees of conviction, saw a much weakened Britain as more likely to serve their interests inside than outside the EEC. Harold Wilson was able to secure useful expressions of support for continued British membership at a Commonwealth conference in 1975. Invocations of the past were thus of little use to opponents of the EEC; the argument that membership would injure the nation's sovereignty did not appear to possess much validity in 1975; a black portrayal of Britain's economic prospects within the EEC did not carry with it much promise that they would be any better, if indeed as good, if Britain left. British conservatism was now working in favour of the Marketeers. The anti-Marketeers with the most plausible case to argue were those who favoured a more socialist Britain: it was not easy to imagine Britain making a speedy transition to become a larger Sweden or a smaller Japan. But strongly socialist solutions appealed to only a small minority in 1975, and the prominence of left-wingers among the anti-Marketeers helps to account for the size of the vote for the EEC. Basically, however, it would seem fairest to conclude that most people found the issue too complicated, and were content to follow the lead of the politicians they trusted most. In such a contest the combined forces of Wilson, Heath, Callaghan, Thorpe and Jenkins easily outweighed Foot, Powell and Benn. Heath, despite his recent loss of the Tory leadership, enhanced his stature as a national figure.[9]

In the referendum of 5 June 1975 about 64 per cent of the population voted. All areas supported entry save Shetland and the Western Isles, and only two voted in favour by less than 55 per cent. The average affirmative vote was 67 per cent. As a footnote to international reactions it is noteworthy that the Soviet Union should have been hostile to British membership whereas Communist China, with its interest in a strong EEC to help balance Russia, welcomed it. British membership of the EEC provides one of the few tidy stopping points in this book, and even then its significance is in many ways no more than formal or symbolic. The first years brought more disappointments than satisfaction for enthusiasts on both sides of the Channel. Too few British firms were equipped to exploit the openings provided for them by membership. In many ways entry only highlighted still more the weaknesses in British industry and salesmanship. Preoccupation with domestic problems left the government with little inclination, opportunity or means to play a positive role in the Community.

A survey on 'imperial aggression' published by the Soviet Defence Ministry in June 1976 listed Britain as the world's worst postwar aggressor in terms of numbers of conflicts and incidents. Britain was unlikely to hold that 'record' much longer. Already the Duncan Report in 1969 had been arguing the need to remodel British overseas missions to meet the requirements of a middle-ranking and essentially European state. At no time down to the mid-1970s was Britain in possession of such effective government organizations to promote her overseas economic interests as many European competitors, and especially Japan with its Ministry for International Trade and Industry. Britain required comparable facilities for the identification of export opportunities and the subsequent synthesis of the necessary financial, production and sales resources. Changes were afoot, even in the Foreign Office, and it was unlikely that political and strategic issues would be able to overshadow economic issues in British overseas policy-making in the fourth quarter of the twentieth century to the degree which they had in the third.

Northern Ireland, 1970–4

The efforts of the Heath government to relieve the troubles in Ulster resulted in a political edifice which did not long outlive the Conservatives' electoral defeat in February 1974. The situation had been deteriorating when they took office. On 6 July 1970 Eire's Foreign Minister, Dr Hillery, made an unprecedented secret visit to a Catholic area in Belfast. He said later that Catholics in Northern Ireland felt themselves to be living in a hostile region. 'I visited them because they needed reassurance that they are not alone and I felt they should not regard themselves as being totally without support.' British efforts to disarm the IRA and to restrain the Orange Order encountered fierce resistance from the first and virtually no cooperation from the second. On 10 August, with fears mounting that the right-wing of the Ulster Unionists was about to force the resignation of the Prime Minister, Major Chichester-Clark, the Home Secretary clearly intimated that direct rule from London would follow the overthrow of the government. The latter continued to prepare legislation for the reform of local government, but it was a vain endeavour. Catholics and Protestants in Belfast who lived in areas where they felt exposed to violence at the hands of the other side moved – perhaps 12 per cent of the population in three years. The first British soldier was killed on 5 February 1971; forty-two more had died by the end of the year as the Provisionals' strategy began to unfold. A new government under the astute Brian Faulkner from 23 March 1971 still failed to unite all the Protestant elements. The initiation of internment without trial from 9 August, in an attempt to cripple the IRA, further inflamed Catholic opinion. The Social Democratic and Labour Party (SDLP) refused to join in political talks while internment lasted. In September 1971 the Catholic hierarchy attacked both the IRA and internment. Relations between London and Dublin seemed at their worst.

The violence at least forced the three governments to try to come together. There was a unique meeting of the three Prime Ministers at Chequers at the end of September. The reunification of Ireland by peaceful democratic means was accepted as a legitimate political aim.

All spoke out against violence and in favour of Catholic–Protestant reconciliation. Edward Heath, in his Lord Mayor's banquet speech of 15 November, agreed that union might come about if a majority in the North constitutionally expressed themselves in favour. Harold Wilson went much further with ideas of reciprocal North and South, Catholic and Protestant concessions, and a movement towards Irish unity over a period of perhaps fifteen years. The price of union might include the ending of what the Ulster Protestants regarded as the 'theocratic' elements in the constitution of Eire and the inclusion of a united Ireland in the Commonwealth. Eire and Britain were about to become partners in the EEC in any case.

As so often in conflicts of this kind, the situation had to get worse before enough people were sufficiently frightened or appalled to try to talk constructively – that is, beyond the rather academic level hitherto followed. A bomb explosion in the centre of Belfast injured sixty-two people on 3 January 1972: on the 30th soldiers killed thirteen people at the time of an illegal civil rights' march in Londonderry. This was 'bloody Sunday'. Three days later the British embassy in Dublin was razed to the ground in the presence of 30,000 people. The government of Eire demanded the withdrawal of British troops from the North. In these circumstances London had no option but to review its policies. Opinion in America and Catholic opinion within the EEC could not be ignored. When the Ulster government would not agree to the total transfer of the control of the security operations to London, direct rule was instituted from 1 April, for one year in the first instance. Internment was to be phased out and regular plebiscites held on the existence of the Border. William Whitelaw became Secretary of State for Ireland. The moves damaged the British government's relations with Protestant opinion in Ulster, but it was imperative that the confidence of Dublin should be regained and perhaps too that of some of the Catholics in the North.

By this time the Ulster Protestants were divided between those who were prepared to cooperate cautiously with the British government (these were led by Brian Faulkner), those who seemed ready to consider an independent Ulster in certain circumstances (then led by William Craig), and those who advocated the complete integration of Ulster within the United Kingdom (led by the Rev. Ian Paisley and supported by Enoch Powell). In May 1972 the Protestant Ulster Defence Association also began to make its presence felt, so that the province seemed on the brink of civil war as extremism gained ground in both camps. There were some sectarian gun battles, but the violence mainly took the form of bombings and shootings; pubs were especially popular targets. The British government could draw comfort only from its improving relationship with Dublin. A referendum had been conducted in Eire on the question of entry to the EEC. The IRA had opposed entry, but no less than 84 per cent of those who had voted had favoured the EEC. Subsequent elections in the Republic in February 1973 confirmed in power a National Coalition made up of the Fine Gael and Labour parties. The new government, headed by Liam Cosgrave, was less divided on policy concerning the North, and relations with Westminster continued to improve, helped by the British white paper of 20 March 1973 (Cmnd 5259) with its promises of a new Assembly and a power-sharing executive for the administration of Ulster. The elections for the Assembly in June 1973 were disappointing for all those who were hoping that a new cooperative spirit might begin to emerge in the North. The elections underlined the divided state of the old Unionist party, with a remnant under Faulkner moving towards the SDLP and the Alliance Party in a desperate bid to create a centre coalition. Their electoral backing, however, appeared all too inadequate.

Long negotiations preceded the formation of the executive. It was finally announced on 21 November 1973 that this was to consist of six of the Faulkner Unionists, four from the SDLP and one from the Alliance party. Faulkner was chief executive, with Gerry Fitt of the SDLP as his deputy. Violence and intimidation continued (the total killed in 1973 was 251 compared with 467 in 1972, and the IRA were also becoming active in England). Tripartite talks nevertheless opened on 5 December at Sunningdale in Berkshire between the British and Irish governments and the new executive. Four days of talks brought agreement that a Council of Ireland should be set up, Dublin and Belfast each having seven representatives. Dublin agreed that the status of Northern Ireland could not be changed until the majority wished it (a plebiscite in March 1973 had demonstrated that over half of the population of the province opposed union with the South). Police cooperation was envisaged between North and South. The executive took office at the end of the year, but two months later its credibility was badly damaged in the British general election when Unionist opponents of the Council of Ireland (fighting as a coalition under the title of the United Ulster Unionist Council) won a sweeping electoral victory. In the second half of May 1974 a general strike organized by the Ulster Workers Council (another Protestant force) destroyed the last shreds of authority possessed by the executive. It was prorogued on 29 May. Wilson's third ministry had to make a fresh start perhaps buoyed up by only one hope – that the violence itself, so long as it remained inconclusive, might ultimately persuade enough people to seek a new compromise. It was not much of a hope. Meanwhile, apart from the cost in lives and bomb damage, the conflict was adding to the already considerable economic and social problems of the province. In 1975 over one-third of the population was described as living in a state of 'economic disadvantage' and in substandard housing. The average for the United Kingdom was more like one-fifth.[10]

The new Conservatism in operation

The Conservatives provoked much criticism by their emphasis on the need for a more selective approach to the social services. Universalists argued that this would lead to lower standards and to the revival of old attitudes towards the poor and among the poor themselves. Nevertheless the government strove to implement much of the Seebohm Report, and instituted the Family Income Supplement to try to bridge part of the gap between the low paid and the basic income which the authorities reckoned all families should be receiving. Legislation in 1972–3 provided housing allowances to try to ease the lot both of council and private tenants with rents beyond their means. There were more frequent reviews of the effects of inflation on pensioners. A comparison made between London and Dortmund in 1973 found that infant mortality was lower in the former, and that while there was a smaller percentage of poor in Dortmund, the provision of basic minima in London was more satisfactory. Nevertheless, British spending on the social services, health and welfare, as a percentage of the national income remained the lowest of all members of the EEC save for Eire. State retirement benefits were generally better in Europe. In Germany a man could normally retire on about 60 per cent of his former income; in Britain the state pension stood at about one-third of the average manual wage in 1973.[11] About 1.75 million pensioners were in need of supplementary benefit, and Help the Aged claimed in 1975 that about one million old people were living below the official poverty line. In general it was estimated that at the end of the Conservative tenure of office about one in twelve of the British population was, to varying degrees, dependent on supplementary benefits of one kind or another.

Even so, by the 1970s, there had been a significant redistribution of the nation's wealth since 1938 and certainly since the beginning of the century. Much depended on the mode of calculation, but if pension rights were included the poorest 90 per cent of the population, who had possessed only about 8 per cent of the nation's wealth in 1900–13, possessed 54 per cent in 1972. If pension rights were excluded, the top 5 per cent of the population owned over half the nation's wealth. The Royal Commission on Income and Wealth reported in 1975 (Cmnd 6171–2) that some income redistribution had occurred since 1949, and at a rather faster rate between 1938 and 1949. Since 1938 the top 10 per cent of the population's share of post tax income had fallen from 34.6 per cent to 21 per cent. Estimates provided by *The Times* on 14 April 1975 of the disparities in incomes of those in public employment showed much levelling between 1938 and 1974, with the span falling from one to thirty-five to one to ten. The range was narrower in Sweden and still more in Denmark. The erosion of differentials between manual workers and professional and managerial people, and between skilled and unskilled narrowed sharply between 1970 and 1976 in terms of net pay. The latter, of course, was not necessarily the only source of income, but the question was being widely debated in the mid-1970s as to how much further the net pay of the managerial and professional classes could be held back without a serious loss of morale and initiative. A significant drain of talent abroad could not be ruled out. Conservative hopes from 1970 of being able to provide more incentives had had no lasting effects, their own income policies from 1972 being a contributory factor among many. The same period also witnessed a marginal redistribution in favour of female workers, though restrictions on their hours of work and their inability to undertake the heaviest manual work limited the effects of the equal pay for equal work legislation as it came into effect between 1970 and 1975. The year 1975 also witnessed the passage of a Sex Discrimination Act and the establishment of an Equal Opportunities Commission.

In the eyes of the government the key to the removal of poverty, and indeed to Britain's other problems, lay in the successful modernization of the economy. Little turned out as it hoped. In less than four years of office it was obliged to recast many of its policies. (Harold Wilson, not unacquainted with the experience himself, coined the description 'U-turns' for these changes of course: Edward Heath, with his yachting experience, might rather have thought of himself as tacking away from hidden reefs and a lee shore in a force ten gale.)

The first upset came almost at once. In 1968 Rolls Royce had signed a fixed-price contract (with the backing of the Labour government) to supply the engines of the American Lockheed TriStar airliner, then under development. The projected engine, the RB 211, was a very ambitious undertaking. Rolls Royce tried to offer both technical advantages over American competitors and a lower price-tag. Deliveries were due in 1971. There was almost no margin for error. Sir Denning Pearson justified the gamble for the company: 'Building a new engine would not guarantee we stayed in business. Not building one would certainly guarantee that we went out of business.' Certainly without the RB 211 Rolls would have been excluded from one of the most important segments of the aero-engine market. The British since 1945 have too often attempted projects beyond their powers. Given the expertise of Rolls, and the anticipated market for large airliners, the RB 211 choice was a wiser decision than many others in the history of Britain and aerospace since 1945. Unfortunately there were technical difficulties. The company was overstretched and undercapitalized compared with its American rivals. There were other weaknesses. Extra government backing was necessary in November 1970. Three months later the situation was so serious that only a massive state commitment could save the firm. The government chose nationalization and a review of the RB 211 contract as the best way forward.

The difficulty of leaving so-called 'lame ducks' to their fate arose again in the middle of 1971 when Upper Clyde Shipbuilders (a product of a previous attempt at reorganization and rehabilitation by the Wilson ministry) faced financial disaster. A government plan to close two of the four yards, with a probable reduction in the workforce from 8,300 to 2,500, led to a workers' takeover of the Clydebank yard on 30 July. All four yards were finally saved in 1972 (one being diverted to the construction of oil rigs), though there was still some loss of jobs. British shipbuilders in any case were soon confronted by a world crisis in the industry when the mid-1970s brought a sharp drop in the demand for ships and a vast surplus in world shipbuilding capacity. But for the Heath government in 1972, with unemployment breaking through the dreaded one million mark in January for the nation as a whole, not to mention the special problems of the Glasgow area, immediate problems were too pressing to speculate on upward or downward trends in world shipping demand. The government had lost Bromsgrove in a parliamentary by-election in 1971, and had seen a safe majority in Macclesfield decimated. The Conservatives had also fared badly in the 1971 local elections. Efforts to stimulate the economy and consumer spending with tax cuts in 1971 had been slow to take effect, while industrial profitability (and hence industrial investment) had been constricted to some extent by the promise made by two hundred large firms in July 1971 to limit price increases to 5 per cent as their contribution to the fight against inflation. Even a record balance of payments surplus was clouded by the disappearance of the competitive edge imparted by devaluation in the course of 1971. Many firms continued to show a disappointing lack of interest in foreign markets.

The government had taken a battering in more ways than one in 1971. Unemployment did nothing to discourage strikes or inflationary wage settlements. The country was witnessing many experiments in local or group opposition to unpopular actions by government and other organizations. It was a period of employees' 'work' or 'sit-ins'; of varied expressions of student unrest in the context of their own institutions or the wider world. Nor were the middle classes themselves models of deference, a successful battle having been previously waged against the siting of London's third airport at Stansted. Fewer people were prepared to bow so readily as in the past to market forces or to those traditionally or institutionally invested with authority. Motives varied. Anarchists and left-wing extremists were active but relatively few in numbers. They were helped by the mood of the times. Doubts about the adequacy of existing institutions and decision-making bodies had already been reflected in the work of, for instance, Samuel Brittan in *Left or Right* (1968), in Christopher Mayhew's *Party Games* (1969), or Wedgwood Benn's Fabian pamphlet, *The New Politics: a socialist reconnaissance* (1970). Benn wrote of the need for new approaches to secure more popular involvement, including the possible use of referenda. Tendencies of this kind can be traced back to the 'angry' movement in the mid-1950s, to their satirical successors in the early 1960s, to the Committee of One Hundred and the anti-Vietnam demonstrations. Instant publicity blew many incidents up out of proportion: incidents also fed upon each other. It was in such an uncertain and excitable atmosphere that the Heath government attempted a radical reform of industrial relations.

Industrial relations

The Heath ministry was determined to grasp the nettle of union militancy. Much public support appeared to be forthcoming for such a step. But such support was not easily translated into effective power. Strong union opposition was unavoidable, and the government apparently ignored warnings from civil servants well versed in labour questions. Among ministers there was little real familiarity with union affairs. The Cabinet might have reflected on labour relations during the war years – an attempt to imprison and fine union officials in a colliery strike in Kent in 1941 had been a fiasco. Failure in war conditions did not augur well for legislation at a time when militancy seemed to 'pay' and when hitherto moderate unions felt themselves of necessity driven to join the 'paper chase'. Much, indeed, could be achieved without strikes: overtime bans and working to rule could often be very effective. Grassroots Conservative opinion, however, demanded action, and the Cabinet itself believed that legislation on industrial relations was an essential part of its strategy to modernize Britain. If successful the rewards would have been considerable. Even failure had its uses (though the government would not have seen it in this light) in that it demonstrated that a particular route was a dead-end. Without the attempt the debate would have dragged on and the temptation to act on these lines would have persisted.

The government asserted the main principle of the Industrial Relations Bill to be that of 'collective bargaining freely and responsibly conducted'. The government wished to make all agreements on industrial affairs legally enforceable, unless there was express written provision to the contrary. It wanted powers for the Secretary for Employment to appeal to a National Industrial Relations Court in the event of a strike which posed a serious threat to the national interest. But the spontaneity with which many strikes, especially unofficial ones, arose could not thus be legislated out of existence. Indeed, a bill designed to restrain unrepresentative minorities could in fact strengthen their influence by alienating others. The legislation had other disturbing features from the unions' point of view. 'In many respects the Act was seen by unions as seeking to set the individual above the group, and to make his rights pre-eminent.'[12] The Act provided a bill of rights for individuals against unions including the right not to be a member. On many grounds unions could be exposed to legal action and the payment of compensation. The National Industrial Relations Court was to have the status of a High Court to deal with offences under the new legislation. If some union claims were strengthened, these worked mainly to the advantage of only a minority in the movement; one innovation which did survive the fall of the Heath government was the new protection against unfair dismissal.

The Industrial Relations Act was carried through Parliament only after 450 hours of embittered debate. It absorbed one-third of the government's legislative time for the session. The royal assent was given on 6 August 1971. The response of employers and most unions was at first fairly cautious. Employers were loath to invoke the Act. Victor Feather for the TUC insisted that 'trade unionists respect the rule of law', though a minority pressed for defiance, often on the ground that 'bad law' should not be accepted. Non-cooperation and non-registration under the terms of the Act gradually became the accepted union response, though a decisive lead from the bigger unions was necessary to overcome the doubts of others. Unions were not in practice penalized for non-registration whereas registration brought suspension from the TUC and the ultimate threat of expulsion. Even so unions were allowed to defend themselves if necessary before the National Industrial Relations Court, and a great deal of the union resistance to the Act was essentially passive. Yet the opposition of only a few key unions could be decisive, and there remained the general point made by Labour MP Brian Walden, that the outcome must be unsatisfactory when there had been no meeting of minds: individualism was in direct conflict with collectivism.[13] Victor Feather recalled the breakdown in preliminary talks between government and TUC. 'The atmosphere was one of lack of co-operation both ways.'[14] The Act was a gift to all extremists and militants of the left: it was a useful rallying point for the Labour party and for the restoration of its somewhat tattered relationship with the big unions. The government's critics did not always make sense; many were blinkered and emotional. But they were often closer to realities than the ministers.

In the early months of 1972 the nation was more divided than at any time since the General Strike of 1926. Yet a report issued by the Department of Employment on 2 December 1976 claimed that even in 1971–3 only about 2 per cent of manufacturing plants were affected by strikes. The mood, however, was ugly in many sectors of society. The *Annual Register* for 1972 spoke of an atmosphere of 'bitterness, lawlessness, and, at times, even violence' permeating Britain. The national coal strike which began quietly enough on 9 January 1972 escalated dramatically in February. The miners began picketing power stations to prevent the movement of coal stocks once it was clear that a strike confined to the pit would have no speedy effect. The accidental death of a picket, emotional scenes in the Commons, violent clashes at a Birmingham coke depot between police and 'flying pickets' followed. Power stations began to shut down through want of coal; the government secured emergency powers on 14 February, but also appointed a committee of inquiry. An opinion poll on the 16th suggested that public sympathies lay strongly with the miners (perhaps by three to one), and the government gave way. It was necessary to triple the National Coal Board's offer of £2 a week before a settlement was reached.

Some Conservatives condemned this as a fatal concession to union militancy. With other unions stepping up their claims, the battle against inflation, it was said, was lost at this point. In one sense this was true. The miners had greatly strengthened the whole union movement against the government. It might be tempting, according to one's political opinions, to draw parallels with appeasement in the 1930s. Yet the most scholarly studies of British foreign policy in that era have revealed that there were no easy solutions, whatever the failings of the policy-makers. Critics must learn to tread with equal caution in the early 1970s. In 1972 the government was in a weak position from almost every point of view. The miners' case was not unreasonable in the context of the times. They out-generalled the Cabinet, but they also drew the important conclusion that such drastic tactics might misfire a second time. The government itself began to trim its sails with an early approach to the TUC on 9 March 1972. Its problems were acute, with inflation unchecked and the prospect of accelerating wage increases. Yet there were over one million unemployed, and on 13 March a £32 million trade deficit had to be admitted for the previous quarter.

Nevertheless the budget was reflationary, and still more dramatic was the creation of an Industrial Development Executive to inject over £1 billion into new industrial developments in 1973-6. A Minister for Industrial Development was appointed. The abolition of Labour's Industrial Reorganization Corporation appeared more doctrinaire and premature than before. Massive government aid for the regions was once again to be forthcoming. The Industry Act of 1972 represented a major revival of government intervention in the economy. For the rest of its tenure of office the Heath ministry found itself caught up more and more with pricing and investment in both the private and public sectors of industry. A limited interventionist step to solve one problem often uncovered or generated further problems. Aid to one firm made it harder to refuse the next. Restrictions on prices created problems of cash flow and investment. Government aid encouraged unions to bid up wages in expectation of still more help. Meanwhile foreign unease over the state of the economy grew, and there was heavy selling of sterling in June 1972. The government, to obtain more economic elbow room (that is, to prevent a balance of payments crisis bringing expansion at home to an end), 'floated' the pound on 23 June. Promises of an early return to a fixed parity came to nothing.

At home one labour crisis followed another. A wage dispute involving 200,000 railwaymen led to a work-to-rule in mid-April. The government applied to the NIRC first for a cooling-off period, and then in the second half of May for a secret ballot. The railwaymen complied, and voted by almost six to one in favour of industrial action – an obvious government defeat in a battle conducted in accordance with its own rules. Another attempt to apply the Act arose out of a dispute over the kind of labour that could be employed in the packing of containers destined for shipment overseas through the ports of Liverpool, Hull and London. Dockers, fearing for their jobs, claimed the work as theirs and 'blacked' containers not 'stuffed and stripped' by themselves. An appeal to the NIRC was followed by a running battle which reached its climax in July 1972 with the imprisonment of five dockers, an almost total stoppage of work in the nation's docks, and with sympathetic action beginning to spread to other unions. An impasse was avoided by the Official Solicitor who secured the release of the five men. But it was another setback to the government and another demonstration of the inefficacy of its legislation. In 1972 the number of working days lost through strikes reached a new postwar record of 24 million – more than 1968–70 combined.

The government redoubled its efforts to secure the voluntary cooperation of the TUC as well as of the CBI in restraining inflation and in striving for faster growth and greater national efficiency. The unions as a whole also seemed anxious to reduce the temperature, though obdurate over the Industrial Relations Act. The TUC began to suspend unions which had registered. The Labour party conference in Blackpool in October found the left in the ascendant, with Michael Foot securing a record vote in the constituency elections to the NEC. But the parliamentary party could not ignore its continuing failure to regain public confidence. Its divisions and the strength of the left contributed to a Liberal by-election gain at its expense in October (the Liberals also gained a seat from the government two months later). Again there was some talk of a possible Liberal coalition with the non-socialist wing of the Labour party. But Harold Wilson appeared content to give the left its head, with only an occasional restraining tug on the reins to ensure that the party took no decisive steps which would seriously limit its freedom of manoeuvre in the future. Meanwhile the government's negotiations with both sides of industry were breaking down in the autumn of 1972. The Cabinet were seeking a package that would reconcile growth with the restraint of inflation, but not even an offer to discuss the Industrial Relations Act would shift the unions from their insistence on price controls without wage restraint. The CBI could offer nothing on price restraint without union cooperation on wages. The tripartite talks were indefinitely adjourned on 2 November. Soon after the Cabinet announced a three month freeze on pay, price, rent and dividend increases during which legislation could be introduced for a longer-term solution. At the time wages were rising well ahead of prices and output. There was also a balance of payments deficit for the year of over £650 million, partly the result of the increases in world commodity prices from the end of 1971.

The oil crisis and the miners' strike

With the passage of time it will become possible to see more clearly just how great a divide the years 1973–4 were in British history – whether or not they represent a significant break in the course of events since 1945 and the real end of the postwar era. At the very least the dramatic developments of 1973–4 ushered in an unexpected election, the fall of a government, a period of acute political uncertainty, and the worst recession since that which followed the Wall Street crash of 1929. These were developments which no government could reasonably have foreseen, but the question must still be faced as to the overall wisdom of the Heath Cabinet's general strategy in 1973, and its handling of individual crises. The year opened with the government white paper of 17 January 1973, *The Programme for Controlling Inflation: the second stage* (Cmnd 5205). This introduced a plan for price, profit and income controls over the next three years. These were to be administered by a newly created Pay Board and a Price Commission. Phase One was already in operation: Phase Two of controls would operate from April, with strict limits laid down concerning the permissible range of price and incomes increases, and with statutory powers to penalize breaches. Resistance to this policy was at first neither serious nor effective. The TUC conference in September, however, made union cooperation with the government dependent on the restoration of free collective bargaining. It also demanded statutory price controls and food subsidies. The CBI wanted less strict price controls, their Director-General insisting that industry needed 'higher dividends, room to make bigger agreements'. For the general public food prices had risen by one-third since 1970, house mortgage interest rates reached an unheard-of 11 per cent in September 1973, while inflation was running at over 10 per cent a year. From October there was also the threat both of oil shortages and of a continuing spiral of oil price increases. Phase Three of the government's battle against inflation, which was to come into effect from November, was thus likely to encounter many more difficulties than Phase Two.

Meanwhile the government had been hoping for a continuing rise in output and productivity, and the budget of March 1973 had been formulated accordingly. It was basically neutral. *The Economist* of 10 March indeed favoured tax cuts and other stimulants lest the expansionist momentum should be lost and there should be a return to stop–go. There was in fact a growing debate as to whether or not the economy was in danger of overheating, and whether the time had arrived for some deflationary measures. Peter Jay wrote in *The Times* of 7 May 1973 of 'The boom that must go bust'. A new dimension was introduced by the rapid growth of credit both at home and abroad. As early as June 1972 Professor Alan Walters had condemned 'the explosive money supply' situation. The Treasury view remained that the money supply, though important, was not the prime cause of inflation. The miners' strike had occurred before the main expansion of the money supply. Severe monetary restraint would jeopardize the ministry's hopes of a 5 per cent growth rate. Only later was it widely felt that the Treasury's approach to monetary policy had been too lax.[15] Much of the increased liquidity was used in property speculation and not for productive investment. Soaring property values and large if nominal profits increased popular suspicion of business in 1973–4 and lessened electoral support for the Conservatives at a critical moment. On the general conduct of industry Edward Heath complained in 1973:

When we came in [to office], we were told that there were not sufficient inducements to invest. So we provided inducements. Then we were told people were scared of balance of payments difficulties leading to stop–go. So we floated the pound. Then we were told of fears of inflation. And now we are dealing with that. And still you are not investing enough.

Long-term causes of this investment caution have been noted, but Heath had reason to feel impatience.

Meanwhile from the spring of 1973 the financial experts continued to debate the course which the government should adopt. Those who favoured deflation were opposed by the government, the Opposition, the TUC and the CBI, *The Economist* and the *National Institute Economic Review. The National Westminster Bank Quarterly Review* had some reservations, though broadly it supported the policy of growth. In August 1973 it thought the government in an extraordinarily difficult situation, but any serious braking would revive fears of stop–go. It did advocate some restriction of the money supply to discourage home demand in favour of exports. But *The Economist* and *NIER* continued to argue that deflation would solve none of Britain's long-term problems. With a floating pound there was now much more room for manoeuvre. The government, though it made some economies, was afraid that cuts in the social services or tax increases would merely fuel wage demands and injure the efforts to reduce inflation. Deflationary measures would not operate at once, and might well strike the economy when it was already on the downswing. There were great hopes that the world boom in commodity prices would burn itself out, if not in 1973 then in 1974. The government had had great difficulty from 1971 in persuading industry to expand. Its drastic increases in public expenditure had been accompanied by the assurance that these could be eased back as the economy picked up, but the government felt far from assured as to the outcome were it to attempt considerable cuts in the circumstances of 1973. The public borrowing needs for 1973–4 remained around £4 billion.

The vulnerability of both the British economy and government to any further shocks was thus all too evident. Even before the oil price explosion the rise in world commodity prices (they trebled between 1971 and 1974) was creating serious balance of payments problems. Then in October 1973 came the agreement of the oil-producing countries to increase prices by 75 per cent. This was announced on 8 October, two days after the outbreak of war between Israel and the

Arabs. While the Arab oil states were determined to use the oil weapon in the struggle against Israel, some increase in oil prices would have occurred in any case. A sellers' market in oil had been developing since 1970. Some movement of the terms of trade in favour of the producing states was long overdue, but in 1973–4 it took place with such violence that it plunged the western world into its greatest postwar economic crisis. At the end of 1973 the price of oil by a further 130 per cent. For Britain, although her visible and invisible exports increased by some £2.5 billion in 1973, her imports rose by £4 billion. In terms of a rise in volume, exports almost matched imports. It was the change in the terms of trade that was critical. The *NIER* in November 1973 conceded that unemployment had fallen since 1972 rather faster than expected and that growth (at about 4.5 per cent a year) was somewhat less than expected. This suggested less potential output and efficiency in the economy than it had originally estimated, but it was broadly satisfied with the trends in consumption, investment, British unit costs compared with their competitors', and in import and export volumes. The two real threats to the government's strategy in its view were the revolution in oil and other commodity prices and in any attacks on the government's prices and incomes policy at home. The government saw matters very much in this light, though *The Spectator* on 24 November was scathingly critical. The recourse to higher interest rates was only partly designed to restrain the money supply: the rates were also 'to attract foreign capital needed to fuel the domestic inflation deliberately created by the Government in its gamble for growth'. There should be a return to the true Conservative policies of 'free markets, balanced budgets and independent enterprise'. But orthodoxy of this kind provided no answers for the hard-pressed government at the end of 1973.

The Cabinet opted essentially for a continuance of its existing policies: an endeavour to restrict British inflation levels to the lowest that were feasible, and to ensure that British exports remained as competitive as possible. Phase Three of the prices and incomes policy came into effect in November. Above all it strove to restrict most pay increases for the coming year to around 7 per cent, though special cases were envisaged, and there were also special threshold payments for every rise of 1 per cent in the retail price index over 6 per cent. But the government was under pressure to concede exceptional rises to the power station engineers, the gas workers and the miners. Trouble was also impending on the railways, and the government's only comfort towards the end of the year was an opinion poll lead of some 5 per cent over Labour (though only of 40 per cent backing among the electorate as a whole) and the capture of Govan in a by-election by the SNP from Labour. The wrangling in the ranks of the Opposition was so serious that on 26 November 1973 Harold Wilson intervened to try to restore some order. He had cause to, since in the last week of October and still more in November tentative thoughts were beginning to circulate among senior Conservatives on the pros and cons of an early election. This interest was naturally prompted by fears of a drastic acceleration in the rate of inflation from the spring of 1974 which would make a later appeal to the country inadvisable.

If such ideas were circulating they were not shared by the Prime Minister. Faced by overtime bans by the power engineers and the miners the government announced emergency measures to conserve electricity on 13 November. A month later it announced its intention to introduce a three day week for most workers from the end of the year with the aim of cutting the consumption of electricity by one-fifth. The Chancellor of the Exchequer introduced an emergency budget on 17 December. State spending was to be cut by £1,200 million a year; there were some credit restrictions but tax increases were marginal. The budget was criticized by some as too mild, and as failing to communicate to the public the real seriousness of the situation. But to *The Economist* of 22 December and others it was on the right lines. Tax increases would trigger off the threshold agreements under phase Three of the incomes policy and by squeezing incomes could well increase hostility to the incomes policy itself. It was estimated that the earnings of many of the oil producers would be in excess of what they could use in the short term. Much would be banked; some of it in London. The great British need was to develop the competitiveness and potential of British industry so that it would be well placed to seize export opportunities now and in the long run. Deflation would only add to unit costs and increase discontent in Britain. But to complement the mild budget, success was vital for Stage Three of the government's income policy. In many of its calculations the government seemed wildly optimistic. Sir Michael Clapham, President of the CBI, went so far as to declare on 11 December that the nation should abandon its growth plans and concentrate on survival: currently the nation was 'walking on the edge of a precipice'. But there was something to be said for the Cabinet's approach. Any other policy was likely to damage its standing in the country still more. Something might turn up. Britain was not the only industrial nation afflicted by the oil crisis. Indeed, by careful diplomacy Britain was avoiding significant oil shortages as Arab producers cut back supplies in the struggle to isolate and weaken Israel.

At home the government had some success too. The grievances of the power engineers were resolved. But in the eyes of the Cabinet the credibility of its incomes policy turned essentially on the outcome of the struggle with the miners. With the oil crisis the nation needed all the coal that could be dug. This enhanced the bargaining position of the miners. But many Conservatives were also tempted by the confrontation with the miners to see this as possibly the best issue on which the government could fight in the remaining one and a half years of its term. One had to be highly optimistic to hope for an improvement in the nation's economic situation within that period. Pressure for an early election to be held on the theme of 'who rules Britain?' thus steadily developed. The demand was at first successfully resisted by the Prime Minister and other key figures in the Cabinet. But with a dispute on the railways leading to one day strikes, and with the miners' ballot resulting in an 81 per cent vote for a strike, the government's options were being steadily eroded. An electioneering atmosphere pervaded Westminster, Whitehall and the media.

The elections of 1974

Among those reported to be doubtful concerning the wisdom of a clash with the miners was Mr Harold Macmillan. 'It's very unwise, you know, to take on the Vatican, the Brigade of Guards or the NUM', was his alleged comment.[16] The government's consultations with the TUC on the crisis, however, broke down on 4 February. The miners' executive called for a strike from the 9th. The government therefore decided on 7 February to call an election for the last day in the month. In one respect it perhaps weakened its hand by announcing an immediate special study of the miners' case under the new relativities procedure of the Pay Board. The government would accept its recommendations. Such a move was probably vital to resolve the miners' strike – its strain on the economy could not be long endured – but the timing of the announcement was controversial. Many asked why an election had to be held first. What the government of course needed was an early end to the strike but in such circumstances that major concessions to the miners would not lead to a general wages scramble in which the whole credibility of its incomes policy was undermined. It therefore hoped to balance concessions to the miners with an impressive electoral mandate which would provide some basis for a long-term strategy in the fight against inflation and to meet the broader economic crisis. Heath resisted the pressure for an early election from many in his own party until he could see no other way to maintain the effectiveness of his government. This would seem the most reasonable interpretation of his actions. On 12 February he put the government's case in these terms: 'The issue is whether this country is now going to return a strong Government with a firm mandate for the next five years to deal with the counter-inflation policy, a firm incomes policy, which Parliament will approve.' Britain was certainly in need of effective government by one party or a coalition, but popular disillusionment with both main parties, the attitudes of the parties themselves, and the vagaries of the electoral system conspired to prevent either possibility.

Conservative efforts to present the election as a battle between moderates and extremists (as defined by themselves) was less successful than hoped. Labour roused itself from its self-destructive internal feuding to fight the election with some tactical skill. It was able to help shift the emphasis in the campaign from the issues of 'who governs' and the miners' strike to the government's overall record and the dramatic rise in prices, not least in their effects on housing and food. There was an 'unacceptable face of capitalism' to be exploited that had not really been in evidence since 1945. Labour moderates concentrated on bread-and-butter issues whereas the left wing assiduously courted the traditional and natural supporters of Labour. The party manifesto had reflected the new strength of the left, with more reference to nationalization, and the redistribution of wealth and power in favour of the working classes. But there was much in the overall record of the government to stir traditional Labour supporters to vote, and it was significant that the polls could discover only about 20 per cent support for more nationalization, save for North Sea oil and gas where about two-fifths favoured public ownership. Rather less opposed Phase Three of the government's incomes policy and favoured the ending of the Industrial Relations Act, proportions which were remarkably close to the final Labour share of the poll on 28 February. Indeed, judged by its performance in the elections between 1945 and 1970, its 1974 electoral campaign had been a disaster in terms of electoral appeal. Labour had secured fewer votes than at any time since the war: its share of the poll was a mere 37 per cent (its previous worst postwar performance had been in 1959 with nearly 44 per cent). In so far as Labour had mobilized its basic supporters, the influence of its left wing had lost it the support of many of the centre so assiduously courted by Attlee, Morrison and others since the 1930s. In the light of past electoral experience, Labour's fate in February 1974 should have been akin to that of 1935, if not worse.

But Labour's failure was equalled and in some ways exceeded by that of the government. Here the tactics of Labour's moderates (and perhaps the caution of the miners' leaders themselves) may have paid off in that the opposition of a clear majority of the country to most of Labour's programme did not result in a closing of the ranks behind the government. Where fear of Labour was too weak to unite its opponents, faith in the Conservatives was too limited to provide a substitute. With different (that is, earlier) timing of the election, or with a little more luck, the government might have won a majority, but the strength of the Liberals and the nationalists was always such that it would not have been an impressive victory in terms of the share of the votes cast. There would have been a political mandate, but not necessarily commensurate with the government's needs. It would not have been comparable with that obtained by the National government in 1931. The long-term erosion of the basic strength of both main parties has already been discussed. Public morale was low. The strong desire to see inflation controlled, the varied fears of union strength and militancy, the opposition to left-wing extremists – all these were accompanied by doubts as to the ability of the government to achieve its aims and by a reluctance to face the costs that might be called for in their implementation. The majority of voters were thus confused and uncertain, and also insufficiently impressed by the government's record since 1970, both in the management of the economy and in its handling of industrial relations, to rally hopefully behind its leadership. Even in the first half of February the polls suggested no more than around 45 per cent support for the Conservatives, with the Liberals running strongly from the outset.

Incidents during the campaign helped to rob the government of such advantages as it possessed. Enoch Powell, five days before the election, denounced both the overall policies of the government and its specific case for an election. He further declared his intention to vote Labour as the only party offering the nation the chance for second thoughts on entry to the EEC. Labour's promise of a 'fundamental renegotiation' of the terms of entry was indeed one of its most popular moves – nearly two-thirds of those polled were in favour. On 26 February the Director-General of the CBI spoke (as he thought, privately) in favour of the revision or replacement of the Industrial Relations Act.[17] Recently published figures showed a record trade deficit; a misleading story was published suggesting that miners' incomes had been overestimated. Nor was the government helped by the announcement of record profits by some firms and banks. Given the closeness of the result even small episodes might have had unusual significance.

The turnout on 28 February was 78 per cent, the highest since 1959. Labour secured 301 seats from 11,646,391 votes, the Conservatives 296 from 11,872,180. The Liberals produced far and away their best postwar performance, with nearly one-fifth of the votes (6,054,744) but only fourteen seats. The SNP and Plaid Cymru won seven and two seats respectively, sharing over 800,000 votes. When account is also taken of the intervention of the United Ulster Unionist Council and other parties in Northern Ireland the decline of the two main parties can be graphically illustrated. In the elections between 1945 and 1970 Labour and Conservatives had secured never less than 87 per cent of the votes cast, and almost 97 per cent in 1951. In 1974 they won no more than 75 per cent between them. Labour had lost half a million votes since 1970; the Conservatives one and a quarter million. The outcome of the February election also left the constitutional experts buzzing in that given the new distribution of seats among the parties, not even the largest and the next but one could in combination command a majority in the Commons – an unprecedented situation. Edward Heath, probably unwisely, explored the possibility of a coalition with the Liberals. This would not have given him a majority. It did expose divisions within the Liberal ranks. Labour therefore took office on 4 March 1974 as the largest single party, yet with its smallest share of the poll since 1931. Even in Wales, its strongest centre, its share of the vote had slumped below half.

The government could not be other than an interim one, the politicians – if not necessarily the nation – being indisposed as yet to accept that the political game might have to be played according to new rules and conventions, at least for the time being. Labour's assets were few. They took office at a time when the nation's morale was so low that even the appearance of some success might suffice to enable the party to win an early election. The new government might be able to feed the hope that it could cooperate with the unions and so avoid the damaging confrontations of the early 1970s. Much was made of Labour's 'social contract' with the unions. In contrast to 1964, Labour could now field a very experienced ministerial team. Harold Wilson took up the premiership again in a less theatrical and impetuous manner. James Callaghan, Roy Jenkins and Denis Healey were an impressive and complementary trio. Michael Foot's rebellious past could prove an asset in office. Yet a second appeal to the nation in October 1974 only marginally improved the situation for the new government. Labour secured an overall majority of three with a lower share of the poll (39.2 per cent) than in 1923 or 1929 (though not February 1974) and with a drop in total votes compared with the previous election. Their strength was based on the collapse of the Conservative vote to under 10.5 million (a drop of nearly 1.5 million since February) and a weakening of the Liberal challenge. The nationalists made further progress, the SNP taking second place from the Conservatives in Scotland with 30 per cent of the vote (though with only eleven seats to the Conservatives' sixteen). Labour's share of the vote in Scotland had fallen to a little over 36 per cent. In the United Kingdom as a whole, less than 30 per cent of the entire electorate had voted Labour in October.

Britain in 1974

Not surprisingly there was much speculation in the mid-1970s as to the political future of the United Kingdom – whether parliamentary democracy as it had been known since 1918 could long survive, and whether indeed the United Kingdom might ultimately be fragmented into as many as four new states. As recently as 1973 Richard Rose had written that 'today one might journey to England to seek the secrets of stable, representative government',[18] whereas in May 1975 an American television commentator was putting the question as to whether Britain was 'drifting slowly towards a condition of ungovernability' and 'sleepwalking into a social revolution'. In Britain parallels were freely drawn with, for instance, the dangers facing Britain in 1939–40. The editors of the *National Westminster Bank Quarterly Review* in November 1974 thought the national mood in the summer of 1974 akin to that in 1939: 'There has been the same mixture of foreboding, unwillingness to face reality, and a desire to do something and get it over. Meanwhile, with familiar landmarks shifting, planning for the long-term future has been well nigh impossible.'

A tutor in British politics might well have been tempted in the mid-1970s to introduce students to his subject with a good textbook on the Middle Ages, with special reference to the reign of King Stephen. Indeed, Professor W. J. M. Mackenzie had earlier been so impressed by the rise of great ungovernable interests outside the state that he had written of the development of a 'new medievalism' in which the state was 'submerged by the interests'. He thought such a system 'technologically conservative and its political horizon is limited to problems familiar to the ordinary man in his daily business'. It was, he concluded, highly vulnerable to external shocks.[19] Samuel Brittan in the *British Journal of Political Science* of April 1975 feared that group competition could ultimately generate such intolerable inflation as to destroy parliamentary institutions. Appreciation of these dangers brought about a remarkable measure of cooperation between the TUC and the Labour government in the summer of 1975, though to what long-term effect one cannot as yet guess. Certainly there seemed to be emerging in the mid-1970s a greater national readiness to agree that the country's problems were more complex and deep rooted than most had been hitherto prepared to accept. Where radical changes had been proposed, the problems of implementation had been underestimated. There was too great a tendency to engage in isolated criticism of the unions, management, the Civil Service, schools and universities, or that mysterious being 'the Establishment' without sufficient reference to their interaction upon each other and the many other influences to which they were subjected. Interest in the educational background of top French civil servants and even in their more direct experience of industry was not sufficient in itself. The French and British Civil Services were what they were because both they and related aspects of life in the two nations had evolved in particular ways over long periods of time. Only to a limited extent were they masters of their own fates in the present.

The British people had set out in the later 1940s to reshape their future with some confidence as well as with some forebodings. They were more often victims of their own past (both in home and foreign affairs) than they were prepared or wished to recognize. There were also important divisions of interest and over the scale of priorities. Apart from the obvious clashes between Labour and Conservative, employee and management, there were many rifts within those and other groupings. The British solution was often that of compromise, though this did not necessarily protect weaker groups such as the pensioners, small shopkeepers and those without strong unions. The large numbers below or near the official poverty line in the early 1970s bear eloquent testimony to this. But for those with power the situation was very different if rarely wholly satisfactory. Power was widely diffused in Britain after 1945 and in some ways became more so with the passage of time. Increases in the powers of the central government could also add to its difficulties by increasing its responsibilities. As the public came to expect more of the central government, so it became more critical and resentful in its moments of disappointment. Politicians and voters came to prey upon each other, fuelling unrealistic promises and hopes. The rivalries and differences of Labour and Conservative were moderated by the harsh necessities of office, but they were still sufficient to bring some significant discontinuities in policy and priorities. In so far as there was a broad accommodation within the framework of the welfare state and mixed economy (and to this must be added down to the late-1960s the pretensions of a great power) at least from the early 1950s, and at times before, it was deemed prudent to allow satisfaction of the main interests to run at least a little ahead of the generation of the resources for their support.

In their turn successive governments might be excused for feeling that much of their expenditure had been undertaken for the purpose (directly or indirectly) of strengthening the nation's economy, but that they in their turn had been failed by management, employees or even educationalists. The right levers had been pulled to little or no effect. Subsidies and aid had too often propped up industries without resulting in basic improvements: increased educational expenditure in universities and polytechnics had not strengthened the engineering profession, for instance, as much as had been intended. Lack of continuity from government to government – even discontinuities within a single ministry – helps to explain the disappointing effects of much state aid, as well as weaknesses within industry itself. Certainly it is otherwise difficult to explain so large a drop in real terms of new manufacturing investment in 1970–1 when the Conservatives suddenly introduced a new system of incentives to replace the cash grants under Labour. Only extraordinary efforts by the Heath government restored the level of real investment by 1973–4 to that achieved under Labour in 1969–70. But other forces were also at work throughout the period from the mid-1960s which were helping to erode long-term business confidence. There were the corrosive effects of inflation and mounting labour unrest. Increases or changes in taxation added to industry's uncertainties. The outcome for British manufacturing industry as a whole was a disturbing fall in profitability. Tne National Economic Development Organization concluded early in 1976 that, with adjustments for inflation, the return on assets employed had dropped from an unimpressive 10 per cent in 1965 to a mere 6 per cent in 1973. These low returns were likely to have been a serious impediment to new investment (despite various government inducements); indeed, some companies had been using up capital to maintain current operations.

Statistics are elusive, fickle creatures, made more so by their creators and users, all inhabiting a world of subtle changes and distortions which perhaps only the pen of Lewis Carroll could capture. Nevertheless by the mid-1970s there was emerging a fair measure of agreement, if with varying degrees of emphasis, that employment and investment in the more obviously and directly productive sectors had been allowed to fall too much in relation to other occupations and services. The unproductiveness of much of the non-manufacturing sectors was sometimes exaggerated. Tourist, banking, insurance and invisible earnings of many kinds have to be considered, while the producing industries themselves were dependent on a variety of services. Nevertheless, in terms of balance, and given the way in which so much British industry appeared to be languishing, the need for some adjustments in resources in favour of industry appeared essential. Far more of the wealth created by British industry was absorbed by wages, salaries and taxes than in Japan. Such new investment as was possible in British industry on average proved about half as productive as that in western Europe. More investment *per se* was thus clearly not the only answer. If some firms were not held back by failings in management, engineering and sales staff, or the general workforce, they could be held back by the environment in which they were required to operate, from the failings of components' manufacturers to the deleterious effects of many aspects of government action. The absorption of too much top quality personnel into the public sector, for reasons of higher status, better or more assured incomes, and for a variety of other reasons, was in itself a factor of considerable importance.

Comparisons of the public sector, of public expenditure, or taxation and of other public impositions on individual incomes with those in other European countries did not necessarily suggest that overall there were striking differences between Britain and her neighbours. But there were many significant differences in detail. Just as there could be disincentives to investors, so also there could be to a great number of individuals – and not merely to the well-to-do. The tax burden of the average married couple had more than doubled between 1960 and 1975 (that is in terms of a percentage of total income). Increased impositions in western Europe were usually offset by a continuing sense of rapidly increasing personal prosperity. Elaborate social services and heavy public expenditure were more easily borne by dynamic economies.

Yet, as the elections of 1974 revealed, the economic disappointments brought confusion among the mass of middle-of-the-road opinion rather than any disposition to swing to extremes. One of the main characteristics of the Welsh and Scottish nationalist parties was their basic moderation and respect for conventional British political practices and ideas. Anthony Crosland argued in *Socialism Now* (1974) that deep surveys of opinion were failing to unearth any potential mass revolt against the current social and economic systems. *Social Trends* (no. 4, 1973) recorded that about half those interviewed declared themselves well satisfied with their jobs, and a further third as fairly satisfied. The sharp increase in strikes from 1968 must be seen mainly in the context of growing concern over incomes in a period of rapid inflation. It is true that many white collar workers were becoming more interested in unions and more actively involved in strikes, but it was as premature to write of the 'proletarianization' of the bourgeoisie as it had been earlier to write of the embourgeoisement of the skilled working classes. Social and political attitudes were certainly becoming more confused and ambiguous. By 1970 perhaps one-fifth of all manual workers thought of themselves as in some way middle-class: 40 per cent of all manual workers who were home-owners described themselves as Conservatives.[20] But in any case R. T. Mackenzie and A. Silver in their study of a sample of working-class voters in the later 1960s found few references to socialism or to a new social order; working-class support for Labour arose mainly out of class loyalty and/or expectations of greater benefits. Most Labour voters saw themselves or their party as in no way deviating significantly from the dominant values in the British political system. By 1970 Richard Rose thought that only just over half the electorate were voting according to their social class, and that basic social characteristics provided less guide to party loyalties than in the average European democracy.[21] If Labour drew nearly half its regular voting strength from strongly class conscious voters, and if class attitudes remained stronger in Wales and in the old industrial areas, the success of nationalist parties in Scotland and Wales, the Liberal resurgence early in 1974, Conservative strength in 1970, and the pattern of voting in 1974 all pointed to the growing strength, if also the growing fluidity, of the centre.

Such was the condition which coincided with the growing feeling and reality of conflict and confrontation in the early 1970s. The distribution of power was becoming more complex, and was beginning to strain traditional institutions and conventions. But the strife arose mainly out of the desire to maintain the *status quo*, whether in terms of the preservation of jobs in decaying industries or areas, the maintenance or advancement of living standards in an era of inflation and slow growth, the preservation of existing work privileges, or union claims in the face of efficiency experts and the Industrial Relations Act. So-called extremists and militants gained influence and followings in such circumstances, but it was as yet premature to identify permanent trends either among the followers or among the militants themselves. The Jack Jones of the mid-1970s appeared in a very different guise from the Jack Jones of a few years earlier. As the appreciation gradually grew of the scale of the crisis facing Britain in the middle of the decade so the initial reaction was one of caution by the vast majority; the usual reactions were in broad conformity with what a study of British history since 1688 would lead one to expect. Much of course would depend on whether the heterogeneous elements that made up the broad centre could cooperate sufficiently and produce a workable synthesis. Much would depend on the patience and continuing generosity of foreign states and central bankers.

Keynes remarked of the Great Depression at the end of 1930, 'what has occurred is not exactly an accident; it has been deeply rooted in our general way of doing things'. The British had done many notable things since 1945. By and large the national wealth and income per head had roughly doubled. At least down to 1967 unemployment had been held below 2.6 per cent (save in 1963). Before the war it had rarely dipped below 10 per cent. The achievements in welfare, health and education had not been unimpressive, if often the subject of controversy. But much of this had been based upon the remarkable expansion of the world economy, and especially that of the western nations since 1945. Other states, in the same environment, had done better both in economic growth and in the provision of social services. Britain's share of world trade in manufactured goods in 1963 had not been far short of that of West Germany – it had stood at about 15 per cent. By 1974 Britain's share at just under 9 per cent was half that of West Germany and less than that of France. Between December 1971 and October 1976 sterling had depreciated by over 40 per cent against other major currencies. Two analyses in 1976, by NEDO[22] and C. F. Pratten, revealed that British manufacturing productivity per worker had risen since 1954 by only 2.9 per cent a year as against 4.6 in West Germany. About half the German advantage was attributed to behavioural causes such as fewer industrial disputes and restrictive practices, better use of personnel, and personal efficiency. But it also seemed clear that many of West Germany's advantages arose from wider causes than what occurred in the factories themselves. As for Britain's nationalized industries, their performance varied widely compared with the private manufacturing sector. Assessments were complicatd by their special financial problems, but in terms of output per employee gas and electricity had outperformed the private sector from the mid-1960s, improvements in coal and on the railways had tailed off in the early 1970s, while output had stagnated or declined in the nationalized steel industry.[23]

In world affairs, judged against other imperial powers in the past as well as in the post-1945 era itself, Britain had conducted a retreat from empire with relatively little bloodshed and with a fair measure of realism in the light of rapidly changing circumstances. The retreat was less orderly and less carefully planned than was often suggested; indeed Britain was frequently only a few steps ahead of disaster. Furthermore the inheritance of the successor states was less satisfactory than many claimed. But by and large the withdrawal from empire was effected without too many drastic mistakes along the way. With respect to Europe, if the decision to enter the EEC was the right one, it was taken too late. Admittedly for Britain to have moved in that direction earlier would have required imaginative statesmanship of the highest order: the delays after 1963 were not mainly the fault of the British. In the defence of Europe Britain at first pursued her national interest sensibly and well from 1946 in so far as other distractions permitted. But for much of the 1950s and 1960s Britain was halfhearted in her European commitments and she was fortunate that circumstances did not exact a severe penalty in consequence. As for the Anglo-American relationship throughout the whole period, this was more ambiguous in its effects on Britain than was always appreciated. Critics often attacked it for the wrong reasons; that is, because they were anti-American and not because they were trying to see it within the broad perspective of British interests. As for Britain's contribution to the western alliance, if this became less satisfactory in the 1970s, this was now because of the nation's growing economic weakness.

Britain from 1945 to 1974 had made the transition from the weakest of the major powers to the ranks of the medium states. In the process she had not shrugged off, as many people hoped she would, all the weaknesses that had resulted from her being the pioneer industrialized nation, as well as a world power. If the movement to her lower status had been largely accomplished by 1974, her consolidation in that new position was far from complete.

Notes and references

(Full bibliographical details are given in the Bibliography, pp. 339ff.)

Chapter 1. Introduction to the postwar era

1. Sked and Cook, pp. 159–60
2. Mowat, pp. 495 ff.
3. J. M. Keynes, pp. 377 ff.
4. Strachey (1), p. 253
5. Sayers, chapters 2–3
6. Sabine, p. 285
7. Titmuss (1), pp. 67–8
8. Hancock and Gowing, p. 542
9. Hutchison, pp. 28–9
10. W. O. L. Smith, p. 137
11. Robbins, p. 193
12. Sayers, p. 141
13. McCallum, p. 238
14. Medlicott (2), p. 469
15. Donoughue and Jones, pp. 339–43
16. Campbell, pp. 417–18
17. Gladwyn, chapter 8
18. Van der Pol, vii. 128, 175
19. M. Foot, pp. 32–4, 228
20. Woodward (1), pp. 524–7
21. *Ibid*, p. 567
22. Harriman, pp. 508–9, 523–30

Chapter 2. Labour and world affairs

1. Hancock and Gowing, p. 546
2. *Ibid*, p. 551
3. Sayers, p. 484
4. Gardner, p. 384
5. Dalton, pp. 85–7
6. Goldsworthy, pp. 184 ff.
7. Gopal, i. 342 ff.
8. Brecher, pp. 62 ff.
9. Dalton, pp. 101, 105
10. Howard, pp. 238–9; Xydis (2), pp. 240–3, 317–18, 348, 406–7
11. Williams (3), p. 171
12. *Ibid*, pp. 154 ff.
13. *Foreign Relations* (1947) iii. 6, 14–19
14. *Ibid* (1947) iii. 29–31, 268 ff.
15. *Ibid* (1947) iii. 43 ff.
16. Williams (3), pp. 178–9; see also Hourani, pp. 9 ff.

17. *Foreign Relations* (1947) v. 499–500
18. *Ibid* (1947) i. 753–4
19. Gupta, p. 288
20. *Foreign Relations* (1947) v. 578
21. *Ibid* (1948) iii. 765–9
22. *Ibid* (1947) v. 625
23. Snetsinger, *passim*
24. Williams (1), p. 20
25. Hourani, p. 19
26. *Foreign Relations* (1948) iii. 1100

Chapter 3. The domestic policies of the Labour government

1.   Marwick (1), p. 339
2.   Dow, pp. 223–7
3.   Pollard, pp. 368–76
4.   Hancock and Gowing, p. 452
5.   Rogow, pp. 49 ff.; seg also Blank, chapter 4
6.   Rogow, p. 68
7.   *Ibid*, p. 45
8.   Sherman, pp. 111–14, 122–4
9.   Harriman, pp. 550–1
10. Gowing, ii. 57
11. Donoughue and Jones, p. 355
12. Chester, pp. 43–4
13. Buxton, pp. 476–97
14. *Foreign Relations* (1947) iii. 497–8
15. Donoughue and Jones, p. 356n.
16. Thompson and Hunter, pp. 15, 45 ff.
17. Donoughue and Jones, pp. 400–3
18. *Ibid*, p. 402
19. Rogow, pp. 167–70
20. C. H. Lee, pp. 157–8
21. Marshall, p. 83
22. Gregg, p. 81
23. M. Foot, p. 195
24. Donoughue and Jones, p. 432
25. *Ibid*, p. 409
26. Dow, p. 33
27. Wigham (2), pp. 99, 101
28. Winch, p. 285
29. Jay, pp. 137–8
30. Mackintosh, pp. 494–5
31. *Foreign Relations* (1948) iii. 1067–71
32. Blank, p. 90
33. Shonfield (2) p. 88
34. Donoughue and Jones, p. 438

Chapter 4. The cold war and the decline of Labour

1.   J. E. Smith, p. 515
2.   *Foreign Relations* (1948) iii. 1113 ff.
3.   *Ibid* (1948) iii. 1073–5, 1091–1108, 1113 ff.
4.   *Ibid* (1948) iii. 1–6; (1947) iii. 818 ff.

5. *Ibid* (1948) iii. 13, 22
6. *Ibid* (1948) iii. 767-9, 844
7. *Ibid* (1948) iii. 57-8, 298
8. *Ibid* (1948) ii. 806
9. *Ibid* (1948) ii. 899-900, 982
10. M. Foot, pp. 230-1
11. *Ibid*, p. 229
12. *Foreign Relations* (1949) ix. 1-260, especially pp. 6-11, 57-61
13. Dalton, pp. 316-18
14. Donoughue and Jones, pp. 481-3
15. Waites, pp. 268-9
16. Williams (3), pp. 227-8
17. M. Foot, p. 259
18. Nicholas, p. 119
19. Dalton, p. 339; Shinwell, pp. 202-3
20. Weaver, pp. 210 ff.
21. R. A. Butler, p. 132
22. Nicholas, pp. 4, 327 ff.
23. M. Foot, pp. 288-9, 293-5
24. Dow, p. 54
25. M. Foot, p. 302
26. D. Acheson, pp. 435, 444; McDonald, p. 123
27. Tsou, p. 575
28. M. Foot, pp. 312-15; Haseler, p. 117
29. Haseler, p. 121n.
30. Dow, pp. 54 ff.
31. See below pp. 114-15
32. *Spectator*, 24 January 1964
33. Crossman (2), i. 129; Shinwell, pp. 206-7
34. Macmillan, iii. 355
35. Donoughue and Jones, pp. 501-3
36. Butler (1), pp. 20-1
37 This is the highest vote recorded by any party in British electoral history down to 1976.

Chapter 5. The return of the Conservatives

1. Macmillan, iii. 361-6
2. Birkenhead (2), p. 276
3. Dow, p. 70
4. Macmillan, iii. 380, 382
5. Dow, p. 181
6. *Ibid*, p. 83n.
7. Beer, p. 323
8. Chester, pp. 998 ff.
9. Hunt, p. 56; Mallaby (1), pp. 41-3
10. Avon, pp. 32-4
11. McDonald, p. 133
12. Kovrig, pp. 83-6
13. Avon, pp. 73-4
14. *Ibid*, p. 34
15. Macmillan, iii. 468-72, 702 ff.
16. Jessup, p. 202
17. Parmet, pp. 354-81; Guhin, pp. 242-51
18. Avon, p. 123
19. *Ibid*, pp. 87 ff.

20. Williams (3), pp. 249–50; *see also* Macmillan, iii. 342
21. Ramazani, p. 192
22. Donoughue and Jones, pp. 497–9, 503–4; Shinwell, p. 210
23. On African colonial economies see especially Duignan, chapters 16 and 18
24. Low, iii. 110
25. Franklin, pp. 13–14, 58, 64, 83–4
26. Miller, pp. 275–6

Chapter 6. Crises and recovery

1. Moran, p. 675
2. Stuart, p. 178
3. Avon, pp. 267–9
4. Harrison, pp. 224 ff., 238–57
5. Donoughue and Jones, pp. 529–30
6. Rogow, p. 1
7. Dow, p. 78
8. Avon, pp. 286–7, 314, 326
9. *Ibid*, pp. 321–3
10. Macmillan, iv. 9
11. *Ibid*, iv. 13–15
12. Blank, p. 137
13. Macmillan, iii. 639
14. Parmet, pp. 478 ff.
15. Eisenhower, ii. 85, 99, 664–81
16. Piers Dixon, pp. 277–8
17. Avon, p. 498
18. *Ibid*, p. 428
19. Dayan, pp. 174, 180–2
20. Epstein, pp. 141–52
21. Gore-Booth, pp. 227–32
22. Macmillan, iv. 111; K. Young, p. 96
23. Macmillan, iv. 154
24. Macmillan, iii. 614
25. *Ibid*, iii. 622, 643–7
26. Avon, p. 363
27. Kennan, ii. 252–5
28. King (1), p. 21 and note
29. Gladwyn, pp. 288 ff.
30. Macmillan, iv. 185, 212
31. Nicolson, iii. 335
32. Gamble, pp. 150, 152
33. Dow, p. 97; Brittan, p. 132
34. Macmillan, iv. 363–72; Worswick, p. 58; Fisher, p. 122
35. See Dow, pp. 108–9; Worswick, pp. 55–8
36. Hutchison, pp. 137–52
37. Shonfield (1), pp. 279–80
38. Brittan (2), p. 140
39. D. E. Butler (3), p. 9
40. *Ibid*, p. 16
41. Klein, chapter 3
42. See Goldthorpe *passim*
43. Henderson, pp. 11–12
44. Heclo, pp. 261–74
45. Hackett, pp. 200–2

46. Titmuss (4), pp. 160–3
47. J. Montgomery, p. 146
48. *The Times*, 7 Aug. 1976

Chapter 7. The Macmillan era

1. M. Foot, p. 547
2. *Ibid*, chapter 15
3. *Ibid*, pp. 625–7
4. Shinwell, pp. 228–30
5. Kilmuir, pp. 308–9
6. Mallaby (1), p. 45
7. D. E. Butler (3), pp. 198, 200
8. Haseler, pp. 166–77
9. *Ibid.*, especially chapters 8–9
10. Macmillan, iv. 704–5
11. Hagen and White, p. 13
12. Cairncross (1), pp. 30–4 and chapter 8
13. Brittan (2), pp. 141–3
14. Blank, pp. 124–5
15. Brittan (2), p. 86
16. Brittan (2), pp. 151–3; Blank, pp. 172–5
17. Brittan (2), pp. 165–79; Denton, pp. 116–17; Pollard, pp. 480–1
18. Fry, p. 61
19. Coleman, pp. 92–116
20. G. Turner, p. xi
21. Baker, p. 182
22. Meier, p. 91
23. *The Times*, 2 Nov. 1973
24. Pollard, p. 422
25. Eldridge, p. 117
26. Pollard, p. 419
27. Meyer, pp. 327 ff.
28. Lipton, pp. 138–9

Chapter 8. Britain and world affairs, 1957-63

1. Macmillan, iv. 437
2. Kolodziej, p. 265
3. Macmillan, v. 250 ff.
4. Barker, p. 155
5. Macmillan, iv. 298–9
6. *Ibid*, iv. 341
7. Morgan, pp. 88–92
8. Macmillan, v. 71, 79–81
9. *Ibid*, v. 55
10. *Ibid*, v. 113
11. *Ibid*, v. 324
12. Kolodziej, p. 80
13. Macmillan, vi. 346–55; Piers Dixon, p. 282
14. Mayne, p. 273
15. Macmillan, vi. 367, 374
16. P. Darby, pp. 143–5
17. McDermott, pp. 154–5

18. Blundell, pp. 253 ff.
19. Macmillan, v. 118–19
20. Birkenhead (2), pp. 340–2
21. Macmillan, vi. 290
22. Mboya, p. 130
23. Birkenhead (2), pp. 342 ff.
24. Welensky, pp. 296–7
25. Macmillan, v. 133
26. Franklin, p. 233
27. M. Foot, p. 623
28. Schlesinger, pp. 304 ff.
29. Sorensen, p. 597; Slusser, pp. 114–17, 183–5
30. Northedge, p. 292

Chapter 9. The transition from Conservative to Labour, 1962-6

1. Macmillan, vi. 85
2. *Ibid*, vi. 84 ff.
3. *The Political Quarterly* (1961) p. 210
4. Grainger, p. 219
5. McKie, p. 29
6. Brittan (2), p. 180
7. Rose (1), pp. 110 ff. A survey in 1975 found Marx, Tawney and Shaw in the lead (*The Times*, 2 Nov. 1976).
8. Bogdanor and Skidelsky, pp. 107–13
9. Crossman (2), i. 27, 118
10. Butler (4), p. 297
11. Booker, p. 233
12. Butler (10), especially pp. 77, 469, 478, 488
13. Butler (4), p. 155
14. Brittan (2), p. 182
15. Davis, p. 24
16. H. Wilson, p. 6
17. Beckerman, p. 24
18. *Ibid*, p. 25; Wallace (2), pp. 157–61
19. Crossman (2), i. 27–116
20. H. Wilson, p. 33
21. C. King, i. 58
22. Brechling and Wolfe, pp. 28–9
23. Crossman (2), i. 489
24. Butler (5), pp. 62–4, 94

Chapter 10. Withdrawal on all fronts

1. Butler (6), p. 9
2. Crossman (2), i. 294, 567 ff.
3. Davis, p. 107
4. Crossman (2), i. 94–5, 117, 354; ii. 156, 181–2
5. Barker, p. 271
6. Crossman (2), i. 179 ff.
7. H. Wilson, pp. 83, 85, 204
8. Pearson, iii. 139
9. Gore-Booth, pp. 361–2
10. *Spectator*, 18 Feb. 1966 and 14 April 1967

11. Crossman (2), i. 95
12. O'Neill, p. 60
13. Macmillan, vi. 268
14. Mackie, *passim*
15. Crossman (2), i. 456
16. Gore-Booth, p. 330
17. H. Wilson, p. 479
18. Macmillan, vi. 327, 329
19. Crossman (2), i. 356, 361, 407, 432
20. Pearson, iii. 284–5
21. Crossman (2), i. 382; ii. 116–17, 138–42; Wallace (2), pp. 83–4
22. H. Wilson, pp. 558–9
23. Miller, pp. 442–50
24. Pearson, iii. 289
25. Crossman (2), i. 443 ff.
26. H. Wilson, pp. 293, 296–7
27. Crossman (2), ii. 303, 320–1, 335
28. *Ibid*, ii. 336–7
29. Strange, pp. 306–7

Chapter 11. Industrial reorganization and industrial relations

1. Rose (3), pp. 112–13
2. Crossman (2), i. 533
3. Zuckerman, p. 45
4. Hackett, pp. 224–7; Meyer, pp. 275–7
5. *Financial Times*, 11 Feb. 1976
6. Johnson, p. 146
7. For this section see generally S. Young, K. D. George, Beckerman, Hodges, Newbould, Bacon, Channon, and Meyer
8. Heller, pp. 280 ff.
9. See especially C. H. Lee, R. J. Dixon, and Cheshire
10. See especially Brand, Kellas, and Stacey
11. Brittan (2), p. 226
12. Crossman (2), ii. 134, 239–40, 335
13. Davis, p. 142
14. Beckerman, p. 276
15. Davis, p. 108
16. H. Wilson, p. 444
17. Crossman (2), ii. 552 ff.
18. *Ibid*, ii. 597 ff.
19. *Ibid*, ii. 621 ff.; H. Wilson, 479–81
20. Strange, p. 259
21. H. Wilson, pp. 586–7
22. Beckerman, p. 297n.
23. Wallace (2), p. 168
24. Compare H. Wilson, pp. 640–61 and P. Jenkins

Chapter 12. The United Kingdom at the end of the 1960s

1. See especially O'Neill, Callaghan, Moody, and Rose (2)
2. Rose (2), *passim*
3. O'Neill, p. 135
4. See Fogelman, *passim*, and Johns, chapter 2

5. *The Times*, 26–30 July 1976; D. J. Smith, Patterson, and Hill
6. V. George, pp. 55–6
7. Titmuss (4), pp. 160–3
8. M. Young, p. 161
9. Philip, p. 245

Chapter 13. The Heath government

1. Cairncross (2), pp. 79–80
2. *National Institute Economic Review* (Feb. 1971) p. 4
3. Sewill, pp. 30–1
4. *The Times*, 3 Nov. 1976
5. Kitzinger, p. 197
6. *Ibid*, p. 29
7. *Ibid*, pp. 97–8
8. Kolodziej, pp. 413–16
9. Butler (9), *passim*
10. *The Times*, 24 September 1976. By November 1976, 1,600 had been killed i Northern Ireland.
11. M. Young, p. 7
12. Thompson and Engleman, p. 44
13. *Ibid*, pp. 27–8
14. *The Observer*, 1 Aug. 1976
15. Harris and Sewill, pp. 13–24, 36–49
16. *The Times*, 28 Feb. 1976
17. *The Times*, 2 July 1976
18. Rose (3), p. 16
19. Rose (1), pp. 59–62, 275
20. Butler (11), pp. 72, 92, 97, 188–9, 194 etc.
21. Rose (3), pp. 170, 270
22. NEDO: *The UK and West German Manufacturing Industry, 1954–72* (1976) *passim*
23. *The Guardian*, 19 Nov. 1976

Further reading

Bibliographical details are given in the Bibliography, pp. 339 ff.)

The literature that might be consulted on British history since 1945 is vast and continually growing. Students will find Havighurst (1976) *Modern England, 1901–70* an invaluable bibliographical handbook. In the brief list that follows an endeavour has been made to strike a balance between good introductory works, books that are particularly stimulating, or are notable for the strength of their analytical treatment, or for their factual content. But it is also a very personal selection.

By way of introduction it is important that the student should appreciate the degree of continuity in British history in the twentieth century, and indeed from earlier times. With this in mind Medlicott (1976) *Contemporary England* is most useful since it covers the whole period from the first world war. Marwick (1968) *Britain in the Century of Total War* makes some interesting suggestions, while for detail on the war years, 1939—45, the student should turn to Pelling (1970), *Britain and the Second World War* and Addison (1975) *The Road to 1945*.

Recent general studies of the years since 1945 are provided by Monk (1976) *Britain 1945-70* and Proudfoot (1974) *British Politics and Government*. Much useful information is contained in *The Annual Register*, with *Keesing's Contemporary Archives* as another invaluable source, especially as a guide to major government white papers and reports. Sub-periods are interestingly dealt with in Sissons (1963) *The Age of Austerity*, Bogdanor and Skidelsky (1970) *The Age of Affluence*, and McKie and Cook (1972) *The Decade of Disillusion*. James (1972) *Ambitions and Realities* provides a thoughtful portrait of the 1960s, and there are some thought-provoking ideas on the earlier period in Hartley (1963) *A State of England*.

For British politics the Nuffield Election Studies of each general election from 1945, and also of the 1975 Referendum, by McCallum and Readman, Nicholas, and especially by Butler with various partners, supply much background detail as well as the basic information for and analysis of each election. The many memoirs of politicians and other leading figures vary sharply in value, as do the biographies. None equals the scale or general overall quality of Macmillan (1966–73) *Memoirs*, though there is much of substance in Avon (1960) *Memoirs . . . Full Circle* and Dalton (1962) *High Tide and After*. Some insights into the later 1960s can be gained from a careful comparison of H. Wilson (1971) *The Labour Government, 1964-70* and Crossman (1975-6) *Diaries of a*

338 *Further reading*

Cabinet Minister. The most soundly researched biography is Donough-hue and Jones (1973) *Herbert Morrison,* and though too sympathetic to his subject M. Foot (1973) *Aneurin Bevan* is both instructive and readable. Williams (1961) *A Prime Minister Remembers* contains points of interest, and both Birkenhead (1969) *Walter Monckton* and Fisher (1973) *Iain Macleod* are workmanlike. Two studies concerning the Labour party which deserve particular attention are Haseler (1969) *The Gaitskellites* and Harrison (1960) *Trade Unions and the Labour Party since 1945.* For their opponents see Lindsay and Harrington (1974) *The Conservative Party, 1918–70.*

British foreign policy since 1945 is dealt with in an admirably complementary fashion by Northedge (1974) *Descent from Power* and (more analytically) by Frankel (1975) *British Foreign Policy, 1945–73.* There are stimulating chapters in Leifer (1972) *Constraints and Adjustments in British Foreign Policy,* while P. Darby (1973) *British Defence Policy East of Suez* is essential reading for an understanding of Britain's final retreat from her pretensions to act as a world power. On imperial and Commonwealth questions one should particularly note Goldsworthy (1971) *Colonial Issues in British Politics, 1945–61,* J. M. Lee (1967) *Colonial Government and Good Government, 1939–64,* Gupta (1975) *Imperialism and the British Labour Movement,* and Miller (1974) *Survey of Commonwealth Affairs, 1953–69.*

The general evolution of the British economy is usefully explored by Pollard (1969) *The Development of the British Economy, 1914–67,* Phillips and Maddock (1973) *The Growth of the British Economy, 1918–68,* and Youngson (1967) *British Economic Growth.* Postan (1967) *An Economic History of Modern Europe, 1945–64* might be used for comparative purposes. On more specific questions one should consult Dow (1968) *The Management of the British Economy, 1945–60,* Brittan (1969) *Steering the Economy,* Beckerman (1972) *The Labour Government's Economic Record, 1964–70,* Strange (1971) *Sterling and British Policy,* Hutchison (1968) *Economics and Economic Policy in Britain, 1946–66,* and Rogow (1955) *The Labour Government and British Industry, 1945–51.*

Gregg (1967) *The Welfare State* provides an introduction to the social history of the period, as well as touching on other issues. Social policy can be profitably studied in Marshall (1975) *Social Policy in the Twentieth Century,* Robson (1976) *Welfare State to Welfare Society,* and in Forder (1971) *Penelope Hall's Social Services of England and Wales.* On the evolution of British society see Johns (1972) *The Social Structure of Modern Britain,* Halsey (1972) *Trends in British Society since 1900,* and Klein (1967) *Samples from English Culture.*

Bibliography

Abel-Smith, B., and Townsend, P., *The Poor and the Poorest*, Bell, 1965.

Abrams, M., and Rose, R., *Must Labour Lose?*, Penguin, 1960.

Acheson, A. L. K. *et al.*, eds. *Bretton Woods Revisited*, University of Toronto Press, 1972.

Acheson, Dean, *Present at the Creation*, Hamish Hamilton, 1970.

Addison, Paul, *The Road to 1945: British politics and the second world war*, Cape, 1975.

Adenauer, Konrad, *Memoirs, 1945-53*, Weidenfeld and Nicolson, 1966.

Aldcroft, D. H., *British Transport since 1914: an economic history*, Newton Abbot: David and Charles, 1975.

Aldcroft D. H. and Fearon, P., *Economic Growth in Twentieth-Century Britain*, Macmillan, 1969.

Alexander, K. J. W., 'The political economy of change', *Political Quarterly* (January–March 1975) pp. 7–24.

Allen, V. L., *Militant Trade Unionism*, Merlin Press, 1966.

Allen, V. L., *Trade union leadership: based on a study of Arthur Deakin*, Longmans, 1957.

Annual Register, Longmans, 1946 ff.

Armytage, W. H. G. (1) *The Rise of the Technocrats*, Routledge and Kegan Paul, 1965.

Armytage, W. H. G. (2) *Four Hundred Years of English Education*, Cambridge University Press, 1970.

Arnold, Guy, *Towards Peace and a Multiracial Commonwealth*, Chapman, 1964.

Artis, Michael, *see* Beckerman.

Attlee, C. R., *As It Happened*, Heinemann, 1954.

Avon, Lord, *The Memoirs of Sir Anthony Eden: Full Circle*, Cassell, 1960.

Bacon, R. W. and Eltis, W. A., *The Age of US and UK Machinery*, NEDO Monograph, 1974.

Baker, Sir John, 'The Engineer in the UK,' *Progress* (1964), pp. 182–4.

Barker, Elizabeth, *Britain and a Divided Europe, 1945-70*, Weidenfeld and Nicolson, 1971.

Beckerman, W., ed. *The Labour Government's Economic Record, 1964-70*, Duckworth, 1972.

Beer, S. H., *Modern British Politics*, Faber, 1965.

Begg, H. M., Lythe, C. and Sorley, R., *Expenditure in Scotland, 1961-71*, Scottish Academic Press, 1975.

Beloff, Nora, *Transit of Britain*, Collins, 1973.

Benn, A. Wedgwood, *The New Politics: a socialist reconnaissance*, Fabian Society, 1970.

Bennett, Neville, *Teaching Styles and Pupil Progress*, Open Books Publication, 1976.

Berrington, H. B., *Backbench Opinion in the House of Commons, 1945-55*, Oxford: Pergamon Press, 1973.

Bevan, A., *In Place of Fear*, Heinemann, 1952.

Birkenhead, Lord (1), *The Prof. in Two Worlds: the official life of Viscount Cherwell*, Collins, 1961.

Birkenhead, Lord (2), *Walter Monckton: the life of Viscount Monckton of Brenchley*, Weidenfeld and Nicolson, 1969.

Blank, S., *Industry and Government: the Federation of British Industries in politics, 1945-65*, Farnborough: Saxon House, 1973.

Blundell, Sir Michael, *So Rough a Wind,* Weidenfeld and Nicolson, 1964.
Bogdanor, V. and Skidelsky, R., *The Age of Affluence, 1951–64,* Macmillan, 1970.
Bohlen, Charles, *Witness to History, 1929–69,* New York: W. W. Norton, 1973.
Booker, Christopher, *The Necrophiliacs,* Collins, 1969.
Boyd, F., *British Politics in Transition, 1945–63,* Praeger, 1964.
Bradbury, M., *Eating People is Wrong,* Secker and Warburg, 1959.
Braddock, J. and B., *The Braddocks,* Macdonald, 1963.
Brand, Jack, *Local Government Reform in England and Wales, 1888–1974,* Croom Helm, 1974.
Brecher, M.,'India's decision to remain in the Commonwealth', *The Journal of Commonwealth and Comparative Politics* (March 1974) pp. 62 ff. and (July 1974), p. 229.
Brechling, F. and Wolfe, J. N., 'The end of stop–go', *Lloyds Bank Review* (January 1965) pp. 23–30.
British Economy: Key Statistics, 1900–70, published for the London and Cambridge Economic Service by *Times* Newspapers, no date.
Brittan, S. (1), *Left or Right,* Secker and Warburg, 1968.
Brittan, S. (2), *Steering the Economy: the role of the Treasury,* Secker and Warburg, 1969.
Broadman, Robert, *Britain and the People's Republic of China, 1949–74,* Macmillan, 1976.
Broadway, F., *State Intervention in British Industry, 1964–8,* Kaye and Ward, 1969.
Brockway, A. F., *Outside the Right,* Allen and Unwin, 1963.
Brown, George, *see* George-Brown, Lord.
Bryant, Sir Arthur, *Triumph in the West, 1943–6,* Collins, 1959.
Bullock, Sir Alan, *The Life and Times of Ernest Bevin,* vol. ii, *Minister of Labour,* Heinemann, 1967.
Bulmer-Thomas, I., *The Growth of the British Party System,* vol. ii, *1924–1964,* John Baker, 1965.
Burn, Duncan, *The Steel Industry, 1939–59,* Cambridge University Press, 1961.
Butler, D. E. (1), *The British General Election of 1951,* Macmillan, 1952.
Butler, D. E. (2), *The British General Election of 1955,* Macmillan, 1956.
Butler, D. E. (3) and **Rose, R.,** *The British General Election of 1959,* Macmillan, 1960.
Butler, D. E. (4) and **King, A.,** *The British General Election of 1964,* Macmillan, 1965.
Butler, D. E. (5) and **King, A.,** *The British General Election of 1966,* Macmillan, 1966.
Butler, D. E. (6) and **Pinto-Duschinsky, M.,** *The British General Election of 1970* Macmillan, 1971.
Butler, D. E. (7) and **Kavanagh, D.,** *The British General Election of February 1974,* Macmillan, 1974.
Butler, D. E. (8) and **Kavanagh, D.,** *The British General Election of October 1974,* Macmillan, 1975.
Butler, D. E. (9) and **Kitzinger, U.,** *The 1975 Referendum,* Macmillan, 1976.
Butler, D. E. (10) and **Stokes, D.,** *Political Change in Britain,* Macmillan, 1969.
Butler, D. E. (11) and **Stokes, D.,** *Political Change in Britain: the evolution of electoral choice,* Macmillan, 1974.
Butler, R. A., *The Art of the Possible,* Hamish Hamilton, 1971.
Buxton, N. K., 'Entrepreneurial efficiency in the British coal industry between the wars', *Economic History Review* (1970), pp. 476–97.
Cadogan, Sir Alexander, *The Diaries of Sir Alexander Cadogan 1938–45,* ed. D. Dilks, Cassell, 1971.
Cairncross, Sir Alec, (1) *Britain's Economic Prospects Reconsidered,* Allen and Unwin, 1971.
Cairncross, Sir Alec, ed. (2) *Inflation, Growth and International Finance,* Allen and Unwin, 1975.
Callaghan, J., *A House Divided: the dilemma of Northern Ireland,* Collins, 1973.
Campbell, Thomas C. and Herring, George C., eds. *The Diaries of Edward R. Stettinius Jr., 1943–6,* New York: Franklin Watts, 1975.
Camps, Miriam, *Britain and the European Community, 1955–63,* Oxford University Press, 1964.

Cardwell, D. S. L., *The Organization of Science in England,* Heinemann, 1972.
Carpenter, L. P., *G. D. H. Cole: an intellectual biography,* Cambridge University Press, 1973.
Carter, C. F. and **Williams, B. R.,** *Industry and Technical Progress,* Oxford University Press, 1957; *Investment and Innovation,* Oxford University Press, 1958; *Science in Industry,* Oxford University Press, 1959.
Caves, R. E. *et al., Britain's Economic Prospects,* Brookings Institution, Washington, 1968.
Chandos, Lord, *The Memoirs of . . . ,* Bodley Head, 1962.
Channon, D. F., *The Strategy and Structure of British Enterprise,* Boston: Harvard Business School, 1973.
Chapman, Brian, *British Government Observed,* Allen and Unwin, 1963.
Cheshire, P. C., *Regional Unemployment Differences in Great Britain,* Cambridge University Press, 1973.
Chester, Sir Norman, *The Nationalization of British Industry,* HMSO, 1975.
Clegg, H. A., *The System of Industrial Relations in Great Britain,* Oxford: Blackwell, 1972.
Cohen, C. D., *British Economic Policy, 1960–9,* Butterworths, 1971.
Coleman, D. C., 'Gentlemen and Players', *Economic History Review* (1974), pp. 92–116.
Cooke, C., *The Life of Richard Stafford Cripps,* Hodder and Stoughton, 1957.
Cooper, A. Duff, *Old Men Forget,* Hart-Davis, 1955.
Court, W. H. B., *Coal,* HMSO, 1951.
Crosland, A., *Social Democracy in Europe,* Fabian Tract 438, 1975.
Crosland, A., *Socialism Now,* Cape, 1974.
Crosland, A., *The Conservative Enemy,* Cape, 1962.
Crosland, A., *The Future of Socialism,* Cape, 1956.
Crossman, R. (1) *New Fabian Essays,* Turnstile Press, 1952.
Crossman, R. (2) *The Diaries of a Cabinet Minister, 1964–8,* Hamish Hamilton and Cape, 1975–6, 2 vols.
Dalton, Hugh., *High Tide and After,* Muller, 1962.
Darby, John, *Conflict in Northern Ireland,* Gill and Macmillan, 1976.
Darby, P., *British Defence Policy East of Suez, 1947–68,* Oxford University Press, 1973.
Davies, Christie, *Permissive Britain,* Pitman, 1975.
Davis, W., *Three Years Hard Labour,* Deutsch, 1968.
Day, A. C. L., *The Future of Sterling,* Oxford University Press, 1954.
Dayan, Moshe, *The Story of My Life,* Weidenfeld and Nicolson, 1976.
Denton, G. *et al., Economic Planning and Policies in Britain, France and Germany,* Allen and Unwin, 1968.
Dixon, Piers, *Double Diploma: the life of Sir Pierson Dixon,* Hutchinson, 1968.
Dixon, R. J. and **Thirlwall, A. P.,** *Regional Growth and Unemployment in the United Kingdom,* Macmillan, 1975.
Donoughue, B. and **Jones, G. W.,** *Herbert Morrison: portrait of a politician,* Weidenfeld and Nicolson, 1973.
Dore, R. P., *British Factory: Japanese Factory,* Allen and Unwin, 1973.
Dow, J. C. R., *The Management of the British Economy, 1945–60,* Cambridge University Press, 1968.
Duignan, P. and **Gann, L. H.,** eds. *Colonialism in Africa, 1870–1960,* vol. iv, Cambridge University Press, 1975.
Edwards, Angela and **Rogers, A.,** *Agricultural Resources: an introduction to the farming industry of the United Kingdom,* Faber and Faber, 1974.
Eisenhower, D. D., *The White House Years,* Heinemann, 1963–6, 2 vols.
Eldridge, J. E. T., *Industrial Disputes,* Routledge and Kegan Paul, 1968.
Epstein, L. D., *British Politics in the Suez Crisis,* Pall Mall Press, 1964.
Ferguson, S. and **Fitzgerald, H.,** *Studies in the Social Services,* HMSO, 1954.
Finer, S. E., *Anonymous Empire: a study of the lobby in Britain,* Pall Mall Press, 1958.
Fisher, N., *Iain Macleod,* Deutsch, 1973.
Fogelman, K., ed. *Britain's Sixteen-Year Olds,* National Children's Bureau, 1976.

Foot, Michael, *Aneurin Bevan, 1945-60,* Davis-Poynter, 1973.
Foot, Paul, *Immigration and Race in British Politics,* Penguin, 1965.
Forder, A., *Penelope Hall's Social Services of England and Wales,* Routledge and Kegan Paul, 1971.
Foreign Relations of the United States, Washington: US Government Printing Office.
Frankel, J., *British Foreign Policy, 1945-73,* Oxford University Press, 1975.
Frankfurter, F., *Roosevelt and Frankfurter: their correspondence, 1928-45,* Bodley Head, 1968.
Franklin, H., *Unholy Wedlock: the failure of the Central African Federation,* Allen and Unwin, 1963.
Fry, G. K., *Statesmen in Disguise: the changing role of the administrative class in the British Home Civil Service, 1853-1966,* Macmillan, 1969
Gaitskell, Hugh, *Socialism and Nationalization,* Fabian Tract, 1956.
Gamble, A., *The Conservative Nation,* Routledge and Kegan Paul, 1974.
Gardner, R. N., *Sterling-Dollar Diplomacy,* Oxford University Press, 1956.
Gaulle, Charles de, *War Memoirs: Salvation, 1944-6,* Weidenfeld and Nicolson, 1960.
Gaulle, Charles de, *Memoirs of Hope,* Weidenfeld and Nicolson, 1971.
George, K. D. and **Ward, T. S.,** *The Structure of Industry within the EEC,* Cambridge University Press, 1975.
George, Victor, *Social Security and Society,* Routledge and Kegan Paul, 1973.
George-Brown, Lord, *In My Way,* Gollancz, 1971.
Gladwyn, Lord, *The Memoirs of . . . ,* Weidenfeld and Nicolson, 1972.
Glubb, Sir John, *A Soldier with the Arabs,* Hodder and Stoughton, 1957.
Goldsworthy, D., *Colonial Issues in British Politics, 1945-61,* Oxford: Clarendon Press, 1971.
Goldthorpe, John H. *et al., The Affluent Worker: industrial attitudes and behaviour,* Cambridge University Press, 1968; *The Affluent Worker in the Class Struggle,* Cambridge University Press, 1969.
Gopal, S. *Jawaharlal Nehru, 1889-1947,* Cape, 1975.
Gore-Booth, Paul, *With Great Truth and Respect,* Constable, 1974.
Gowing, M. M., *Independence and Deterrence: Britain and atomic energy, 1945-52,* Macmillan, 1974, 2 vols.
Grainger, J. H., *Character and Style in English Politics,* Cambridge University Press, 1969.
Gregg, P., *The Welfare State, from 1945 to the present day,* Harrap, 1967.
Guhin, M. A., *John Foster Dulles,* Columbia University Press, 1972.
Gupta, P. S., *Imperialism and the British Labour Movement, 1914-64,* Macmillan, 1975.
Guttsman, W. L., *The British Political Elite,* MacGibbon and Kee, 1963.
Hackett, J. and **A-M.,** *The British Economy: problems and prospects,* Allen and Unwin, 1967.
Hagen, E. E. and **White, S. F. T.,** *Great Britain: quiet revolution in planning,* Syracuse University Press, 1966.
Halsey, A. H. (1) *Ability and Educational Opportunity,* HMSO, 1961.
Halsey, A. H., ed. (2) *Educational Priority,* HMSO, 1972.
Halsey, A. H., ed. (3) *Trends in British Society since 1900,* Macmillan, 1972.
Hancock, W. K. and **Gowing, M. M.,** *The British War Economy,* HMSO, 1949.
Hanham, H., *Scottish Nationalism,* Faber, 1969.
Harriman, W. Averell, *Special Envoy to Churchill and Stalin, 1941-6,* Hutchinson, 1976.
Harris, Nigel, *Competition and the Corporate State: British conservatism, the state and industry, 1945-64,* Methuen, 1972.
Harris, R. and **Sewill, B,** *British Economic Policy, 1970-4,* Institute of Economic Affairs, 1975.
Harrison, M, *The Trade Unions and the Labour Party since 1945,* Allen and Unwin, 1960.
Hartley, A., *A State of England,* Hutchinson, 1963.
Haseler, S., *The Gaitskellites,* Macmillan, 1969.
Havighurst, A. F., *Modern England, 1901-70,* Cambridge University Press, 1976,

bibliographical handbooks, no. 5.

Hayward, J. and **Watson, M.**, eds. *Planning, Politics and Public Policy: the British, French and Italian experience,* Cambridge University Press, 1975.

Headey, B., *The Job of the Cabinet Minister,* Allen and Unwin, 1974.

Heclo, H., *Modern Social Politics in Britain and Sweden,* Yale University Press, 1974.

Heffer, E., 'Labour's future', *Political Quarterly* (1972), pp. 380–8.

Heller, R. and **Willatt, N.**, *The European Revenge,* Barrie and Jenkins, 1975.

Henderson, I., ed. *The New Poor,* Owen, 1973.

Hill, Clifford, *Immigration and Integration: a study of the settlement of coloured minorities in Britain,* Oxford: Pergamon Press, 1970.

Hodges, M., *Multinational Corporations in National Development,* Farnborough: Saxon House, 1974.

Hoffman, J. D., *The Conservative Party in Opposition, 1945–51,* MacGibbon and Kee, 1964.

Hogg, Q. (1) *The Left was Never Right,* Faber, 1945.

Hogg, Q. (2) *The Case for Conservatism,* Penguin, 1947.

Hourani, A., ed. *Middle Eastern Affairs no. 4,* Oxford University Press, 1965.

Howard, H. N., *Turkey, the Straits and U.S. Policy,* Johns Hopkins University Press, 1974.

Hunt, Sir David, *On the Spot,* P. Davies, 1975.

Hutchinson, G., *Edward Heath: a personal and political biography,* Longman, 1970.

Hutchison, T. W., *Economics and Economic Policy in Britain, 1945–66,* Allen and Unwin, 1968.

Ingham, K., *A History of East Africa,* Longmans, 1965.

Ingram, Derek, *Partners in Adventure,* Pan Books, 1960.

James, R. R., *Ambitions and Realities: British politics, 1964–70,* Weidenfeld and Nicholson, 1972.

Jay, Douglas, 'Government control of the economy', *Political Quarterly* (1968), pp. 134 ff.

Jenkins, Peter, *The Battle of Downing Street,* Knight, 1970.

Jessup, Philip C., *The Birth of Nations,* Columbia University Press, 1974.

Johns, E. A., *The Social Structure of Modern Britain,* Oxford: Pergamon Press, 1972.

Johnson, Harry G., *Technology and Economic Interdependence,* Macmillan, 1975.

Kellas, J. G., *The Scottish Political System,* Cambridge University Press, 1975.

Kennan, G., *Memoirs,* Hutchinson, 1968—73, 2 vols.

Keynes, J. M., *The General Theory of Employment, Interest and Money,* Macmillan, 1936.

Keynes, Milo, ed. *Essays on J. M. Keynes,* Cambridge University Press, 1975.

Khrushchev, N. K., *Khrushchev Remembers,* Deutsch, 1971.

Kilbride, Sir Alec, *From the Wings,* Cass, 1976.

Kilmuir, Earl of, *Political Adventure,* Weidenfeld and Nicolson, 1964.

King, A., ed. (1) *The British Prime Minister: a reader,* Macmillan, 1969.

King, A. (2) 'Overload: problems of governing in the 1970s', *Political Studies* (1975) pp. 284–96.

King, Cecil, *The Cecil King Diaries, 1965–70,* Cape, 1972.

Kirkman, W. P., *Unscrambling an Empire, 1956–66,* Chatto and Windus, 1966.

Kirkpatrick, Sir Ivone, *The Inner Circle,* Macmillan, 1959.

Kitzinger, U., *Diplomacy and Persuasion: how Britain joined the Common Market,* Thames and Hudson, 1973.

Klein, Josephine, *Samples from English Culture,* Routledge and Kegan Paul, 1967, 2 vols.

Kolodziej, E. A., *French International Politics under de Gaulle and Pompidou,* Cornell University Press, 1974.

Kovrig, Bennett, *The Myth of Liberation: east-central Europe in U.S. diplomacy and politics since 1941,* Johns Hopkins University Press, 1973.

Lee, C. H., *Regional Economic Growth in the United Kingdom since the 1880s,* McGraw-Hill, 1971.

Lee, J. M., *Colonial Development and Good Government, 1939–64,* Oxford: Clarendon Press, 1967.

Leiber, R. J., *British Politics and European Unity,* University of California Press, 1970.

Leifer, M., ed. *Constraints and Adjustments in British Foreign Policy,* Allen and Unwin, 1972.
Lindsay, T. F. and **Harrington, M.,** *The Conservative Party, 1918–70,* Macmillan, 1974.
Lipton, M., *Assessing Economic Performance,* Staples Press, 1968.
Livingstone, James M., *The British Economy in Theory and Practice,* Macmillan, 1974.
Lovell, John and **Roberts, B. C.,** *A Short History of the TUC,* Macmillan, 1968.
Low, D. A., *History of East Africa,* Oxford University Press, 1963–73, 3 vols.
Lowndes, G. A. N., *The Silent Social Revolution: an account of the expansion of public education in England and Wales, 1895–1965,* Oxford University Press, 1969.
McCallum, R. B. and **Readman, A.,** *The British General Election of 1945,* Oxford University Press, 1947.
McDermott, G., *Leader Lost: a biography of Hugh Gaitskell,* Leslie Frewin, 1972.
Macdonald, D. F., *The State and the Trade Unions,* Macmillan, 1976.
McDonald, I., *A Man of The Times,* Hamish Hamilton, 1976.
Mackenzie, R. T. and **Silver, A.,** *Angels in Marble,* Heinemann, 1968.
Mackenzie, W. J. M., *see* Rose (1).
McKie, D. and **Cook, C.,** *Decade of Disillusionment: British politics in the 1960s,* Macmillan, 1972.
Mackie, J. A. C., *Konfrontasi: the Indonesia–Malaysia Dispute, 1963–6,* Oxford University Press, 1974.
Mackintosh, J. P., *The British Cabinet,* Stevens and Sons, 1968, 3rd Edition, Stevens 1977.
Macmillan, Harold, *Memoirs, 1914–63,* Macmillan, 1966–73, 6 vols.
Mallaby, G.,(1) *From My Level,* Hutchinson, 1965.
Mallaby, G.,(2) *Each in his Office: studies of men in power,* Leo Cooper, 1972.
Manderson-Jones, R. B., *The Special Relationship: Anglo-American Relations and Western European Unity, 1947–56,* Weidenfeld and Nicolson, 1972.
Marshall, T. H., *Social Policy in the Twentieth Century,* Hutchinson, 1975.
Marwick, A. (1) *Britain in the Century of Total War, 1900–67,* The Bodley Head, 1968.
Marwick, A. (2) *see* Sked and Cook.
Mayhew, C., *Party Games,* Hutchinson, 1969.
Mayne, R., *The Recovery of Europe,* Weidenfeld and Nicolson, 1970.
Mboya, Tom, *Freedom and After,* Deutsch, 1963.
Medlicott, W. N. (1) *British Foreign Policy since Versailles, 1919–63,* Methuen, 1968.
Medlicott, W. N. (2) *Contemporary England,* Longman, 1976.
Meier, R. L., 'Research as a social process', *British Journal of Sociology* (1951) ii, 91–104.
Meyer, F. V., *et al.,* *Problems of a Mature Economy,* Macmillan, 1970.
Miliband, R., *Parliamentary Socialism,* Merlin Press, 1964.
Miller, J. D. B., *Survey of Commonwealth Affairs, 1953–69,* Oxford University Press, 1974.
Millis, W., ed. *The Forrestal Diaries,* Cassell, 1952.
Milne, R. S. and **Mackenzie, H. C.,** *Straight Fight,* Hansard Society, 1954.
Mitchell, Joan E., *Britain in Crisis, 1951,* Secker and Warburg, 1963.
Monk, L. A., *Britain 1945–70,* Bell, 1976.
Monroe, E., *Britain's Moment in the Middle East, 1914–56,* Chatto and Windus, 1963.
Montgomery, J., *The Fifties,* Allen and Unwin, 1965.
Montgomery, Viscount, *Memoirs,* Collins, 1958.
Moody, T. W., *The Ulster Question, 1603–1973,* Cork: Mercier Press, 1973.
Moon, Penderel, ed. *The Viceroy's Journal,* Oxford University Press, 1973.
Moran, Lord, *Churchill: the struggle for survival,* Constable, 1966.
Morgan, R., *The United States and West Germany, 1945–73,* Oxford University Press, 1974.
Mowat, C. L., *Britain between the Wars, 1918–40,* Methuen, 1968.
Murray, K. A. H., *Agriculture,* HMSO, 1955.
Nabseth, L. and **Ray, G. F.,** eds. *The Diffusion of New Industrial Processes,* Cambridge University Press, 1974.
NEDO, *The United Kingdom and West German manufacturing industries, 1954–72,* 1976.

Nettley, J. P., *see* Rose (1).
Newbould, G. D., *Management and Merger Activity*, Liverpool: Guthstead, 1970.
Nicholas, H. G., *The British General Election of 1950*, Macmillan, 1951.
Nicolson, N., ed. *Harold Nicolson, Diaries and Letters*, Collins, 1966–8, 3 vols.
Northedge, F. S., *Descent from Power: British foreign policy, 1945–73*, Allen and Unwin, 1974.
Nunnerley, David, *President Kennedy and Britain*, Bodley Head, 1972.
Nutting, A., *No End of a Lesson*, Constable, 1967.
O'Farrell, P., *England and Ireland since 1800*, Oxford University Press, 1975.
O'Neill, T., *The Autobiography of . . .*, Hart-Davis, 1972.
Orwell, George, *Animal Farm*, Secker and Warburg, 1945.
Pandey, B. N., *The Break-up of British India*, Macmillan, 1969.
Parkinson, J. R., *The Economics of Shipbuilding in the United Kingdom*, Cambridge University Press, 1960.
Parkinson, M., *The Labour Party and the Organization of Secondary Education, 1918–65*, Routledge and Kegan Paul, 1970.
Parmet, H. S., *Eisenhower and the American Crusades*, New York: Macmillan, 1972.
Patterson, S., *Immigration and Race Relations in Britain, 1960–7*, Oxford University Press, 1969.
Peacock, A. T. and Wiseman, J., *The Growth of Public Expenditure in the United Kingdom*, Allen and Unwin, 1967.
Pearson, L. B., *Mike: the memoirs of . . .*, University of Toronto Press, 1972–5, 3 vols.
Pelling, H. (1) *America and the British Left*, Black, 1956.
Pelling, H. (2) *Britain and the Second World War*, Collins, 1970.
Pelling, H. (3) *Winston Churchill*, Macmillan, 1974.
Pelling, H. (4) *A History of British Trade Unionism*, Macmillan, 1976.
Pelling, H. (5) *A Short History of the Labour Party*, Macmillan, 1976.
Perham, M., *Colonial Sequence, 1949 to 1969*, Methuen, 1970.
Philip, Alan Butt, *The Welsh Question: nationalism in Welsh politics, 1945–70*, Cardiff: University of Wales Press, 1975.
Phillips, G. A. and Maddock, R. T., *The Growth of the British Economy, 1918–68*, Allen and Unwin, 1973.
Pollard, S., *The Development of the British Economy, 1914–67*, Arnold, 1969.
Postan, M. M., *An Economic History of Western Europe, 1945–64*, Methuen, 1967.
Priestley, J. B., *English Journey*, Heinemann, Gollancz, 1934.
Proudfoot, Mary, *British Politics and Government, 1951–70*, Faber, 1974.
Punnett, R. M. *Front Bench Opposition*, Heinemann, 1973.
Ramazani, R. K., *Iran's Foreign Policy, 1941–73*, University of Virginia Press, 1975.
Ray, G. F., *The Diffusion of New Industrial Processes*, Cambridge University Press, 1974.
Robbins, Lord, *Autobiography of an Economist*, Macmillan, 1971.
Robinson, Joan, *After Keynes*, Oxford: Blackwell, 1973.
Robinson, John A. T., *Honest to God*, SCM Press, 1963.
Robson, W. A., *Welfare State to Welfare Society*, Allen and Unwin, 1976.
Rodgers, W. T., ed. *Hugh Gaitskell, 1906–63*, Thames and Hudson, 1964.
Rogow, A. A., *The Labour Government and British Industry, 1945–51*, Oxford: Blackwell, 1955.
Roll, Eric, *A History of Economic Thought*, Faber, 1973.
Rose, R., ed. (1) *Studies in British Politics*, Macmillan, 1969.
Rose, R. (2) *Governing without Consensus*, Faber, 1971.
Rose, R. (3) *Politics in England Today*, Faber, 1974.
Roth, A. *Heath and the Heathmen*, Routledge and Kegan Paul, 1972.
Sabine, B. E. V., *British Budgets in Peace and War, 1932–45*, Allen and Unwin, 1970.
Sachar, H. M., *Europe leaves the Middle East, 1936–54*, New York: Knopf, 1972.
Sampson, A., *The New Anatomy of Britain*, Hodder and Stoughton, 1971.
Sandford, C. T., *National Economic Planning*, Heinemann, 1972.
Sayers, R. S., *Financial Policy, 1939–45*, HMSO,1956.
Schlesinger, A. M., *A Thousand Days*, Deutsch, 1965.

Sewill, B., *see* Harris, R.
Sherman, Martin J., *A World Destroyed: the atomic bomb and the great alliance*, New York: Knopf, 1975.
Shinwell, E., *I've Lived Through It All*, Gollancz, 1973.
Shonfield, A. (1) *British Economic Policy since the War*, Penguin, 1958.
Shonfield, A., (2) *Modern Capitalism*, Oxford University Press, 1965.
Short, A., *The Communist Insurrection in Malaya, 1948-60*, Muller, 1975.
Silver, Eric, *Victor Feather, TUC*, Gollancz, 1973.
Sissons, M., ed. *Age of Austerity*, Hodder and Stoughton, 1963.
Sked, A. and **Cook, C.**, eds. *Crisis and Controversy*, Macmillan, 1976.
Slusser, R. M., *The Berlin Crisis of 1961*, Johns Hopkins University Press, 1973.
Smith, David J., *Racial Disadvantage in Britain*, PEP, 1974.
Smith, Jean Edward, ed. *The Papers of General Lucius D. Clay: Germany, 1945-9*, Indiana University Press, 1974.
Smith, W. O. Lester, *Education in Great Britain*, Home University Library, 1949.
Snetsinger, J., *Truman, the Jewish Vote and the Creation of Israel*, Stanford: Hoover Institute Press, 1974.
Social Trends, no. 4 HMSO, 1973.
Sorensen, T. C., *Kennedy*, Hodder and Stoughton, 1965.
Stacey, Frank, *British Government, 1966-75: years of reform*, Oxford University Press, 1975.
Strachey, J.(1) *Contemporary Capitalism*, Gollancz, 1959.
Strachey, J. (2) *The End of Empire*, Gollancz, 1959.
Strange, S., *Sterling and British Policy*, Oxford University Press, 1971.
Stuart, James, *Within the Fringe*, Bodley Head, 1967.
Sturmey, S. G., *British Shipping and World Competition*, Athlone Press, 1962.
Swann, D. *et al.*, *Competition in British Industry*, Allen and Unwin, 1974.
Terraine, J., *The Life and Times of Lord Mountbatten*, Hutchinson, 1968.
Thomas, H. (1) *The Suez Affair*, Weidenfeld and Nicolson, 1966.
Thomas, H. (2) *John Strachey*, Eyre Methuen, 1973.
Thompson, A. W. J. and **Engleman, S. R.**, *The Industrial Relations Act*, Martin Robertson, 1975.
Thompson, A. W. J. and **Hunter, L. C.**, *The Nationalized Transport Industries*, Heinemann, 1973.
Titmuss, R.(1) *Problems of Social Policy* HMSO, 1950.
Titmuss, R. (2) *Income Redistribution and Social Change*, Allen and Unwin, 1964.
Titmuss, R. (3) *Choice and the Welfare State*, Fabian Tract, 1967.
Titmuss, R. (4) *Commitment to Welfare*, Allen and Unwin, 1968.
Townsend, Peter, *Labour and Inequality*, Fabian Society, 1972.
Tsou, Tang, *America's Failure in China, 1941-50*, University of Chicago Press, 1963.
Tugendhat, C. and **Hamilton, A.** *Oil: the biggest business*, Eyre Methuen, 1975.
Turner, G., *Business in Britain*, Penguin, 1971.
Turner, H. A. *et al.*, *Labour Relations in the Motor Industry*, Allen and Unwin, 1967.
Urry, T. and **Wakeford, J.** *Power in Britain*, Heinemann, 1973.
Vaizey, J., *The History of British Steel*, Weidenfeld and Nicolson, 1974.
Van der Pol, J., *Selections from the Smuts Papers*, vol. vii, Cambridge University Press, 1973.
Waites, N., ed. *Troubled Neighbours: Franco-British relations in the twentieth century*, Weidenfeld and Nicolson, 1971.
Walker, P. Gordon, *The Cabinet*, Cape, 1970.
Wallace, W. (1) 'The management of foreign economic policy in Britain', *International Affairs* (April 1974), pp. 251-67.
Wallace, W. (2) *The Foreign Policy Process in Britain*, London: Royal Institute of International Affairs, 1975.
Watt, D. C., *Personalities and Policies*, Longman, 1965.
Wavell, Lord, *see* Moon, P.
Weaver, Finlay, 'Taxation and redistribution in the United Kingdom', *The Review of Economics and Statistics* (August 1950), pp. 210 ff.

Welensky, Sir Roy, *Four Thousand Days: the life and death of the federation of Rhodesia and Nyasaland,* Collins, 1964.

Wigg, Lord, *George Wigg,* Michael Joseph, 1972.

Wigham, Eric (1) *What's Wrong with the Unions?* Penguin, 1961.

Wigham, Eric (2) *Strikes and the Government, 1893–1974,* Macmillan, 1976.

Williams, F. (1) *The Triple Challenge* (Heinemann, 1948).

Williams, F. (2) *Ernest Bevin,* Hutchinson, 1952.

Williams, F. (3) *A Prime Minister Remembers,* Heinemann, 1961.

Wills, A. J., *An Introduction to the History of Central Africa,* Oxford University Press, 1973.

Wilson, B. R., *Religion in a Secular Society,* C. A. Watts, 1966.

Wilson, Harold. *The Labour Government, 1964–70,* Weidenfeld and Nicolson, and Michael Joseph, 1971.

Winch, D., *Economics and Policy,* Hodder and Stoughton, 1969.

Woodward, Sir Llewellyn (1) *British Foreign Policy in the Second World War* HMSO, 1962.

Woodward, Sir Llewellyn (2) *British Foreign Policy in the Second World War,* vol. iii, HMSO, 1971.

Woolton, Lord, *The Memoirs of . . . ,* Cassell, 1959.

Wootton, Barbara, *End Social Inequality,* Kegan Paul, 1941.

Worswick, G. D. N. and Ady, P. M., *The British Economy in the 1950s,* Oxford University Press, 1962.

Xydis, S. G. (1) *Greece and the Great Powers, 1944–7.* Thessaloniki, 1963.

Xydis, S. G. (2) *Cyprus: reluctant republic,* Hague and Paris: Mouton, 1973.

Young, K. *Sir Alec Douglas Home,* Dent, 1970.

Young, M., ed. *Poverty Report '74,* Temple Smith, 1974.

Young, S. and Lowe, A. V., *Intervention in the Mixed Economy: the evolution of British industrial policy, 1964–72,* Croom Helm, 1974.

Youngson, A. J., *British Economic Growth, 1920–66,* Allen and Unwin, 1967.

Zhukov, G. K., *The Memoirs of Marshal . . . ,* New York: Delacorte Press, 1971.

Zuckerman, Sir Solly, *Scientists and War,* Hamish Hamilton, 1966.

Index

South Africa, 32, 96, 120, 197, 200–1,
233, 237–8, 240, 261, 300
South East Asian Treaty Organization
(SEATO), 112, 127, 194
Soviet Union, 1, 13, 28; and origins of
the Cold War, 14, 18–22, 26–7,
34–8, 67, 70–5; and Middle East,
32–3, 39–43, 113, 115, 131, 186,
195–6, 244; and China, 75, 111,
137–8; and the western powers in the
1950s, 85–7, 91, 94, 104–7, 136–9,
157, 185–8; and Berlin and Cuban
crises, 183, 203–4; in 1960s, 136,
200–1, 203, 231–3, 236, 239–40;
in 1970s, 299–300, 304; and nuclear
weapons, 49, 74–5, 85, 87, 127, 183,
203, 230–1
Spaak, Paul, 139–40
Spain, 72, 178
Standard of living, 6, 61, 80–1, 83–4, 94,
102–3, 127–8, 145–8, 151, 154–5,
214–16, 224, 262, 281, 293, 326–7
Stanley, Oliver, 27
Stalin, Joseph, 17, 20, 75, 106
Steel industry, 46, 78–80, 89, 91, 100–1,
128, 145, 148, 151, 173–4, 218, 223,
248, 291, 327
Sterling; problems of in 1940s, 24–8,
37–8, 44–5, 66–9, 71; in the 1950s,
83, 89, 96–8, 113, 128, 130, 135,
139–43, 145; in the 1960s, 163, 165,
167, 188, 194, 196, 202, 211, 219–21,
223, 228–9, 239–40, 244–5, 259–63;
and the EEC, 300–1; in the 1970s,
313, 327
Stewart, Michael, 228, 241–2
Stokes, Richard, 114, 216
'Stop-go' economic policies, 163–5, 173,
211, 213, 316
Strachey, John, 4, 90, 128, 154–6, 212
Strang, Sir William, later Lord, 20, 302
Strange, Susan, 262
Stuart, James, later Lord, 123
Sturmey, S. G., 175
Sudan, 39, 115
Suez; British base at, 39–40, 42, 109,
113–16; canal, 32, 132–6, 140–1, 153,
156, 158, 179, 182, 185, 194, 201;
and closure of the canal in 1967, 230,
234
Sukarno, President, 235
Sweden, 5, 72, 168, 172, 175, 184–5,
264, 304, 308
Switzerland, 184–5
Syria, 131, 195

Taiwan, 87, 110, 137

Tanganyika, 196–7
Tate and Lyle, 80
Tawney, R. H., 10
Taxation, 5; and Attlee government, 45,
68–9, 80, 89; and Conservatives
(1951–64) 95, 98–9, 128, 142, 144–5,
158–9, 166–7, 210; and Labour
(1964–70) 220, 227–8, 230, 262–3,
281, 293; in the 1970s, 289, 296–7,
310, 316, 318, 324–5
Technical colleges, 11–12, 147
Technology, Ministry of, 214, 252, 255
Television, 127, 147, 150, 210, 215–16,
272, 287–8, 292
Templer, Field-Marshal Sir Gerald, 113
Textile industry, 48, 50, 151, 174, 188,
256, 290
Thailand, 111, 203
Thatcher, Margaret, 218
Thomson, George, later Lord, 242, 299,
303
Thorneycroft, Peter, later Lord, 121,
143–4
Thorpe, Jeremy, 304
Titmuss, Richard, 150, 279
Tizard, Sir Henry, 48, 49
Tizard, Jack, 286
Torrington, 144
Tory Reform Committee, 7
Town and Country planning, 8–9, 58–9;
see also New Towns
Townsend, Peter B., 278–9
Trade; postwar problems, 8–9, 16, 23–6,
35, 37–8, 44–7, 57, 66–9, 77, 269;
in the 1950s, 83–4, 89, 94–8, 100,
121, 128–30, 140, 145, 162; in the
1960s, 164, 166–7, 201, 220, 223–4,
228, 231, 239, 241–2, 247, 249–50,
252–3, 255–7, 260, 262–3, 293; in the
1970s, 296, 316–18, 321, 327; *see also*
Balance of payments, and individual
industries
Trade unions; in the 1940s, 6, 10, 16,
44, 50, 52, 55, 66, 68, 70, 75, 80;
in the 1950s, 125–6, 129–30, 143–4,
150, 154, 159–61; in the 1960s,
165–7, 180, 222–3, 228, 275, 293;
in the 1970s, 296–8, 302, 323; *see
also* Industrial relations
Trades Union Congress (TUC), 6, 9,
19–20, 51–2, 67, 70, 75, 83, 88–9,
100, 125–6, 130, 142–3, 150, 184,
188–9, 222–3, 262, 264, 266–7, 298,
312–16, 319, 323
Transport, 48, 53–4, 100–2, 145, 167,
248, 276, 290
Treasury, 8–9, 12, 18, 21, 34, 36, 46–7,